Foreign Policy of India and Asia-Pacific

Foreign Policy of India and Asia-Pacific

Edited by

K. Raja Reddy

Professor, Centre for Southeast Asian and Pacific Studies,
Sri Venkateswara University, Tirupati.

New Century Publications
New Delhi, India

NEW CENTURY PUBLICATIONS
4800/24, Bharat Ram Road,
Ansari Road, Daryaganj,
New Delhi – 110 002 (India)

Tel.: 011-2324 7798, 6539 6605
Fax: 011-4101 7798
E-mail: indiatax@vsnl.com • info@newcenturypublications.com
www.newcenturypublications.com

Editorial office:
LG–7, Aakarshan Bhawan,
4754-57/23, Ansari Road, Daryaganj,
New Delhi – 110 002

Tel.: 011-4358 7398

First Published: **2012**

ISBN: **978-81-7708-289-0**

Published by New Century Publications and printed at Salasar Imaging Systems, New Delhi.

Designs: Patch Creative Unit, New Delhi.

PRINTED IN INDIA

ABOUT THE BOOK

Asia-Pacific region is home not only for economic power houses like India, China and Japan but also for the emerging economies like Indonesia and Vietnam. Flash points like the South China Sea and Korean peninsula highlight the vulnerability of the region's security landscape.

India—which is witnessing high growth rate—is regarded as a strong and enduring Asia-Pacific partner. India's foreign policy is geared to meet the demands of the interdependent world whose watchwords are peace and development.

This volume contains 21 research papers—authored by scholars in the field—which provide invaluable inputs of ideas, facts and figures about Asia-Pacific region. The volume will be useful for academicians, students, analysts, business executives, policy planners and the general reading public interested in seeking deeper insights into the emerging dynamics of Asia-Pacific region.

ABOUT THE EDITOR

K. Raja Reddy is Professor at the Centre for Southeast Asian and Pacific Studies, Sri Venkateswara University, Tirupati. He teaches Vietnamese History, Indian Foreign Policy and Regional Organisations in Asia-Pacific. He is the author of *Vietnam: Struggle for Unification, 1954-1975* and *Vietnam Women: Past and Present* and is the Editor of *India-ASEAN: Foreign Policy Dimensions for the 21st Century*.

Professor Reddy has organised national and International seminars besides participating and presenting scholarly papers at various national/international conferences/seminars. He has visited a large number of countries including Vietnam, United States, Thailand, Singapore and Malaysia. He is presently engaged in research on India's bilateral relations with China and strategic partnership with Vietnam.

Contents

CONTRIBUTORS

A. Lakshmana Chetty	Former Director, Centre for Southeast Asian and Pacific Studies, Sri Venkateswara University, Tirupati.
A.N. Ram	Former Secretary, Ministry of External Affairs and Chairman CSCAP India, New Delhi.
B. Srinivasulu	Associate Professor, Department of Economics, Yogi Vemana University, Kadapa.
C. Ravindranatha Reddy	Centre for Southeast Asian and Pacific Studies, Sri Venkateswara University, Tirupati.
C. Sheela Reddy	Assistant Professor, Department of Political Science and Public Administration, Sri Venkateswara University, Tirupati.
D.S. Rajan	Director, Chennai Centre for China Studies, Chennai.
E. Subbarama Krishnaiah	Research Scholar, Centre for Southeast Asian and Pacific Studies, S.V. University, Tirupati.
G. Jayachandra Reddy	Associate Professor, Centre for Southeast Asian and Pacific Studies, Sri Venkateswara University, Tirupati.
G. Vijay Kumar Reddy	Assistant Professor, Centre for Southeast Asian and Pacific Studies, Sri Venkateswara University, Tirupati.
G.V.C. Naidu	Centre for South, Central, Southeast Asian and South West Pacific Studies, School of International Studies, Jawaharlal Nehru University, New Delhi.
Ganganath Jha	Centre for South, Central, Southeast Asian and South West Pacific Studies, School of International Studies, Jawaharlal Nehru University, New Delhi.
Kripa Sridharan	Head of Research-Asia, Infosight Singapore Pvt. Ltd. Singapore.

M. Prayaga	Assistant Professor, Centre for Southeast Asian and Pacific Studies, Sri Venkateswara University, Tirupati.
Mala Selvaraju	Department of East Asian Studies, Faculty of Arts and Social Sciences, University Malaya, Kuala Lumpur, Malaysia.
N. Amareswaran	Department of Education, Sri Venkateswara University, Tirupati.
P. Munirathnam Reddy	Centre for Southeast Asian and Pacific Studies, Sri Venkateswara University, Tirupati.
Rabindra Sen	Department of International Relations, Jadavpur University, Kolkata.
Rajaram Panda	Chief Programme Officer, Japan Foundation, New Delhi.
S. Utham Kumar Jamadhagni	Senior Lecturer, Department of Defence and Strategic Studies, University of Madras, Chennai.
Sudhir Singh	Dyal Singh College, University of Delhi, New Delhi.
Syed Ali Mujtaba	Chennai-based Correspondent of MIZIMA, a pro-democracy news network specializing on Burma related news.
Tridib Chakraborti	Department of International Relations, Jadavpur University, Kolkata.
V. Ramesh Babu	Assistant Professor, Centre for Southeast Asian and Pacific Studies, Sri Venkateswara University, Tirupati.
V. Suryanarayan	Senior Professor and Director (Retd.), Centre for South and Southeast Asian Studies, University of Madras, Chennai.
Y. Yagama Reddy	Centre for Southeast Asian and Pacific Studies, Sri Venkateswara University, Tirupati.

PREFACE

In the world of extreme changes, Asia Pacific is projected as the most dynamic region in the 21st Century. The countries of the region are linked through geographical contiguity and sea lane connectivity. Though the region appears highly divergent in terms of cultures and customs, a close look reveals strong cross-cultural footprints across the countries of the region particularly Southeast Asia. After India became proactive in cultivating its relations with the countries of the region in the last decade of the previous century, Asia Pacific provided an opportunity for its deeper involvement in strengthening economic, political and cultural relations with the individual countries and also the region as such.

Amidst the complex maze of developments, a critical factor that needs greater attention is the nature of evolving the US policies in the region, within the larger framework of global unipolarity. The US-led unipolar movement is in the second decade and it is unlikely that this status will change in the next few decades despite economic rise of China, which is expected to overtake US as the world's largest economy by 2040. Nonetheless, the American overall preponderance and its ability to influence developments across the global arena, are unlikely to be seriously challenged. The US continues to be the single largest source of new and advanced technologies and no country is more attractive than the US to lure the best and brightest from all nooks and corners of the world. Former Soviet Union was the only country that came close to challenge the US military might.

India—which is witnessing high growth rate—is regarded as a strong and enduring Asia-Pacific partner. India's foreign policy is geared to meet the demands of the interdependent world whose watchwords are peace and development.

I place on record my deep sense of gratitude to all the scholars for their worthy contributors to this volume. Thanks are also due to the following eminent academicians for their help, encouragement and co-operation at every stage of the completion of this volume: Professor A. Lakshmana Chetty, Professor Y. Yagama Reddy, Professor C. Ravindranatha Reddy, Professor P. Munirathnam Reddy, Dr. Jayachandra Reddy, Dr. M. Prayaga, Dr. Vijay Kumar Reddy, Dr. Ramesh Babu, Dr. Padmaja and Professor N.J. Richard.

Finally, I thank Mr. Sandeep Sury, Chief Executive, New Century Publications, New Delhi, for bringing out this volume so elegantly.

Tirupati
29 June 2011 K. Raja Reddy

1

Domestic Imperatives of India's Growing Engagement with Southeast Asia

A.N. Ram

India's Look East Policy, launched in the early 1990s under the direction of former Prime Minister, Shri P.V. Narasimha Rao, in its evolution, has passed through three distinct phases. In the first phase, from around 1992 to 1997, India's nascent partnership with the Association of Southeast Asian Nations (ASEAN) expanded and got deepened from limited sectoral dialogue in four identified areas to full dialogue partnership in 1995 to encompass a much broader canvas. This phase saw a structured and institutionalized framework for partnership to develop between India and ASEAN. Also during this period, India was admitted as a full member of the ASEAN Regional Forum (ARF) in 1996, a dialogue platform mainly for discussing regional security issues with the participation of all ARF members, regional and extra-regional. This phase, significantly, was marked by a quantum leap in India's bilateral relations with the ASEAN countries through an expansion of trade, technology and investment exchanges; frequent exchange of high level visits starting with Prime Minister, P.V. Narasimha Rao's historic visit to Thailand in 1993 to other Southeast Asian countries followed by a gradual thawing of relations after the unfortunate misunderstandings largely caused by India's policy on Kampuchea and Indo-China.

The ASEAN countries too were looking for an opportunity to take full advantage of India's economic reforms and the opening up of the Indian economy. In the case of India, her economic imperatives propelled the Look East Policy. The international environment too, after the cold war, was propitious enough for India and ASEAN, to resume a reinvigorated partnership for which our Look East Policy and ASEAN's Look West Policy provided the impetus for a new relationship based on evolving convergences and the imperatives of profound post cold war strategic, economic and political changes underway.

The second phase, from approximately 1998 to 2002, can be described as a period of missed opportunities and our failure to consolidate and build upon our promising partnership with ASEAN. The 1998 Pokharan-II tests created a climate of unease, if not apprehension, among some ASEAN countries. Economic and commercial exchanges plateaued and even declined in some cases. The impediments to freer flow of investments, trade and tourism, perceived to have been caused by rigid Indian domestic laws became the root cause of India's inability to attract greater ASEAN involvement with India. Projects like the TATA-Singapore (SIA) Airline tie-up to augment capacity and induct technology failed to take off. There were also difficulties in the finalization of some other infrastructure, high technology and agriculture projects and not much progress was being achieved in working out new and more liberal trade and investment regimes. To add to all these, the intensity and frequency of high level exchanges and dialogue came down. This was also a period when foreign policy, apparently, was driven by other preoccupations and priorities.

Happily, this period of hiatus was brief and ended in the early 2000s with India's growing economic, political and military clout and the present manifest potential of the Indian economy in the context of globalization. This could be described as the promising third phase of India's Look East Policy. India's bilateral relations too with the ASEAN countries began to show an upward trend. Countries like Singapore and Thailand were the first to seize the moment and to advocate a much greater role for India in the Asia-Pacific.

With political stability and growing clout, India was able to focus once again on the revival and reinvigoration of our Look East Policy. It was, therefore, not surprising that in 2002, India-ASEAN full dialogue partnership was unanimously raised to Summit level dialogue (ASEAN+I), an arrangement so far reserved only for Japan, South Korea and China (ASEAN + 3) has been extended to India though India is not a part of the ASEAN+3 dialogue structure. By joining this exclusive arrangement, India meant to achieve a much higher level of partnership with an involvement in Southeast Asia. India and ASEAN, at the Laos Summit in 2002, agreed with each other on an ambitious Vision document for partnership up to 2020.

At the Bali Summit, (2003) India promptly endorsed the ASEAN Treaty of Amity and Cooperation (TAC) and the proposal to declare Southeast Asia as a Zone of Peace, Friendship and Neutrality (ZOPFAN), a long pending expectation of ASEAN. It was at Bali again that India announced its intention to enter into a Framework Agreement for Free Trade (FTA) with ASEAN. Bi-lateral FTA with Thailand and Comprehensive Economic Cooperation Agreement (CECA) with Singapore are now ready to be implemented; and simultaneously, India has commenced discussions on Investment Protection, S&T, HRD and joint Tourism Promotion Agreements with ASEAN. Accompanying this, there has been a steady growth in India's two-way trade (now estimated to be around US$ 40 billion) and in the investment relations with the ASEAN countries. The India-ASEAN Joint Business Council (JBC) has also been energized to play an important part in this process. High level bilateral visits were also intensified. India's participation in ASEAN Post Ministerial Conferences (PMCs) and at ARF conclaves also became much more substantive and meaningful.

The first East-Asia Summit (EAS), held in Kuala Lumpur in 2005, and the subsequent EAS summit meetings furthered

India's integration process with the Asia-Pacific countries, including China, Japan, South Korea and Australia, besides the ASEAN countries, also contributing to the growth in India's bi-lateral relations with the Asia-Pacific countries. India's membership of sub-regional arrangements like the Bay of Bengal Initiative for Multi Sectoral Technical and Economic Cooperation (BIMST-EC) and Mekong-Ganga Cooperation (MGC) are now an integral part of this process. The Indian Ocean and its waterways connecting it to the Pacific and to the West to Africa, Europe and beyond, are of common interest to us and bring us together in fora like the Indian Ocean Regional Association for Regional Cooperation (IOR-ARC). Simultaneously, at the track-II and inter-governmental levels, similar discourse is taking place in Asia-Pacific organizations like the Council for Security Cooperation in the Asia-Pacific (CSCAP) of which India has been a member since 2000, Asian Cooperation for Development (ACD), the Chiang Mai Initiative etc. Happily, India is now a full-fledged participant in the Asia-Europe Meeting (ASEM) from which India was initially kept out because of reservations on the part of one or two ASEAN countries.

This signifies the changed perception of India. It is noteworthy that in this third phase, currently in progress, India this year has finalized a Free Trade Agreement on goods with ASEAN (two way trade is expected to get doubled by 2015), bilateral Free Trade Agreements with Singapore and Thailand and investment agreements with some other countries. Tourism flows have also gone up significantly. India-ASEAN relations are poised for a major all round surge forward and thus the changed international strategic and economic imperatives make this partnership now indispensable.

Until about late 1980s, it had been customary to look at India-ASEAN relations largely through a shared civilizational, cultural and historical prism. Unfortunately, modern day nation states and regional entities do not always see their international relations in anything like a narrow paradigm. A relationship devoid of fundamental mutuality of interest and deep and sustainable manifest content, is unlikely to prosper in the contemporary context. Even though India-ASEAN relations go back into antiquity and have been nurtured by unique bonds, our modern diplomatic relations are comparatively recent, having been established only after India's independence. The imperative of cold-war geo-politics inevitably drew India and ASEAN apart as both started looking at each other from the cold-war prism. India was seen as being too closely tied to the Soviet apron strings and decisively on the other side of the cold-war divide and the non-alignment was seen to be synonymous with anti-Americanism.

There was very little bilateral content in this ancient relationship to mitigate the pulls and pressures of the cold-war divide. India, on the other hand, viewed ASEAN as an integral part of the US led strategic alliance, inimical to its own interests in a vital neighbouring region. Both continued to drift apart, maintaining only minimal correct relations with virtually no warmth being devoid of any significant political, strategic, cultural or commercial congruence. The 1980s saw a further distancing and diminishing of the bilateral relations as India's policy on Kampuchea—a close neighbour of Thailand and Indochina—was seen to be unfriendly and inimical. The relationship dipped to a new low of apathy. The perception that a poverty-ridden India was too embroiled in sub-continental problems, did not help matters. China was beginning to emerge as a major factor in Southeast Asia and comparisons between India and China were inevitable. It was only after Prime Minister P.V. Narasimha Rao had launched his historic and path breaking "Look East Policy" at the end of the cold-war and visited Thailand and other ASEAN countries in 1993 in pursuance of this policy, that relations both bilaterally and regionally with ASEAN began to improve gradually. Reservations in ASEAN were so deeply entrenched that it required a deft and subtle diplomacy- and patience-to break barriers.

Likewise, Prime Minister Rao's visit to Thailand in 1993, was path breaking. After 1993, there was no looking back and India's all-round relations with ASEAN began to grow multi-dimensionally, particularly in areas like trade and investments, tourism, HRD, science & technology and thus a new kind of partnership was evolved. The time had come for the two great neighbours, India and ASEAN, to catapult their somewhat low content and low intensity relationship into a meaningful, mutually beneficial and sustainable partnership based on India's respective national, sub-regional, regional and international imperatives so that the new post Cold-War convergences would make India and ASEAN indispensable partners.

The post-Cold War strategic and security landscape has dramatically altered the perspectives of countries and regions, including India and ASEAN. Today, Russia (erstwhile Soviet Union) and the United States are no longer adversaries both having cast the shadow of their rivalry over Southeast Asia and elsewhere. The US, the sole super power, has emerged as the pivot of this new global and regional architecture and the cold-war military alliances have become largely irrelevant. Europe has begun reshaping its relations with its Eastern neighbours as also with its NATO partners. The non-aligned movement has all but withered away. China has emerged as a major factor on the international scene, particularly in the Asia-Pacific. Japan seems to be in search of a new and enlarged role in the Asia-Pacific. India is emerging as at once a regional and global player with over-arching relationships. India's emergence from nuclear isolation following a unique and a kind waiver granted to it by the Nuclear Supplier's Group (NSG) on September 6, 2008, is bound to further positively impact on India-ASEAN relations. India will, no doubt, be seen as a major global and regional factor capable of playing a significant role in Asia-Pacific affairs.

Where do India and ASEAN go from here? Both India and ASEAN need an uninterrupted period of peace in a secure and stable politico-strategic-economic environment. The economic growth and social stability of the two regions is contingent upon this. That the Indian Ocean and the Bay of Bengal space our common maritime boundaries and sea-lanes and that Myanmar is India's good neighbour, are factors that cannot be ignored in our strategic and security calculus and discourse. India and ASEAN have a common interest and a role to play in ensuring and maintaining peace, prosperity and stability in this region. In the larger Asia-Pacific regional context, both the regions as major trading entities and importers of oil and energy, need to work together to ensure the safety and freedom of the sea-lanes passing through the Indian Ocean and Southeast Asia. Energy security is a major concern as both the regions depend heavily on oil imports. Both India and ASEAN face similar and common environmental challenges and need to cooperate in controlling and combating global warming and other ecological and environmental challenges.

Recently, at the Bali Summit on climate change, both India and ASEAN had taken similar positions in advocating a purposeful policy response. Both are victims of natural disasters, as demonstrated by the devastating Tsunami that struck the region in 2004, and both need to carry the process of regional cooperation and coordinated action forward. Since India's political stability, security and economic well-being are firmly anchored in the Asia-Pacific and in the Gulf to India's west, India has a deep and abiding common interest in peace and stability in this larger region as well. India's foreign, security and defence policies cannot afford to be oblivious of the fact that India's extended neighbourhood remains an area of tension and rivalry and, therefore, is of crucial importance to India's own peace, security and development. Central Asia should be seen as a part of this extended neighbourhood just as the Asia-Pacific is. Therefore, for example, recent events in Indonesia, East-Timor, Afghanistan, Fiji, the Gulf, West Asia, Pakistan, Iraq and elsewhere in our extended neighbourhood, are matters of common concern to India and call for a common and coordinated approach/policy, wherever possible.

The Indian Ocean Rim Association for Regional Cooperation (IOR-ARC) and its space are also of common interest to both India and ASEAN. It is noteworthy that in the post cold-war era, India has been emerging as a major regional and global player with extremely supportive cooperation arrangements with the United Sates, Europe and Russia. India's relations with China have also improved considerably and both the countries are cooperating in significant new areas, including the Asia-pacific. India's pivotal role in the Indian Ocean region and Southeast Asia has been enlarged in recent years and India is helping to safeguard the security of the Indian Ocean area, particularly the sea-lanes, and the sea-lane arteries of Southeast Asia. India now is also one of the recognized nuclear weapon powers of the region and has a stake in preserving peace and stability of its neighbourhood. In this context, the vastly improved relations between India and China augur well for regional and international peace.

It must also be remembered that India is a major politico-economic-military power with over-arching interest in the peace and stability of the larger region. India's growing economic, military and knowledge clout is bound to become a major factor for the maintenance of peace in our extended neighbourhood. While India does not wish to be seen as a counterpoise to China in Southeast Asia, India's growing strength-military and economic being in the interests of Southeast Asia, is necessary for peace and stability in Asia. ASEAN is one of the fastest growing economies of the world and is a strategically important partner in a fluid neighbourhood. It is a pluralistic multi-ethnic and multi-religious democracy which faces challenges, domestic and external, similar to India's. India and ASEAN, therefore, need to exchange views and cooperate in the shaping of this new emerging architecture in our region. India's strength should be seen as a force to minimize the vulnerabilities of Southeast Asia, particularly as India has no hegemonistic designs or a vested agenda in this friendly region. This is the essence of India's evolving strategic partnership and hence, the crucial importance of India- ASEAN relations.

Initially, India's Look East Policy was premised more on economic rather than on strategic considerations. More recently, however, India has expanded her low level links with the Asia-Pacific to include political, defence, maritime, strategic and hitherto unexplored areas of economic cooperation. The Look East Policy, in other words, has now acquired a strategic dimension. India's domestic priorities and concerns are now an integral and indispensable core element in its Look East Policy. Southeast Asian countries too are beginning to see strategic congruences evolving with India. India, to them, provides an additional option and an enhanced comfort level. Their own Look West Policy takes into account India's potential political and military strengths, apart from her enormous economic and other attractions. The growing non-economic convergences include areas such as the war against global and regional terrorism and extremism, trans-national crime, cross border subversion and insurgencies and maritime cooperation, including safety of sea lanes, ports, economic zones etc. The economic convergences also go beyond traditional trade and commerce and now include areas such as energy security, HRD, environment, S&T and the new emerging areas of the knowledge economy. India is appearing to look attractive and a new imperative is beginning to become evident.

On her part, India is now increasingly looking at its growing relations with her eastern neighbours from the prism of her domestic compulsions, particularly in the North East and in the Andaman Sea. Strictly speaking, India's Look East Policy should take off from her North East, a point rightly emphasized by the Minister for North East Region, Shri Mani Shankar Aiyer. Some of these problems are now recognized, and have historical transnational dimensions and implications. Peace and normalcy in the North East, for example, cannot be fully restored and ensured without the cooperation of Bangladesh, Nepal, Myanmar and Thailand. This region is unique and has always had transnational links. Subversion and terrorism, drugs and its nexus with crime and trans- border trade and economic links, for example, have to be seen in a historical and traditional context. Over 95 percent of the borders of India's Northeast are with foreign countries, a reality India can ill afford to ignore. While there is no precise estimate of trans-border informal trade, it is widely believed that it is larger than formal trade.

There are other trans-border links too based on cultural affinities, tradition, connectivity and ethnicity that have governed relations between the North-East of India and the neighbouring countries. Likewise, the security of the Andaman Sea, the sea-lanes and India's economic zone will need sub-regional cooperation with countries like Thailand, Myanmar, Indonesia and Bangladesh. Cooperation in preserving the ecology, environment and the unique fragile bio-diversity of this region also form an imperative, which India cannot afford to ignore. This region has emerged as a hub of piracy, poaching and maritime crimes. Even intelligence gathering by foreign powers in this space is said to have increased. If China's growing influence and presence (China has military bases in Myanmar close to India and plans to augment her military presence in this strategic space) in this region are to be contained and managed, strategic links with India's eastern neighbours are indispensable. This is the rationale of India's renewed Look East policy in this third phase in the contemporary context. The Asia-Pacific now again is India's strategic partner.

Apart from the North-East and the Andaman & Nicobar (A&N) Islands, among the other domestic challenges that make it imperative for India to get her partnership with Southeast Asia deepened, there are combating domestic and international terrorism, trans-national crime and its nexus with drugs, fundamentalism and extremism, illegal migration and transfer of laundered money, small arms, human trafficking etc. Some countries/groups also indulge in clandestine trade in sensitive technologies and materials and there is a growing network of proliferation of lethal materials through State and non State actors, a matter of concern to both India and ASEAN. Both are also victims of cross border terror, trans-national crime and drug trafficking. India shares a 1600 km. long land border and a long maritime boundary and common space with SE Asia. Both are dependent on cooperation to fight these destabilizing forces. Indeed, both face terrorist and criminal elements that are common, often externally inspired and supported. Indian terrorist groups often take shelter and set up operational bases in countries like Myanmar, Bangladesh and Thailand.

The North-East terrorist groups have close ethnic and other ties with groups operating in Myanmar, Bangladesh and Northern Thailand. These concerns, therefore, have trans-border dimensions which can only be met through cooperation, joint action, intelligence sharing and even a joint mechanism at the political, policing and military levels. Likewise, India's neighbours too could benefit from cooperation with India. Bangladesh, though not an ASEAN country, has emerged as a major hub of terrorism and also needs to be brought within the ambit of institutionalized sub-regional cooperation arrangements.

Both ASEAN and India are fast growing economies which need increased trade, investment and technology access and avenues and both have an abiding interest in open non-discriminatory and non-protective trade and a level playing field which is what they are trying to secure at the Doha Round Trade Negotiations. The present system is heavily weighted in favour of the developed countries and both India and ASEAN seek a greater voice in a restructured global economic order. For India and ASEAN to prosper, to progress and to improve the quality of life of their peoples, it is necessary to forge a common front of similarly placed developing countries. Both are energy deficient and need to promote energy security. India's impressive economic growth could be seriously hindered if the on-going energy crunch and high prices of oil continue. India has done commendable work in developing non-conventional and alternate energy sources.

This experience and expertise could be shared with ASEAN. Also, the imminent agreements on civil nuclear energy offer an exciting opportunity and option. The security and safety of the seas and the sea-lanes so necessary for trade and energy requirements makes it imperative for India and ASEAN to cooperate in ensuring and enhancing energy security. Cooperation in maritime security is also necessary to fight criminal elements, poachers and to protect economic zones and fisheries. The Coast Guards and the Navies of India and ASEAN already have augmented their cooperative arrangements but much more needs to be done to evolve better coordinated and more effective arrangements. Defence cooperation is a part of these arrangements.

A major current domestic concern with international and cross-border ramification is cooperation in preserving the environment and countering the effects of climate change. Climate change cannot be effectively countered by national efforts alone. India and ASEAN are neighbours who share the same geographical space, common seas and face similar climatic challenges. Unless the effects of climate change are countered and controlled collectively, India's very existence will be threatened. This should become an important part of the continuing discourse. India and ASEAN need to get their efforts redouble, to tackle this problem through cooperation. Likewise, cooperation in dealing with the natural and man made disasters is the only way to tackle the issues like the Tsunami, earthquakes, oil spills etc.

The Indian Diaspora, particularly in Southeast Asia, is a major bridge between their adopted countries and India. They have contributed much to their adopted countries and today have the capacity and wherewithal to promote links–economic, commercial and cultural–between India and ASEAN. The Overseas Chinese, though greater in numbers, are a major source of foreign investments in China; the overseas Indians too are now beginning to invest in India. One day, in the not too distant future, they could become the best insurance for closer friendship and cooperation between India and ASEAN. The domestic spread effect of the Indian Diaspora's growing involvement with their home country could become a significant trigger for socio-economic development and growth of their original home states in India. They will also increasingly become an instrument of promoting friendship between India and their adopted countries.

The progress and rapid growth of India and ASEAN depends on peace and stability in our extended neighbourhood. Both have a vested interest in promoting peace and stability. For my part, I visualize a unique partnership evolving between India and ASEAN, based on the shared civilizational bond and growing strategic, political, defence, economic and cultural congruences. Both seek peace, development, disarmament, stability and are partners in trade and commerce, combating terror and crime, promoting maritime and energy security, jointly working to fight the adverse effects of climate change and, above all, in nurturing and enriching the civilizational bond through growing people to people contacts, educational and cultural exchanges, tourism and jointly exploring the frontier areas of Science and Technology.

India-ASEAN partnership in the coming years, is poised to become a major factor in the strategic landscape of the Asia-Pacific. India and ASEAN together with the other Asia-Pacific countries are now recognizing mutual advantage and the inevitability of together building and maintaining regional peace, security and stability and in evolving a new secure regional strategic and economic architecture in the shared extended neighbourhood. The countries of the Asia-Pacific, notably, China, Japan, South Korea and Australia will, in their own interest, have to build an overarching Pan-Asia-Pacific partnership with India and ASEAN if this space is to realize its promise and potential. India, arguably, is no longer peripheral to the Asia-Pacific and should be seen as an integral part of this new emerging architecture. The pursuit of India's national and domestic interests in furthering and shaping its Look East engagement is no longer an option but an imperative for India, in partnership with the Asia-Pacific.

2

Southeast Asia's Reciprocal Engagement Strategy: External Actors and Regional Security

Kripa Sridharan

Introduction

This paper aims to understand and to explain the motivations and mechanisms of reciprocal engagement in the context of Southeast Asia's international relations. The dynamic interaction between regional and extra-regional powers will be highlighted in the paper with particular reference to the Association of Southeast Asian Nations (ASEAN) anchored security and cooperative forums that have emerged in the last two decades and impacted great power relations. The rise of India and China and its implications for regional stability will also be discussed. Inevitably, the discussion will also factor in the convergence and divergence of interests between the major powers themselves.

There are multiple definitions of engagement both in a conventional dictionary and also in the foreign policy context. As with many such broad concepts that describe inter-state relations their meaning tends to be vague, imprecise and even contradictory. Engagement can be of a positive kind engendering cordiality but it can also be a negative strategy employed to neutralise the emergence of new power centres. [1] In Southeast Asia the engagement policy is deemed to be a constructive force and is defined in terms of reciprocity—the region engages the major powers and desires the major powers to engage the region in a similar manner. In short, it wants the major powers to remain connected with the region and to take an active interest in its security and development.

Some scholars, however, find the term engagement

inadequate to explain Southeast Asian states' linkages with the great powers. Evelyn Goh argues that omni-enmeshment is a better term than engagement, by which she means "the process of engaging with a state so as to draw it into deep involvement into international or regional society, enveloping it in a web of sustained exchanges and relationships, with the long term aim of integration". [2] Omni-enmeshment is more intense than engagement with a goal of redefining and remoulding the identity of target states. The difficulty with the concept of enmeshment, however, is that it evokes a negative feeling such as, someone getting embroiled in an unpleasant situation without an escape route. This is certainly not what the Southeast Asian states seek in their relationship with the great powers. They regard engagement as a positive process that serves the interests of both the local and outside powers. [3] Given this, a more appropriate term to describe the approach of the Southeast Asian states towards the major powers would be *reciprocal engagement.* This essentially means they are eager to engage outside powers and would like the outside powers to reciprocate their gesture in full measure. The region's leaders see benefit in such reciprocity and often point this out to the target states.

For instance, in 2008, Singapore's Minister Mentor Lee Kuan Yew emphatically said to his western audience that the West should engage Asian powers so that they become common stakeholders in the fight against security threats. [4] In the past few years, Southeast Asia has been worried that the US is less than forthcoming in its policies towards the Asia Pacific region at a time when China is galloping ahead with its outreach policy towards the entire continent and beyond. Ideally, Southeast Asia would like all the major powers to build a healthy stake in the region's strategic future. What they fear most is to be pushed into a situation where they are forced to choose between the major powers or take sides in their rivalry. A stable multi-polar regional system is their preferred choice and these states have sought to get the external powers to share a common regional platform. ASEAN-driven forums have been useful in drawing together Asia's rising and established powers. Cordial relations between them are considered vital for regional order and stability. As Singapore's Minister of Foreign Affairs, George Yeo notes:

If there is a major clash between existing and emerging powers, Southeast Asia will be affected and may be balkanized. For this reason, a large part of our diplomatic energy is concentrated on fostering good relations with the major powers and building an architecture of peace and cooperation around ASEAN in Asia. We are a strategic region for all the major powers–the US, China, Japan, India and Europe. [5]

Southeast Asian states do not want their region to be an arena where the interests of great powers collide, nor do they want the region to be ignored by outside powers. They are equally averse to the idea of any one power dominating the region. They feel that the best way to avert these possibilities would be to see a balanced presence of all the major powers in the region and to encourage them to participate in the region's evolving strategic architecture. Well-intentioned off shore powers are also regarded as a bulwark against an unduly assertive local or extra-regional power. The strategy of reciprocal engagement is regarded as serving these multiple goals. At this juncture, one might legitimately ask why should the extra-regional powers bother about Southeast Asia. What attraction does the region hold for them?

Southeast Asia's Significance

Southeast Asia draws global attention because of certain compelling factors. With a gross domestic product of US$ 883 billion and a combined population of five hundred and seventy five million people, its significance is self-evident. The region is also of considerable geo-political importance to the US, the European countries and the three major Asian powers, China, India and Japan. A considerable proportion of the world's trade and energy supplies transit through the region. One third of global trade and 80 percent of China and Japan's oil supplies pass through the Straits of Malacca. The sea lanes that straddle the region have become critical points of attention especially in the wake of terrorist threats that have now become a universal concern. The safety of the sea lanes is now more than a Southeast Asian concern. Walter Lohman of the Heritage Foundation points to the importance of Southeast Asia:

Southeast Asia's half-billion people reside in the most dynamic area of the world. China, a rising economic and military power with an economy of more than US$ 2 trillion and a population of over 1 billion, sits on their northern doorstep. India, another billion-person nation, is outside their western door. Japan, which has the world's second largest economy, and South Korea, a country with such energy that it maintains an economy the size of India's with only 5 percent of India's population, are each a short flight away. [6]

Southeast Asia is a relatively prosperous region which has witnessed an impressive decline in poverty levels. Trade barriers throughout the region are low and the regional states are wedded to the idea of closer regional integration. There have been no violent military conflicts between the states in the region for the last two and a half decades and there is a general consensus among the regional states that the use of force should be avoided to resolve disputes. This does not mean that these states are bereft of intra-state conflicts but that such conflicts have not spilled over to the external arena to embroil the neighbours in a direct fight. These are impressive achievements that have not gone unnoticed by external powers. On their part, the regional states are equally keen to explore the areas of common concern with their external partners and would like them to contribute to the region's future. This has resulted in a web of multi-dimensional interactions between the regional and extra-regional states.

ASEAN states have been very practical in accepting the

reality of external actors' penetration of the region and its benign as well as deleterious effects. They have been resourceful in providing an arena for these actors to meet and engage in useful bilateral discussions on the sidelines of regional meetings. They have tried to impress upon them that Southeast Asia's success in maintaining a conflict-free environment can be a model for the wider Asia-Pacific region which can be promoted in a spirit of cooperation alone.

Southeast Asia has been a region of importance for external actors ever since a fairly long time. This was clearly apparent during the Cold War period, when the two super powers competed with each other for a dominance in a region that was for anything nicknamed the 'Balkans of the East'. The US and the Soviet Union had created their own alliance structures in the region and were keen to maintain their influence through them. Their policies and the regional states' inclination to draw closer to one super power or the other in effect, created a differentiated Southeast Asia, divided between Communist Indochina (dominated by the pro-Soviet Vietnam) and non-Communist members of ASEAN. Even though ASEAN had an uncertain beginning and was buffeted by bilateral problems between the member-states, it gradually stabilised itself and became more purposeful. 1976 was a watershed when the first ASEAN summit was convened and two important initiatives emerged: the Declaration of ASEAN Concord and the Treaty of Amity and Cooperation in Southeast Asia (TAC). While the Indochina half of Southeast Asia was embroiled in conflicts, the ASEAN states focused on economic development and trod the path of prosperity. ASEAN also made a mark as a deft 'diplomatic community' sternly opposing Vietnam's invasion of Cambodia and fervently keeping the issue alive in international forums. ASEAN's success in the diplomatic front and the economic achievement of the member countries raised the region's international profile in the 1980s and early 1990s.

ASEAN states persistent effort to isolate Vietnam and

bring about a change in its Cambodia policy, bore fruit eventually. This was considerably facilitated by the momentous changes that occurred in the international system. The implosion of the Soviet Union in 1991, gradually led the successor Russian state to reassess its foreign policy options. One prominent policy revision was with respect to the alliances. This meant that the allies such as Vietnam, could no longer rely on Russia's patronage and support. This in turn prompted Hanoi to re-evaluate its own external commitments. Its Cambodia policy was one of the most critical areas of reorientation. It led Vietnam to withdraw its forces from Cambodia in the early 1990s, thus paving the way for a reconciliation between the two halves of Southeast Asia. Once this was accomplished, Vietnam sought integration with ASEAN and became its seventh member in 1995. ASEAN became an important vehicle for regional reconciliation following the end of Sukarno's regime in the 1960s and Vietnam's entry into ASEAN in 1995, was yet another instance of the regional reconciliation. With Vietnam joining ASEAN, the dream of one-Southeast Asia, a long cherished goal, came closer to realisation.

However, in the immediate aftermath of the Cold War, the region's relevance to external powers seemed doubtful. America's attention was focused on the Gulf, following Iraq's invasion of Kuwait in 1990. The Soviets, being mired in their domestic problems, became desperate enough to cut their own losses abroad. This resulted in their decision to get out of Afghanistan. This was also a period, when Eastern Europe underwent momentous changes. The transformations in Eastern Europe were more absorbing to the Americans and the Europeans than any development in Asia. In fact, the super powers' dwindling interests in Asia, raised fears of a potential competition for influence among the major Asian powers. Southeast Asian states in the early 1990s, were seriously worried that China, Japan and India would jostle for dominance and their rivalry could be detrimental to the interests of regional peace and order. One way to prevent such an eventuality, was to engage these powers, and at the same time, to persuade the US, to remain committed to the region.

Relevance not Relegation

The major worry for Southeast Asia in the wake of the Cold War, was to protect its threatened relevance. After the demise of the Cold War and the resolution of the Cambodian conflict, ASEAN tried to hasten the pace of regional integration and emerge as a cohesive entity. Since ASEAN states' security and economic links with the West/US were strong and were considered vital for the continued prosperity of the region, they felt that it was imperative to keep these powers engaged in the region's development. They could only hope to do so if the ASEAN region had something to offer in return. Robust economic integration could have provided some incentives, but ASEAN's record was dismal on this score. While ASEAN was still a long way off from concluding a regional free trade agreement, North America and Europe were moving further in this direction. The North American Free Trade Agreement (NAFTA) and the 1992 Maastricht Treaty, raised eddies of anxiety for Southeast Asia. These arrangements were unsettling to the export-dependent economies of Southeast Asia and they feared the ill-effects of these inward looking trading blocs. This forced the ASEAN members in 1992 to sign the Framework Agreement on Enhancing ASEAN Economic Cooperation. This was an undertaking to create an ASEAN Free Trade Area (AFTA) in fifteen years' time. Once in place, this was expected to raise the region's attractiveness to foreign investment, particularly from its western trading partners. ASEAN leaders referred to the need for such a move because of the imperatives of an interdependent world, which required meaningful partnership with stronger economic powers. Not surprisingly therefore, the 1992 Singapore Declaration noted:

While ASEAN's cooperative relationships with the

dialogue partners have made significant progress, ASEAN should strengthen existing dialogue mechanisms and develop new ones where necessary for the enhancement of economic relations with these countries, especially ASEAN's major economic partners. [7]

A similar anxiety about the relevance arose in the wake of the 1997 regional economic crisis. ASEAN's need to reinvent itself became even more critical at that point. The threatened irrelevance was exactly the opposite of what ASEAN had enjoyed earlier, when it was perceived as the most successful regional organisation and as one that had contributed to the region's stability. If the 1997 crisis had exposed ASEAN's ineffectiveness more worrying than this, was the political fallout of the crisis such as the collapse of the Suharto regime in Indonesia and the chaos that followed. The fear that the region would be written off by the external powers became palpable and grew worse when the region was hit by multiple crises. Alongside the economic and political challenges, came the environmental disaster in the form of the haze pollution. This was triggered by the Indonesian forest fires in 1997 and 1998 and added to the region's woes. As opposed to the earlier image of a dynamic and vibrant region, Southeast Asia wore an embattled look. With every negative development, the urgency to reinvent itself, grew perceptibly. The regional states struggled to engage external economic partners on terms that would benefit Southeast Asia and forestall the possibility of its marginalisation.

Once again, the engagement imperative seemed uppermost in ASEAN's calculation because that was regarded as one of the best options for regional growth and stability. Apart from the economic imperatives, there was also an eagerness to attain the goal of one Southeast Asia. As a solid ten-member grouping, with a vast market and some very prosperous members, the region's allure was expected to rise. While membership expansion could not be accomplished in 1997, the aim was achieved in 1999. By then, the Southeast Asian economies were no doubt, showing signs of recovery though the regional integration remained elusive. However, the eagerness to move in that direction, at least for some states, remained a top priority.

Yet another push to accelerate the integration process was made in 2003, as reflected in the Declaration of ASEAN Concord II in Bali. The Concord envisaged the creation of a 'dynamic, cohesive, resilient and integrated ASEAN Community,' by the year 2020. (The three pillars of the ASEAN community are political and security cooperation, economic cooperation and socio-cultural cooperation). [8] An economically integrated ASEAN was viewed as something vital to enhance Southeast Asia's international relevance and strategic weight. Engaging the external powers would only be possible if the region's economic attractiveness is bolstered. This is a goal which the ASEAN states were, and still are, desperate to attain though the impediments remain. In the absence of a tightly integrated community, fears of relegation loom large.

Changing Distribution of Global Power and America's Perceived Neglect

Southeast Asia's external security context consists of traditional and newer actors. The United States and Japan have had a regional presence since a long time. Japan was an economic partner of consequence to the region while the US supported a fuller range of interests encompassing political, security and economic concerns. Currently, the region's external security setting is rather crowded. While the US continues to be a dominant force, its position is being challenged by China. The latter's geographical proximity and increasing capabilities render a sharper edge to its relentless regional quest. Japan is no longer the economic model for the region and it is clearly behind China in attractiveness, but it has legitimate ambitions to play a greater role in the region's future. India has emerged as a new player of significant relevance and is now courted assiduously and ardently by some Southeast Asian states.

A dramatic change in perceptions and interactions has occurred between China and Southeast Asia in the last few years. Much of this has resulted from the changes in the global distribution of power which has seen the balance of economic power shifting out of the US and Europe, to Asia. This is mainly because of the fantastic transformation and performance of the Chinese economy. It would seem that the US is yet to internalise and devise a suitable strategy to respond to these changes. Because of its pre-occupation with the war on terror and other distractions, the US has not been fully engaged with Southeast Asia. ASEAN states are deeply concerned about America's neglect of the region, especially as their eagerness to keep the United States involved in the region, stems both from economic and security concerns.

American policy makers admit, that the US cannot afford to ignore China's increasing influence in the Southeast Asian region. Its economic reach has grown enormously in the last few years as if it now wants to vie with political influence. [9] One line of argument is, that the burgeoning influence of China is the direct result of the low priority that the US has assigned to the region. From this follows the prescription, that the US should strengthen its policy towards Southeast Asia. [10]

It has been widely noted that the 1997 economic crisis was a turning point in the region's relations with the US and China. While the US showed little sympathy and failed to provide necessary and timely help to the affected countries, China came forward with bilateral loans and pointedly avoided devaluing its currency. Since devaluation would have added to the region's woes, refraining from such a policy enabled China to reap tremendous good will. American relations with the region suffered also because of Washington's insouciance towards Chinese activities in the South China Sea in 1995 and 1999. This was unsettling to the regional states. The third dampener was the East Timor crisis in which America took an extraordinary interest but this only resulted in widening the gap between the US and Indonesia. The US Congress sharply responded to the allegations of atrocities committed by the Indonesian army in East Timor by cutting off the aid that helps in the army's training but thereby earned Indonesia's displeasure. All in all, in comparison to the healthy state of relations that had existed earlier between the US and the Southeast Asian states, the late 1990s was noticeably sclerotic.

The subsequent period has also not seen any marked reversal in America's perceived indifference towards the region. Washington's obsessive concern with the war on terror not only added to the feeling of neglect but also opened up the space for China to enhance its profile in Southeast Asia. The decision by the US Secretary of State Condoleezza Rice to skip the ARF meeting a couple of times, reinforced the perception of neglect. ASEAN leaders openly expressed their disappointment in terms of nonchalance on America's part. [11] America's lack of commitment was being seen as a threat to the Asian balance even though Southeast Asian states did not openly verbalise the fear of a hyper active China. It is significant that the new Obama administration sought to correct this flaw in policy, by despatching the American Secretary of State, Hillary Clinton to Asia, soon after it came to power. Secretary Clinton's visit to Indonesia in February 2009, was expected to raise the level of engagement with the Asian region. As the well known Indonesian strategic analyst Jusuf Wanandi noted, the visit was indicative of the importance attached to Indonesia by the US which was eager to discuss issues related to non-proliferation, the global financial crisis and the problem of China's role. [12] China's subtle moves to establish itself as a paramount power in the region is a palpable concern.

China's Engagements in the Region

Clearly, the inroads that China is making into Southeast Asia, have implications for the US. But not everyone in the US policy-making circle regards China's forward thrust in the region in negative terms. People perceive this, as a natural consequence of its growing economic muscle. They are also aware, that China enjoys the advantage of geographical proximity to Southeast Asia. It is argued that Beijing's integration with the region could ultimately help in advancing one of the goals of the US, which seeks China's socialization. Deeper involvement with the multilateral arrangements in the region, could result in China's deeper commitment to the cooperative norms espoused by the regional states.

On the other hand, a well-entrenched Chinese presence in Southeast Asia is regarded in ominous terms by some observers, who are worried that the region under China's spell might leave little space for the US to pursue its objectives. [13] The main concern in these formulations is how China will use its rising influence and power. Some see China adopting a conscious policy to exclude the US not only from Southeast Asia but also from the wider Asia-Pacific region. The clutch of initiatives which was mooted by it in 2005, seemed to confirm this surmise. These included a joint military exercise with Russia; multilateral search-and-rescue exercises in Hong Kong; a pointed advice to the US during the Shanghai–Six meeting to withdraw its military forces from Uzbekistan and the most telling of all, the decision to keep the US out of the East Asia Summit. [14] As One American Analysis Notes:

China has demonstrated a remarkably deft ability to use its policy tools, literally manoeuvring the United States out of its seat at a growing number of international fora. Furthermore, China has become an important provider of security assistance, and the presence of its military far from home is becoming commonplace. If Beijing has its way and Washington continues to neglect Southeast Asia, American military and security guarantees will soon be redundant to the Chinese presence. [15]

Apart from the apparent forward thrust in China's Southeast Asia policies that directly challenge the US,

Washington is no less handicapped by widespread anti-US sentiments in some of the ASEAN countries. One Southeast Asian scholar lists the lapses in the following terms: "(America's) soft power is continuously eroding and the US administration is not making efforts to expand its relations with the region beyond terrorism and the proliferation of weapons of mass destruction. US economic policies and relations with ...Southeast Asia are unattended. Education and culture, which have been so important to appreciate US leadership, have been limited due to migration policies. Support for democracy and human rights, which the US has been championing, have become rhetoric (sic) or are wrongly implemented". [16]

There is little doubt that China has been actively scaling up its regional level interactions with Southeast Asia. During the 2002 China-ASEAN summit, a number of significant agreements were signed between the two sides: the Declaration of Conduct in the South China Sea; Joint Declaration on Cooperation in the field of Non-traditional Security Issues and, the Framework Agreement on Comprehensive Economic Cooperation. China acceded to the Treaty of Peace and Amity in 2003. Some of these undertakings are path breaking since they commit China to abide by the conflict-mitigating mechanisms perfected by the ASEAN states. Endorsement of these norms reflects a commonality in the views of the signatories about the significance of cooperative security.

Such reassurances have naturally produced dividends in other areas. In 2004, ASEAN leaders agreed to recognise China as a full market economy and in the same year, they signed an Agreement on Trade in Goods and an Agreement on Dispute Settlement Mechanism. Overall, China's regional level initiatives have complemented its bilateral commercial interests and interactions.

The ASEAN platform allows Beijing to project a credible image of itself as a responsible rising power. China's diplomatic endeavour to convince the states on its periphery of its benign intentions has stood it in good stead. Since ASEAN is a recognised regional entity that anchors several Asia-wide regional dialogues and forums, China gets an opportunity to display its 'soft power' skills to the world at large. Beijing has achieved a spectacular image-makeover within a short span of time. Historical antipathies and suspicions nurtured by its smaller neighbours, are now in the process of being replaced by amity and trust. This is not only because of China's economic attractions but also its willingness to be flexible on hardcore issues like subscribing to a regional code of conduct and tailoring its economic policies by paying heed to the larger interests of the region. Beijing desperately wants to dispel the 'China threat' theory and therefore chants the multilateral mantra.

It has not been unusual for regional elites to compare the regional presence and performance of China and the US especially, since the 1990s, only to draw worrying conclusions. For instance, Singapore's Senior Minister Goh Chok Tong observed that the number of mechanisms between ASEAN and China since the time the latter became a formal partner of ASEAN in 1996, amounted to 27, while the US, which has enjoyed a formal relationship with ASEAN since 1977, can boast of just seven US-ASEAN bodies, which meet rather infrequently. [17]

Steady progress has also occurred in the China-ASEAN Free Trade Agreement. Mooted in 2001, it has made an extraordinary progress in seven years. An early harvest programme encompassing trade in goods came into effect in July 2005.The two sides signed a trade in services agreement in January 2007. [18] China-ASEAN trade crossed the US$ 100 billion mark in 2005 and reached US$ 202.6 billion in 2007. China -ASEAN free trade area is expected to materialise before the targeted date of 2010. While this is regarded as good news by ASEAN countries, they are nevertheless keen that the Trade and Investment Framework Agreement (TIFA) signed between the US and ASEAN, culminates in a Free

Trade Agreement soon. Analysts point out that an enhanced TIFA might "strengthen the hands of Asean trade partners as they negotiate on a full China-Asean FTA". [19]

The growing push by China and Washington's complacent attitude, are regarded as detrimental to the long term interests of both America and Southeast Asia. The US position in the past few years is derided by some American analysts as a "policy without a strategy" that cries for immediate correction. This line of argument is countered by those who feel that the idea of the Chinese ascendancy over the US, has been made much to the extent of generating the exaggerated fear. David Shambaugh observes: "It would be hasty to assume that China's obvious economic heft accompanies equally influential political and diplomatic influence...China's geo-economic strategy in Asia also has practical limitations because the country remains very poor, as Chinese leaders themselves admit". [20]

Obviously, China is not allowed to have anything all its way in the region because, not all the ASEAN states are sanguine about a pro-active China. One example of ASEAN's wariness about China was evident in its decision not to take up China's offer of acceding to the Southeast Asian Nuclear Weapons Free Zone (SEANWFZ) regime. China was told that the region would prefer a simultaneous accession by all the nuclear powers. ASEAN countries are aware of the negative consequences of too tight an embrace by China and this is one of the reasons for their stressing the sensible idea that a balanced presence of all the major powers would be the most desirable option. By highlighting Beijing's ever expanding role, they want to make sure that the US and Japan remain committed to the region. India has also been added to this list now.

The repeated calls for a policy reversal have begun to produce some effect. The US has come to realise that its approach has given rise to the impression that it was forfeiting the region. The visit by Condoleezza Rice to Indonesia, when she lavishly praised that the country's democratic transformation and the moderate face of Islam that it exhibits, underscored America's eagerness to impress upon the Southeast Asians that Southeast Asia remains vital to its interests. Rice assured her hosts that "the US was eager to work with ASEAN" and that it would particularly like to see Indonesia playing a leadership role in the region. [21] This charm offensive by the US unfortunately, was perceived by some observers as a belated effort to catch up with China, which has now become Jakarta's major economic partner. Fortunately, a reversal in America's approach to Asia is now more clearly discernible. The region's priorities rather than US priorities are being stressed by the new Obama administration. Unlike in the preceding administration of President Bush, terrorism is no longer the central or main issue of concern and the US is willing to make its bilateral moves more comprehensive in the region. [22]

To some extent, American moves are reactive and largely prompted by Beijing's Asian forays. This was perhaps more true under President Bush than it is now. However, China is keen to disabuse this notion by claiming that its policies are not aimed at displacing the US. It says that on the contrary, it has always welcomed the "American presence in the Asia-Pacific region as a stabilizing factor". [23] Beijing cites its own weakness as a major impediment for entertaining any ideas of dominance. By its own admission, it will take China 100 years to catch up with today's developed nations which also means that the 'China threat theory' is vastly overblown. And secondly, China's leaders emphasise that when China becomes powerful, it will remain amiable. In other words, it will ascend peacefully.

Beijing's claim of its peaceful rise is acknowledged by the ASEAN countries. They stress that a prosperous China will also be a responsible China but at the same time, they are eager to see that the US stays committed. They are also convinced that a China which is firmly embedded in the region's normative order, will be less susceptible to cause any mischief. As Carlyle A. Thayer perceptively notes:

ASEAN can be expected to work harder at shoring itself up as an effective regional organisation in order to better manage increasing interdependence with China. ASEAN's attempt to develop a sense of partnership with China will contribute to China's regional integration and thereby help strengthen the regions' multilateral architecture. Although China favours the current ASEAN+3 framework, ASEAN is likely to push for enhancing the East Asia Summit process in order to counterbalance China's overwhelming influence. [24]

Experts are keen to point out that the US under President Obama, should regard China as 'a responsible stakeholder, especially in regional initiatives' and despite certain gaps in their policies, there are several shared objectives that can be bolstered to their mutual advantage. [25]

Japan and Southeast Asia

At one time, Japan had been Southeast Asia's economic model and provider. Japanese aid, trade and investment helped the regional countries to notch up impressive growth figures. But this is now being challenged by the Chinese juggernaut. A shift from a yen-based to a yuan-based influence, is now palpable. The bursting of the bubble economy in the 1990s, left Japan in a very weak condition to continue with the kind of economic interactions that had been the norm between Tokyo and the Southeast Asian countries. As Japan's economic woes continued unabated China's economy boomed which drew ASEAN's attention. As mentioned earlier, the last few years have seen China, edging out Japan as the economic partner of choice for the region.

However, Japan's economy in the last couple of years has begun to look up partly because of the reforms that it undertook in the wake of its economic downturn. Charged by a revitalised economy and being aware of China's aggressive economic initiatives in the region, Japan is now trying to regain its clout by pursuing the Free Trade Agreement (FTA) route. It has signed an FTA with Singapore, but the negotiations with other ASEAN countries like Thailand, Malaysia and Indonesia, are proceeding rather slowly because of disagreements over agriculture and investment issues. The framework talks on ASEAN-Japan FTA, have also not made much headway. As opposed to China's pursuit of the FTA with ASEAN, resulting in a huge market of 1.8 billion people and GDP of 2 trillion US dollars by 2010, the Japanese effort was inward looking, since the benefits were always toted in terms of Japanese, rather than Southeast Asian gains. Japan has been keen to consolidate a Tokyo-cantered economic framework as a way to balance the rapid strides made by China in the economic sphere, but this has proved hard to pull off given Japan's special interests and the scars left by the 1990 economic woes. It was announced last year that a comprehensive FTA between Japan and ASEAN would enter into force by December 2008.

ASEAN states are disappointed by the slow progress of the Japan-ASEAN Closer Economic Partnership (CEP) in comparison with the pace of the Chinese initiative. [26] At the same time, some in Southeast Asia see a silver lining in the cloud of Sino-Japanese rivalry. They feel that this will spur Japan to seek a vigorous reengagement with the region. It is felt that Japan would not have bothered to move on the CEP but for China's 2002 dramatic initiative. [27] The region feels reassured by the improvement in bilateral trade figures with Japan which has climbed from US$ 99 billion in 2000 to US$ 135.9 billion in 2004.

Apart from the expectation that Japan will regain its former position in the region's economy, a more vital hope is that China and Japan will develop a stable relationship. Despite the strong economic links between these two East Asian neighbours, their political relations have been marred by mutual recriminations. Hardy perennials like the row over Japanese history text books, insufficient apology for war time atrocities, visits by Prime Minister Koizumi to the Yasukuni Shrine (which honours the country's Class A war criminals), US-Japan alliance commitments and their implications for Taiwan, the claims over Senkaku Islands and Tokyo's endeavours towards becoming a 'normal' country, have all contributed to the worsening of ties. China's opposition to Japan's bid for a Security Council seat, has riled the Japanese who openly articulate the 'China threat' theory. The traditional bilateral meeting between China and Japan–usually held on the sidelines of the annual ASEAN Summit–was cancelled in 2005, much to the dismay of the ASEAN states.

Although Sino-Japanese relations have become relatively more steady now, as evidenced in the April 2007 visit by Premier Wen Jiabao to Japan, where his deft diplomacy calmed the ruffled feathers, and more recently, in the positive signals that emanated from the Prime Minister Taro Aso's government. [28] China continues to be concerned about the depth of the US-Japan strategic alliance which is a cornerstone of Japan's security policy. China regards it as a Cold War relic which is irrelevant now. The Southeast Asian states do not share this view and on the other hand feel that the US commitment to Asia tends to be strengthened by such ties. This is one more way of keeping the US tethered to the region.

Indian Connection

Apart from persuading the US to stay the course in Asia as a reinsurance factor, the Southeast Asian states have also been encouraging India's engagement with the region. They are aware of the potential rivalry between China and India but since the relations between the two Asian giants are reasonably stable now, they feel that engaging India would not cause any destabilisation. They are also acutely aware of the fact that both the Asian giants are ascendant powers and their rise could be leveraged to the benefit of the region.

At the same time, they also think of the benefits of India's presence in the region as a counterpoise to China. The larger implication of India's strengthening ties with the US and Japan is also evaluated from this angle. In particular US-India partnership is perceived in positive terms by most ASEAN states. India's Look East policy has thus acquired an added value to the region. In the last two decades, India - Southeast Asia relations have matured considerably.

The free trade agreement concluded between India and ASEAN, after nearly six years of negotiations, has boosted the prospects of even closer ties between the two sides. [29] Trade between them is expected to surpass the US$ 50 billion by 2010. India-ASEAN trade in 2007-08 was around US$ 38.37 billion and is slated to rise to US$ 48 billion, this year.

India's Look East policy, the most overtly articulated foreign policy by the Indian government in 1991, has been a substantial success. India is now engaged with the region along several dimensions–from economic, cultural, diplomatic, to strategic and security links. Its defence and security outreach in Southeast Asia, is particularly noteworthy.

Unlike in earlier times, India feels less awkward about discussing its strategic vision and security interests in the wider Asia-Pacific region. For instance, in his speech at the 5th IISS Asia Security Summit, the then Defence Minister, Pranab Mukherjee observed: *"India's role is crucial for ensuring and maintaining long-term peace, stable balance of power, economic growth and security in Asia.*" It is a core state whose role is crucial for the economic well-being, institution building, collective and cooperative security, economic integration and trade expansion and political and civilisational dialogue, essential for a growing Asia. It straddles the land and maritime spaces between East and West, and provides potential energy and trade corridors to Central Asia and the Indian Ocean region". [30] (Emphasis added).

India and the ASEAN countries also share a common objective in working towards a norm-based regional system. In the last ten years, India has been an active subscriber of regionalist endeavours led by ASEAN. New Delhi's trans-regional journey has not only made it take an active interest in the region's activities, but it has also provided it with an opportunity to pursue its policy of engaging the major international actors on a regular basis, during the annual meetings of ASEAN-led forums. A sort of linear progression has occurred in India's involvement in Southeast Asian regionalism at both the formal and informal levels. These could be labelled as *first and second generation* linkages. India's sectoral partnership with ASEAN, which was then upgraded to a full dialogue status followed by membership in the ASEAN Regional Forum (ARF), rightly belong to the first category and these have been amply covered in the literature. The institutionalisation of India-ASEAN annual summit and India's inclusion in the East Asia Summit, fall within the second category. They are still in the process of evolution, but by no means inconsequential.

Engagement and Community-Building

While ensuring that the region had an all-encompassing regional institution, the ASEAN states have continuously promoted the idea that the regional organisation should not function in isolation. Towards this end, they have gone to great lengths to engage extra-regional powers not only bilaterally but also through multilateral forums.

External powers acknowledge the leading role played by ASEAN, to keep Asian regionalism on the move. One example of the importance they attach to ASEAN is, the appointment of a dedicated ambassador to ASEAN which has been appreciated by ASEAN.

The ASEAN Secretary General, Surin Pitsuwan, "thanked ASEAN's Dialogue Partners for their faith and confidence in ASEAN and its peoples". The U.S., Australia, New Zealand, and Japan, have announced the appointment of their respective Ambassadors to ASEAN to work directly with the ASEAN Secretary-General and the ASEAN Secretariat in Jakarta. "These appointments demonstrate the confidence and goodwill of these countries for ASEAN and its peoples. We certainly appreciate their gesture of goodwill and we expect more Dialogue Partners to follow their lead" said Dr. Surin. [31]

Southeast Asian states understand that developments affecting all the major powers, will be crucial for the future of Asia's international politics. Situated between a vibrant but unstable Northeast Asia and an economically resurgent South Asia, the Southeast Asian states rightly regard themselves as Asia's bridge builders. This is not an empty claim as they have exerted to create multiple forums, where states from all the three regions and beyond, congregate at regular intervals.

ASEAN thus enables the Southeast Asian countries not only to sustain a conflict-free environment, but also to reach out to the major powers to meet and address their intersecting concerns within ASEAN-led conclaves. By doing so, it also opens up the way to integrate them in the construction of regional order as conceived by the ASEAN states themselves. The important multilateral security and cooperative forums are the ASEAN Regional Forum (ARF), ASEAN+3 (APT), Asia-Europe Meeting (ASEM), Shangri-La Dialogue, and East Asia Summit (EAS).

One of the first endeavours, of the kind in the aftermath of the Cold War and the uncertainties it spawned, was the ARF which had met for the first time at the level of foreign ministers in 1994, in Bangkok. Subsequent meetings were held annually in each of the ASEAN countries on the basis of rotation. It is a forum for consultation and confidence building and currently comprises 27 countries from Northeast Asia, Southeast Asia, South Asia and Australasia. It is the only region-wide security forum and complements the existing bilateral security arrangements in the region.

During the second meeting of the ARF in 1995, a concept paper was adopted outlining a step by step approach for cooperative security starting with confidence building measures, to preventive diplomacy and mechanisms for conflict resolution. Several proposals for confidence building were identified and divided into two lists–Annex A included those measures that could be explored and implemented in the immediate future and Annex B contained an indicative list of other proposals to be explored over the medium and a long term. Under this head, certain concrete initiatives in counter-terrorism and maritime security cooperation, have been undertaken.

The ARF arose as an effort to cope with the uncertainties of the post-Cold War security situation and was intended to 'socialise' the major powers, particularly China, to adhere to the norms of a restrained and predictable behaviour. Modelled on the ASEAN, the ARF does not use any rigid or formal structures to promote cooperation. The guiding principles of this multi-lateral dialogue arrangement are informality and flexibility as it seeks to raise the comfort-level of members. In many ways, the ARF has imported the ASEAN culture, particularly the 'ASEAN Way' of interaction, and extended it to a broader platform. [32]

No doubt, the ARF as a forum for regular dialogue, has been useful but critics say that it is merely a talk shop, since no serious issues are addressed in the forum. It cannot be otherwise because, there are no provisions to address, let alone for resolving the key sources of conflict in the region: South China Sea, Taiwan or the Korean Peninsula. Any noteworthy progress on these issues is impossible given the norm of non-interference in the internal affairs of other countries which is at once an inviolable ASEAN principle and an ARF principle. China's well known positions on the South China Sea and Taiwan as its internal affairs, naturally preclude these issues from being even raised in the meetings. As Desmond Ball notes:

The ARF is very much an ASEAN (that is, Southeast Asian) creature in both substantive and procedural terms. Its mechanisms are not well suited for serious dialogue about, let alone resolution of, Northeast Asian security issues...The major powers in Northeast Asia, for instance, cannot be expected to pay much attention to a body in which two-thirds of the members are extra-regional and extra-subregional, at least where issues affecting their important security interests are involved. [33]

Of the three stages of cooperative security, progress on preventive diplomacy has been minimal and regarding the third stage, the conflict resolution seems totally beyond its capacity right now. Among the major powers, the United States has played a truant for a couple of times, which is an indication of the less importance that it gives to the conclave. ARF's institutional deficit is much too glaring to excite some of the external powers.

In sum, it is a broad tent security forum comprising two dozen states from near and far. Much like ASEAN, it is strong on confidence building and consensus engendering activities, rather than possessing "a remit for regional problem-solving". [34] Nonetheless, its record of achievements lies in the "expansion of the Forum from 18 to 24 members, with others clamouring to join; the inclusion of defence officials in the ARF's activities; the strengthening of the Forum with an ARF unit in ASEAN's Jakarta Secretariat; the signing of the Declaration on the Conduct of parties in the South China Sea, and the readiness with which the Forum was mobilised to cooperate on counter-terrorism measures such as interdicting terrorist financing and beefing up maritime security". [35] No doubt, the evaluation of the ARF, is very much subject to the perspective one adopts–realists perceive its performance as inadequate but constructivists share a more optimistic view about its efficacy, much like what ASEAN has been in the context of Southeast Asia.

Apart from the ARF, ASEAN states also engage their East Asian neighbours through the ASEAN-Plus Three (APT) cooperative forum. The APT initiative was a culmination of a process that started with the idea of an East Asian Economic Grouping (EAEG) as proposed by Prime Minister Mahathir. It met with strong opposition from the US. The idea did not receive any support from Japan and Indonesia either. Therefore, it was dropped and later, it resurfaced in the form of an East Asian Economic Caucus (EAEC). The caucus was envisioned as a consultative forum within the APEC platform. But the 1997 regional financial crisis brought home the necessity of a regional response which neither ASEAN nor APEC managed to provide. Their ineffectiveness prompted a search for a better way to address the mounting challenges faced by the regional economies and the answer was found in APT. [36] The APT knits together the Northeast and Southeast Asian regions.

The first APT Summit was convened in December 1997 to look into the possibility of financial cooperation. APT's first notable achievement was the Chiang Mai Initiative (CMI) of May 2000, which was a currency swap arrangement. ASEAN's existing currency swap framework was expanded to include China, Japan and South Korea. The other component of the CMI was the expansion of the ASEAN surveillance process to include the three Northeast Asian countries. For the time being, this seems the only way of nudging the core Northeast Asian states - China, Japan and South Korea–in the direction of regionalism.

But even this is not assured. The uncertainty in Sino-Japanese relations bodes ill for any major breakthrough in regional cooperative efforts in the near future. The diplomatic tiffs that occur from time to time between China and Japan and between Japan and Korea are not altogether conducive to regionalism to emerge and bloom in that part of Asia. Arguably, a regional organisation might be a good mediating influence in such situations. Conflicts may be mitigated and relations steadied through some norm building. Highlighting the need for a suitable forum where these disputes could be raised, one commentator noted: "...the Northeast Asian states can perhaps take a lesson from the ASEAN experience and think of setting up a body aimed at not only addressing present difficulties but also promoting amity and cooperation in the long run. Moves to set up such a Northeast Asia dialogue have yielded limited results so far." [37]

In the absence of such a forum, the APT provides an alternative. ASEAN states are well aware that instability in Northeast Asia and its adverse effects will not be confined to that region alone. Two major unresolved issues with vast potential for an open conflict, are the China-Taiwan issue and the Korean dispute. By drawing in all the interested parties into a dialogue platform, ASEAN is trying to ensure that a predictable environment is created in the region. The APT process has grown considerably stronger and now has forty eight mechanisms that coordinate sixteen areas that fall within its purview. A special APT unit was established in the ASEAN Secretariat in December 2003.

Northeast Asia lacks a regional organisation. The Northeast Asian states have failed so far to create one and the prospects of regionalism do not look very bright there, even though it is not bereft of regionalization (i.e. interactions across borders initiated and dominated by private businesses as seen between Japan, China and South Korea.). The Southeast Asian region, on the other hand, has the best record on regional cooperation among the three regions. South Asia is a mix of the two–there is a regional organization which is twenty years old but interactions among the member-states resemble the Northeast Asian situation. The presence of a regional organization, in other words, has not materially changed the regional environment in South Asia as it has done in Southeast Asia.

Several scholars who have detailed the slow and uncertain progress in regionalist endeavours in Northeast Asia list several reasons for the failure of regionalism in that part of Asia. [38] Though Northeast Asia and East Asia are used interchangeably by informed observers, the main members of these regions are China, Japan, North and South Korea, Mongolia and the Russian Far East. A glaring lack of trust among the core members of the region, excessive attention to domestic and local priorities, irreconcilable national identities and enduring bilateral problems have come in the way of creating a common regional platform in Northeast Asia. Judged from the common requirements underpinning economic regionalism Northeast Asia seems to possess them all in ample measures. A relatively high level of prosperity, eagerness to integrate with the international economy, complementarity among the states, robust intra-regional trade and inter-sub-regional cooperation, are all present there and they should have pushed the region towards integration. Given this, the promised land of regionalism should have been within the grasp of the countries.

But, as one scholar notes: "Nationalism was, indeed, the culprit along with unresolved tensions between globalization and regionalism and insufficient local vitality for decentralization to become a positive force for regionalism. The dream of a single, economically integrated region dissolved in a caldron of great-power rivalries and divided countries torn by narrow notions of national interest and distrust." [39]

The Six-Party talks that began in 2003, involving the two Korean states, the US, China, Japan and Russia, to find a solution to North Korea's nuclear programme, have the potential to evolve as a formal institutional mechanism. South Korean President Roh Moon-hyun commented that the breakthroughs in the talks not only augur well for resolving the North Korean nuclear problem but could also lay "the foundation of peace and security in Northeast Asia. In the future, the Six-Party Talks should evolve into a Six Party Foreign Ministers Talks, and at a separate forum, the directly involved parties should convene to discuss the permanent peace regime on the Korean Peninsula". [40] The three key Northeast Asian states have so far been unsuccessful in creating any formal cooperative mechanism. As Kishore Mahbubani observes: "As a consequence, the only fora where the three Northeast Asian leaders can meet comfortably and discuss common challenges have been the meetings convened by ASEAN, especially ASEAN+3". [41]

The reason advanced for ASEAN's interest and ability to provide such a forum, is its experience in conflict mitigation. Mitigation is not the same as resolution or settlement. It is a minimalist strategy but vital for maintaining an environment where disputes can be addressed informally and contained, before they overwhelm the region. This is ASEAN's badge of honour and the one, which it likes to promote beyond the region. As Singapore's Minister for Defence Rear-Admiral Teo Chee Hean explains:

The ASEAN countries have learnt through hard experience and current practice, how to forge cooperation out of conflict. They have also learnt that to have a voice on regional and international issues, the ASEAN countries have to work together and speak with one voice. It is this unique combination of a pivotal geographical position at the crossroads of Asia; a history of forging cooperation out of conflict; and being no threat to anyone but able to act collectively to influence events, that gives ASEAN a unique role to play in the evolving security architecture in Asia. [42]

While the APT has a distinct East Asian focus which China particularly favours, it is not altogether comfortable for some ASEAN states to promote exclusionary regionalism. [43] In order to broaden the base of cooperation and to engage as many external powers as possible, a new pan-Asian forum called the East Asia Summit (EAS), was crafted in December 2005. EAS brought together the leaders of ASEAN, China, Japan, South Korea, Australia, New Zealand and India, under a common umbrella. It is a forum for a strategic dialogue to address the challenges facing the East Asian region. The US is not part of the grouping and one of the reasons for that is that it was unwilling to sign the TAC. One of the qualifications for EAS membership is an accession to TAC.

Supporters of EAS regard it, as a first step in the creation of an East Asian Community (EAC). But EAS had its fair share of trouble, even getting off the ground because of China's reservations about including India and the others in the summit. Beijing ideally prefers strengthening the APT process and managing the creation of an EAC, under its leadership to anything else. It is not particularly in favour of letting EAS take the lead in community creation. Towards this end, it suggested that the EAS should have a differentiated structure, divided between core and peripheral tiers. [44] This did not find any endorsement from ASEAN. China had to accept reluctantly the reality of equal membership for all. Indonesia, Singapore and Japan were particularly keen that the summit should include India, Australia and New Zealand so as to make it more inclusive and outward-looking. ASEAN also made sure that the summit was held in Southeast Asia following the annual ASEAN summits. [45] Earlier, China had made a bid to host the summit but this was ruled out by the ASEAN states. ASEAN insists that it should be the driving force for regional community building effort in the Asia-pacific region. Even though ASEAN states are drawing closer to China, they are also wary of too tight an embrace by Beijing.

India is enthusiastic about its participation in the Summit. On the eve of his departure to Singapore to attend the Third EAS Summit, Prime Minister Manmohan Singh said:

This Summit is one of the most ambitious exercises of community building and integration ever attempted in Asia. The East Asia Summit has identified five areas of cooperation –energy, education, finance, avian influenza and national disaster mitigation. India has taken and is ready to take many initiatives in these areas. The Summit is likely to adopt a Declaration on Climate Change, Energy and the Environment. The Summit is also expected to discuss regional and international issues, and future directions for cooperation. East Asia is home to some of the fastest growing economies of the world. The creation of a cooperative framework in East Asia will have a profound impact on the global economy and international relations. India's role in the success of this enterprise is crucial. [46]

Assessment and Conclusion

Southeast Asian states, though small powers, have achieved a reasonable measure of success in keeping the region relevant to outside powers. Although they do not have identical views on the role of external powers, they agree in general, that they have to engage them or become irrelevant. The core ASEAN states differ in their perception of external threats. While Indonesia, Singapore and Vietnam have reservations about China's role despite their friendly relations with it, Malaysia and Thailand are more sanguine about Beijing's regional thrust. Similar differences over the role of the US are also palpable in the region, although they all share the view that the US is globally more influential than China. India's presence is also perceived differently by different regional states. Of the Southeast Asian countries, Singapore has done its utmost, to engage India and to persuade India to play a more active part in the region's development. Malaysia is more reserved about giving India a greater profile in the region. Indonesia partly shares Singapore's views on India presence in Southeast Asia mainly because of the China factor. Therefore, it would be incorrect to assume that there is a monolithic thinking on the engagement of outside powers by regional states.

Engaging the western powers is not without its problems in ASEAN. For Myanmar, the US and the European countries are particularly irksome because, they are critical of the junta's dismal record on human rights and democratisation. Except for China and to some extent India, Myanmar has no reason to welcome the engagement of other outside powers. Although the core ASEAN states have ignored Myanmar's reservations on this score, they cannot be totally impervious to a fellow member's opposition to a policy, however uncomfortable that might be. This was painfully evident, when the United Nations

Special Envoy for Myanmar, Ibrahim Gambari's address to the EAS had to be abruptly cancelled by ASEAN because of Myanmar's serious objections, and it cannot be denied that was embarrassing to the region. [47]

The engagement policy is also problematic in another respect–it may not be what it is made out to be. It could merely be a diversion strategy to hide the inadequacies of the regional integration efforts. Instead of deepening the regional integration process ASEAN states are keener on outreach efforts. Dialogue partnerships, Post-Ministerial Conference (PMC) or the ARF, are all seen as a way of drawing the attention away from the shortcomings of the association. A more meaningful regionalism leading to greater cohesion and consolidation should be the top priority, instead of merely expanding the regional platform for external actors. In the absence of consolidating an integrated Southeast Asia, they have been expending their energies in broadening the ASEAN-anchored forums which are mostly talk shops.

This naturally raises questions about reciprocal engagement's efficacy. Southeast Asian countries are more eager to engage outside powers, in particular, the United States, than the outside powers are to engage it. This is certainly the case with the United States. America's level of attention has dipped, while China's has ballooned, leading to a different set of anxieties for the regional states. Notwithstanding the strategic importance of Southeast Asia, its pull is not felt equally by all external powers.

All said, Southeast Asia has not done too badly by following the reciprocal engagement strategy. Some credit must be given to its management skills for not letting the region become an arena for great power confrontation. Instead, the energies of the Southeast Asian states are concentrated in harnessing the strength of these powers for the benefit of the region's stability and order. Through engagement, they have also been able to devise certain collective cooperative strategies to address both traditional and non-traditional threats, confronting the region. This does not however mean, that regional security or stability can be taken for granted. Given its geographical location, Southeast Asia's stability is very much dependent on the choices made by the established and emerging powers–if they clash, the region will feel its adverse impact but if they pursue a harmonious policy, it will redound to the credit and benefit of the region.

End Notes

1. For an excellent review of the meaning of engagement see David Capie and Paul Evans, *The Asia-Pacific Security Lexicon,* (Singapore: ISEAS, 2002), pp.108-135.
2. Evelyn Goh, "Great Powers and Hierarchical Order in Southeast Asia: Analyzing Regional Security Strategies," *International Security,* Vol. 32 (3) Winter 2007/2008, p. 121.
3. The positive nature of engagement notwithstanding, it should be pointed out that the idea of 'flexible engagement' that the Thai foreign minister, Surin Pitsuwan floated in 1998 to modify ASEAN's non interference principle and to use diplomacy to address certain domestic issues of member states, was regarded as a negative strategy by the ASEAN states, who refused to embrace it.
4. Lee Siew Hua, "MM to West: Enlarge, Engage Asian Powers," *Straits Times,* September 24, 2008.
5. "Europe's Role in the 21st Century," Speech by George Yeo, Minister for Foreign Affairs, Hamburg, March 13, 2007, http://beyondsg.typepad.com/beyondsg/2007/03/minister_george_1.html.
6. Walter Lohman, "Guidelines for US Policy in Southeast Asia," *Backgrounder #2017,* March 20, 2007, http://www.heritage.org/research/AsiaandthePacific/bg2017.cfm
7. Singapore Declaration. January 28, 1992, http://www.aseansec.org/5120.htm.
8. "Declaration ASEAN Concord II," Bali, Indonesia, 7 October 2003, http://www.aseansec.org/15159.htm.
9. Statement by Deputy Assistant Secretary Eric G. John, Bureau of East Asian and Pacific Affairs, Before the House Subcommittee on Asia and the Pacific, September 21, 2005.
10. Catharine E Dalpino, "China's Emergence in Asia and

Implications for US Relations with Southeast Asia," Statement Before the US Senate Foreign relations Committee, June 7, 2005.

11. "US Misses Rare Chance to Discuss Security Issues with Asia," Channel News Asia, July 23, 2005 http://www.channelnews asia.com/stories/afp_asiapacific/view/159453/1/.html.
12. Geoff Thompson, "Hillary Clinton to visit Jakarta, Strengthen US-Indonesia Link," *Australian Broadcasting Service,* February 18, 2009, http://www.abc.net.au/pm/content/ 2008/s2495177.htm.
13. John Mearsheimer, "Why China's Rise Will not be Peaceful," September 17, 2004 http://johnmearsheimer.uchicago.edu/ pdfs/A0034b.pdf.
14. Phillip P. Pan, "Rumsfeld Chides China for Mixed Signals," *Washington Post,* October 20, 2005.
15. Dana R. Dillon and John J. Tkacik, Jr., "China and ASEAN: Endangered American Primacy in South Asia." *Backgrounder #1886,* Washington, DC: The Heritage Foundation, October, 19 2005.
16. Jusuf Wanandi, "Recent Strategic Developments in East Asia," *Jakarta Post,* March 2, 2006.
17. Goh Choc Tong, "Constructing a New East Asia," speech at an Asia Society Conference, Bangkok, *Straits Times,* June 10, 2005.
18. Carlos H Conde, "ASEAN and China Sign Trade Services Accord," *International Herald Tribune,* January 14, 2007, http://www.iht.com/articles/2007/01/14/business/asean.php.
19. Richard P Cronin, "A New US-ASEAN Trade Track," *Wall Street Journal Asia,* February 9, 2006, http://www.stimson.org/southeastasia/?SN=SE20060215955.
20. David Shambaugh, "The eagle's Grip on Asia Still Holds," *Straits Times,* April 25, 2005.
21. *Straits Times,* March 18, 2006.
22. See John Brandon, "Analysing America's Role in China, Indonesia and Singapore," *Weekly Insight and Features from Asia, Asia Foundation,* February 18, 2009, http://asiafoundation.org/in-asia/2009/02/18/analyzing-americas-role-in-china-indonesia-singapore.
23. Foreign Minister Tang Jiaxuan's statement quoted in David Shambaugh, "China Engages Asia," *International Security,* Vol.

29(3), Winter 2004, p. 91.

24. Carlyle A Thayer, "Southeast Asian Reactions to China's Peaceful Development Doctrine: Indonesia, the Philippines and Thailand," *NBR Analysis,* Vol. 8 (5), April 2008, p. 13.
25. Tianjian Shi and Meredith Wen, "Avoiding Mutual Misunderstanding: Sino-US Relations and the New Administration," *Policy Brief* , Washington DC: Carnegie Endowment for International Peace, January 2009, http://www.carnegieendowment.org/publications/index.cfm?fa=view&id=22617&prog=zch.
26. "The Future of East Asian Cooperation," speech by Prime Minster Lee Hsieng Loong, Tokyo, May 25, 2005 http://www.aseansec.org/17474.htm.
27. Takashi Kitazume, "ASEAN Sees the Brighter Side of Japan-China Leadership Rivalry," *Japan Times,* March 10, 2005.
28. Zang Tuosheng, "Positive Signals on Sino-Japanese Ties," *China Daily,* December 12, 2008, http://www.chinadaily.com.cn/opinion/2008-12/16/content_7308019.htm.
29. P.S. Suryanarayana, "India-ASEAN Clinch a Free Trade Agreement," *The Hindu,* August 29, 2008, http://www.hindu.com/2008/08/29/stories/2008082956371500.htm.
30. "Growing India and its Impact on Regional and World Matters," Defence Minister Pranab Mukherjee's Address at the 5th IISS Asia Security Summit, Singapore, June 3, 2006, http://www.idsa.in/speeches_at_idsa/ShangriLa030606.htm.
31. "ASEAN Embarks on New Era – ASEAN Charter Fully Ratified," Press Release, ASEAN Secretariat, October 21, 2008, http://www.aseansec.org/22022.htm.
32. Amitav Acharya, "Ideas, Identity and Institution-Building: From the ASEAN Way to the Asia-Pacific Way," *The Pacific Review,* Vol. 10 (13), 1997, pp. 319-346.
33. Desmond Ball, "Security Cooperation in Asia-Pacific: Official and Unofficial Responses" in Annelies Heijmans, Nicola Simmonds and Hans van de Veen (eds.), *Searching for Peace in Asia-Pacific: An overview of Conflict Prevention and Peace building Activities,*(Boulder: Lynne Reinner, 2004), p. 45.
34. M. Leifer, "Regional Solutions to Regional Problems?", in Gerald Segal and David S.G. Goodman (eds), *Towards Recovery*

in Asia-Pacific, (London: Routledge, 2000), p. 113.

35. Khong Yuen Foong, "The ASEAN Regional Forum: Still Thriving After All These Years," *IDSS Commentaries*, 46, 27 July, 2005, p. 2.
36. Douglas Webber, "Two Funerals and a Wedding?: The Ups and Downs of Regionalism in East Asia and Asia-Pacific after the Asian Crisis," *The Pacific Review,* Vol. 14 (3), 2001, pp. 339-372.
37. K. Kesavapany, "Asean Proves to be Regional Blessing", *Straits Times*, April 18, 2005.
38. See the following: Gilbert Rozman, *Northeast Asia's Stunted Regionalism: Bilateral Distrust in the Shadow of Globalisation,* (Cambridge: Cambridge University Press, 2004); Claes G. Alvstam, "East Asia: Regionalisation Still Waiting to Happen?," in Shulz, Soderbaum and Ojendal *op.cit.*; Hank Lim and Chyungly Lee (eds.), *The Emerging North-South Divide in East Asia: A Reappraisal of Asian Regionalism,* (Singapore: Marshall Cavendish, 2004).
39. Rozman, *op. cit.,* p. 2.
40. Roh Moon-hyun, "On History, Nationalism and Northeast Asian Community," *The Asia-Pacific Journal: Japan Focus,* May 19, 2007, http://japanfocus.org/products/details/2424.
41. Kishore Mahbubani, "Asia's Geopolitical Competence," *Livemint,* February 18, 2008, http://www.livemint.com/2008/02/18000125/Asia8217s-geopolitical-comp.html.
42. See Singapore's Minister for Defence, Rear-Admiral Teo Chee Hean 's speech, "ASEAN and Asia's Regional Security Architecture," delivered at the Munich Conference on Security Policy, February 10, 2008, http://www.securityconference.de/konferenzen/rede.php?id=220&sprache=en&.
43. Shulong Chu, "The East Asia Summit: Looking for an Identity," *Brookings Northeast Asia Commentary,* February 1, 2007, http://www.brookings.edu/opinions/2007/02northeastasia_chu.aspx.
44. Mohan Malik, "East Asia Summit: More Discord Than Accord," YaleGlobal Online, December 20, 2005, http://yaleglobal.yale. edu/display.article?id=6645.
45. Martin Walker, "Battling for the New Asia," *The Globalist,* April 6, 2005, http://www.theglobalist.com/StoryId.aspx?StoryId=4479.

46. See PM's Statement prior to his departure to Singapore to attend the EAS, 19 November 2007, http://www.meaindia.nic.in/cgi-bin/db2www/meaxpsite/coverpage.d2w/coverpg?sec=ss&filename=speech/2008/06/06ss01.htm.
47. "ASEAN Cancels Gambari Speech," *Al Jazeera,* 20 November, 2007, http://english.aljazeera.net/news/asia-pacific/2007/11/2008525142458452226.html.

3

India and ASEAN: Evolving a New Culture

Ganganath Jha

India and ASEAN–geopolitically linked to each other, have been constantly getting the areas of their cooperation enlarged, though they have miles to go by to get their vision of "Asian Century" fulfilled. Their urge to have a common concern for emerging challenges has been justifiable and successful in certain areas but the problems of sustainable development, environmental pollution and terrorism have been on the increase. While the theories of peace and conflict are discussed at the academic level, the radical elements are actively supporting unrest and turmoil as if the terror groups are determined to sabotage the gains of the civilized world in South and Southeast Asia. Besides, the threat of terrorism, the rising population, hunger, and illiteracy have contributed to an erosion of social values. Hence the countries in the region have to give their attention to building up of a common consensus to work together in the broader interests of humanity. India and ASEAN have been keen to work for regionalism, peace and development and in that endeavour, a renewed feeling of brotherhood with new inputs is essential. This requires an evolving of a new culture of universal brotherhood and humanitarianism of a high order. There is a need to forge a system in which each partner is trusted and the scope of violence, minimized.

India adopted the policy of Look East in 1992 and extended the hand of cooperation with eastern neighbours. Although it was deeply embroiled in attending to its economic and security problems, India's initiative of Look East enthralled ASEAN and the response was in terms of an offer of Sectoral Partnership. This event proved a landmark in creating new spirits for regional cooperation. The ASEAN has been working for community building and the Treaty of Amity and Cooperation (TAC), ASEAN Concord I and ASEAN Concord II are aimed at minimizing the scope of conflict and creating a desirably common approach. Every partner of the ASEAN is required to make commitments to TAC, but the question is to what extent those resolutions impact the attitudes of terrorists? What needs to be done for maintaining peace and promoting prosperity? There is a need to generate new ideas, which may help in building creative and positive environment for peace and prosperity to prevail. The concept of universal prosperity and happiness as propounded by Vinoba Bhave (Sarbodaya) for example, is an ideal worth considering and cherishing, but to implement them needs vision and charisma, which are rare.

Talking about Mahatma Gandhi or Vinoba Bhave in the present day world, may not look realistic especially in market-worshipping western World and the community minded Islamic world. The developments since 9/11 have alarmed the international community. Al Qaida in the Arab world and Jemaah Islamiyah (Ji) in Southeast Asia are supporting Islamic terror. Jehad is foremost and topmost in their agenda. The realists led by the US, tried to subdue Al Qaida Jehadis through military means in Afghanistan and Iraq and that proved counter productive. Hence cultural approach assumes importance. China used its traditional wisdom to cement ties with ASEAN in the post-financial crisis era. It subjected its usual assertiveness to some kind of dilution and adopted accommodative attitude to the crisis-ridden ASEAN countries. It began extending an enormous support to ASEAN, showing its preparedness to share the problems. It adopted a cultural approach with a touch of Buddhism and Confucianism to provide help to crisis resolution. China's humanitarian attitude endeared the ASEAN partners. This helped the evolution of a culture of Sino-ASEAN cooperation which ultimately enabled China to emerge as the largest trading partner in 2006. ASEAN successfully recovered from the crisis and gave fitting answer to all those who criticized ASEAN model and "Asian values" in the aftermath of the crisis.

Asia is richly endowed with resources and manpower. It has natural rights to be on the top of the development index, but unless a culture of cooperation and accommodation is evolved in South Asia, the projection of "Asian Century" will remain elusive. The eminent persons, comprising Ban Ki Moon, Lee Kuan Yew, Mahathir Mohammad, Thaksin Shinawatra and Manmohan Singh, are endowed with ideas and vision and they can provide necessary input for the agenda of Asian Century. Ban Ki Moon is experienced and renowned for his opinion on Asian Community building. Although Mahathir's anti-West rhetoric looked negative, he remained charismatic. Lee as an architect of Singapore, has exceptional qualities. His advice has helped Vietnam's boom in recent years. Again Thaksin's rural development ideas have gathered popular support and Manmohan Singh as an architect of India's economic liberalisation, has put India on development path. They are all exceptionally qualified but when and how they can work in a team and advocate effective governance for development and unleash a new culture, are hypothetical projections. The establishment of common currency, common parliament, common markets etc are required for the development of Asian nations and that is possible only if the regional leaders work out consensus, plans and programmes for collective and common good.

In 1992, when India joined ASEAN as a sectoral partner, it was a step in the right direction. For decades before 1992, India and ASEAN indulged in polemics and this situation was fully exploited by China. The US ever since the signing of Shanghai communiqué (1972), had extended tacit support to China in expanding influence in the ASEAN region. India's economic and security relations remained dismal. However, when the sectoral partnership started, India's trade, investment and tourism ties immediately picked up momentum. Both took important steps to lend a boost to economic and cultural ties. This event prodded Pakistan to seek ASEAN partnership. In 1993, Pakistan was also offered sectoral partnership but it took years between Pakistan and ASEAN to choose the sectors of cooperation. Pakistan was also restrained by ASEAN to keep its bilateral disputes with India outside the purview of the sectoral partnership.

This was frustrating for Pakistan because Pakistanis tend to use every international fora—the United Nations, (UN) Organization of Islamic Conferences (OIC) or South Asian Association for Regional Cooperation (SAARC)—for bashing India. The SAARC proved a failure for regional cooperation because of India-Pakistan disputes. Kashmir remained volatile and trans-border terrorism was supported by one against another. The ASEAN leaders knew about it and therefore, opposed their entry in any form in the ASEAN. But when India was accepted as a sectoral partner, it was difficult to ignore the case of Pakistan. It is understood that before offering the partnership, Pakistan was categorically told that the Association is exclusively for economic cooperation, and all contentious bilateral disputes are not within the purview of sectoral partnership. Pakistan accepted the conditions of the ASEAN and did not raise its voice against India through ASEAN forum. Islamabad was satisfied neither with trade nor with investment relations, because it does not invite comparison with India.

India is geopolitically connected with ASEAN states through land borders of 1600 kilometres with Myanmar and maritime borders of thousands of kilometres with ASEAN states in the Indian Ocean alongside the Bay of Bengal. India's trade with ASEAN countries has been increasing because of its contiguity with Myanmar, Thailand and Indonesia. The fixed targets for Indo-ASEAN trade are the US$ 50 billion by 2010. India's trade volume with ASEAN was US$ 38 billion in

2007. Pakistan's trade with ASEAN shows upward trends particularly with Malaysia and Indonesia, but the overall volume was merely US$ 342 million (2004). Although the trade volume marginally increased thereafter, it is around one billion US dollars only (Shivpun Singh, 2005). Pakistan had been an aligned partner of Southeast Asian states through SEATO in the past, but it failed to exert its economic influence in the region to overtake India. What is disturbing and annoying is that the countries in the region today seem to give the impression of conniving at the Pakistan's role behind the scenes in supporting Taliban and Mujahideen violence to spread the gospel of Islam.

ASEAN's policy to cultivate relations with India turned out to be a landmark step because it facilitated the emergence of India as a worthy partner for regional cooperation. The sectoral partnership was proved to be so rewarding, that ASEAN decided within a period of two years, to upgrade it into a full dialogue partnership in 1995. This enabled India to participate in ASEAN Post-Ministerial Conferences and also to get the membership of ASEAN Regional Forum (ARF). This event proved catalytic for improving ties as it laid the solid foundations for economic, cultural and strategic linkages to be promoted. ASEAN-India working group looked for cooperation in the new areas such as health and pharmaceuticals, social security and rural development in addition to trade, investment, tourism, science and technology. The development in relations created a new ethos and culture of cooperation which was thoroughly missing during cold war years.

The ASEAN in the post Cold War era, took another landmark decision to cultivate Vietnam and other Indo-Chinese neighbours and by way of bringing them to the ASEAN fold. It was not an easy decision because Vietnam had been isolated for its actions in Cambodia (1978). It was projected by one and all as hegemonistic and hostile for decades. The US had evolved "domino theory" as its crusade against Vietnam and the ASEAN was projecting it as a common threat and an exporter of violent revolution in the region. But after the demise of the Soviet Union, ASEAN discovered a convergence of interests with Vietnam, as the globalisation and the emerging new world order posed challenges to both ASEAN and Vietnam without discrimination. Thus, there was a consensus to the effect that Vietnam should not be further isolated, that both Vietnam and ASEAN should face the challenges of globalisation collectively.

Vietnam welcomed the gestures of the ASEAN leaders and took necessary steps to subject its system to reform and to accommodate the grievances of the adversaries having been satisfied with the reforms in Vietnam, ASEAN offered its membership. As Vietnam was ready to accept, it became integrated with the ASEAN in 1995. Vietnam proved a trustworthy partner of the ASEAN ever since, and has shared responsibilities with other partners. It is devoted to turning the impoverished Indo-China region into a market place and is supporting growth triangle proposals. Vietnam is in the forefront of Mekong Basin Development initiative, East-West Corridor or any projects connected with developments of Cambodia, Laos, Myanmar and Vietnam (CLMV). All this has been possible because of the change in the attitudes of ASEAN and the end of the policy of bleeding Vietnam White. Vietnam has signed ASEAN Treaty of Amity and Cooperation, Free trade agreements and all conventions to combat terrorism. These developments have given birth to a new culture of Southeast Asian fraternity and cooperation, which is a necessary condition to build environment for "Asian Century".

Another area of relief is the suspension of polemics over South China Sea. There were overlapping sovereignty claims in the Spratlys region and China had used its military to throw out Vietnamese from Truong-Sa (1988) and the Philippines from Kalayaan (1992). In 1995, when Vietnam joined ASEAN and China became a dialogue partner, cooperation was explored amongst the contestants. Several conferences on the problems of South China Sea in Jakarta conveyed ASEAN concern and track II diplomacy had moderating impact on China. The ASEAN claimants were not averse to joint exploration and exploitation of resources in the contested areas and they were not interested in doing anything that would be detrimental to the Chinese interests. ASEAN established a special committee to formulate a code of conduct for the South China Sea to be observed by all claimants to the Spratly islands. A draft code of conduct was approved in 1999 which had the approval of the majority.

China, insisting that it would adopt the proposed code only as a set of guidelines and not as a legally-binding document, resolved not to strengthen its presence on the islands. However, in November 2002, ASEAN and China's foreign ministers adopted a Declaration on the conduct of Parties in the South China Sea agreeing to promote a peaceful environment and durable solutions for the area, to resolve territorial disputes by peaceful means, to refrain from undertaking activities that would aggravate existing tensions, and to initiate a regular dialogue of defence officials. Sinologist, Bronson Percival (2007) has explained this phenomenon by saying, "China has thoroughly adjusted to the 'ASEAN way". It places contentious issues (such as conflicting claims in the South China Sea) temporarily to the side, places process before product, and welcomes efforts to build an East Asian Community".

China adopted a benevolent attitude towards ASEAN in the post-financial crisis (1997) era. The crisis had a devastating impact on Indonesia, Thailand and other countries. China preferred the policy of accommodation with ASEAN in the place of assertiveness. It refused to devalue its own currency, and contributed to IMF rescue plans. It agreed to provide additional financial support to Thailand. It did not attach any conditions for its financial contributions whereas the US did attach strings while contributing to the IMF.

Again the ASEAN exports to traditional markets which had stagnated due to the financial crisis, needed outlets. China provided them an outlet and support and thus there was a rapid rise in China-ASEAN trade which ultimately helped in redeeming the region out of the crisis. China bravely faced the challenges posed by the financial crisis and endeared herself to the ASEAN countries through generosity and overtures. Its role during the crisis, indeed paved the path for the establishment of China-ASEAN Free Trade Area, which is destined to remove all tariff barriers by 2015. This will cover the area of 2 billion people with a combined GDP of US$ 3 trillion and a trade of over US$ 1.5 trillion.

In 2004, the trade between ASEAN-China was of US$ 103 billion and that of the US$ 136 billion. However, the ADB reports in 2006 suggested, that China surpassed the US and became the largest trading partner. The trade volume then was US$ 189 billion which was increased further to US$ 202 billion in 2007. This is the figure of China and Hong Kong taken together. ASEAN-China trade has suggested, that they have taken proper steps to create a common market, which is necessary for the rise of Asia, but correspondingly the progress in creating proper conditions for trade and investment in South Asia, is abysmal. The insurgency in Mizoram, Nagaland, Manipur and Assam is being abetted by the political leaders for petty gains and the divisive elements who are prominently in plenty. It may be easy to blame New Delhi for disturbances in the country but explanation is simplistic in terms of the ethnicity, religion, culture and history of the people in Northeast which display an amazing diversity. People there are sensitive about their identity and ethnocentricity. Thus, we find that the gateway which geographically connects India with Southeast Asia is often disturbed.

Again Bangladesh, which is adjoining Southeast Asia via Northeast is witnessing the undesirable growth of Islamic fundamentalism. They too are busy indulging in a tirade against India occasionally and thus are restrained from doing anything which is advantageous to India. Besides geopolitical factors, there are some infrastructural gaps on India-ASEAN frontiers. India in comparison to Japan and China, was much late in taking initiatives to get the transportation linkages with Southeast Asia strengthened. It began to do so only after 1991 but Japan started its friendship drives following the Fukuda doctrine (1976). China initiated programmes to cultivate friendship with ASEAN as soon as it adopted the policy of Four-Modernization (1978). India was late in establishing its infrastructure for cooperation with ASEAN. Satu P. Limaye (2003) has rightly observed that "India's economic ties with ASEAN are in their infancy partly because India's trade liberalization started recently and is far from complete. Moreover, India-ASEAN trade has been growing steadily—30 percent in the past three years". Indo-ASEAN trade stood at US$ 10 billion in 2002. On the other hand, ASEAN trade with the United States stood at US$ 120 billion, with Japan US$ 116 billion, with China US$ 70 billion, and with Korea US$ 32 billion in the same year.

It is interesting that Pakistan which continues to remain the sectoral partner of ASEAN is keen to get its ties strengthened. Pakistani leaders are visiting ASEAN countries and negotiating free trade agreement while Malaysia and Singapore have been supporting Pakistan in the Association. Pakistan has come out with its policy initiatives in the name of "Strategic Vision East Asia Initiative" (2003) and is trying to send its overtures. It is pleading for full dialogue partnership status. However, the main hurdle in that endeavour is that the level of trade relations are so low (less than one billion) that ASEAN has delayed its decision.

The ASEAN countries are interested in South Asian markets and an entry can be secured if there is peace and stability in the region. Any rapprochement between India and Pakistan, will fetch huge and secure market to ASEAN. It will provide a master key to the conflict resolution in different parts of South Asia. Naturally, it will suit the interests of the region and our East Asian neighbours. It will open vast opportunities for trade and investment. The normalization will require Pakistan's acceptance of existing frontiers with India and adherence to the principle of non-interference in the affairs of a neighbouring country. India and Pakistan both would be benefited if the relations become mutually cooperative. This point has been very well illustrated by *Business Times* of Singapore, which stated that "a booming economy and improving ties with India will help Pakistan build bilateral alliances in Southeast Asia".

Pakistan is at a crossroads today. The political turmoil after the exit of General Parvez Musharraf and the split between Nawaz Sharif and Asif Ali Zardari indicate political instability in that country. We cannot expect any visionary initiative of Pakistan towards India by way of dispensation. However, if there is confidence building and cooperation between India and Pakistan, it will prove path breaking not only for the conflict resolution of Kashmir but also for the prosperity of South Asian region, which is otherwise most impoverished.

Indian profile in the ASEAN region is satisfactory because India has been taking initiatives to evolve culture of cooperation under Look East Policy. The concept of Look East was advocated by P.V. Narasimha Rao, I.K. Gujral and Atal Bihari Vajpayee, the three Prime Ministers of India successively. Although Sukarno, Phibun and Roxas also advocated "Look East" in 1940's, their emphasis and objectives were different from India. 'Look East' for an Indian is connected with his traditions that his Sun God is in the East, and if he offers prayers to the rising sun in the morning everyday, he will be healthy wealthy and wise. Southeast Asia is geographically located in the East and is an important component of our traditional folklores by all means. It was identified as central to India's foreign policy in the entire Asia-Pacific. India's look east had three-pronged approach.

First to renew political contacts with the ASEAN partners;

second, to increase economic interaction (trade, investment, science and technology, tourism etc.) and third, to forge defence links with ASEAN partners as a means to get political and strategic interests and understanding enhanced. Indian think-tanks are reviewing the notion of economic security, self-reliance and national interests in the light of developments in the post-cold war era. As a nation of one billion people, India cannot afford to remain a marginal player in the global economy, as measured, for instance, by our share in the world trade or income. Commensurate with her size and civilizational characteristics, India is willing to assume greater role in global affairs and world economy. Look East policy is endeavoured to fulfil those aspirations and it has already evoked positive response in the ASEAN region.

The meaning and contents of Look East policy were defined by Narasimha Rao himself during his tenure as the Prime Minister of India (1991-1996). His speech delivered on 8 September 1994 in Singapore, was a milestone to influence the opinion of Southeast Asians where he spoke about endogenous and exogenous nature of the problems, which were a matter of common concern and common interests and they were:

1. interpretations of sovereignty, whether over the oceans, in outer space, over territory, resources etc.;
2. frictions arising out of differing cultural perceptions – as we witnessed in the case of Michael Fay;
3. massive needs and demands of relatively underdeveloped populations and migratory tendencies, with no respect for national boundaries;
4. confrontational postures on a broad range of fundamental issues related to trade barriers, currency stabilization, international aid and investment flows; and
5. intensification of the debate over linkages between issues such as human rights, labour-laws, environmental protection and resource management, liberal information flows etc, in political and economic relationship.

Southeast Asian countries were also looking for suitable answers to the aforementioned issues but Indian premier pointedly articulated "the increasing tendency on the part of dominant powers to assume that they cannot only define the means, but even the ends, of collective international endeavour. This has been revealed in the form of intrusive prescriptions in the areas of social regulation, dissemination of knowledge, technological development and even domestic administration. The worst part of this tendency is that on closer scrutiny, it can be easily shown to be based on unsympathetic half-knowledge." Indian Prime Minister's speech was widely applauded because he pleaded for combining synergies between India and ASEAN and spoke about the broad parameters of cooperation in diverse areas.

In retrospect, we find that both India and ASEAN having broadened the scope of their cooperation, have gained from their interaction. When India became the sectoral partner of the ASEAN in 1992, the mindset of bureaucrats in ASEAN and mandarins in the Ministry of External Affairs, had not sufficiently changed but the developments in the years following, proved positive. It is heartening to find broader understanding on matters of regional concern, whereas India failed to generate similar response through SAARC. It is very difficult to evolve consensus within SAARC, whereas ASEAN has a consensus over matters of regional concern and stringent punishment to be given to the culprits. Here, however, India's strategic and economic cooperation with ASEAN will be evaluated, and it is in order to mention about institutional arrangements which have placed the relations on the right track.

India and ASEAN have set up a number of institutional mechanism to facilitate economic relations. Joint trade committees which had come into existence after 1992, have been renamed as Joint Business Commissions. Besides, ASEAN-India Business Council and ASEAN-India Joint Management Committee are coordinating economic exchanges. ASEAN-India Trade Negotiation Committee and ASEAN-India Economic Ministers' Meetings have been providing inputs for fruitful economic contacts. After the elevation of India into a dialogue partner status, ASEAN-India Joint Cooperation committee and India-ASEAN Working Group on Trade and Investment had been established. They provide suitable advice about various areas of economic relations with positive results. There is ASEAN-India Fund also, to support the lectures of important ASEAN leaders in India and that of Indians in the ASEAN region. It has been supporting exchange programmes and track II process to strengthen relations so that India ultimately becomes an integral part of the proposed ASEAN Economic Community.

The ASEAN has been a dynamic regional grouping and has been incorporating new ideas to strengthen the feeling of togetherness in economic and security matters. Although ASEAN objectives were enshrined in the Bangkok Declaration (1967) on the eve of ASEAN summit meeting in 2003, they adopted another declaration, known as "Bali concord II', which made the signatory states committed to the creation of an ASEAN Economic Community, an ASEAN Security Community, and an ASEAN Socio-cultural community. These objectives allotted various kinds of commitment to the existing economic cooperation frameworks, regional plans of action and Initiatives for ASEAN Integration (IAI), and outlined plans for the creation of an Integrated ASEAN Economic Community (AEC) by 2020 that would entail the harmonization of customs procedures and technical regulations by the end of 2004, the removal of non-tariff trade barriers and the establishment of a network of free-trade-zones by 2005; and the progressive withdrawal of capital controls and strengthening of intellectual property rights. ASEAN economic and trade ministers worked closely to produce a 'roadmap' for the integration of 11 sectors identified as priority areas in the AEC plan of action, namely agriculture, air travel, automotive, electronics, fisheries, healthcare, information technology (IT), rubber, textiles, tourism and wood.

The dialogue partners were expected to facilitate the endeavour of the community building so that they would prove to be useful for the grouping. India, being always keen to act as a relevant partner, began to articulate through various forums, some valuable inputs. It is understood that Indian leadership wanted to get relations with ASEAN fortified, while the latter wanted to actively engage India vis-à-vis China to develop a more balanced relationship (Rahul Sen and Mukul G. Asher, 2004). It was also believed that India's economic structure was largely complementary (service oriented) to ASEAN economies (light manufacturing) and if the level of relations are enhanced, both sides would be benefited (Mukul G Asher, 2003). Indian Prime Minister, Vajpayee had noted that the ASEAN countries have begun to develop regional dominance in certain areas of technologies and wished India and ASEAN to exploit their respective synergies. As a market, ASEAN is attractive for Indian exporters because of its geographic proximity, conducive to shorter delivery schedules and lower freight costs.

With a sizable population of Indian origin, and a shared sense of historical, cultural and religious commonalities, the emerging economic linkages between India and ASEAN are bound to be multifaceted and deep-rooted. Moreover, the new breed of Indian migrants to Southeast Asia are likely to be software engineers, financial analysts and management professionals who will increasingly play an influential role in connecting ASEAN with South Asia. (Faisal Yahya 2003). With this projection in mind, both decided to hold India-ASEAN Summits every year. The first summit was held in Phnom Penh (2002) and the second summit was held in Bali (2003). Prime Minster Vajpayee attached great importance to addressing the agenda of those meetings and took initiatives to fortify relations. He wanted to break new grounds of cooperation besides approving the recommendations of

ASEAN-India working Group (2001) to pursue cooperation in new areas, such as health and pharmaceuticals, social security and rural development.

After India-ASEAN Summit at Bali in 2003, India signed the Treaty of Amity and Cooperation and thereby signed a joint Framework Agreement for comprehensive economic cooperation and supported the establishment of an Indo-ASEAN regional trade and investment area including the setting up of an ASEAN-India Free Trade Area in goods, services and investments. The objectives of the framework agreement included (a) strengthening and enhancing economic, trade and investment cooperation,(b) liberalizing and promoting trade in goods and services and (c) facilitating economic integration within ASEAN. Various new issues of cooperation were discussed in the field of agriculture, biotechnology, and human resource development and both sides adopted the joint declaration for cooperation to combat international terrorism. The framework agreement also provided agreement on trade in goods towards progressive tariff reduction in 105 agreed items. Tariff reduction for ASEAN-6, namely, Brunei, Indonesia, Malaysia, Philippines, Singapore and Thailand, was to be completed by 2007 and for the CLMV by 2012. The idea of an FTA with a ten-year time frame was mooted by India during the first summit. However, the idea of FTA carries certain issues of negative listing, rules of origin and the level of tariff reduction on agricultural commodities. Those issues are yet to be resolved.

A framework agreement for the creation of FTA with Thailand was signed in 2003, under which 84 items could be imported from Thailand at 50 percent of the normal rate of duty prevailing in India. Similar agreement was signed with Singapore. The framework agreement is to be signed with CLMV countries, MGC and BIMST-EC also. India took an active interest in Thailand's initiative for Asian Bond Fund and provided US$ 1 billion as a modest contribution to consolidate India's partnership with the ASEAN. The framework agreement for comprehensive economic cooperation is indeed a landmark document through which India provided "fast-Track" tariff concessions to ASEAN partners. The proposal was to achieve US$ 30 billion target for India-ASEAN trade by 2007, which stood nearly at US$ 10 billion in 2003. India also offered to run daily flights to major Indian cities including New Delhi, Kolkata, Mumbai and Chennai. The proposal to hold Car Rally had also been made on the eve of India-ASEAN summit, which was flagged off from Guwahati in the following year. This Car Rally proved the geographic connectivity of India with Southeast Asia through a land route.

The third India-ASEAN summit was held in Vientiane in 2004. The participants signed a partnership pact for Peace, Progress and Shared Prosperity containing a long-term vision for boosting trade, investment, tourism, culture, sports and people to people contacts. It also included Action Plan touching upon the entire gamut of political and security cooperation, including food, human resources, energy, finance, science and technology, IT, communication technology, health and agriculture. Prime Minister Manmohan Singh on the eve of the summit said, that a "long-term partnership agreement with ASEAN would provide a new dimension to our relations. He said that new India is on the horizon and the future lies in working together with our neighbours in the East, with whom we have profound civilization ties" (2004). At the same time, he spoke about linking East Asia with ASEAN for the community building. This was an idea which was meant to give an Asian touch to the existing regional arrangements. Whether it was proper to be revealed at ASEAN-India Summit is an issue to be debated.

India's trade relations with ASEAN are expanding. From US$ 2.4 billion in 1991-92, it reached US$ 23 billion by 2005-06. It is understood that as and when FTA will be implemented in letter and spirit, the volume of trade will exceed the targets. The Chinese have already signed FTA with the ASEAN and with this they have established a combined market of 1.7 billion people, regional GDP of US$ 2 trillion and international trade worth US$ 1.2 trillion. China's trade with ASEAN in 2004 was about US$ 70 billion and now it is increasing rapidly. They have certain advantages over India in the ASEAN region, but it is suggested that if FTA with India becomes operational, it would also be a market of 1.5 billion people and the regional GDP of US$ 1.5 trillion. India and China are also exploring the feasibility of an India-China bilateral FTA on the pattern of ASEAN. If the agreement is signed, it may complement India-ASEAN free-trade proposals. At the same time, it will brighten the prospects for better economic and security understanding and confidence building. It is interesting to note, that the Communist Party leaders in China are solidly supporting new economic zones and FTA proposals whereas the Communist Party leaders in India are not approving of the idea of the establishment of Special Economic zones or FTA. They are the important partners of Manmohan Singh led government, they had been playing the obstructionist role since 2004.

India's major export items to the ASEAN market are gems and jewellery, machinery and instruments, dyes, semi-finished iron and steel, oil meals, drugs, pharmaceutical and fine chemicals, transport equipments, electronic goods, inorganic/organic/agro chemicals, non-ferrous metals, plastic and linoleum products, manufacture of metals, man-made yarn fab & made ups, meat and preparations, cotton yarn, fabrics and madeups. India's major items imported from ASEAN are electronic goods, vegetable oils, organic chemicals, wood and wood products, coal, coke and briquettes, non-electrical machinery, transport equipment, metal ferrous ores & metal scrap, artificial resins, plastic materials, printed books, pulses, electrical machinery, and non-ferrous metals, etc. India's trade with ASEAN countries is hovering around 7-9 percent of its total trade every year (Bhattacharya, 2006).

Bilaterally, the trade between India and Singapore has

been increasing. From US$ 6.6 billion in 2004-05, it has reached US$ 8.7 billion in 2005-06. India's trade figures with Thailand have increased from US$ 1.22 billion in 2000-01, to US$ 2.2 billion in 2004-05. As far as Indonesia is concerned, the trade figures increased from US$ 3.9 billion in 2004-05 to US$ 4.3 billion in 2005-06. Similarly, trading figures with Malaysia have increased to the extent of making Malaysia as one of the top ten investors in India. Again, the trade between CLMV countries and India is increasing substantially. However, it is investment relations which have to be attended to, with utmost care. The environment has been disturbed especially after the suspension of Tata-Singapore Airline project and that of special economic zone at Nandigram, Haldia, where Indonesia's Salim group has lot of stakes. Despite obstacles, avenues are explored to strengthen investment relations. Malaysia and Singapore are major investors in India. Malaysia has made substantial investments in expanding capacities in selected infrastructural areas such as logistics, highways, and ICTs in India. On the other hand, Singapore has made investments in health care, real estate and tourism. Their technology park in Bangalore has created a positive environment for investments in India.

There are several areas of collaboration between India and ASEAN countries which can prove mutually beneficial. For example, energy, edible oil, pharmaceuticals, IT and BT are prospective areas of joint ventures. It is commonly understood, that the Indian Origin entrepreneurs own the largest palm oil refinery in Malaysia, the largest carbon-black manufacturing units in Thailand and a large number of textile factories in Indonesia (Yahya, 2003). One the other hand, Tata, Reliance, Birla and Ranbaxy are noted Indian companies which are potential investors in the ASEAN region. Indian companies are ready to invest in auto-components sector in Thailand, on motor vehicles and energy sector in Indonesia and Vietnam, and on Information and Communications Technology (ICT) in the Philippines.

In food processing, forest products and cooking oil, there are abundance of scope for collaboration with Indonesia, Malaysia and Myanmar. 'Malaysia and Indonesia are major palm producers and Thailand has much expertise in food processing industry-particularly in deep sea fishing and other marine related activities'. The information technology (IT) is an area, where India has advantages and Singapore's Info-Comm Development Authority has signed an MOU with NIIT. Entertainment and multi-media especially films and TV programmes of India are popular in the ASEAN region. The collaboration in those areas could be fruitful to both the sides. Both India and ASEAN can be benefited if there are investments in drugs, pharmaceuticals and human resources.

Foreign Direct Investment (FDI) from the ASEAN region is trickling in slowly in limited areas and it is mainly meant for infra-structure building, hotels and tourism services, heavy industries, chemicals, fertilizers and food processing. Total Indian FDI in the ASEAN region is merely US$ 225 million and that of ASEAN in India, US$ 2 billion (Shekhar 2007). India has attached importance to infra-structure development to connect India with ASEAN. India intends to build railways and roadways from New Delhi to Hanoi and Kolkata to Singapore directly. Tamu-Moreh road connecting India and Myanmar through highways is to be expanded to facilitate trade and people-to-people contacts. This is intended to facilitate greater movement of people from across the eastern borders and wants to welcome tourists and pilgrims visiting Sanchi, Sarnath, Bodh Gaya, Nalanda and other parts of India.

Indians find landmark developments in economic relations with ASEAN and similarly India's linkages in the security matters have witnessed positive developments. When SEATO or Five Power Defence Pact was signed, it had cold-war parameters. However, when the ARF was established (1993), it reflected regional concerns of security. Brunei meeting of the ARF (1995) defined a framework for the future of ARF. It was to be evolved in three stages (a) the promotion of confidence building (including disaster relief and peace keeping activities), (b) the development of preventive diplomacy, and (c) the elaboration of approaches to conflict resolution. In 1996, India got the membership of ARF and it has been participating in its activities. The ASEAN wanted India, China and other actors in the Asia-Pacific to engage in regional security matters and to build a consensus on broader issues of common concern. Indian participation in ARF can be understood in the following areas:

- Confidence Building,
- Maritime Cooperation, and
- Combating Terrorism.

For confidence building, India regularly participates in ARF Senior Officers' Meetings (ARF-SOM) and Inter-Sessional Support Group Meetings for confidence Building Measures (ISG on CBMs), the Council for Security Cooperation in Asia-Pacific (CSCAP) and other forums. The participants deliberate on transnational organized crimes such as drug trafficking, terrorism or counter-terrorism, maritime piracy, and illegal movement of the nuclear, chemical, biological and other materials. In view of a perfect and proper understanding of India's security concerns in the ASEAN region Pakistan has been prevented from taking Kashmir dispute to find a place in the deliberations of ARF. The staunch support of ASEAN became tacit when India went in for Pokhran II as most of the states did not join Japan or Australia for Trade embargo. Although Western reactions were vociferous, ASEAN did not pass any resolutions against India. The US, the UN, the EU Australia and Japan indulged in strong criticism of Indian experimentation and called for adherence to non-proliferation, but majority of ASEAN partners felt that if China can experiment its nuclear weapons or North Korea can do so , why not India?

Pokharan II was a clear indication of India's emerging status as a nuclear weapon state and its potential to influence strategic developments in the region. The nuclear testing was not viewed as a threat, but as an asset. The countries in Southeast Asia could find India's contribution in a more positive perspective as far as fighting against terror is concerned, compared to the United States, for example (Acharya, 2006). Equally important is the fact that India has been able to assure the regional states on its manifest neutrality and its desire to keep South Asian issues out of the ambit of ASEAN or ARF. Although India has refused to sign the Comprehensive Test Ban Treaty (CTBT), as a nuclear-weapon state, it was willing to respect the nuclear-free status of Southeast Asia by converting this recognition into a de jure commitment. ASEAN states appreciate Indian gestures in strengthening their security profile. India's substantive role in preventing sea piracy and terrorism has been appreciated.

India has established a naval base at Andaman Islands, called Fortress Andaman (FORTAN). This is strategically located in the waterways that pass through Southeast Asia connecting Bay of Bengal to East Asia. This waterway connects Indian Ocean with the Pacific and thus FORTAN has lot of implications on the politics of Malacca Straits. The maritime threats, sea piracy, smuggling and terrorism–in the region are matters of common concern and both India and Southeast Asia cooperate to grapple with those threats. India welcomed Indonesia, Malaysia and Singapore, to have joint naval exercises at Andaman in the post-Cold War era (1991). This proved a good exercise for confidence building between India and the ASEAN states. India was encouraged to establish defence ties with some of the ASEAN states and Malaysia was the first to sign MOU for defence cooperation in 1993. This was for training Malaysian air force personnel and at least 100 pilots came for training (Naidu, 2006).

In the same year, India and Singapore made arrangements for training and for joint exercises of their naval personnel with Indian counterparts. India had agreed to provide anti-submarine warfare training to Singapore's naval personnel also. Thailand has availed itself of the strategic expertise of the

Indians after acquiring an aircraft carrier. On the other hand, Vietnam is trying to build up its navy with Indian expertise, and has been seeking technological support for an upgradation of MIG-21 fighters. Similarly, defence cooperation with Indonesia, Laos and Myanmar has also started taking place. India had supplied anti-insurgency defence equipments to Myanmar and has transferred two BN-2 Defender maritime aircraft to Myanmar (2007). There is coordination of search and rescue operations at sea and an establishment of inter-operability with navies of other ASEAN states. The most important aspect of Indian navy's role is the protection of sea lanes of communication in the Indian Ocean region. As articulated in India's Naval Doctrine of April 2004, India's maritime policies have been made clear. The doctrine is premised on the necessity to build cooperative maritime security with the countries on the shores of the Indian Ocean with regard to challenges encompassing safe flows of trade and energy as well as threats of terrorism (Acharya, 2006).

After ASEAN-India Summit in 2003, both sides have given focussed attention on security cooperation. They agreed for joint operations to protect sea lanes and for pooling resources in the event of war against terrorism. The military contacts and joint exercises that had already started in 1991, were expanded into full fledged defence cooperation. India has got an access to various ports in Southeast Asia for enhancing the level of cooperation. India and ASEAN have signed a joint Declaration for Cooperation in combating international terrorism (October, 2003) and accordingly, they have agreed for (a) an exchange of information (b) legal and enforcement matters (c) institutional capacity augmentation and (d) training. India has also signed the Treaty of Amity and Cooperation in 2003 and repeated its commitment to maintenance of peace and stability of the region. The ASEAN countries are convinced about India's role in the region and they have looked complimentarily to support one another.

However, combating terrorism is a difficult task. The

terrorists have their concealed network and websites and they are active in India and Southeast Asia. In certain cases, they have popular support also, and it is difficult to contain them. India has a long history of fighting terrorism, but Indians have succeeded only in a few cases. Kashmir, for example, has been a centre of terrorist activities led by Laskar-e-Toiba (Let) and Harkat-ul-Jihad-al-Islami (HUJI) and their political settlement is not in sight. They get regular supply of arms and ammunitions from across the border and Pakistan has been supporting them at the international fora without any hesitation. It is understood that Al-Qaeda had funded the establishment of training and indoctrination centres for the spread of terrorism in Afghanistan, Pakistan, the Philippines and Indonesia to create jihadi forces. They were also supported by the government in Pakistan and Bangladesh initially. Abu Sayyaf group (ASG) and Moro Islamic Liberation Front (MILF) in the Philippines had Al Qaeda connections. Jemaah Islamiyah (JI) in Indonesia was also inspired by Al Qaeda, which had several groups to spread terror in different parts of Southeast Asia. Again Kumpulan Militant Malaysian (KMM) and Majelis Mujahidin Indonesia (MMI) Pattani National Liberation Front (Thailand) had jihadi squads, suicide bombers and indoctrinated fanatics to be sacrificed in the name of Islam.

Following 9/11, Asia became the main focus of counter-terrorism, and the terrorists began to retaliate. Their attacks on Indian Parliament (2001), suicide attacks at the tourist resort in Bali (2002), the bombing of Marriot Hotel (2003) and Australian Embassy (2004) in Jakarta, the explosion in Super Ferry 14 in the Philippines (2004) and various suicide attacks on security establishments in Kashmir, Jaipur, Bombay, Bangalore and Delhi are big challenges for the security establishments. The threats of transnational terrorism and the imperatives for global coordination have been a challenging task. The terrorists in the ASEAN region have revealed that they were trained in Afghanistan, Pakistan and Bangladesh

.Whether it is JI, LeT Or HUJI, they have got specialized training and at present most of them are based in SAARC countries. On the other hand, the intelligence reports suggest that criminal groups in Southeast Asia do supply arms and ammunitions to insurgent groups in India's northeast such as ULFA, as well as to the Liberation Tigers of Tamil Elam (LTTE) in Sri Lanka (Acharya 2006). The ULFA in Assam and other separatist groups are using sophisticated weapons which are regularly supplied through the porous borders at the Myanmar frontiers. It is difficult to identify various criminal outfits which supply arms to rebels. Again the countries in the region have not been able to stop the sources of their funding which very often comes in the name of welfare activities from inside and outside the country. There are a number of West Asian countries which have been sending assistance to promote Mosque and Madrasah activities and it is difficult to exercise surveillance over its expenditure and place them for audit.

Terrorism is against the ethics of civil society. It attempts to destroy business centres, communication channels and to sabotage every infrastructure of growth. It is barbaric in approach against its adversaries and intends to restructure society to promote nothing but hatred and terror. Although the terrorists try to take the help of religion to attain their objectives, it is a retrogressive development to be discarded. India and ASEAN are committed to combat terror, but till the combating is sincerely coordinated by India, Pakistan, Bangladesh and ASEAN and effectively monitored by the appropriate agencies without fear or favour, the endeavour will remain incomplete and unfulfilled.

Finally, we find that the balance sheet of economic relations is satisfactory. Although negotiations over FTA are still in the bargaining process, the fact that China and Japan are going to implement FTA proposals in near future, will surely have positive impact on Indian decision makers. India has a vision to emerge as a developed nation by 2020 and this objective will automatically pave the path for mutually beneficial economic cooperation with ASEAN and other partners. However, the security cooperation is not satisfactory. The ASEAN may be actively trying to nab their terrorists and cooperating with one another in tracing the hideouts of Jemaah Islamiyah or Abu Sayyaf or remnants of Al Qaida supporters, but there are certain pockets in South Asia, where the terrorists have got the protection of state in the name of religion. There are some who, for the sake of "vote bank politics" argue by way of seeking protection to certain religious or fanatic groups, irrespective of whatever they do. There must be a regional consensus over certain issues of regional concern and regional actors should try to spell out those norms in this age of globalisation. The developments in South Asia have an impinging impact on the overall situation of Southeast Asia and vice versa and the matters of grave security and economic implications should not be overlooked.

ASEAN has evolved a sophisticated mechanism to resolve separatist movements and a reference to them would be in order here. They, at the outset, tried to understand the genesis of secessionist movements and tried to effectively contain them through a coordinated action in which national efforts were supported by regional initiatives. Again, an acceptance of the principles of non-interference in the internal affairs of the neighbouring countries makes all the partners desist from supplying weapons to insurgents or from providing sanctuaries. In this context, a reference to ASEAN's two important resolutions, namely, "Declaration of ASEAN Concord", and "Treaty of Amity and Cooperation in Southeast Asia" (1976), is important.

The ASEAN Concord (1976) observed that the stability of each member state and of the ASEAN region is an essential contribution to international peace and security. Each member state resolves to eliminate threats posed by subversion to its stability, thus paving the way for the national and ASEAN resilience to gather additional strength. Again, it has been observed, that the member states, in the spirit of ASEAN solidarity, shall rely exclusively on peaceful processes in the settlement of intra-regional differences. Again, the Treaty of Amity and Cooperation (TAC) evolved a code of conduct to minimize the scope of conflict. Article 2 stated that in matters of maintaining relations with one another, the high contracting Parties shall be guided by the following fundamental principles:

1. Mutual respect for the independence, sovereignty, equality, territorial integrity and national identity of all nations;
2. The right of every state to lead its national existence free from external interference, subversion or coercion;
3. Non-interference in the internal affairs of one another;
4. Settlement of differences or disputes by peaceful means;
5. Renunciation of the threat or use of force; and
6. Effective cooperation among themselves. (TAC, 1976).

The Treaty of Amity and Cooperation further resolved, that "in the event no solution is reached through direct negotiations, the High Council shall take cognizance of the dispute or the situation and shall recommend to the parties in dispute appropriate means of settlement such as good offices, mediation, enquiry or conciliation." The High Council may, however, offer its good offices, or upon agreement of the parties in the dispute, constitute itself into a committee of mediation, enquiry or conciliation when deemed necessary, the High Council shall recommend appropriate measures for the prevention of deterioration of the dispute or the situation.

Besides passing these resolutions ASEAN members tried to cultivate ASEAN spirit of cooperation and sincerely worked for confidence building. They expressed their strong faith in ASEAN partners and kept vigil on their borders. When Vietnam militarily intervened in Cambodia, the ASEAN partners rallied their support to the *de jure* rulers to oppose Vietnamese occupation. Whatever compulsions or motive that Vietnam had in deciding upon the military intervention to overthrow genocidal Khmer Rouge from power, it became a case of interference in the internal affairs of a neighbouring country. Vietnam's action did not get ASEAN approval. In 1986, Vietnam reviewed its policy and in 1988, withdrew from Cambodia which paved the path for its reconciliation and cooperation with ASEAN.

To conclude, it can be observed that the ASEAN has evolved mechanism for conflict resolution and confidence building, which works. ASEAN has consensus over matters of regional concern and for dealing with issues of sustainable development successfully. South Asians, on the other hand, are left far behind in that endeavour. They always take one step forward and another backward, and hence there is stagnation and underdevelopment. The endeavour to bring gas pipeline from Myanmar to India via Bangladesh or Iran-Pakistan and India gas pipeline proposal, proved a failure because of the opposition of one or the other of SAARC partners. The endeavour of free trade, upgrading of roadways, highways and railways and other communication network amongst SAARC countries is delayed because of political strategic differences.

Singapore's Prime Minister, Goh Chok Tong once portrayed India as one Wing of ASEAN's jumbo jet and China and Japan as the other Wing (2002). It was generous on his part to project India as equally important as East Asian neighbours, despite India's low ranking in development matters. Although India has immense resources, vast expertise, and manpower, it has suffered because of faulty management, corruption and socialist drives. It is universally recognized that India has appropriate scientific and technological expertise which, if mobilized properly, can substantially contribute to India's modernization. India has a huge market with approximately 500 million middle class population who believe in free market system. Its potential to act as an effective wing of ASEAN is possible, but this objective is interlinked with issues of regional understanding, peace and prosperity.

The ASEAN has played an important role in integrating India and in strengthening the ethos of regional cooperation, which is bound to pay dividends in future. Singapore's role to campaign for India's sectoral partnership in 1992, Thailand's role in supporting India in BIMSTEC or ASEAN's tacit support for Pokharan II, were crucial developments in confidence building in India-ASEAN relations. The arrival of Salim Group of Industries from Indonesia, and the involvement of Singapore, Malaysia and Thailand in joint ventures, have increased the mutual confidence in each other. Again, the increasing cooperation in the traditional or non-traditional security matters, joint exercises and sharing of military intelligence, have been of high order. The increased level of cooperation in the political, economic, security and cultural areas, have generated new spirits. We have faith in "ASEAN way", and if it is accepted as a norm, it will certainly help in community building in the SAARC region. Both India and ASEAN are advertently working in that direction and the projection is that India will be an integral part of a common market by 2020.

References

Satu P. Limaye, "India's Relations with Southeast Asia Take a Wing," *Southeast Asian Affairs 2003*, pp. 39-51.

Frederic Grare and Amitabh Matoo, *India and ASEAN: The Politics of India's Look East Policy*, (New Delhi 2001).

G V C Naidu, "India and Southeast Asia," *World Focus*, 2006, pp. 16-20.

Swapan K. Bhattacharya, "India's Economic Relations with the ASEAN countries," *World Focus,* 2006, pp. 28-32.

Faizal Yahya "India and Southeast Asia: Revisited," *Contemporary Southeast Asia,* 2003, pp. 79-103.

Arabinda Acharya, "India and Southeast Asia in the age of Terror: Building Partnership for Peace," *Contemporary Southeast Asia*, 2006, pp. 297-321.

Sudhir Devare, *India and Southeast Asia: Towards Security Convergence*, (Singapore, 2006).

Rahul Sen, Mukul G. Asher, Ramkishen S. Rajan, "ASEAN-India

Economic Relations," *Economic and Political Weekly*, 2004, pp. 3297-3307.

Vibhanshu Shekhar, "India-ASEAN Relations: An Overview", *IPCS*, 2007, pp. 4-7.

K S Nathan, *India and ASEAN: The Growing Partnership for the 21st Century*, (Kuala Lumpur, 2000).

Ganganath Jha, "India's Relationship with Southeast Asia," *Dialogue Quarterly*, 2004, pp. 157-68.

The text of the Speech Delivered by Prime Minister P V Narasimha Rao, 8 September 1994 at Singapore.

Text of Treaty of Amity and Cooperation in Southeast Asia, 24 February 1976, Bali, Indonesia.

Text of Declaration of ASEAN Concord, 24 February 1976, Bali, Indonesia.

Saeed Ahmed Rid, "Pakistan's Look East Policy: Opportunities and constraints," *Regional Studies*, Winter, 2006-07, pp. 64-92.

Times of India, 29 August 2008.

Aparna Shivpuri Singh, *Business Times,* 23 June 2005.

Bronson Percival, *The Dragon Looks South: China and Southeast Asia in the New Century*, (Praeger Security International, Westport, 2007), p. 9.

Satu P. Limaye is Director of Research, Asia Pacific Centre for Security Studies, Hawaii, USA.

Satu P. Limaye, n.1, p. 43.

Goh Chok Tong, Text of his speech in the first ASEAN-India Summit, Phnom Penh, 2002.

4

Regional Cohesion of ASEAN after Four Decades

Tridib Chakraborti

The history of Southeast Asia is a narrative of fracas and indistinctness. Since the end of the Second World War, this region has been engulfed in cold war politics, which largely prevented the countries of the region from functioning independently and in a concerted manner, for the accomplishment of their holistic success. Each country of this region got encumbered with some problem or the other, all the time encountering and struggling with countless influences-constructive or venomous–both from within and without. After more than five decades of nation building, in spite of diverse histories, political and social systems, religious beliefs, and cultural backgrounds, the countries of Southeast Asia could retrospect and introspect with complacency at their manifold achievements.

Many of these countries also countenanced series of severe setbacks and disappointments. While some of them were infuriated with prolonged armed struggle, political upheavals, blood-spattered military coups and separatist struggles, which had followed as usual, the corollaries of race/ethnic conflicts, poverty and under-development, domination of ruling party on the minority community, religion (mainly the ascent of Islamic fundamentalism), historical legacy, opium and drug-related menace, human trafficking etc., others enjoyed unprecedented economic augmentation and development, wealth and affluence. Despite this plethora of sweet and sour historical reminiscences, the nation-states of Southeast Asia endeavoured to maintain a somewhat peace and sustained security through their indigenous regional organization like the Association of Southeast Asian Nations (ASEAN), which was established on August 8, 1967, in Bangkok, at the initiative of the five original member countries, namely, Indonesia, Malaysia, the Philippines, Singapore, and Thailand.

While Brunei Darussalam joined the Association on January 8, 1984 and Vietnam on July 28, 1995, Laos and Myanmar became members on 23 July 1997 and Cambodia on April 30, 1999. The Bangkok Declaration united the ASEAN member countries in a joint effort to promote the economic cooperation and the welfare of the people in the region. This Declaration clearly set out the guidelines for ASEAN's activities and defined the aims of the organization and also represented the collective will of the nations, to bind themselves together in friendship and cooperation through mutual efforts and sacrifices, in order to secure their peoples' peace, freedom and regional prosperity. After more than four decades of its performance based on the principles of trial and error, ASEAN emerged as one of the most successful experiments in the realm of regional organization in the Asia-Pacific region. Moreover, through its policy of trial and triumph, it has come to play a very constructive and prominent role in developing a sense of regional identity in Southeast Asia.

During its more than 42 years of existence, ASEAN experienced a host of nuisance, like the genocidal act of the Pol Pot regime during 1975-78; Vietnam's invasion of Cambodia; transmigration and influx of refugees; drugs, human trafficking and transnational crimes; East Timor crisis; Myanmar's military repression; transnational problems such as the forest fires in Indonesia, low intensity conflicts and terrorism; Muslim separatist movement in Southern Thailand and the Philippines; Thailand's devaluation of the Baht; Cambodia's Coup d'etat in 1997; sacking of Anwar Ibrahim, Malaysian Deputy Prime Minister, in the 1990's; the financial crisis of 1997; gender discrimination; the ill impacts of globalization and lopsided multilateral trade regimes like the WTO; Asian Values syndrome; rising Islamic fundamentalism; new forms of terrorism; uneven economic status among ASEAN members; natural calamities like 'Tsunami' and earthquakes; poor human rights records, territorial claims etc. Despite their long drawn experiences, the ASEAN members, on many occasions, unfortunately failed to resolve some of these issues. Consequently, they pragmatically generated acute and critical comments on the governmental policies of the respective countries to resolve the crises, in doing which they inevitably confronted questions about ASEAN's regionalism idea and its principles of non-interference and non-confrontation.

The volcanic eruption of antipathy took place, when Surin Pitsuan, the then Foreign Minister of Thailand, challenged the basic premises of ASEAN's central principle of non–intervention and called for a change at the ASEAN Foreign Ministers' Meeting held in July 1998. Surin Pitsuan proposed to review the implementation of the principle of non-intervention in ASEAN, which did not represent a sudden turn-around in the attitudes within the region, towards ASEAN's diplomatic norms and practices. This was something that had already been built up within the previous decade. He demanded that the ASEAN members be allowed to openly discuss each other's domestic affairs, if these had an impact, outside their borders. He dubbed his proposal as "constructive intervention" and a month later, at the ASEAN Ministerial Meeting in Singapore, to remove the impression that he was suggesting a modification of the principle of 'non-intervention', re-christened the idea as 'flexible engagement'. In the Singapore Meeting, Pitsuan made it clear that ASEAN must adhere to the principle of non-intervention, but, simultaneously, find a way to deal with new problems and challenges which threaten to affect and damage ASEAN's credibility, if left unapprised and unanswered: "The principle of non-intervention is not the real issue…the real issue is how we can work together in dealing with the new challenges of a new millennium." [1]

This proposal of Surin Pitsuan received the support of the Philippines. Domingo Siazon, the then Foreign Minister of the Philippines, in a statement, said: "The policy of non-intervention is a universally accepted concept governing relations between countries. However, in view of growing integration, events have trans-boundary effects which have an impact on other countries." He further added that Surin's proposal of "flexible engagement would not divide and weaken ASEAN. We should be mature enough." Unfortunately, the Thai Foreign Minister's proposal was strongly opposed by the rest of the ASEAN members who advocated "constructive interventions" in certain regional issues. They viewed the Thai initiative as a 'non starter'. Following this debate, the Singapore meeting decided, as a compromise, to have "enhanced interaction" in future. The phrase "Enhanced interaction", was not clearly spelt out, but presumably, it meant more candid and frequent exchanges of views in private. In the next Ministerial Meeting, held in July 1999 in Singapore, the ASEAN Foreign Ministers exchanged their views related to issues that have an adverse impact on the neighbourly relations.

However, nearly all members regarded the retention of the principle of non-intervention as essential, since it stresses "mutual respect for independence, sovereignty, equality, territorial integrity and national identity of all nations". Their emphasis on the principle of non-intervention had originated in 1971, when the ASEAN members, through the concept of the Zone of Peace, Freedom and Neutrality (ZOPFAN), had recognized the right of every state, large or small, to lead its national existence free from outside interference, lest its freedom, independence and integrity should be affected adversely, and declared that the neutralization of Southeast Asia is a desirable goal.

The ZOPFAN Declaration provided a standard example of

the emerging ASEAN way of consensus, compromise, and avoidance of rigid reciprocity and rejection of legally binding obligations. [2] This idea of maintenance of nation-state sovereignty was further fortified by Article 2 of Chapter I of the Treaty of Amity and Cooperation (TAC) adopted at ASEAN's First Heads of Government Summit in 1976, which primarily aimed at promoting perpetual peace, everlasting amity and cooperation among their people, that would subsequently contribute to their strength, solidarity and closer relationship for practical necessity, in the absence of which, the Association would become irrelevant and incompetent to address the real world changes and challenges. In the TAC, ASEAN member countries accepted the following fundamental principles in their relations with one another, as mentioned hereunder:

1. Mutual respect for the independence, sovereignty, equality, territorial integrity and national identity of all nations;
2. The right of every state to lead its national existence free from external interference, subversion or coercion;
3. Non-Interference in the internal affairs of one another;
4. Settlement of differences or disputes by peaceful means;
5. Renunciation of the threat or use of force; and
6. Effective cooperation among themselves. [3]

Thus, the TAC mostly served as a code of conduct for an interface between the ASEAN member countries in Southeast Asia. It was also a non-aggression pact, as the accession of non–ASEAN states was explicitly allowed. Chapter IV of the TAC dealt with "Pacific Settlement of Disputes", making its signatories obliged to settle disputes "through friendly negotiations" and consultation. Following this Treaty, ASEAN, through its multifarious activities, gradually emerged as a successful economic organization in Southeast Asia. To the ASEAN members, its 'ASEAN Way' is not at all a typical conflict resolution mechanism, but a thing that evolved as a conflict avoidance instrument, by relying on the software arms of regional understanding rather than on the hardware elements of formalized, rule-based instrumentalities. During its long years of experience, ASEAN has never been visualized as a mechanism for conflict settlement and conflict resolution. It has rather been able to establish itself successfully in conflict mitigation. The signing of the ASEAN Charter in November 2007, which seeks to establish ASEAN as a legal entity and formally move the region towards an EU-style economic community by 2015, has greatly increased ASEAN's institutional capacity and ability for autonomous action.

However, from 1976 to the present day, ASEAN in its day to day functioning, faced a plethora of internal and external problems with regional and transnational ramifications, and these troubles have occasionally caused serious tensions among themselves and divided the countries of Southeast Asia. Issues like Cambodia's Coup d'etat in 1997; the sacking of Malaysian Deputy Prime Minister, Anwar Ibrahim in the 1990's, East Timor crisis; Myanmar's military repression; transmigration and influx of refugees; drugs, human trafficking and transnational crimes; Thailand's devaluation of the Baht; etc. failed to resolve the regional differences. However, this splitting up among the ASEAN members, does not mean that the performance of ASEAN during its forty-two years of existence, dismally failed to establish itself as a strong and successful regional organization in global politics. There are a number of cases, where ASEAN performed quite proficiently and successfully to demonstrate its ability and strength to tackle many outstanding critical issues, both regional and transnational in nature. Issues like the problem of forest fires and trans-boundary environmental pollution, terrorism after 11 September, South China Sea problem, Cambodia crisis in 1979, financial crisis in 1997, minimizing the gap between the rich and poor of ASEAN members, etc. were taken into prime consideration. In all these cases, the ASEAN members took a number of initiatives and strove to resolve them entirely on the basis of dialogue, consultation, cooperation, engagement, mutual interaction and regional consensus, without breaking away from the principle of non-intervention.

ASEAN's Accomplishment: Cases of Regional Cohesion

The first issue was related to the South China Sea imbroglio. The South China Sea (SCS) remains a major contentious matter among the countries of the Asia-Pacific region. The maritime disputes in the South China Sea have been characterized by strategic, diplomatic and economic considerations. The territorial claims in this region (particularly in regard to the Paracel and Spratly islands) among the various disputing countries owing to their strategic importance appeared to be the gravest threat in the last part of the 20th Century and the early part of the 21st Century. China has been the main claimant over the issue of territorial sovereignty in the SCS and also the principal and potential source of threat and uncertainty for the ASEAN countries. The other claimants include the ASEAN countries and Taiwan. The Philippines, Malaysia and Brunei claim specific parts of the South China Sea, while China, Taiwan and Vietnam claim all of its island, islets and reefs; China appears to claim the submerged features as well. In fact, there remains virtually no unclaimed area in the South China Sea. The claims and counter claims over the island in the South China Sea culminated in numerous clashes among the disputing countries, of which, the clash between Vietnam and China in Paracel islands in 1974, the quarrel between Vietnam and China in Spratly islands in 1988 and the conflict between China and the Philippines in Mischief Reef island in 1995, are the most significant. [4]

Owing to these severe conflicting disputes, ASEAN as a regional grouping, was forced to undertake initiatives and formulate coherent policy in the face of such a crisis, because such frequent disputes threatened the peace and stability of the region as a whole. Moreover, with the collapse of the former Soviet Union in 1991 and the gradual withdrawal of the naval forces and military deployments from Vietnam by Russia and simultaneously the phased withdrawal by the US from its former naval and air bases in the Philippines (because of the failure to hold negotiations on new terms for continual use of the bases) resulted in a major power vacuum in the region of Southeast Asia. This made China a powerful actor in the region, likely to fill in the vacuum and establish its domination over the region, not only to pose a threat to the security of the Southeast Asian countries, but also to increase the possibility of Beijing resorting to the use of force in the settlement of disputes in the South China Sea. Besides this, many States in this region feared that Beijing intends to establish the entire South China Sea as a "Chinese Lake".

It is a fact that the conflict management approaches with reference to South China Sea's Paracel and Spratlys islands, differ considerably. One reason is that the Paracel conflict is de facto considered to be a bilateral issue between China and Vietnam, whereas the Spratly dispute is considered to be a multilateral dispute. Furthermore, attempts at negotiations between China and Vietnam have displayed that the latter wants to include the Paracel issue on the agenda, while the former is not amenable. The archipelago, being in the full control of China, the latter recognizes no issue to be there, to negotiate. The role that ASEAN can play is rather a complex exercise, since four of its member states–Brunei Darussalam, Malaysia, the Philippines and Vietnam–pursue sovereignty claims to all, or parts of the Spratly archipelago. This naturally exhibited a situation in which ASEAN cannot play the role of a third party mediator between China and the other claimants. Nevertheless, the condition in the South China Sea has been brought onto the agenda in the context of the ASEAN–China dialogue, after the ASEAN members in July 1992, signed the ASEAN Declaration on the South China Sea, in Manila. In this Manila Declaration, the ASEAN members did not deal with the problem of sovereign jurisdiction but initiated an effort to disseminate an informal code of conduct based on self-restraint, the non-use of force and the peaceful resolution of disputes.

It relied on the norms and principles primarily introduced in the ASEAN Treaty of Amity and Cooperation (TAC) of 1976. [5] Thus, this informal code of conduct for the South China Sea was based on the notions of conflict management and avoidance of conflict, rather than conflict resolution. Despite the overlapping claims, the member states shared an interest in promoting a tranquil solution to the territorial dispute in the South China Sea. At the ASEAN Foreign Ministers' meeting held in July 1999, in Singapore, the Philippines and Malaysia, for the first time brought about a proposal for a 'regional code' with respect to the security and economic issues over the Spratly group of islands in South China Sea.

However, this draft 'code of conduct' was described mainly as an intra-ASEAN document and ASEAN planned to widen its reach by incorporating China's cooperation and ideas. By this principle, the ASEAN members propose to seek the extension of these principles through the espousal in future, of a Regional Code of Conduct for the South China Sea covering all ARF members, by which they would liquefy tensions with reference to this issue. China, after its initial repudiation for several times, finally signed the Code of Conduct on 4 November 2002. The Declaration on the Conduct of Parties on South China Sea was a 10-point programme, which was adopted by the governments of the member states of ASEAN and the People's Republic of China (PRC). It re-emphasized the need to peacefully settle the South China Sea dispute, and agreed to "refrain from action of inhabiting on the presently uninhabited islands, reefs, shoals, cays, and other features."

In addition, ASEAN and the PRC pledged to resolve territorial issues peacefully and to "respect freedom of navigation in and over-flight above the South China Sea." [6] This Declaration was in itself a triumph, since it was the first political document concluded between China and ASEAN over the South China Sea issue, bearing a positive significance for enhancing mutual trust between the two sides, and also a progressive step towards the resolution of the crisis, as China for the first time, signed a multilateral declaration with ASEAN over the issue, which it had earlier rejected. But, the November 2002 China-ASEAN agreement has been encumbered with problems. First, the Declaration is merely a political statement, not a legally binding document. If one party violates a provision, there is no method for enforcement. Secondly, the statement fails to mention any geographic scope, specifically concerning the Spratly or Paracel Island chains. Finally, the language of the Declaration on the Conduct of Parties in the South China Sea is so compelling that it prompts the signatories to commit themselves to cooperative conduct, though history shows that this is unlikely to happen every time.

However, Beijing's accession to the TAC in October 2003 and Tokyo's promise in December of the same year to ratify the document, clearly demonstrates that multilateralism—via ASEAN—is working. Furthermore, the Eleventh ASEAN-China Summit held on November 20, 2007, at Singapore, stressed the early implementation of the Declaration for adopting a Regional Code of Conduct for the South China Sea eventually. In this meeting, the ASEAN member countries further reaffirmed their determination "to the early and full implementation of the Declaration on the Conduct of Parties in the South China Sea (DOC), towards the eventual adoption of a Regional Code of Conduct in the South China Sea." In addition, the ARF also played a crucial role as a multilateral platform, in trying to achieve Beijing's cooperation in the resolution of the South China Sea crisis, through various negotiations and discussions.

Thus, the decades-old South China Sea problem has been temporarily resolved and at present, there is no sign of any tension or clash among the claimants. The drastic alteration of the global order and the prominence of economics as a major determining factor in bilateral relations rather than politics, have largely reduced the tensions that had existed in the South China Sea. Besides this, the tragic September 11 terrorist attacks have unexpectedly brought new stability in the SCS. The event provided an opportunity for an improvement of the relationship between the United States and China. The event also shifted the regional security focus from the conventional security issues to the non-conventional issues, in particular, the threat posed by international terrorism. In addition, there have been other developments after the September 11 terrorist mayhem, which have the potential to affect peace and stability in the SCS, in a positive way. These developments include the emergence of a stronger US defence capability in the SCS and a US-led security and military alliance in Southeast Asia; the strengthening of military relations between the United States and the three claimants in the SCS, namely, the Philippines, Malaysia, and Vietnam; the start of the U.S.—India strategic relationship; the revival of the U.S.—Pakistan political and military relations; a growing *rapprochement* between the United States and Russia; and the deployment of the Japanese navies in the SCS and the Indian Ocean.

In resolving this crisis, ASEAN's adherence to regional cohesion played a key factor to reduce this tension and generated a favourable and congenial environment in the region. Its initiative of the code of conduct undoubtedly shows a desire of the different parties involved, to pursue their individual claims by peaceful means, as well as openly denounces the use of force in the South China Sea. In that sense, it contributes towards the easing of tensions between the claimant states. By putting off the question of boundaries, it also increases the possibility of reaching agreements on joint oil exploration and development schemes, as well as of achieving the restoration of peace through collective means and at the same time it keeps the principle of maintenance of sovereignty of each country intact, in the region.

Thus, the South China Sea dispute can be characterized as one, striking balance among sovereignty, development and security interests of ASEAN, based on regional cohesion. In fact, the ASEAN members followed a coherent policy, based on the principles of non-intervention, to momentarily resolve this kind of a dazzling regional tension in the Asia-Pacific region. At present the overall situation in the SCS has become more stable and the possibility of any serious armed conflict has lessened to a large extent. In the changing global order, the regional security issues have shifted more towards the discussion of non-traditional, comprehensive, cooperative, and human security matters, including piracy, marine environmental protection, shipping safety and navigation, maritime terrorism, and joint development of natural resources in the South China Sea region. This affable development has, no doubt, served the region's interests to an enormous point.

The second issue is Haze Crisis. The issue of environmental security as a prime attribute of policy shaping, did not become a chief subject of study for the countries of Southeast Asia during the first three decades of the cold war. Its environmental attentiveness slowly evolved in the 1970s, after the 1972 Stockholm UN Conference on the Environment. Following this conference and with a desire to initiate a regional sustainable development programme internationally, the United Nations Environment Programme (UNEP) Commission, in its Asia–Pacific regional advisory team meeting, held in 1977, outlined an Asian Sub-regional Environment Programme (ASEP), in the wake of which, the countries of Southeast Asia—mainly the ASEAN members, took a number of important pledges on environment for the sustainable use and management of natural resources. At the Fifth ASEAN Ministerial Meeting on Environment of 1992 in Singapore, the ASEAN members held that those industrial countries should extend environmental aid and proficiency to the developing nations in their quest for ecologically sound development.

The meeting also emphasized the responsibility of the developed countries to provide the developing nations with new financial resources, as well as an access to the environmentally sound technology at the consessional and preferential terms. Through this Singapore Declaration, the ASEAN members pledged "to play an active part in protecting the environment by continuing to cooperate by promoting the principle of sustainable development and integrating it into all aspects of development". Unfortunately, the implementation of these environmental declarations has not been an effective exercise for the countries of Southeast Asia. This weak implementation effort could be attributed to the lack of an internal environmental monitoring system within the framework of ASEAN itself as a regional organization. However, the most important factor behind the lack of implementation of ASEAN's Environmental declarations was that the individual countries continued to put greater stress on the preservation of their national sovereignty and the recognition of their developing country status. Such an exclusivist consciousness often compromised with the environmental concern of the ASEAN members, in spite of international pressure to make concrete contributions to the protection of the earth. [7]

The situation was drastically altered with the issue of an environmental understanding percolating deeply in the minds of Southeast Asian countries, following the scourge of smoke pollution due to forest fires in some parts of Southeast Asian region in 1997 and 1998. This smoke hazard, which was ultimately converted into the transboundary haze problem, consequent on the pollution of the smoke, dust, moisture and vapour suspended in the air, being sufficient to spoil, visibility, and originating in the large-scale forest and land fires, has been the most idiosyncratic principally crippling environmental trouble facing the ASEAN countries in the post-Cold War years.

These large-scale fires that caused trans-boundary haze,

are often deliberately set by large plantation companies and farmer settlers who come from the more densely populated provinces of Indonesia and are provided homesteads in these provinces, and who have joined the traditional shifting cultivators living in the region for a long time, clearing small sites of planting crops until the soil's nutrients have been exhausted and then moving to other sites by using fire as the most economical way of converting forest land for cultivation. This resulted in several large-scale forest fires and haze episodes since the early 1980s, particularly during the dry seasons of 1982-83, 1987, 1991, 1994 1997, 1998, 2000, 2005, and the most recent one in 2007 which caused severe damage well beyond the destruction of forest land and ecosystems. In fact, these land and forest fires in Southeast Asia destroyed more than 3 million hectares of peat lands.

However, the 1997 and 1998 smog crisis produced by forest fires in Indonesia's Kalimantan and Sumatran provinces of Jambi, Riau and elsewhere, largely engulfed the entire region of Southeast Asia and posed a stern challenge to every aspect of ASEAN's character and modalities. This unscheduled outburst of haze from forest fire took a heavy toll on travel, environment and human life, apart from causing public health disaster in the region with a sharp increase in the number of patients treated for respiratory ailments, lung and heart diseases, reduced fertility and damage to the nervous system, blood cells and kidneys. Such health concerns turned many Southeast Asians decidedly impatient with their leaders. Besides this, serious transport accidents appeared more than co–incidental during this smog period: a Garuda Airbus collided into a mountainside on the approach to Medan in Sumatra, killing all 256 passengers on board. Also, in the unclear Straits of Malacca, a small Indian cargo vessel hit a supertanker and killed 20 of the former ship's crew. Further, many traffic accidents were exacerbated by this haze catastrophe. In Indonesia's easternmost province of Irian Jaya, severe drought had caused staple food crops to fail in the highlands, which resulted in an estimated minimum of 500 deaths from mass starvation. [8]

The most immediate impact of this haze calamity was a sharp blow to Southeast Asian tourism the affected countries, being Malaysia and Indonesia. Many advisors in European and North American countries had warned their citizens against visiting countries hit by the polluted air, particularly Malaysia, Indonesia and Singapore. Many foreign countries and multinationals like Ericsson and General Electric etc. evacuated the expatriates from these countries and also caused devastating loss of national wealth of Indonesia and its surrounding neighbours, estimated to be more than US$ 9 billion.

Further, this smog crisis destroyed more than 20,000 hectares of land-laying waste to small holdings, National Park and commercial plantations, mostly in Kalimantan. It also ravaged more than 300,000 hectares on the islands of Borneo, Java, Sulawesi and Sumatra and the economic damage in log and timber destruction was estimated at US$ 912 million. Besides this, a variety of damages such as decreased quality of life, losses of biodiversity and atmospheric impacts are difficult to monetize. Fire-related smoke haze episodes also reveal a social component: a large part of the population in Southeast Asia does not have the financial means to buy protective measures such as respiratory masks and air conditioning, nor are they able to refrain from outdoor work when air pollution is high. An undue hike in the medical treatment costs of haze related diseases [9] only added to the agonies of the victims.

The regional smog events in the seasons of 1982-83, 1987, 1991 and 1994 in Indonesia thoroughly disturbed the environmental condition of the Southeast Asian region. This typical Indonesian forest fire and smoke caused large scale health and safety problems not only in Indonesia, but also in Singapore and Malaysia, and impelled the countries of ASEAN to accept measures to overcome this calamity in the form of the "ASEAN Cooperation Plan on Transboundary Pollution," which was accepted in October 1994, at the ASEAN Ministerial Meeting on the Environment convened in Kuching, Malaysia. As a follow-up action to the decisions, the Government of Malaysia hosted on "ASEAN Meeting on Transboundary Pollution" in June 1995 in Kuala Lumpur. In this meeting, it was agreed that regional understanding on and the appreciation of the impact of transboundary pollution/haze and the need for capacity building and cooperative efforts to combat transboundary pollution/haze would be taken into account. This meeting agreed to develop an Asian cooperative plan in order to address the transboundary pollution issue, which contained, among others, the following:

1. Comprehensive measures for prevention, management and control;
2. Establishment of an early warning system including identification of focal points for information exchange;
3. Building up of national and regional institutional capacity; and
4. Establishing cooperative links with developed countries to assist ASEAN's efforts. [10]

The most important aspect of this meeting is the avoidance of any reference to the promotion of forest conservation or protection as a means of minimizing the generation of smoke. Following this meeting, a 'Haze Technical Task Force' came into being at the Sixth Meeting of the ASEAN Senior Officials on the Environment (ASOEN), held in September, 1995. The Prime objective of the work of the task force was to operationalize and to implement the measures recommended in the Asian Cooperation Plan on Transboundary Pollution relating to atmospheric pollution, including particularly the problem of fire and smoke. This meeting further reiterated the aim of disseminating information on fire prevention and containment, including making satellite data on actual fires available. But, in spite of these resolutions on haze problem, the mechanisms used by them, were unfortunately moved in a desultory manner.

However, things have gone along different path after the 1997 and 1998 epidemic eruption of haze calamity produced by forest fires in Indonesia's Kalimantan and Sumatra, which bitterly overwhelmed the entire region of Southeast Asia and practically posed a harsh challenge to every aspect of ASEAN's fabric and modalities. Mutual solidarity on the part of ASEAN governments and a preference for indirect diplomacy have practically collapsed in the context of seriousness of the problem. This prolonged haze crisis has confronted ASEAN for the first time with a serious multilateral problem and clearly revealed itself as a major breakdown of environmental management not just for Indonesia but also for ASEAN as a whole. In fact, ASEAN for the first time was caught between rhetoric and reality, and the haze crisis brought the issue of environmental degradation back to the top of the political agenda. Since the problem affected most of the countries of ASEAN, there was a big question mark about ASEAN's "Principle of Non-Intervention in the Affairs of another Nation." [11]

As against such background of the haze problem over the years, in November 1997, the Senior Officials of the ASEAN countries in a meeting, agreed to a regional division of labour. Accordingly, Singapore was to take the lead in monitoring the fire hazards, Malaysia was to concentrate on the fire prevention measures and Indonesia on the strengthening of the fire fighting capability. Following this meeting, the ASEAN Environment Ministers met in Singapore on 22-23 December 1997 and adopted an ASEAN Regional Haze Action Plan (RHAP) to address the problem of smoke haze in the Southeast Asian region, caused by land and forest fires. In this meeting, the members of ASEAN had also agreed on the region's joint effort to combat fires and smoke haze and further avowed that ASEAN member countries would continue to look after the environment in their quest for economic development, while at the same time, work closely to set up for future environmental challenges, especially those arising from the effect of climate change.

Revealing these countenances of understanding, this meeting espoused a Regional Haze Action Plan and identified three main objectives to develop better management and enforcement so as to prevent fires, to institute cooperative mechanisms to monitor fires, and to build fire-fighting competence. Thus, the signing of RHAP was a turning point in the region's effort to thwart and to alleviate the damage from the periodic trans-boundary haze. To implement the RHAP, in July 1999, the ASEAN Environment Ministers met in Singapore and fully approved the Implementation Plan for the RHAP and undertook several initiatives and recorded major achievements, which are as follows:

1. Monitoring of Fire and Haze Pollution: The centrepiece of RHAP's monitoring activities is a network of national and regional level institutions that include the ASEAN Specialized Meteorological Centre (ASMC), national meteorological agencies, and other related agencies in the region. It was agreed that the ASEAN Secretariat's RHAP-Coordination and Support Unit, would continuously monitor the haze situation on a regular and region-wide basis and share information through its website with a direct link to the ASMC, and a database of upcoming ASEAN events. [12]

2. Immediate Action Plans: The Immediate Action Plans (IAPs) are designed to help local government units and the communities in developing comprehensive action plans for forest fire and haze management. The IAP for West Kalimantan was completed, with the aid of funding and technical support from Australia.

3. Law Enforcement Programmes: Large scale haze crisis that caused transboundary pollution problem was often set by either small farmers or large plantation companies, to clear land at nominal cost and effort. Besides this, regional collaborative efforts to enhance the region's capacity for law enforcement actions were taken to overcome these irregularities. These included the establishing of the SRFA Legal Group on Law and Enforcement in the Southeast Asian region.

4. Public Awareness Programmes: In April 1999, the ASEAN members accepted a "zero-burning" policy and urged all members to enforce the laws and regulations on this policy. Following this decision, dialogue sessions for raising an awareness of the zero-burning practices and techniques among plantation companies, were undertaken and attempts were made to establish a regular forum for maintaining the dialogue sessions with plantation companies. Thus, with the establishment of RHAP, the ASEAN has laid out the cooperative framework and detailed operational plans to deal with the transboundary haze pollution in the region. It is also a major initiative of ASEAN's firm determination to actively tackle the problem.

Following this agreement, on June 10, 2002, all the ten ASEAN member countries in Kuala Lumpur signed the ASEAN Agreement on Transboundary Haze Pollution. The agreement came into force on November 25, 2003. However, having taken part in the negotiations and signed the agreement, Indonesia did not ratify the agreement, which remains the main centre of haze crises. Most of the ASEAN members felt that Jakarta's refusal to ratify this agreement is incomprehensible, irresponsible and an unfriendly act especially as the Indonesian government's repeated assurances of action in the past to prevent a recurrence of the haze nightmare, have been hopelessly ineffective. Besides this, ASEAN's effort in cooperation on haze pollution was exhibited at the Ninth ASEAN Ministerial Meeting on Haze (AMMH) held on June 11, 2002 in Kuala Lumpur, where the Environment Ministers discussed and finally decided on actions to be taken on fire prevention and control in Peatlands. As a result, the ASEAN Peatland Management Initiative (APMI) was developed with various partners and endorsed by the ASEAN Senior Officials on the Environment-Haze Technical Task Force (ASOEN-

HTTF) in February 2003.

Finally, on November 10, 2004, the 11th ASEAN Ministerial Meeting on Haze took place in Hanoi, Vietnam. In this meeting, the ASEAN Ministers reviewed the enhanced cooperation in addressing land and forest fires and the resulting trans-boundary haze pollution and expressed their satisfaction regarding the substantial progress in regional collaborative activities, such as the inventory of fire-fighting resources, the ASEAN Peatland Management Initiative, publication and dissemination of zero-burning and controlled burning practices, early warning information systems, standard operating procedures for monitoring assessment and joint emergency response etc. [13] They also stated their environmental commitments in the Hanoi Plan of Action and, more explicitly, through the Strategic Plan of Action on Environment for 1999-2004.

This action plan mainly deals with the prevention, mitigation and monitoring of land and forest fires and trans-boundary haze; conservation of natural resources and biodiversity; protection of marine and coastal environment; the implementation of multilateral environmental agreements; and the promotion of environmental awareness, information and education. However, the fact remains that the present legacy lies with Indonesia which is yet to ratify the ASEAN Agreement on Trans-boundary Haze Pollution, and that naturally reveals a soft weakness of ASEAN, as a political and technical body. Indonesia's participation in the ASEAN Haze Agreement is essential and so, an enforcement and liability clause should be incorporated because those, who are responsible for the fires, should pay adequate reparations to those who suffer the consequences of the haze. This "bite" is desirable to ensure that all the declarations and action plans have been made effective enough.

Recently, on October 22, 2008, at Phuket, Thailand, the Sixth Meeting of the Sub-Regional Ministerial Steering Committee (MSC) on Trans-boundary Haze Pollution took place, wherein the Environment Ministers and their representatives from Brunei Darussalam, Indonesia, Malaysia, Singapore and Thailand, participated. This meeting highly appreciated Indonesia's efforts in effectively implementing its Plan of Action (PoA) in dealing with trans-boundary Haze pollution and congratulated Indonesia for achieving its 50 percent hotspot reduction target as of mid October 2008, compared to 2006. The Meeting also noted that, while there has been an increase of hotspot activities in the region, there was no significant corresponding increase in trans-boundary haze. This is attributed to the concerted mitigation actions taken to restrain the fires and to better the normal weather conditions.

Thus, in spite of these limitations faced by ASEAN members, it is clear that the haze is no longer an individual undertaking of the ASEAN countries, especially as it receives a coordinated and concerted response from all the members of ASEAN. The haze issue, for the first time, has undoubtedly formulated a collective response to a regional environmental problem in Southeast Asia, based on regional solidity.

The third Issue has been that of terrorism. The internal security troubles in the socio-political structure of Southeast Asia do not form a topical experience. These problems originated mainly in ethnic/ race conflicts, poverty and under-development, domination of ruling party on the minority community, religion (mainly rise of Islamic fundamentalism), historical bequest, opium and drug related issues, etc. The exhibit of these internal security problems has often led to eruptions of insurgency and low intensity clashes followed by terrorism. In Southeast Asia, these social unrests—be it in guerrilla form, terrorism and/or low intensity war—often vary from one country to another and the occurrence of these momentous inner security challenges are analytic of the lack of authenticity of the nation-state in Southeast Asia. In particular, the sternness of the separatist challenges in Indonesia and the Philippines specify their basic tenderness leaving the issue whether they become Balkanized and failed states unclear. More importantly, there is an interactive element in the internal rebellions: for instance the problems in Moluccas Islands, Irian Jaya and Aceh, Southern Philippines, Myanmar, Malaysia (PAS), Southern Thailand Pattani movement etc., often create mistrust, dissection and anxiety among the neighbouring countries of Southeast Asia, resulting in sharp conflicts of opinions and interests, and thereby hoisting obstructions towards the realization of a regional security community and a united front against the low intensity conflict and terrorism that have cropped recently in the region.

The terrorist activities of Abu Sayyaf Group (ASG), the Jemaah Islamiah, the Moro Islamic Liberation Front (MILF), the Laskar Jihad, the Front Pembela Islam (Islamic Defenders Front-FPI), the New People's Army (NPA), and the Kumpulan Mujaheddin Malaysia (KMM), the Pattani United Liberation organization (PULO), New PULO, the Barisan Revolusi Nationale (BRN), Majelis Mujahidin Indonesia (MMI) etc., an alliance of about 100 militant and radical groups, have practically disturbed the entire security situation of Southeast Asia. [14]

Actually, the emergence of a regional fundamentalist Islamic terror network centred through Jemaah Islamiya in Indonesia, and its connections with most of the above-mentioned groups have often twisted the distrust, dissection and anxiety both within and outside the region. These links are primarily based on shared experiences of senior commanders in the anti-Soviet Afghan War in the 1980s and 1990s. Today, they manifest themselves in joint training, recruitment, financial help, and operational cooperation and often engross themselves in direct and indirect links with the terrorist outfits in the Middle East, including Al-Qaeda. These myriad groups have sporadically exploited local grievances and grafted themselves onto the pre-existing ethnic conflicts, thereby forming a dodgy symbiotic understanding with local insurgents. Their networking position was further strengthened by the concentration of large Muslim population, influenced by fundamentalist Islamist theology, permeable borders, botched societies and scrawny ascendancy in the region. They offer local fighters an access to funds and to know-how and receive in return, a base from which they can wage their own brand of jihad.

The manifestation of jihid among the Islamic radical groups in Southeast Asia, is not the same as that of their counterparts elsewhere in the world. Southeast Asian Islamic radicals focus more on political aspects of jihid than just the religious and tactical aspects, such as the methods of attack, as in the case of their counterparts in the Middle East. Southeast Asian groups would renounce violence and focus on political means as long as the end result is the establishment of Islamic state or the implementation of Islamic jurisprudence. In fact, there is no explicit aversion on their part for achieving these objectives through the existing political framework. [15] The emergence of the rebel groups within the nation-states of Southeast Asia as well as their external links clearly revealed the foremost weakness of the post-colonial configuration of Southeast Asia. [16] After the September 11, 2001 incident in the United States, the internationalization of the concept of terrorism, low intensity conflicts, insurgency predicament and transnational crime, have become important and dynamic themes of regional politics in Southeast Asia. Following this event, President George Bush described Southeast Asia as a second front in the 'global war on terror' [17]

This was not astounding in this region since the countries like Malaysia, Thailand and the Philippines are already marked significantly in Al-Qaeda's network and a hub of global terrorist activities spanning from East and Southeast Asia to Australia. But the fact remains that the threat of terrorism in this region has been mainly emanating from the domestic constraints and not related to global matters. This resulted in an awfully explosive nature of the security in the region. The ASEAN members, in the context of this bumpy budding threat, identified the acts of terrorism as a menace in the process of their regional cohesion, and sternly felt the need to deal with international terrorism in the post-September 11 world and to exploit its ability to forge a coherent message on this issue, important not only for the sake of regional security, but also for the long-term viability of the organization itself. Since this incident, the ASEAN countries have taken important counter-terrorism measures to resolve this international menace, though a clear difference of opinion on approach to terrorism was perceptible among them. Unlike Singapore, the Philippines and Thailand, Indonesia and Malaysia with predominantly Muslim populations, expressed their reservation against the US strategy to counter terrorism in this region.

At the national level, the Indonesian government treated the issue of terrorism as a political subject, and acknowledged this threat as existential in nature. It was also unwilling to connect itself to US views on global terrorism. Malaysia, on the other hand, expressed its serious reservation regarding linking terrorism with Islam, and resolutely considered that terrorism has been essentially transnational in character and is an artefact of Western misdeeds against the broader Muslim community. It also refused to accept the links of Malaysian religious and political organizations to the global Al-Qaeda network. However, Singapore maintains an uncompromising posture on the general issue of terrorism because of its multi-racial state character. It blindly supported the US way of handling the issue of terrorism, in view of its exclusive economic interests. Thailand and the Philippines on the other hand, are tending to downplay terrorism for the sake of domestic politics. The conflicts in these countries, however, are mostly ethno-nationalist in nature, resulting largely from an abortive integration of the Muslim population into the mainstream.

Thus, a tendency exists to identify these conflicts as domestic insurgencies with local implications rather than part of the global jihad with wider ramifications. [18] Therefore, in spite of their differences in viewpoint, the ASEAN members at the regional level have taken certain important initiatives to reduce the threat, posed by terrorism. On October 11, 2001 in Singapore, at the Third ASEAN Ministerial Meeting on Transnational Crime (AMMTC), the Ministers "strongly condemned all acts of terrorism, in particular the terrorist attacks of September 11, 2001 on the US, which led to the loss of innocent lives of people of various nationalities and destruction of properties", and called all its member states to ratify all relevant international anti-terrorist conventions.

At the Seventh ASEAN Summit held on November 5, 2001, in Brunei Darussaalam, the member countries signed the ASEAN Declaration on Joint Action to Counter Terrorism. This was ASEAN's initial step to create a unified threat perception of terrorism. The issuance of this statement in spite of sharp disagreements among members is not much surprising, as it might apparently emerge, because the document took a decidedly uncontroversial stance on the broad issue of terrorism. The declaration failed to address the primary sources of dissection within the ASEAN organization, most importantly the methods for fighting terrorism through multilateral cooperation and more directly, the extent to which such regional cooperation would involve the United States. Nevertheless, the Declaration was significant as a statement of the objective and as an acknowledgement that terrorism was a serious long-term issue that had to be faced.

To brand terrorism as a truly regional and global endeavour, the ASEAN related groupings and other regional organization, such as ARF, APEC, ASEAN+3, ASEAN+1 etc. have undertaken a number of schemes, including an apparatus of sharing information and astuteness to develop law enforcement and investigation capabilities of the agencies of respective member countries. One of the early pragmatic initiatives taken by the region was the Agreement on Information Exchange and Establishment of Communication Procedures, which provides anti-terrorism exercises, joint operation to hunt suspected terrorists and formation of a hotline to communicate immediately, signed by Indonesia, Malaysia and the Philippines in May 2002.

Later, Brunei, Thailand and Cambodia have also acceded to the Agreement in 2003. Besides this, the Joint Communiqué issued at the special ASEAN Ministerial Meeting on Terrorism held on 20-21 May 2002, in Kuala Lumpur recalled the 2001 ASEAN Declaration on Joint Action to Counter Terrorism adopted at the Seventh ASEAN Summit in Brunei Darussalam to advance ASEAN's efforts in the global struggle against terrorism. In this meeting, the ASEAN Ministers also committed "to counter, prevent and suppress all forms of terrorist acts in accordance with the Charter of the UN and other International law, especially taking into account the importance of all relevant UN resolutions" and "to follow-up on this communiqué by entrusting the Senior Officials to execute the Work Programme on Terrorism to implement the ASEAN Plan of Action to Combat Transnational Crime approved on May 17, 2002 in Kuala Lumpur which is deemed to be an integral part of this Communiqué and to review its progress at subsequent meetings of the ASEAN Ministers responsible for transnational crime issues." [19]

Moreover, this meeting once again reaffirmed their regional commitment that "the sovereignty, territorial integrity and domestic laws of each ASEAN member country shall be respected and upheld in undertaking the fight against terrorism". As such, the fact that the fundamental principles enshrined in Article 2 of the TAC of 1976, form a key to governing relations among member countries while dealing with any matter, manifested the consciousness in part, of the ASEAN member countries and their respect for these principles. Besides this, ASEAN states, in their various regional and Summit meetings, have taken various other initiatives in order to review and strengthen the national mechanism of the member-countries to combat terrorism, and for carrying out different-counter terrorism training programmes and projects, including psychological operation/ psychological warfare courses for law enforcement authorities and on intelligence procuring, course on bomb/explosive detection, post-last investigation, airport security and inspection.

Furthermore, to overcome this terrorist menace, it has also taken a variety of institutionalized apparatus, like the ASEAN-EU Meetings, the ASEAN-US Meetings, the ASEAN plus three Meetings, the Inter-Sectional Meeting on Counter Terrorism and Transnational Crime and so on, where different avowals and joint communiqués were approved to combat terrorism internationally, while paying due respect to the ASEAN principles of the territorial sovereignty, integrity and non-interference in domestic affairs of the state. However, these counter-terrorism schemes of ASEAN have not been sufficiently effective enough because of their loose organizational structures, the non-binding nature of their agreements, and their tradition of non-intervention in the internal affairs of member-states. Nevertheless, on January 13, 2007, at Cebu, the Philippines, the ASEAN Convention on Counter terrorism was drafted and this pragmatically paved the way for a more legally binding approach to cooperation in counter-terrorism. This Convention provided a framework for regional cooperation to counter, to prevent, and to suppress terrorism, in addition to reinforcing the 2004 Mutual Legal Assistance Treaty–ASEAN's only legally binding agreement related to counter-terrorism, and remained extensively dissimilar to some of the earlier regional proposals.

Thus, the signing of the ASEAN Charter in November 2007, which seeks to establish ASEAN as a legal entity and formally moves the region towards a EU-style of economic community by 2015, once ratified, would greatly increase ASEAN's institutional capacity and ability for autonomous action, including the field of counter-terrorism. So far, only Singapore and Thailand have ratified, although no ASEAN members had any crucial reservations about the convention because they had all agreed to cooperate in combating terrorism. Besides this, ASEAN since 2001 had commenced several centres for combating terrorism in the region, including the Jakarta Centre for Law Enforcement Cooperation, the International Law Enforcement Academy in Thailand, and the Southeast Asia Regional Centre for Counter Terrorism in Malaysia. At present, the members of this organization have achieved some success in degrading the operational capabilities of major terrorist groups such as JI and ASG. [20] Thus, ASEAN's counter terrorism plans have long been hindered by its wobbly organizational configurations, the non-binding nature of its agreements, implications of terrorism as a threat to regional order and its practice of non-intervention in the internal affairs of states. This was further augmented in view of the fear about adverse domestic reactions following the adoption of a US led counter-terrorism strategy on a regional basis in Southeast Asia, after 9/11 incident.

Therefore, the dilemma in countering the terrorist organizations in Southeast Asia took its origin from the fact that ASEAN unity is more important to Southeast Asian countries rather than the war on terrorism. The issue of terrorism has no doubt been treated as a litmus test for ASEAN solidarity, since counter terrorism cooperation severely posed major challenges to its principles of non-intervention. In fact, it is mainly through peaceful dialogue and discussion, consultation and consensus, in line with the fundamental principles of TAC, that a number of declarations have been adopted by ASEAN, setting the stage for a firm and progressive resolution of the problem of terrorism, through constant engagement and trust-inducing actions.

The fourth issue which brought the ASEAN members collectively under one umbrella, has been natural disasters. The episode of earthquake and Tsunami disaster on December 26, 2004, brought not only an unprecedented loss of life and property, but more importantly removed mainly the geographical and environmental boundaries of the nation-states of South and Southeast Asia. This unparalleled catastrophe forced the alertness among the nation states that disaster management has to be integrated into the conventional development and investment efforts, since this Indian Ocean Tsunami has caused mammoth destruction in South and Southeast Asia and in some parts of Africa. This destructive natural disaster brought various governments, international organizations, private sector, humanitarian organizations and community groups under a single umbrella and unfalteringly demonstrated their craving for international cooperation, solidarity and partnership.

It also demonstrated that the nation-states, although segregated by borders, political ideology, race and creed, humanity, possess the inherent instinct to rise to the occasions, if needed. These disasters have further generated complex emergencies that require urgent and coordinated responses from a broad range of state and non-state actors, and unfortunately, many states of South and Southeast Asia, at the initial level, are least prepared to cope with these complex humanitarian emergencies, and virtually lack any regional capability to respond to this disaster and to provide emergency relief, rehabilitation, and reconstruction. However, after its initial shock of this natural disaster caused by the institutional weakness, the countries of this region cultivated a level of solidarity, not frequently witnessed among the members of ASEAN, since the 1997 Asian financial crisis.

This Tsunami disaster, therefore, provides an opportunity to the ASEAN members to come together once again and to act decisively to forge the ASEAN's response to the tragedy and to create an impact of regional cohesion and understanding among themselves, which was temporarily slacked and partially weakened, in view of certain serious internal weaknesses among the member states. In fact, the Tsunami disaster provided an opportunity to regenerate regional cohesion among the ASEAN members, which remains the main backbone of its existence. Thus, apart from dispatching aid quickly to the areas hit by the tragedy, the ASEAN-led Tsunami Summit, held on 6 January in Jakarta, was a clear manifestation of ASEAN solidarity. So far, the outcome of the initiatives taken by ASEAN members to overcome any further disaster in future is the establishment of the ASEAN Regional Disaster Emergency Response Simulation Exercise (ARDEX-05), that commenced in 2005. [21] The simulation exercise is envisioned to be an annual exercise, bringing together several personnel and mobilizing light-to-medium equipment geared toward providing immediate humanitarian assistance to the affected countries in times of natural disaster. Beyond ASEAN, there are also other ad hoc exercises in disaster management, being undertaken within the ARF framework.

After the tsunami disaster in December 2004, the ARF ministers have decided to work together in emergency relief, rehabilitation, and reconstruction, as well as prevention and mitigation efforts in addressing the natural disasters. [22] Besides these regional initiatives, the humanitarian assistance was also provided by external partners to ASEAN, like the United States, European Union, Australia, India and Japan, plus a number of international aid agencies, to overcome this natural catastrophe. Hence, in the aftermath of the tsunami, Southeast Asian countries held a number of meetings and agreed to enhance cooperation in disaster relief, including prevention and mitigation. [23] The ASEAN members, specifically, agreed to mobilize an additional resource to meet the emergency needs of tsunami victims. They also called upon the international community through the United Nations to convene an international pledging conference for sustainable humanitarian relief efforts and to explore the establishment of "standby arrangements" for other humanitarian relief efforts. ASEAN also called on donor countries—the World Bank, Asian Development Bank, and other financial institutions—to provide the necessary funds to support the rehabilitation and reconstruction programs in disaster-stricken areas.

More significantly, in July 2006, the ARF Ministerial Meeting, officials from ARF countries, have discussed the possibility of developing guidelines in improving civilian and military cooperation in humanitarian operations—i.e., natural disasters. It is a fact that the ASEAN leaders have demonstrated their leadership by bringing together their colleagues from around the world to Jakarta, to take stock of what had happened, and charted out the road ahead in hastening emergency relief operations, coordinating the rehabilitation and reconstruction of the affected areas, and thus reinforced the need for prevention and mitigation of natural catastrophes. It further exhibited ASEAN at its best in illustrating the effectiveness and the drive of the organization as well as its openness to external powers. The Tsunami calamity, therefore clearly revealed an innate capacity of the ASEAN members to come together quickly and to display empathy and care for each other in times of severe crisis.

It also proved that when the crunch comes, the ASEAN members could put politics aside and work together in a spontaneous outpouring of shared humanity and regional solidarity. However, in spite of this solidarity, these regional initiatives are not sufficient to stand, if any disasters occur in the region, and for that, one could argue that the region needs more solidarity to do more in the areas of prevention and mitigation by developing an extraordinarily effective regional early warning system to prevent further calamities in coming years. The recent natural disasters in Indonesia and Malaysia in early 2007, the unfortunate lag in response time, resulted in unnecessary loss of lives and human misery. Hence, while regional efforts are being considered to improve disaster management, attention also needs to be focused on improving capacity at the national level. One could suggest therefore, that countries in the region would need to examine their own capacity and perhaps reconsider their own national strategies for disaster mitigation or risk reduction. [24]

The Fifth issue of the regional cohesion of ASEAN has

been the Initiative of ASEAN Integration (IAI) programme. The most critical hurdle of ASEAN is the development gap among member states, which has a powerful impact on the degree of regional engagement. The unequal economic development because of poverty and the existence of wide regional disparities in terms of living standards between countries like Laos, Cambodia, Vietnam and Myanmar on the one hand, and Singapore, Malaysia, Indonesia, Thailand, Brunei and the Philippines on the other, remains another irritable condition in Southeast Asia.

The major reasons behind poverty among the new members of ASEAN (e.g. Vietnam, Cambodia, Laos and Myanmar) are manifold. Among these, lack of entrepreneurs, relatively closed socialist economy, high military spending, forced relocation of people, corruption, lack of access to basic social services, human capital and food security, environment degradation, high illiteracy rate, transition from command to market economy, high population density, exclusion of indigenous groups etc., are principally responsible factors for economic vulnerability of these states. Although the governments of these countries introduced poverty alleviation programmes through National Plans to combat their poverty, these endeavours failed to improve their overall economic condition, unlike the attempts of the other developed members of ASEAN towards the same end. The various poverty alleviation programmes of these countries received further jolt because of the negative impact of liberalization measures, coupled with the 1997 East Asian Financial Crisis.

Besides this, the new ASEAN entrance members sometimes feel isolated, as a result of their own deficiencies in resources and knowledge while attempting to catch up with the rest of the grouping, particularly in areas of more sophisticated cooperation like free-trade agreements, prevention of infectious diseases, etc. This mindset has been developed among the poor members of ASEAN, because of their very little experience with multilateral cooperation after long years under colonial rule, as well as the socialistic pattern of economic experiment. To overcome as well as to reduce the intra-ASEAN disparities for a stable, prosperous and highly competitive ASEAN economic region for a free flow of goods, services and investments, a freer flow of capital, equitable economic development, and thereby facilitated regional economic integration, the developed ASEAN members have agreed to institute a Road map for Integration of ASEAN (RIA) by way of providing a framework for more logical implementation of the regional programme.

They also pragmatically visualized that for a stable, prosperous and highly competitive ASEAN economic region, reduced poverty and socio-economic disparities must be shrivelled. So, to diminish the intra-ASEAN economic disparities, the rich ASEAN members, in November 2000, agreed to launch four major initiatives which are: the Initiative for ASEAN Integration (IAI), Mekong Basin Development Cooperation, the Joint ASEAN-World Bank Initiative on Mainstreaming Social Development and the ASEAN-UNDP Partnership Facility, and requested all the Full Dialogue Partners to champion and to promote this regional cause. For the implementation of the Initiative for ASEAN Integration (IAI), Vietnam joined other ASEAN members in issuing the Hanoi Declaration on Narrowing Development Gap at the AMM-34 held in Hanoi in 2001. With Vietnam as the chair of the IAI task force, the implementation of IAI has seen a number of results. The IAI currently has 134 projects and over 90 percent of these have received a total committed aid of US $48 million for developing infrastructure, human resources, information technology, tourism, poverty reduction and an improvement of living standards.

On June 2007, Vietnam hosted the second IAI Development Co-operation Forum held to work out a co-operation strategy to implement the IAI in the 2008-2015 periods. Vietnam introduced an important initiative on socio-economic development through the Sub-Mekong Development and Cooperation Programme for poor areas along the East-West Corridor. However, all these efforts and realization of the benefits of these regional initiatives will take time to fabricate a positive outfit. But, these initiatives have been no doubt a clear example of ASEAN's commitment, priority and responses to changing circumstances for the developmental needs of all underdeveloped economies of its new members, and amply manifest its mindset of holistic integration process and regional cohesion of understanding.

Finally, the 'we feeling' of the ASEAN members has been so much prominent that some cases, wherein the regional members failed to resolve many of their bilateral disputes by themselves, have been referred to the International Court of Justice (ICJ), for final decision, for the sake of regional cohesion. For example, the Sipadan and Ligitan dispute between Indonesia and Malaysia was referred to ICJ in November 1998 and the Court issued its verdict in favour of Malaysia in December 2002. Similarly, Pedra Banka islands dispute between Singapore and Malaysia was referred to ICJ in July 2003 and the Court has given its verdict in favour of Singapore in 2008.

These issues clearly reflect the international arbitration and adjudication as a sagacious option of ASEAN to manage the disputes in the capacity of a dispute settlement mechanism. These issues clearly indicate the regional states' preferences for finding a peaceful solution to bilateral problems. Although the critics point out these references of issues to external body as a major weakness of the ASEAN Way, the positive dimension has been that the states have opted for a rational approach for regional cohesion, to make the ASEAN as well as the region safe, peaceful and stable.

Conclusion

The history of ASEAN may be told in terms of a series of important events or milestones, which depict the steady growth of the Association, the expansion of its agenda, and the decisions that have veritably changed the history of Southeast Asia. From a regional grouping that initially had to define itself by what it was not - a regional association that was not a military alliance-ASEAN had become at the end of the 20th century, a dynamic community of nations. At the time of its founding, many predicted that ASEAN would not last long, because many factors were going against it, not the least, the simmering disputes between member countries. But, in the event, ASEAN's consensus-building approach to problems enabled the association to move forward. Each member learned to recognize its stake in the viability of the association. Each recognized the wisdom of ASEAN in not being a supranational government that has authority over its individual members. Each member exercises full sovereignty.

This is why ASEAN decisions are reached either unanimously or consensually. In a broad consensus, one or two members may not fully agree with a proposal but will not object to its being carried out. In aiming to become a "concert of nations" in the new century, ASEAN does not mean to transform itself into a political union under any form of central supranational authority. Each country will continue to preserve its national government and identity in accordance with the ideals and aspirations of its people. However, all ASEAN members are legally bound by the code of conduct embodied in the Treaty of Amity and Cooperation in Southeast Asia, among other agreements. Neither the TAC nor any other agreement, however, requires ASEAN members to change their political systems into any specific homogenized system. ASEAN never assigned to itself, the mission of converting its members to a uniform political set-up. Unlike the European Union, ASEAN did not set any political criterion for its prospective members, to fulfil before admission. After 32 years, on 30 April 1999, ASEAN encompassed all ten countries of Southeast Asia by admitting Cambodia within its orbit.

It is a fact that differences in political systems do not

hinder the strengthening of ASEAN unity and solidarity. On the contrary, ASEAN sees the diversity in its membership as a source of strength and inspiration for fostering a strong sense of community and regional solidarity. All ASEAN members willingly agree to share the responsibility of strengthening peace and stability in Southeast Asia. The success rates of ASEAN on regional cohesion based on the principle of non-intervention remain much higher than those of other regional organizations in the Asian region. The fact is that serious intraregional differences have always been visible among the ASEAN members on many issues. But these intraregional disputes have not led to any war or war-like situation, as had happened in South Asia (e.g. Kargil War in 1998), and never disrupted the regional process at any moment. The uneven power structures in South Asia (mainly between India and others) remain another major weak point of SAARC, which has been more or less invisible in Southeast Asia. And, thus, the countries of Southeast Asia have not faced any major war among themselves. The two wars they had faced were mainly because of extra-regional powers.

Thus, after forty-two years of experience, the habits of cooperation among ASEAN members enabled them to acquire a sense of genuine community. It is a community that prefers dialogue to confrontation. It has established itself as a history of successful diplomatic community which skilfully gave a sharp retort to more or less all external challenges, in spite of divergent strategic perspectives among regional members. The intra-mural collaboration among the ASEAN members has retained its organizational cohesion, because of its nature as an "articulated community." Whether at its early inception, or in the subsequent development, ASEAN has always found a way to allow its declaratory principles to carry the day. Through its experience of more than four decades, ASEAN's regional cohesion has been developed based on all its mechanism including the ARF, conflict prevention and conflict mitigation rather than resolution and post-peace building activities through the inputs of self-restraint, de-augmentation and non-threatening outlook. However, in recent times the ASEAN has also sought to strengthen its internal cohesion through the creation of an ASEAN Charter in November 2007.

This Charter aims at placing the Association on an international legal footing, and moves it to a more rule based-regime, through which it looks as though there needs to be much greater compliance on the part of its members with decisions taken by ASEAN as a group. This has been no doubt ASEAN's supreme achievement that has provided a setting for the peaceful management of disputes among its members, and in this sense, ASEAN represents a much better performance in institutional success in the third world countries and has emerged as a prominent regional organization in the emerging global politics.

End Notes

1. Daljit Singh, "Southeast Asia in 1999: A False Dawn?," *Southeast Asian Affairs: 2000*, (Institute of Southeast Asian Studies, Singapore, 2000), p. 6.
2. Unpublished M.Phil Dissertation by Sushama Ray Karmakar entitled "ASEAN in the Global Order: Dispute Settlement Mechanism and the Way Out," Department of International Relations, Jadavpur University, Kolkata, India, 2008, p. 10.
3. For details see http://www.aseansee.org/64.htm (22 December 2007).
4. For details see "The Territorial Claims in South China Sea: Probing Persistent Uncertainties," in Arun Kumar Banerji and Purusottam Bhattacharya (eds.), *People's Republic of China at Fifty: Politics, Economy and Foreign Relations*, (Lancer's Books, New Delhi, 2001), pp. 171-207.
5. Adopted at the First ASEAN Summit held in Bali in 1976, the Treaty of Amity and Cooperation (TAC) constitutes a norm-based code of conduct that enunciates ASEAN's core principles, including the respect for sovereignty and non-interference in the affairs of other states.
6. David Wiencek, "South China Sea Flashpoint Revisited," *China Brief,* 2:24 (December 16, 2008), http://www.jamestown.org/ pubs/view/cwe_002_024_002.htm.

7. For details see Tridib Chakraborti, "The Environmental Battlefield in Southeast Asia: The Haze Catastrope and Regional Responses," in Purusottam Bhattacharya and Sugata Hazra (eds.) *Environment and Human Security*, (Lancer's Books, New Delhi, 2003), pp. 167-202.
8. Tridib Chakraborti, "Haze Sans Frontiers: The Environmental Calamity, ASEAN Response and India-ASEAN Cooperation on Non-Traditional Security Threats," in V.R. Raghavan (ed.) *India and ASEAN: Non-Traditional Security Threats,* (East-West Books (Madras) Pvt. Ltd, Chennai, 2007), pp. 112-113.
9. *Ibid.* pp. 113-114.
10. *Annual Report: 1994–95,* ASEAN Standing Committee, (ASEAN Secretariat, Jakarta, 1995), p. 41.
11. Tridib Chakraborti, n. 8, pp. 118-119.
12. For details, see http://www.haze–online.or.id/help/chronology.php (26 May 2008).
13. For details, see http://www.haze–online.or.id (19 June 2008).
14. For details see Tridib Chakraborti, "Terrorism and the ASEAN States: A Classificatory and Prescriptive Analysis," Om Prakash Mishra and Sucheta Ghosh (eds.), *Terrorism and Low Intensity Conflict in the South Asian Region*, (Manak Publisher, New Delhi, 2003), pp. 316-356.
15. Amitav Acharya and Arabinda Acharya, "The Myth of the Second Front: Localizing the 'War on Terror' in Southeast Asia," *The Washington Quarterly*, Vol. 30, No. 4, Autumn 2007, p 79.
16. Clive Christie, *A Modern History of Southeast Asia: Decolonization, Nationalism and Separatism*, (Tauris Academic Studies, London, 1996), p. 192.
17. John Gershman, "Is Southeast Asia the Second Front," *Foreign Affairs*, Vol. 79, No. 4, July-August, 2002, pp. 60-74.
18. For details, see Amitav Acharya and Arabinda Acharya, "The Myth of the Second Front: Localizing the 'War on Terror' in Southeast Asia," n. 15, pp. 80-82.
19. For details, see http://www.aseansec.org/newdata/sammter.htm.
20. For details, see http://www.aph.gov.au/library/intguide/FAD/sea.htm.
21. ASEAN Agreement on Disaster Management and Emergency Response, Vientiane, July 26, 2005, http://www.aseansec.org/17587.htm.

22. See *Chairman's Statement of the Twelfth Meeting of the ASEAN Regional Forum* (ARF), Vientiane, July 29, 2005.
23. For details, see Statement from the Special ASEAN Leader's Meeting on Aftermath of Earthquake and Tsunami, Jakarta, January 6, 2005, http://www.aseansec.org/17067.htm.
24. For more on this, see Mely Caballero-Anthony, "Will Asia Heed Warning of Jakarta's Katrina," *Today,* February 7, 2007, at http://www.todayonline. com/articles/170454.

5

Rise of India and its Implications for Southeast Asia

Mala Selvaraju

India Growth: A Brief

Many studies and observations have shown that the 21st century belongs to the Asia Pacific region (i.e. Chee, 1997; Thompson, 1998; World Bank, 1993) in which India and China are the two new rising stars. This can be explained by the extraordinary economic growth of both the countries. In this connection, this paper focuses on India and its rise. India is the twelfth largest country in the world with a GDP of US$ 719.8 billion measured in USD-Exchange rate terms (2005). India is the second fastest economy growing country with a GDP growth rate of 8.9 percent at the end of the first quarter of 2006-07.

The Economist had this to say about India's economic boom, "*...signs of boom are everywhere. Some 5m new mobile-phone connections are added each month. To meet the soaring demand, Nokia ...built a huge factory near Chennai in just five months. Almost every city is seeing frenetic construction. Some 450 shopping malls are being built. ...perhaps one-third of India's 60m-80m square feet of "grade A" office space has gone up in the past 18 months alone. Flights are full, and prices of hotel rooms ruinous.*

(***The Economist***, June 3rd 2006)

The above citation can be seen as an evidence of the emergence of India as global economic powerhouse. It is amazing to note that this relatively poor nation is being closely monitored by the world. The past two decades have witnessed

India's annual growth of 6 percent. It must be noted that this growth was not at all hampered even when the world, especially Asian countries were experiencing tremendous economic slowdown in late 1990's to mid 2000s.

As for the developing countries, the India phenomenon should be viewed as an opportunity rather than a threat. To view India as a threat to be eliminated will only plunge the developing nations into a state of active denial of what is reality and what exactly is happening. Therefore, it is imperative for the developing economies i.e. Southeast Asian countries, to device strategies to tap the opportunities provided by the change in the global economic environment. As such, this paper, therefore, attempts to examine three pertinent issues namely, India's motives toward Southeast Asia; in case of a possible confrontation between China and India, the implication for Southeast Asia; and how the Southeast Asian countries react politically and economically to the rise of India.

India and Southeast Asia

Historically, India had a long history of cultural, economic, and political influence in Southeast Asia. This can be witnessed through the Indian influences in most of the temples in Southeast Asia. But India had lost its regional influences due to colonialism and economic backwardness. India tried to reconstruct its traditional role in the region after gaining independence. Nehru had a "grand strategy for a major-power role during his tenure from 1947-1964. Although deeply aware of his country's serious domestic issues, he still believed that "India is destined to be a key player on the international stage" (Nayar, 2003:115-158).

India aspires to be in the circle of great power politics and it has been constantly searching for an international status. India's nuclear tests in 1998 have shown the Indian muscle. India has also been striving to carve for itself, a permanent seat at the UN Security Council. But India continues to face economic difficulties which make it difficult to play a critical role in the world political economy (Grare, 2004:47). India recognizes the importance of info-tech economy. As Gordon states "India's status as a regional great power will depend to a significant degree on the ability of the nation to improve its performance in the marriage of design and production in high technology areas" (Gordon, 1993:45). As a result, India becomes the centre of info-tech which attracts a large off sourcing from all around the world, especially the United States.

On the international relations front, India is interested in seeking a greater role in the region through engagement forums like BIMSTEC (Bay of Bengal Initiative for Multi-Sectoral Technical and Economic Cooperation) established in 1997, India-Southeast Asian dialogue that had its vogue since 1992 [1], ASEAN Regional Forum (ARF), and East Asia Summit.

Some Indian policy makers and commentators expressed their views that the perception of the Chinese threat in the Asia Pacific Region can push a shared interest between India and ASEAN, Japan, and the United States (Malik, 1995:322). But this statement is not totally correct considering the fact that India has been seeking regional stability for the sake of economic development. In fact, India needs Southeast Asia, to back Indian economic development.

The demise of India's biggest strategic trade partner and energy (oil) supplier, the Soviet Union, required India to develop new strategies and hence, the creation of its Look East Policy in 1991. India has intensified paying its attention to Southeast Asia since 1991, following the "Look East" policy which is not only meant for its political economy survival but also spells the beginning of its realignment in order to shoot into eminence as a member of the Asia Pacific Economic Cooperation (APEC) and Asia Europe Meeting (ASEM) and eventually to join the global market. ASEAN too, started to be more positive towards India in the 1990s to the extent of accepting India in 1992, as a sectoral dialogue partner of

ASEAN. In 1995, India became a full dialogue partner and the following year witnessed as a member of ARF.

India's concentration in this region is more on countries like Cambodia, Laos, Vietnam, Myanmar and Thailand. In June 1997, India together with Bangladesh and Sri Lanka, established cooperation with Myanmar and Thailand aiming at creating a free trade zone among member countries by year 2017. [2] In 2000, India sponsored the "Mekong-Ganges River Cooperation Project" with Cambodia, Laos, Vietnam, Myanmar and Thailand which aimed at promoting cooperation on tourism, culture and education.

India has set up its companies in many parts of Southeast Asian countries, especially Singapore, Malaysia, Indonesia, and Thailand. Bilateral trade has increased from US$ 5.8 billion in 1997, to about US$ 30 billion in 2006. Now, Indian government is negotiating with ASEAN on an Indo-ASEAN Free Trade Agreement. In addition, Indian community network is also strong in Southeast Asia. This Indian community network can create a more favourable condition for strengthening the relations and for promoting mutual understanding between India and Southeast Asia. India's efforts to match the influence of China, Japan and South Korea in Southeast Asian region, were finally rewarded when it became a summit level partner in 2002. In 2004, ASEAN-India Partnership for Peace, Progress and Shared Prosperity, was signed.

To conclude, "Slowly but surely, ASEAN is emerging as central pivot in the Indian view of Asia and its future, and essential to the construction of a security order that will be in India's interests" (Mattoo, 2003:463).

China-India Rivalry

Asian security depends on the bilateral relations between India and China. There are two contradictory views on the bilateral relations between the "rising tiger" China and the "rising elephant" India. Realists such as political and security strategists, look at the bilateral relations between China and India quite negatively. On the other hand, liberalists such as economists and regional institutionalists, have a positive view on Sino-India relations and its impacts on Asia.

Perception of threat to important values and interests, competition for markets, commercial rivalry getting transformed into strategic rivalries, competition over armaments and cultural influence, are the causes of rivalry between the great powers (Thompson, 1999).

Tibet is one of the main causes of conflict between India and China. Agreement on Tibet, signed on April 29, 1954, by New Delhi, formally recognized the Chinese sovereignty over Tibet. But still, India supports Dalai Lama in some ways (Grare, 2004: 52). Another potential cause of conflict is, the border issue. China and India went to war in 1962 because of the border issue. Since then, there has been a period of Sino-Indian Cold War (1962-1976). Pakistan is also one of the factors leading to mistrust and conflict between India and China since China has been inclined to extending some support to Pakistan, the enemy of India. In the1971 war between India and Pakistan that led to the birth of Bangladesh, Sino-Pakistani cooperation was manifest in the diplomatic and military cooperation (Sidhu and Yuan, 2003:19).

Sino-Indian Détente, 1979-1998 resolution of the border issues, resumption of high level exchanges, visits, expanded contacts and cooperation in many areas such as trade, education, and cultural exchanges and two important agreements were reached, i.e. the 1993 Agreement on the Maintenance of Peace and Tranquility, and the 1996 Agreement on Confidence-Building Measures (Sidhu and Yuan, 2003:22). Measures to build confidence between the armed forces of the two countries have been initiated. Cultural and academic exchanges have steadily increased. Bilateral trade has also developed rapidly (US$ 2.9 billion in 2000 and 3.6 in 2001 against US$ 265 million in 1991). However, both the countries are competing for regional dominance and influence in the multipolar world of the 21 Century (Cabestan, 2004: 136; Malik, 1995: 317-355).

Moreover, the future rivalry of the two countries concerns a competition for a regional leadership. Each country views the other, as an expansionist hegemonic power. China cultivates a good relationship with India's neighbours such as Myanmar, Bangladesh, and sometimes with Pakistan (China-Pakistan nuclear cooperation; China supplies Pakistan with nuclear technologies). Such encirclement strategy makes India more suspicious of China (Grare, 2004:.52-3). Taylor argues that "over the long term, India and China...will always tend toward a rival relationship and thus each will seek a security link with a different superpower" (Taylor, 1987:232).

On the other hand, positive thoughts arise regarding the rise of China and India and their bilateral relations. Sridharan argues "Imminent conflict between China and India is much more remote" (Sridharan, 1993:118). "Although New Delhi and Beijing remain wary of each other's long term intentions as both acquire greater economic and military power, neither side finds its fundamental interests served by using openly adversarial terms." (Sidhu and Yuan: 2003:32-33). High level visits were restored and economic and technological development has been progressed. "The current leaders of China and India have determined that they can achieve economic growth and enhanced power most effectively within a peaceful, stable international environment" (Frazier, 2004:306).

China-Indian relations can be categorized into two main streams of thoughts. From economic liberal perspective, they believe that "expanding webs of economic interdependence create a basis for peace and cooperation in the competitive and anarchical state system" (Gilpin, 1987:12) However, the economic nationalists believe that "economic interdependence must have a political foundation and that it creates yet another arena of interstate conflict, increases national vulnerability, and constitutes a mechanism that one society can employ to dominate another" (Ibid., p.13).

China and India both, by all possible means, try to maintain peace and stability in the region for the sake of economic development. Realization that the border and strategic issues can be solved through diplomatic means rather than by force seems to have dawned on both Indian and Chinese leaders who are thus, matured enough, to avoid serious conflict and to live peacefully together in prosperity and happiness.

Consequences of the Rise of India for Southeast Asia

Politically, the rise of India may create some kind of "threat". But it is just short term "threat" or "unrealistic". Once the engagement and interactions take place among the politicians, businessmen, and scholars of ASEAN, China, and India, the perception of "threat" will be dispelled from their minds.

Strategically, the rise of India can create a magnetic effect in the region. India may attempt to exert its influence on some countries considered as the main geopolitical strategic points. ASEAN knows about this effect and its members are doing their best to cooperate and integrate deeper and deeper among themselves. Regarding China's foreign policy towards Indian increasing presence in Southeast Asia, Lijun argues that China would like to use the influence of India in Southeast Asia in order to make a triangle power strategy against the U.S. because China cherishes the theory of one against two (i.e. China Vs. US-Japan) (Lijun, 2006). If this is the case, then both Indian and Chinese presence would not get involved in any more conflict in influencing Southeast Asia politically.

Economically, the rise of India positively helps Southeast Asian countries to develop their own economy through the spill over effect theory. The trade between ASEAN and India has increased remarkably as above mentioned. Indian companies are seeking their investment locations in Southeast Asia and at the same time companies from Southeast Asia are seeking ample opportunities in the huge markets of India. Regional movements of goods and people are increasing day by day. All these economic links lead to stronger mutual interdependence of members of ASEAN and India.

At the same time, the rise of India can take away foreign direct investment from Southeast Asia. Southeast Asian technological development still lags behind that of India. Southeast Asia relies almost totally on FDI in order to improve its technologies. Now Southeast Asia faces the grave issue of losing out to China and India. This creates a big challenge for Southeast Asian countries (Mani, 2005:114).

Southeast Asian Responses to the Rise of India

Southeast Asian countries had been the playing ground for the Great Powers during the Cold War. Southeast Asian region experienced war and armed conflict, markedly Indochina War. Southeast Asia experienced genocide that occurred in Cambodia from 1975-79 which had killed more than 2 millions of people, something unprecedented in the history in twentieth century. All these wars, armed conflicts, and mass killings were mainly caused by the power politics and geopolitics of the great powers, US vs. USSR, in the Cold War period.

Such panic experiences always alert Southeast Asian countries in dealing with big powers. Now in the era of Asia Pacific, India and China are extraordinarily growing in almost all fields–political, economic, and cultural. This would pose unwieldy challenges as well as ample opportunities for Southeast Asia.

ASEAN recognizes the challenges and opportunities arising from the rise of India and the need to achieve integration. ASEAN needs to reform its economy, public administration, and international relations. ASEAN has tried its best to reduce the development gap in the region through issuing and implementing many policies and projects such as ASEAN Free Trade Area, ASEAN Integration Initiative,

ASEAN and the Greater Mekong Sub-regional Development Program, Poverty reduction strategy in the region especially in Cambodia, Laos, Myanmar and Vietnam (CLMV countries).

Rising India creates a competing ground with Southeast Asia for foreign investments and markets. "This could become a severe test of regional cooperation in the decades to come, but it may well be the challenge that the region needs to raise ASEAN to a higher level of cooperation" (Gungwu, 2003: xvii). ASEAN countries need to strengthen their competitiveness. Such a competition affects positively rather than negatively the region at large. It can improve the regional competitiveness in the world market.

Southeast Asia still has comparative and competitive advantages against India. Rising India leads to an increase in labour cost in this country. This can lead to the inflow of Indian companies to the ASEAN countries, especially that of the late comers (Cambodia, Laos, Myanmar, and Vietnam). Southeast Asian countries are aware of such opportunities. Moreover, India increasingly needs to import agricultural products from other countries including those from Southeast Asian region. This creates a lucrative agricultural sector in Southeast Asian countries (except Singapore).

Southeast Asian countries need to reform their economic system from "mass production-based ones relying on unskilled or semi-skilled labour to knowledge-based ones". Such knowledge-based economy requires high quality education which is being implemented in many countries in Southeast Asia (Mani, 2005). This is the best way for Southeast Asian nations to compete with India. Moreover, Southeast Asia needs to improve the competitiveness through the improvement of corporate governance. This is critical for the health of the economic system and the competitiveness of the economy.

Conclusion

Large and proud countries, India and China, do have competing interests in the region. But such conflict of interests will not lead to serious instability in the region. They find ways to cooperate with each other and with other entities in the region to maintain peace and stability.

ASEAN countries stay between the two civilized, powerful, and prosperous India and China. ASEAN countries tackle the challenges created by the competing interests between India and China through deeper integration and economic reform in order to stand safe and healthy amid the two giants. ASEAN must expedite its economic reform and development in order to compete with India and China and to enter into big markets in both India and China. ASEAN needs to improve its education system in order to meet the demand for human resources to gain any entry into the knowledge based economy. In the meantime, Southeast Asia must prepare to welcome the potential large amount of investments from India and China in future.

End Notes

1. At the inception of ASEAN, India was sceptical about the durability of the association (Sridharan, 1993:118). But since the early 1990s India started "Look East" policy toward Southeast Asia, East Asia and the Pacific.
2. Zhao Hong, *India's Economic Relations with ASEAN: Implication for China,* (Kuala Lumpur, University Malaya, 2006), p. 98-99.

References

Brook, Timothy and Luong, Hy V., *Culture and Economy: The shaping of Capitalism in Eastern Asia*, (The University of Michigan Press, Michigan, 2002).

Cabestan, Jean-Pierre, "The Chinese factor: China between multipolarity and bipolarity," in Gilles Boquerat and Frederic Grare (eds.), *India, China, Russia intricacies of an Asia Triangle*, (India Research Press, New Delhi, 2004).

Chan, Steven, *East Asian Dynamism: Growth, Order, and Security in the Pacific Region*, (Westview Press, Oxford, 1993).

Chee, Chan Heng (ed.), *The New Asia-Pacific Order*, (Institute of Southeast Asia Studies, Singapore, 1997).

Cheng, Joseph Y.S., "ASEAN's role in the Chinese foreign policy framework," in Sharon Siddique and Sree Kumar (compiled), *The 2nd ASEAN Reader*, (Institute of Southeast Asian Studies, Singapore, 2003).

Cotterell, Arthur, *East Asia: From Chinese predominance to the rise of the Pacific Rim*, (PIMLICO, London, 2002).

Frazier, Mark W., "Quiet competition and the future of Sino-Indian relations," in Francine R. Frankel and Harry Harding (eds.), *The India-China relations: What the United States needs to know,* (Columbia University Press, New York, 2004).

Frost, Stephen, Hewison Kevin and Pandita Sanjiv, "The Implications for labour of China's direct investment in Cambodia," *Asian Perspectives*, December 2002.

Kyodo News International, April 27, 2005.

Gilpin, Robert, *The political economy of international relations*, (Princeton, 1987).

Gipouloux, Francois, "Globalisation and Regionalization in East Asia: Stakes and Strategies" in Francois Gipouloux (ed.), *Regional Economic Strategies in East Asia*, (Maison Franco-Japonnaise, Tokyo, 1994).

Gordon, Alexander, India's security policy: Desire and necessity in a changing world," in Chandran Jeshurun (ed.), *China, India, Japan, and the Security of Southeast Asia*, (The Institute of Southeast Asian Studies, Singapore, 1993).

Grare, Frederic, "India, China, Russia and the quest for global status: strategic partnership or strategic competition," in Gilles Boquerat and Frederic Grare (eds.), *India, China, Russia intricacies of an Asia Triangle*, (India Research Press, New Delhi 2004).

Gungwu, Wang, "Foreword: New challenges for ASEAN," in Sharon Siddique and Sree Kumar (compiled), *The 2nd ASEAN Reader*, (Institute of Southeast Asian Studies, Singapore, 2003).

Jie, Chen, "Major concerns in China's ASEAN policy," in Chandran Jeshurun (ed.), *China, India, Japan, and the Security of Southeast Asia,* (Institute of Southeast Asian Studies, Singapore, 1993).

Kim, Samuel S., *China and the World: Chinese Foreign Policy Faces the New Millennium*, (Westview Press, USA, 1998).

Lijun, Sheng, "The U.S. factor in China's ASEAN policy," Institute of Southeast Asian Studies, *Trends in Southeast Asia Series: 7*

(2006), (Institute of Southeast Asian Studies, Singapore, 2006).

Malik, J. Mohan, "China-India relations in the Post-Soviet era: The continuing rivalry," *The China Quarterly*, 1995, No. 142.

Mani, A., Creating knowledge based economies in Southeast Asia, *Ritsumeikan Journal of Asia Pacific Studies*, 2005, 54:3, pp. 114-132.

Mattoo, Amitabh, "ASEAN in India's foreign policy," in Sharon Siddique and Sree Kumar (compiled), *The 2nd ASEAN Reader*, (Institute of Southeast Asian Studies, Singapore, 2003).

Nayar, Baldev Raj and Paul, T.V., *India in the world order: Searching for major-power status*, (Cambridge University Press, Cambridge, 2003).

Sidhu & Yuan, Jing Dong, *China and India: Cooperation or conflict*, (Lynne Rienner, Boulder, London, 2003).

Sridharan, Kripa, "India-ASEAN relations: Evolution, growth, and prospects," in Chandran Jeshurun (ed.), *China, India, Japan, and the Security of Southeast Asia,* (Institute of Southeast Asian Studies, Singapore, 1993).

Taylor, Robert, *Greater China and Japan: Prospects for an economic partnership in East Asia*, (Routledge, London, 1996).

Taylor, Jay, *The Dragon and the Wild Goose: China and India*, (Greenwood Press, New York, 1987).

Thompson, Grahame (ed.), *Economic Dynamism in the Asia-Pacific.* (Routledge, London 1998).

Thompson, William R., *Great Power Rivalries*, (South Carolina: University of South Carolina Press, Columbia, 1999).

Umbach, Frank, "ASEAN and Major Powers: Japan and China Changing Balance of Power? ," in Jorn Dosch and Manfred (eds.), *International Relations in the Asia-Pacific: New Patterns of Interest, Power and Cooperation,* (Munster, New York, 2000).

World Bank, *East Asian Miracle: Economic growth and public policy*, (Oxford University Press, Oxford, 1993).

Yahuda, Michael, *The international politics of the Asia-Pacific.* (Routledge Curzon, New York: 2004).

6

Malaysian Indian Society in Ferment

V. Suryanarayan

The unprecedented demonstration by Malaysian Indians before the British High Commission in Kuala Lumpur at the end of November 2007, under the sponsorship of the Hindu Rights Action Force (HINDRAF), has brought into sharp focus the pathetic situation in which the Indian community finds itself in Malaysia today. The HINDRAF is a coalition of 30 non-governmental organizations, committed to the preservation and promotion of the Hindu identity. The coalition had been agitating against what it calls the unofficial policy of temple demolition and the steady introduction of Sharia-based law. The Memorandum submitted to the British High Commission demanded that the United Kingdom should move an emergency resolution in the United Nations, condemning the "ethnic cleansing" taking place in Malaysia. It also appealed that the issue should be referred to the World Court and International Criminal Court of Justice for crimes against its own ethnic minority Indians. In August 2007, the Malaysian Indians had approached the Royal Court of Justice, demanding a compensation of US Dollars, tantamount to 4 Trillion, which works out to the US Dollars of one million to every Malaysian Indian, for bringing his forefathers as indentured labourers and for failing to protect their rights and interests on the eve of Malayan independence.

The Malaysian Government, true to its authoritarian traditions, refused permission to hold the rally, arrested the leaders and used tear gas and water cannon to disperse nearly 35,000 demonstrators. The leaders of the HINDRAF should know that historical wrongs like the indenture system, perpetrated during the colonial era, cannot be undone. Presumably, their objective was to highlight the increasing marginalization of the Indian community in the social, economic, political and cultural life of Malaysia. A Malaysian Indian student, Ananthi, a Rhodes Scholar, reading for her PhD in Oxford University, echoed the feelings of the overwhelming majority of her community, in a letter widely circulated in Malaysia. To quote Ananthi, "It was about being neglected, about not having a seat at the table to bargain, about having a national and communal leadership that we do not trust and is utterly discreditable. It is about saying no to being the forgotten Indians, and not enough of us in our comfortable houses, those of us who worked to manage to work the system to our benefit – stood with the other Indians, who are not so different from us". For the first time, the marginalized Malaysian Indians displayed the power of *Makkal Shakti* (people's power).

This paper is divided into two sections. The first one deals with the changing political dynamics in Malaysia and the second one analyses the factors that have led to the marginalization of the overwhelming sections of the Malaysian Indian community.

It has been rightly said that every issue in Malaysia, whether political, cultural or economic, had always continued to be dominated by ethnic considerations. The entire political system is based on communal politics. The ordinary Malaysian grows up and lives in a pervasive communal atmosphere. While ethnicity would continue to dominate, the nature of political discourse has been changing from time to time, depending upon the changing political dynamics. In order to put the issues in their respective perspective, it is necessary to highlight certain political realities.

The Malays feel that they are the indigenous people (*Bhumiputra*) and, therefore, they have an extraordinary claim for dominance in the political and cultural life of the country. The British colonialists upheld this claim and ruled the country in the name of Malay Sultans, in whom sovereignty was vested. At the same time, as part of imperialist objectives, the British also encouraged a large-scale immigration of the Chinese and Indians for the economic exploitation of the country's natural resources. The existence of a plural society prevented the growth of anti-British feelings as well as a sense of common nationalism in Malaya before the Second World War. As the English novelist Somerset Maugham wrote, "Malaya was a first rate country for third rate English men".

The political awakening of the Malays, in the immediate aftermath of the Second World War, following the introduction of the Malayan Union Proposals (a unitary state to which the Sultans were to cede their sovereignty) and the unity that they forged under the United Malays National Organisation (UMNO) had far reaching consequences. Not only did it compel the British to withdraw the Malayan Union proposals, but it also made it clear, that the Malays would never give up their pre-eminent position in the political life of Malaya. While in later years, the Malay leaders did co-operate with the Malayan Chinese Association (MCA) and the Malayan Indian Congress (MIC), in the larger interests of Malaya as a whole, the dynamic leadership of Malayan nationalism has always remained in the hands of Malays. The Alliance, which was voted to power in 1955, was not an alliance of equal partners; it was an alliance in which the supremacy of the Malays was clearly established. The transformation of the Alliance into *Barisan Nasional* in the 1970's, with the incorporation of various Malay and non-Malay political parties, further reduced the political clout of the MCA and the MIC.

On the eve of Independence in August 1957, the Malays and the non-Malays were roughly equal in numbers (Malays 49.8 percent, Chinese 37.1 percent, Indians 11.1 percent and others 2.0 percent). Over the years, the demographic structure has radically altered to the advantage of the Malays. Higher rate of natural increase and large scale immigration of

Indonesian Malays have contributed to the burgeoning of Malay population. The *Bhumiputras* (Malays plus the indigenous people of Sabah and Sarawak, which were incorporated into Malaysia in 1963) constitute nearly two thirds of the population; the Chinese constitute 23.7 percent and the Indians, 7.1 percent.

An important clue to the understanding of the political economy is the social and political contract arrived at, by the elite of the three communities on the eve of independence. It was assumed that the economic predominance of the Chinese would be offset by the political supremacy of the Malays. It was believed that, with the passage of time, this equilibrium would give way to a more balanced one, when the Malays would play a greater role in the economic life and the Chinese and the Indians would play a greater role in politics. The pre-eminent position of the Malays was enshrined in the Constitution–the retention of the Malay Sultanate, the acceptance of Islam as the State Religion, the constitutional provisions safeguarding the "special rights" of the Malays and the acceptance of Malay as the national and official language. The major concession made to the non-Malays was the conferment of citizenship on them.

The fragility of the Malaysian political system came out into the open on May 13, 1969, when, following the reverses suffered by the Alliance in the general elections, the large-scale Sino-Malay clashes took place in Kuala Lumpur. Emergency was proclaimed and when democratic process was restored following the amendment of the Constitution, Malay political power was further entrenched. The Royal Commission appointed to enquire into the riots, was of the view that the crisis was due to the disenchantment and frustration of the Malays, who were denied the enjoyment of the fruits of independence. In 1970, Malay corporate ownership was a meagre 2.4 percent, compared with 63.3 percent enjoyed by the foreigners, 22.4 percent enjoyed by the Chinese and 10.0 percent by unknown parties. While the overall poverty incidence was high, to the extent of 51.2 percent in 1970, about 76.0 percent of them were Malays. A New Economic Policy (replaced by National Integrity Plan in 2004) was launched to bring about economic transformation, with a particular emphasis on the development of the Malays. In the political sphere, the democratic rights were curtailed, it was made a seditious criminal offence to challenge the special rights conferred on the Malays, the language provisions in the Constitution, the institution of Sultanate and citizenship laws.

Under the leadership of Prime Minister Mahathir (1981-2003) Malaysia underwent a fundamental transformation. From being a producer of primary commodities, Malaysia had become an industrialized country, virtually an economic power house in the ASEAN region. Despite occasional hiccups, for example, during the Asian economic crisis, the country registered an economic growth averaging 8.0 percent. The absolute poverty level came down from 51.2 percent in 1970 to 7.0 percent in 2000. By 1990, the Malay share in the corporate capital went up to 19.2 percent, the Chinese 46.8 percent and the Indians 1.5 percent, the nominee companies 8.5 percent and the balance, owned by the foreigners. To Dr. Mahathir, his strong criticism of American foreign policy in West Asia and Southeast Asia became gratifying.

The negative side of the story was increasing authoritarianism. In addition to continuing criticism of the non-Malays about the pro-Malay and pro-Islamic policies of the government, the discontent also spread to Malay middle class. The first to raise the banner of revolt was Tunku Razaleigh Hamzah, who in 1987 formed a secular Malay party, *Parti Sengamat 46* (Spirit of 46). Subsequently, Razaleigh was readmitted into UMNO. Far more important was the revolt led by Anwar Ibrahim in 1998, who formed a political party called *Kedilan* (Justice Party) under the leadership of his wife. The unfair trial of Anwar Ibrahim, coupled with the third degree treatment meted out to him, has earned him considerable good will in Malaysia and abroad.

After his release, Anwar Ibrahim started speaking in a more democratic idiom, for widening the democratic space, tolerance of dissent and the establishment of a truly pluralist society, with an emphasis on redistributive justice.

He was prepared to champion the non-Malay cause when he promised to abolish the New Economic Policy and to promote equality for all. The cumulative effect was that the ruling *Barisan Nasional* suffered serious reverses in the general election held in March 2008. In the 12th general election, the UMNO and its coalition partners in the Barisan Nasional, suffered unprecedented reverses. It lost its two third majority in parliament. What is more, it had lost its power in four states—Kedah, Perak, Penang and Selangor—besides failing to regain power in Kelantan. What is more, Anwar Ibrahim re-entered parliament by winning the by election in the Permatang Pauh, with a huge majority. Anwar Ibrahim is openly making a bid for power by enticing ruling party members of parliament into his fold. Another important consequence was the decision of Prime Minister Abdullah Ahmad Badawi to expedite the transfer of power to his deputy Najib Abdul Razak.

An important political reality must be highlighted. It is extremely difficult for opposition parties to function in Malaysia. The draconian Internal Security Act, which provides for detention without trial, has been frequently used against opposition leaders, Malay and non-Malay alike. The Internal Security Act is inhuman, because it denies the victim a fundamental human right, the right to a fair trial. Anwar Ibrahim underlined some of the evils of the Malaysian political system in an international conference in New Delhi, few months ago, "What is an election if the political parties in the opposition do not have access to freedom of speech, assembly and movement, necessary to voice their criticisms of the government openly and to bring alternative policies and candidates to the voters? Where I come from, the opposition is barred from the air waves, rallies are not allowed and opposition newspapers operate underground". Prof. Harold Crouch, an astute observer of the Malaysian political scene, has remarked, "It is hard to place Malaysia in a clear cut category between democracy and authoritarianism". He concludes "Malaysia is neither democratic nor authoritarian... as the Malaysian political system has been oscillating between repression and responsiveness".

Having enumerated the changing political dynamics in Malaysia, I now pass on to deal with the complex issues relating to the marginalization of the vast majority of Malaysian Indian community. At the end of the Second World War, the Indians (the term today includes Indians, Pakistanis, Nepalis, Bangladeshis and Sri Lankans) constituted about 14.0 percent of the population of Malaya. Number of them returned to India during the years of the communist insurgency and the dark days following the communal riots in May 1969. By 2,000, Indians numbered 1.8 million, representing 7.7 percent of the total Malaysian population of 21.89 million. According to the Singhvi Committee Report, the total number of Indians in Malaysia is 1,665,000, of which 1,600,000 are Malaysian citizens, 15,000 are non-resident Indians and 50,000 are stateless people. Approximately, 80.0 percent of them are Tamils; followed by North Indians (mainly Sikhs) forming 7.7 percent and Malayalis, 4.7 percent, Telugus 3.4 percent, Sri Lankan Tamils 2.7 percent, Pakistanis and Bangladeshis 1.1 percent and others 0.4 percent. From the viewpoint of religion, Hindus number 81.2 percent; Christians 8.4 percent; Muslims 6.7 percent; Sikhs 3.1 percent; Buddhists 0.5 percent and others 0.1 percent. In the specific context of Malaysia, where Islam, the religion of the Malays, is the State religion, sections of the Muslim community of Indian origin eventually got assimilated into the Malay society.

We should make a distinction between the middle class (mainly non-Tamils and Sri Lankan Tamils) whose standard of living is fairly high and the working class (mainly Tamil) who are poor and are getting marginalized. The working class belongs to the lower castes of the Hindu society like *Adi Dravidar, Vannan, Maruttuvar, Nadar, Vanniyar* etc. The Indians, especially Tamils from the Madras Presidency, were the preferred labourers to develop the rubber plantations, because they displayed unquestioned loyalty and obedience, being content with what they had earned and non-rebellious by nature. Most of them continue to be weighed down by low esteem, which is worsened by lack of interaction between the well-off and the less well-off sections.

A notable feature of the Indian community is its changing socio-economic profile. In 1970, 47 percent of the Indians were engaged in agriculture and 74 percent of them, in the plantations. With rapid economic expansion and diversification of the economy, the plantations have been converted for other purposes, including the construction of luxury homes. The uprooted Indians were only paid a pittance as compensation. They naturally migrated to the urban areas and joined the squatter population. Few years ago, Samy Velu, the President of the Malaysian Indian Congress (MIC), deplored the plight of thousands of estate workers "living in squalor in slums in dozens of long-houses and squatter settlements all over Selangor".

Aliran, the well-known journal of the Malaysian reform movement, provided statistical details, few years ago, which made an alarming reading as follows. Forty percent of the serious crimes in Malaysia are committed by the Indians; there are 38 Indian based gangs with 1,500 active members; during the last few years, there had been a hundred percent increase in the number of Indian gangsters; Indians recorded the highest number of those detained under the Emergency Regulations and banished to Simpang Rengamm prison. In the field of social woes, again, it is the same story. In Kuala Lumpur, 14 percent of the squatters are Indians; they have the highest suicide rates; 41 percent of the vagrants and beggars are Indians; 20 percent of the child abusers are Indians besides 14 percent of the juvenile delinquents.

The communal clashes that took place between the Indians and the Malays in Kuala Lumpur in March 2001 sent shock waves throughout Malaysia. It was the worst ethnic riots since the communal clashes in May 1969. Ethnic tensions in Malaysia are mainly due to Sino-Malay rivalry; but the Indian involvement in 2001 riots (five of the six killed were Indians and the other was an Indonesian) was a sad reminder that in Malaysia's progress towards prosperity, the Indians were being left behind.

The disadvantaged status is clearly visible in the economic sphere. The Chinese are firmly entrenched in trade, business and industry. They are reconciled to the subordinate status in the political life of the country; at the same time, they have sharpened entrepreneurial skills to their credit and thus, have become indispensable. The status of the Malays has steadily improved as a result of the energetic drive of the Malaysian Government since the introduction of the New Economic Policy. In 1970, the Indians owned only 1.0 percent of the share capital in limited companies, while the Chinese controlled 22.5 percent, Malays 1.0 percent and the rest being held by the foreigners. At the turn of the century, the Indians held only 1.5 percent, compared to 19.4 percent of the Malays and 38.5 percent of the Chinese, the balance being held by the foreigners.

The deplorable status of the Tamils is directly related to the poor educational attainments. Though the Malaysian Government has expanded the educational facilities on a larger scale since independence, the fruits of education have not percolated through the disadvantaged sections of the Indian population. The importance of education in the development of disadvantaged sections of population has been highlighted by many writers. It is a means of upward social and economic mobility; an avenue of modernization; an instrument to enrich cultural life and, above all, in the Malaysian context, a means of national unity and integration.

The Indians continue to be the most disadvantaged section

at all levels of education. The Tamil medium primary schools are in a deplorable stage. Single teacher handling multiple classes; ill equipped schools with teachers having no commitment and high drop rates are some of the serious drawbacks. The family life is characterized by alcoholism, violence against women and addiction to Tamil TV Channels. These do not provide a congenial atmosphere for study. As a result, only limited number of Tamil students reaches the university stage. The current intake of Indian students in Malaysian universities is only 6.2 percent, and most of these students hail from non-Tamil and Sri Lankan Tamil sections; the few Indian Tamils, who are lucky to get admission in the Universities, are also from relatively affluent families.

Confounding the complex situation is the general perception that the increasing Islamisation of the country and the destruction of Hindu temples are posing grave threats to the Hindu way of life. Given below are two illustrations which took place in 2003. The first related to Shyamala Sathiaseelan. Shyamala's husband, having embraced Islam, gained custody of his two children and also had them converted to Islam without the permission of his wife. Shyamala's appeal for help from authorities went unheeded. The second case involved Murthy Maniam, a convert to Islam, whose dead body was buried according to Muslim rites by the religious authorities despite his widow's claim that he had remained a practicing Hindu until his death.

The non-Muslim members of the Malaysian cabinet requested the Prime Minister to provide constitutional guarantees for religious freedom, but their appeal was ignored by Prime Minister Badawi. Many Hindus also were deeply hurt when, for the first time, the UMNO General Assembly was held during Deepavali. As Dilip Lahiri, former Indian diplomat has written the UMNO youth leaders brandished and kissed the *Kris* (dagger) and threatened to shed the Chinese and Indian blood, if Malay supremacy was challenged at all. The Hindus also began to feel that the Government was lukewarm on the sensitive question of the destruction of Hindu temples. As a result, the HINDRAF and the allied organizations began to take deep roots in the Hindu community.

In the preservation of the Hindu identity, in the prevailing atmosphere of increasing Islamisation, the temples do play a significant role. The temples and religious festivals are the only visible attachment to traditions and the Hindus cling on to them tenaciously. Needless to suggest, that there is a close nexus between religion and Malay politics. The policies of the Malaysian Government have been double edged. On the one hand, the leaders of the UMNO are committed to the promotion of Islam in all possible ways. Dr. Mahathir has mentioned several times that Malaysia is an Islamic State and the Islamic identity is projected in a flamboyant way both within the country and outside. Such a policy is necessary to mobilize the Malays under the UMNO banner. Otherwise, the Malays will flock to *Parti Islam* (PAS) for leadership and inspiration.

At the same time, the realities of Malaysia and the needs of modernization dictate that the Government must encourage a less exclusivist approach towards Islam. When the desecration of the Hindu temples began in 1978, the most horrendous being the destruction of the *Murugan* temple in Kerling, Prime Minister Hussein Onn came down heavily on the Islamic extremists. But the situation has been allowed to drift during recent years. In its Memorandum, the HINDRAF has pointed out that in every three weeks one Hindu temple is destroyed in Malaysia, the most significant being the demolition of the Mariamman temple in Shah Alam. The Government maintains that most of these temples have been constructed in government owned lands without proper authorization being obtained. But the temples have been functioning for many years; strangely enough, there are no reports of the destruction of Chinese places of worship. Is it because the Chinese are more organized and will hit back if their religious beliefs are tampered with?

The question should legitimately be asked as to what extent the Malaysian Indian Congress (MIC), which represents the Indian community in the government, has succeeded in its primary objective of safeguarding the interests of the Indian community? An Indian observer of the Malaysian scene comes to a dismal conclusion. Factional struggle and disunity had been the major curse of the Indian community. Since its inception in 1946, fight for power, petty politicking and mud slinging had been its major attributes. The rivalry between Devaser and Sambandan; between Sambandan and Manickavasagam; Manickavasagam and Sami Velu; and among Sami Velu, Padmanabhan, Subramaniam and Panditan –brings no laurels to the Indian community. Samy Velu is more interested in ingratiating himself into the Malay leadership rather than championing the legitimate Indian interests and aspirations.

What is more, self-help measures, initiated by the MIC, with much fanfare, have not led to the desired results. For example, the Maika Holdings Bhd, that started in 1982, as an investment vehicle for the Malaysian Indians, incurred heavy losses, resulting in the loss of savings of large number of poor Indians. Frustration and anger against the leadership found expression when the Indian youth began to disturb the functions organized by the MIC; very often, Samy Velu was booed and jeered. How distant the MIC was from the ordinary Indians became evident when the results of the 2008 parliamentary elections were announced. Of the nine MIC candidates of the Barisan Nasional, only three could win their seats, and that too with slender margins, those who were defeated included Samy Velu, the President of the MIC, who had lost the Sungai Siput constituency in the Perak State. The emergence of the HINDRAF has to be viewed against in the backdrop of the alienation of large sections of Indians, coupled with a non-performing MIC.

The unfortunate events in Malaysia naturally attracted the

attention of Indian leaders. Prime Minister Manmohan Singh, Foreign Affairs Minister Pranab Mukerjee and Chief Minister Karunanidhi have expressed concern and regret over the turn of events in Malaysia. Their objective is not to interfere with the internal affairs of a friendly country, but to influence the Malaysian Government to initiate immediate steps for the redressal of long pending grievances. The Malaysian response has been unfortunate. Representatives of the Malaysian Government, including the Prime Minister, have demanded that the Government of Tamil Nadu should keep off from what it considers to be an internal matter of Malaysia. What is the record of the Malaysian Government in this respect? As a leading member of the international Islamic organization, the Malaysian Government has sharply criticized many governments for pursuing policies, which have adversely affected the Moslem communities. The UMNO and the PAS, the two leading Malay parties, have, on several occasions since independence, criticized the policies of the Thai Government which has led to the alienation of the Malay minority in Southern Thailand. The Malay leaders have also criticized the Government of Singapore for pursuing discriminatory policies against the Malay minority in the island. The Malaysian criticism of India, to say the least, is an illustration of the pot calling the kettle black.

The increasing intolerance of the Malaysian Government and its vocal advocacy of OIC sponsored causes have cast a long shadow over India–Malaysia relations. As the former Indian diplomat, Dilip Lahiri has pointed out, on a range of issues affecting India-Southeast Asia relations, Malaysia had been the "most difficult" among the member states of ASEAN. The Malaysian Government is preparing itself to crack down on the HINDRAF; few government spokesmen have started levelling the unsubstantiated charge that the HINDRAF has links with the Tamil Tigers. The perceptive Indian observers of the Southeast Asian scene remember that when General Rabuka began systematically to discriminate against the Indian community in Fiji, in order to justify himself, he was quoting chapter and verse from Dr. Mahathir's book, *The Malay Dilemma.* Few years ago, in Brickfields in Kuala Lumpur, few Indian expatriates, who were working in the IT industry, were rounded up and detained as illegal immigrants, though they had proper documents to prove that they had entered Malaysia through legal channels. The shocked Indian diplomats immediately protested, and the Malaysian Government had to tender an apology for its inhuman behaviour. Turbluent times are ahead in Malaysia and for the Malaysian Indians.

The Malaysian Indian community is at the cross roads today. If the present situation is allowed to drift and deteriorate, the community would suffer untold damages and would be left behind in the economic and educational advancement of the country. If the present hardships are to be overcome, it is important that the Indian community must re-evaluate its role and chalk out a new destiny by sinking its differences and by working as a team. The minority character of the Indian community and its vulnerable position makes such a task all the more urgent and imperative. The Malaysian Government must also view the marginalized and impoverished Indian community with greater sympathy and understanding and ensure that the Indians, to begin with, at least obtain a share equal to their proportion in the population.

7

Geopolitics of Cyclone Relief Efforts in Myanmar

M. Prayaga and A. Lakshmana Chetty

Myanmar, which had already been in the midst of a political storm since 1988, when the military leaders cracked down on a pro-democracy movement killing as many as 3000 people, was struck by the deadly cyclone named *Nargis* on May 2-3, 2008. As the cyclone had left a vast trail of death and destruction behind it, the military government of Myanmar made a call for international aid. The international community, which was deeply concerned about the victims of the disastrous cyclone, swung into action swiftly to distribute the aid directly to the cyclone affected people. The military rulers of Myanmar who had stonewalled Western aid efforts and did not budge even after the UN Secretary General's talks by way of mediation with Senior General Than Shwe, curiously enough, did not mind seeking the assistance of the neighbouring countries such as Bangladesh, China, Thailand and India in their relief efforts. This paper, while shedding light on the Nargis and its dreadful consequences, focuses on the junta's relief effort, the policy it had adopted in accepting the offers of aid, the inbred prejudices against the Western countries it had betrayed, and the predilections for its Asian neighbours, besides probing into the factors that prodded the military leaders to toe a policy course that would make an impact on Myanmar's overall relief effort. An attempt is also made to scrutinize the junta's initiative to hold a referendum on the new Constitution—drafted under its own supervision—in the wake of the devastating cyclone and the global outrage it had sparked off.

Settings

Devastating cyclones are not anything new to the Indian Ocean. In 1883, the Indonesian volcano on the island of Krakatoa, when exploded, triggering powerful tidal waves, killed around 36,000 people. [1] Coming to the recent times, the Bhola cyclone which hit East Pakistan (now Bangladesh) on November 12, 1970, had killed half a million. [2] The super typhoon 'Nina' of 1975 claimed well over one lakh lives in China. [3] The 1991 Bangladesh Cyclone killed at least 138,000 people and rendered as many as 10 million people homeless. [4] In December 2004, a colossal earthquake, 160 km off the Indonesian island of Sumatra, set off giant tidal waves or tsunami which killed well over 229,000 people besides obliterating communities in Thailand, Indonesia and India. [5]

Cyclone Mala of 2006 struck the coast of Myanmar with winds of 185 kmph, causing severe damage and killing 22 people. Next cyclone to hit Myanmar was Nargis, which was slightly weaker than its predecessor but had a significantly greater impact. Cyclone Nargis, which had hit the lower Irrawaddy delta area in early May 2008, was, as claimed by Myanmar Ambassador in Geneva, Wunna Maung Lwin, the "worst cyclone ever to hit his country." [6] According to the United Nations chief Ban Ki-moon, at least 133,000 people were dead or missing while two million more needed shelter, enough food, safe drinking water and medical care. [7] Accompanied by fierce winds and waves, Nargis wiped out vast swaths of the Irrawaddy delta, popularly known as the fertile 'rice bowl' of Myanmar. With the power and phone lines destroyed and roads blocked by the uprooted trees, approach to the isolated areas of the delta was rendered extremely difficult. Since 85 percent of school buildings were either destroyed or severely damaged, children had to attend classes in relief camps and tents. Families and villages obliterated in their entirety, were legion.

Since Myanmar has already achieved notoriety as one of

the world's worst healthcare systems, [8] diarrhoea, malaria and dengue fever spread fast among the cyclone victims making their lives still more miserable. The UN humanitarian agency warned that the "acute environmental issues" set off by the cyclone would "pose an immediate risk to human life and health." [9] The deadly storm not only inundated 5,000 square kilometres of low-lying land in the Irrawaddy delta, but also left about 62,000 people dead or missing. [10] Water systems were overwhelmed with salt water and sewage. Adding to the woes of the farmers of the delta, was the death of many of the draft animals required for planting the rice crop by mid-June. Tens of thousands of people were huddled in Buddhist monasteries and schools.

Yangon, the largest city of Myanmar, was hit hard by the monster storm. Awestruck senior citizens said that they had never seen the former capital so devastated in their lifetimes.[11] With the disruption of electricity supply, most of the 6.5 million residents of Yangon were denied power and water supplies. Highlighting the powerlessness of the households of the main city of Myanmar, a reporter said: "Above all else, Shwedagon Pagoda, perhaps the most magnificent site in Southeast Asia, shines gold upon the blackened city below." [12] In Yangon, "one of Asia's greenest cites," many of the 100-year-old trees were knocked down. According to Reuters report, the storm stripped Yangon of about one third of its biggest trees. [13] Surveying the uprooted trees, a resident of Yangon, Kyaw Win, said ruefully: "This was such a beautiful city, but no more." [14] Storm's 165 kmph winds blew roofs off the hospitals, schools and dwellings and also delivered a body blow to tourism industry, which was already in a bad shape because of military's crackdown on pro-democracy activists in the last 46 years of its rule. A French tourist, Dominique Mas, said: "The problem will be the feel of tourism. People will be afraid to go to a town they think is ruined." Western embassies have also advised their citizens to leave Yangon because of shortages of food, water and fuel. Ei mon Oo, a tour operator lamented: "Business is very bad. The tourists are not coming in and many of the tour destinations are closed". [15]

Junta's Initial Reaction to the Humanitarian Crisis

The India Meteorological Department (IMD), which gave "storm warning" to its counterpart in Myanmar 48 hours before cyclone Nargis made landfall, [16] continued to issue "accurate warnings as frequently as every three hours". [17] Acting on this information, Myanmar officials had begun issuing warnings through press and electronic media since April 29, 2008. But the military government did not take follow up action such as the evacuation of people from vulnerable areas to safer areas. The Generals—who were greatly concerned about the May 10 referendum on the new Constitution drafted under their own supervision which ensured a central role for the Army in politics—[18] displayed, what Timothy Keating, head of the U.S. Pacific Command, described as, 'less serious concern' about the storm. [19] However, shaken by the scale of devastation, the military regime of Myanmar, which had spurned any foreign assistance in the wake of the 2004 tsunami, felt constrained to issue an appeal inviting international aid. On May 5, 2008, i.e. two days after the storm dissipated, at a meeting with foreign diplomats and representatives of the U.N. and international aid agencies, Myanmar's Foreign Ministry officials welcomed international humanitarian assistance and specified the urgently needed things including roofing materials, plastic sheets and temporary tents, medicines, water purifying tablets, blankets and mosquito nets. [20]

Response of the Global Community

The international community, which was gravely concerned over the cyclone Nargis that had caused devastation on a giant scale, readily responded. The UN, Governments and Private aid agencies swung into action.

The United Nations

On May 8, 2008, the UN offered US$ 10 million for cyclone Nargis relief, besides nine helicopters for aid distribution, while two UN Food Programme (WFP) airplanes loaded with medicines, high-energy biscuits and other supplies were already waiting in Yangon for two days for junta's permission to allow materials in. As Richard Horsey, Coordinator of the UN humanitarian aid, has stated, between 30 and 40 visas requested by various UN agencies and private relief groups, were pending with the Myanmar government. Horsey added: "These are mostly people who have key experience in handling disasters of this scale, and so they can bring lessons from other similar disasters." [21]

On May 9, 2008, at the Yangon airport, the Myanmarese officials made bold to confiscate two planeloads of critical aid sent by the WFP and to add injury to this glaring affront, they offered to shoulder "the illegitimately moral responsibility of distributing the supplies." [22] However, international organizations began repeatedly questioning the competence of the military regime to supervise the relief work alone by itself. For three weeks after the storm, the military regime of Myanmar effectively blocked the international efforts to deliver the aid. Even 15 days after the cyclone had struck, none from WHO was permitted to enter Myanmar. UN Secretary-General Ban Ki-moon's efforts to talk to Than Shwe were all in vain as the latter had refused to respond to even Ban's telephone calls. As Ban's two letters to Than Shwe "to find out what's really going on the ground" remained unanswered, the UN chief sent third letter through the UN Humanitarian Chief, John Holmes. [23]

As Shawn W. Crispin of *Asia Times* has pointed out, what was at stake for the UN was its own "relevance and ability to manage global calamities." [24] Ban, therefore, flew into Myanmar's disaster zone on May 22, 2008. Flying in a helicopter over the flooded rice fields he saw how the extent of the disaster had destroyed the dwellings in the delta. Ban said "the main purpose" of his visit was to demonstrate his "solidarity." Ban also availed his visit to press the military leaders to open the doors to the UN and the entire international community, which, as he himself said emphatically, "stand ready to help to overcome the tragedy." In his talks with Prime Minister Thein Sein, and the military dictator General Than Shwe, Ban insisted on the international aid experts being rushed in especially because the crisis had exceeded Myanmar's capacity. [25] General Than Shwe had consented to allow "all aid workers irrespective of nationalities" into the delta. An UN official said: "The General said he saw no reason why that (entry of aid workers into the delta) should not happen as long as they were genuine humanitarian workers and it was clear what they were going to do." Gen. Shwe also agreed to allow the Yangon airport to be used as a logistical hub for aid distribution. [26]

Junta's assurance to Ban did raise the hopes of the international aid agencies only to shatter them soon, when the latter found later that Ban's personal appeal really cut no ice with the generals. Many humanitarian groups were found waiting for visas. France Hurtubise of the International Federation of Red Cross and Red Crescent Societies said that six of the group's foreign staff entered the delta for the first time only on June 4, 2008. She lamented: "For the tsunami (which killed 220,000 people) we had 300 expats in within the first month–compare 300 to six." [27] The position of the WFP was no better either. While the awesome relief effort needed more helicopters to reach the survivors in remote areas, the Generals gave permission on July 3, 2008, to only one helicopter to operate from Yangon, while nine more were allowed to lie idle in the Thai airports. [28]

The United States

The US responded promptly to the crisis in Myanmar by making an initial offer of US$ 250,000. However, the US State Department's request for a Disaster Assistance Response

Team (DART) to visit the hardest hit areas before providing the aid, was turned down by the Generals. The Deputy spokesman of the State Department Tom Casey told the reporters: "We have a DART team that is standing by and ready to go into Burma to help try to assess needs there. As of this moment, the Burmese government has not given them permission to go into the country so that there is a barrier to us being able to move forward." [29] However, Myanmar's military rulers, after initial opposition, agreed on May 9, 2008, to allow a single US cargo aircraft to bring in relief supplies. Gratified Pentagon spokesman Maj. Stuart Upton noted: "We hope that this is the beginning of broader support between the United States and Burma to help the Burmese people." [30]

However, these expectations were baffled when four US Navy ships loaded with relief material, had been waiting at sea since May 13, 2008, to seek permission from the military rulers of Myanmar. According to Admiral Timothy Keating, these ships were capable of delivering 250,000 pounds of relief materials per day by plane, helicopter and amphibious landing craft. The young sailors and marines on board had already gained vast experience with the tsunami at Aceh and the cyclone Sidr in Bangladesh. "So these guys, they know what they're doing and they know how much help they can provide just that quick…And there would be significant material going ashore within an hour", added Timothy Keating. [31] As the junta refused to allow them in, the US military ordered its Navy ships to leave back in June 2008. Visibly upset, Admiral Timothy Keating said:

It is time for the USS Essex group to move on to its next mission. I am both saddened and frustrated to know that we have been in a position to help ease the suffering of hundreds of thousands of people and help mitigate further loss of life but have been unable to do so because of the unrelenting position of the Burma military junta. [32]

The American public and media were so outraged as to recommend an invasion at least to force Myanmar to open.

Madeleine K. Albright, former US Secretary of State, saw the need to "override sovereignty", given the Myanmar government's "criminally neglectful" response to the cyclone. [33] In the *Time*, the magazine, Romesh Ratnesar raised a question: "Is it Time to Invade Burma?" [34]

The military rulers had their own reasons for closing the doors of Myanmar to the US which, being a vociferously vocal critic of junta's Myanmar, had dismissed the latter, as an "outpost of tyranny." [35] President Bush ordered a fresh dose of sanctions against Myanmar just 36 hours before the devastating cyclone Nargis had hit the Irrawaddy delta. [36] A few days later, he signed legislation awarding the Congressional Gold Medal to Aung San Suu Kyi. On this occasion, he said in a message meant for the leaders of Myanmar: "Let the United States come to help you, help the peoples…At the same time, of course, we want them to live in a free country." [37] Two days after Myanmar was lashed by cyclone Nargis, the US First Lady Laura Bush came down heavily on the junta for its "failure to meet the people's needs." [38] The junta suspected that the US leaders were trying to exploit the cyclone situation, only to get democracy restored, by highlighting Myanmar's enfeebled and impoverished response to the cyclone crisis.

The Generals took strong exception to Washington's conditional offer of aid which insisted on the disbursement of its aid by its own officials. *The New Light of Myanmar*, the mouthpiece of the military regime, expressed the perception of the junta of the US intentions thus: "We recognize that US citizens by nature are generous and they make generous donations to every region that has come under a natural disaster." But the most loathsome aspect of the offer, the paper added, was that such assistance "comes with strings attached." The paper also referred to an article on a website which said that Washington wanted to dislodge the military government and seize its oil. [39] It may be mentioned that it was widely believed that the military rulers shifted their capital in 2005, from Yangon to Naypyidaw, a city located in a remote corner of the country, fearing an invasion by the US.

European Countries

European countries did not lag behind in expressing their deep concern for the victims of cyclone Nargis. France offered US$ 309,200 as an emergency aid. Foreign Minister of France, Bernard Kouchnor was ready to travel to Myanmar "to personally testify France's solidarity" with the people of Myanmar. European Union offered US$ 3 million of humanitarian aid in urgency. [40] Total, a leading French firm involved in exploration and extraction of oil and gas in Myanmar, has donated US$ 2 million to the relief effort. [41] The British Premier Gordon Brown pledged that his country would do everything it could, to mitigate the suffering in the disaster-hit Myanmar. [42] Other European countries, celebrities, ordinary people and aid groups have donated generously. France and Britain sent their naval vessels laden with humanitarian aid to Myanmar. The private, Christian-oriented group World Vision, a major international relief agency, has offered US$ 26 million for relief operations lasting for six months. The International Federation of Red Cross and Red Cross Crescent raised US$ 1 million.

Despite this overwhelming response, the help has only trickled in, as the military rulers of Myanmar have made it clear that they did not want the aid to be distributed by the outsiders. Check points were set up on the outskirts of the areas worst hit by the cyclone, thus blocking effectively the entry of foreign aid experts or workers into the regions. A new set of guidelines was issued by the junta on June 10, 2008 requiring repeated contact with the national and local government agencies and the large amounts of paperwork further complicated the relief operations. Brad Adams, Asia Director at Human Rights Watch, said in a statement on June 13, 2008: "The government should be streamlining aid efforts to cyclone victims, not slowing down aid with these new rules." [43]

In the wake of the reports of Myanmar officials' diversion of foreign aid that trickled into Myanmar, heightened the concerns of the Western aid donors, the demand for allowing foreign aid experts into the delta to distribute the aid directly among the cyclone victims, gained further strength. UN spokesman, Michel Montas, said the UN was concerned that some aid sent to Myanmar, might be diverted to people who were not victims of cyclone Nargis. Meeting in Brussels for an urgent meeting on Myanmar, the EU Development Ministers urged the junta "to offer free and unfettered access to international humanitarian experts, including the expeditious delivery of visa and travel permits." [44] Enraged France went to the extent of calling on the Security Council to invoke the UN concept known as the "Responsibility to Protect" (R2P) to authorize foreign delivery of aid shipments to Myanmar's people ignoring Junta's authorization. Even though the French demand was supported by Germany and the UK, some members of the Security Council including China, Russia, Vietnam, South Africa and Indonesia differed from France saying that Myanmar's humanitarian crisis was not an appropriate issue for the Council. [45]

Even Thai Premier Samak Sundaravej's mediatory efforts to convince his Myanmar counterpart Thein Sein in Yangon that Myanmar should open up for international relief operations and ease visa rules for aid workers, were in vain. Thein Sein told Samak: "...his country with 60 million people has a government, its people and the private sector to tackle the problem by themselves. They are confident of dealing with the problem by themselves. There are no outbreaks of diseases, no starvation, no famine. They don't need experts, but are willing to get aid supplies from every country." [46] Western nations' insistence that the aid offer was conditional to allowing entry to aid workers was not acceptable to the military regime. On May 13, 2008, *The New Light of Myanmar* said that the aid from nations who impose economic sanctions against Myanmar and push the UN Security Council to take action against Myanmar, and offer aid "with strings attached", was not at all welcome. [47]

There were various other factors which had gone into the shaping of junta's policy against unhindered access to Western humanitarian groups. Hoping to take entire credit for the relief effort, the military rulers of Myanmar insisted on foreign aid agencies to hand over supplies to the officials of Myanmar who would carryout the distribution work. Professor Monique Skidmore of Australian National University said the generals "are going to do what they can to be seen as helping the population." The junta was also apprehensive that the crisis might provide an opportunity for aid groups to discredit the junta through their distribution of aid "without corruption, nepotism or political favour." [48] Given the fact, that the cyclone-hit areas were strongholds for opposition groups fighting for independence, the military leaders were afraid that if the Western aid workers were allowed, Myanmarese would be exposed "to democracy and compassion, which erodes at the fear and power" that they held over their countrymen. [49]

The generals were worried that the arrival of the UN officials and Western aid experts and workers would "tax the system" in Myanmar which already started facing the logistical problems. Providing "decent accommodation" to a relatively high paid workers, was yet another problem. The junta which was "extremely paranoid and isolated and xenophobic" was concerned that it did not have at its beck and call, many "trusted military officials" proficient in European languages, English in particular, to control or monitor "all kinds of people from all over the world". [50] The sensational stories with the headlines like "Myanmar Cyclone Victims Getting Low-Quality Supplies," "Is it Time to Invade Burma?", "Disaster May Loosen Junta's Grip in Burma" published and broadcast by the Western media and the invocation of R2P [51] by the Western countries, besides the threats of dispatch of naval vessels by the US, France and Britain to force open Myanmar, certainly did not go well with the military rulers. [52]

It cannot be ruled out that in denying any entry to the people of Western world into Myanmar which was being nursed by China to emerge as another Tibet (autonomous region of China), Yangon was conscious of China's desire not to permit the outside world to see for itself Beijing's tightening control over Myanmar. It may be mentioned that China not only had listening posts in Great CoCo Islands but also developed various other ports including Hyangyi, Kyaukpyu and Mergui to berth larger vessels. China has expanded Mandalay and Pegu airfields to receive heavy transports. China has been developing important infrastructural facilities with the ultimate objective of securing maritime access to its landlocked provinces like Yunnan and Sichuan to the Bay of Bengal. More intriguing was the presence of quite a few Chinese military experts in Myanmar's ports and naval bases most of which were "rented" to China. [53]

However, the junta, did not wish to go too far with its policy of denying access to foreign aid agencies and workers for fear of incurring the wrath of the Western world. Therefore, it made certain gestures to pacify the annoyed global community as a whole. Accordingly, on May 17, 2008, the military leaders arranged a trip in favour of the Yangon-based diplomats, to the devastated delta so that they would see for themselves, the Army's relief operations, which, as expected, were a stage-managed and sanitized affair. [54] The diplomats who participated in the tour, expressed their sense of disappointment when they said: "What they showed us looked very good, but they are not showing us the whole picture." [55] Further, on May 19, 2008, Myanmar invited three representatives from each country to visit the cyclone hit-South. Myanmar's Ambassador in Geneva, Wunna Maung Lwin, thanked the "international community" for its "aid and goodwill." [56] On May 19, 2008, Myanmar also gave the WHO, whose officials were earlier not allowed into Myanmar, the upbeat reports on the recovery of the victims of the cyclone disaster.

All measures of Myanmar designed to placate the Western countries, did not seem to have had the desired effect which was very much in evidence in the discouraging response to the appeals for donations. Myanmar's military government sought well over US$ 11 billion in aid for cyclone victims, but international donors needed an access to verify their needs. In support of the global community's stand, ASEAN Secretary-General Surin Pitsuwan said:

The concern is for the international community to pledge assistance. How do we know it's US$ 11 billion? How can we be certain?...Accessibility (therefore) is important to guarantee confidence and verify the damage and needs, otherwise confidence during pledging will be affected. [57]

The UN, however, set a goal of US$ 202 million for its relief efforts. The UN, joined by the government of Myanmar and ASEAN, held aid donors meeting in Yangon on May 25, 2008. But till June 12, 2008 the world body received only US$ 89 million or 44 percent from government donors and about US$ 51 million in pledges was yet to be received. Amanda Pitt, a spokeswoman in Bangkok for UN relief operations, lamented: "Funding is clearly not coming at the rate we would hope." [58] The UN, therefore, has launched on July 10, 2008, the Revised Flash Appeal (based on the post-Nargis Joint Assessment Report (PONJA) [59] for about US$ 500 million for cyclone Nargis relief, but the response was quite disappointing. In stark contrast was the USS 2 billion raised within a week of the 2004 tsunami disaster. [60]

Reasons for the lukewarm global response to cyclone Nargis catastrophe are not far to seek. Western democracies perceived Myanmar as a 'pariah state' with human rights violations. Western nations had been sore about junta's refusal to implement political reforms and the extension of period of detention of democracy icon Aung San Suu Kyi under the pretext of the worst natural disaster. The world body was equally indignant at the junta. Even as the UN was feeling sorry for over a million cyclone victims, who even one month after the cyclone hit Myanmar, had not been provided any relief, the military government claimed that "the relief effort was over and construction has begun." [61] The foreign exchange controls which hindered the flow of aid in cash were decried. [62] By denying visas to foreign aid experts, the generals retarded the flow of aid. By contrast, Pakistan and China, which often viewed Western interference with suspicion, threw open their borders to international aid when earthquakes struck them, so that the expected help was expedited. [63] Yet another factor that hampered the relief effort was the devastating 'Sichuan earthquake' that hit China (just ten days after the cyclone Nargis), and killed as many as 69,136 people and "caused US$ 86 billion in damage, making it the costliest disaster" in the annals of China and the third costliest disaster in the history of the world. [64]

Myanmar's Asian Neighbours: ASEAN

Asian nations, in sharp contrast with their Western counterparts, were cautious in dealing with Myanmar. ASEAN, of which Myanmar was a member, reacted to the crisis of cyclone Nargis spontaneously. On May 5, 2008, ASEAN Secretary-General Surin Pitsuwan, called on all member nations to offer "urgent assistance" to Myanmar: "I am sure Myanmar's neighbours in ASEAN are standing by ready to join the international community to extend help in whatever form the government of Myanmar would like them to do." He emphasized that such an assistance would be "in line with the spirit" of the ASEAN Agreement on Disaster Management and Emergency Response," which was signed in 2005 but yet to be operational. [65] Accordingly, Thailand donated US$ 50,000 in addition to dried food and medicines offered by the Thai military. [66] Thailand also sent a medical team of 30 physicians to Yangon. Incidentally, the Thai team, as claimed by the Thais, was the first bunch of foreign medical staff to be accepted by the generals of Myanmar to extend direct aid to the victims of the delta. [67] Malaysia contributed US$ 1 million, besides humanitarian aid worth RM 500,000. [68] UNICEF Malaysia had set up "Maybank Account" under its "Myanmar Children Cyclone Appeal 2008" campaign.

With a view to highlighting the growing level of international community's frustration with visa regulations and other hindrances, Senior Officials of the ARF held their one day meeting in Singapore on May 9, 2008 and "stressed the importance of speeding up the arrangements to receive and deploy aid, material and relief personnel to the stricken areas." The Senior Officials also urged Myanmar to setup coordinating mechanism to work with aid agencies so as to assess the damages and needs in the cyclone-hit areas and to facilitate the distribution of humanitarian assistance and entry and deployment of rescue and medical personnel and equipment. The statement also said that the ARF members "stand ready to help Myanmar in both relief and reconstruction efforts." [69]

On May 19, 2008, George Yeo of Singapore, which holds the rotating Chair of ASEAN, held an emergency meeting of ASEAN Foreign Ministers wherein it was "agreed to establish an ASEAN-led Coordinating Mechanism." While apparently convincing Myanmar to drop its resistance to large-scale foreign aid, ASEAN also warned donors that "international assistance given to Myanmar, given through ASEAN, should not be politicized." Pleased with the outcome of the ASEAN Foreign Ministers Meeting, Myanmar's Foreign Minister Nyan Win welcomed "the immediate dispatch of medical teams from all the ASEAN countries. Myanmar also invited its ASEAN partners to oversee redistribution of foreign aid. [70]

Expressing its growing concern for the cyclone victims, ASEAN, in association with the UN and Myanmar government, organized an "International Pledging Conference" in Yangon on May 25, 2008, to raise much needed funds for relief effort. The Philippines, with a per capita income of US$ 3730, has pledged US$ 20 million, whereas the US, with a per capita of US$ 45,850, had pledged US$ 29 million. [71] Participants of the Conference took a decision to set up a Tripartite Core Group (TCG) comprising representatives from Myanmar, ASEAN and the UN to coordinate relief efforts. While ASEAN and the countries of Southeast Asia were meticulously cautious in their responses to cyclone Nargis, Southeast Asian Press, which did not seem to have been under compulsion to part with its freedom, was critical of the junta's management of the cyclone crisis. *The New Straits Times* came down heavily on the military administration for its "slothful response" to the disaster which it described as "utterly shameful." Referring, in particular to the "impediments" the regime had erected to the aid agencies, the Kuala Lumpur-based daily thundered:

All regimes and governments are ultimately judged not on their politics or ideologies but how well they care for their people. If the regime wishes to preserve its integrity against foreign influence or, worse, forestall perceptions of how badly it needs foreign assistance at this time, it is dooming its own people to fatal hardship and itself to total disrepute.

It is shameful that such political consideration should even arise in the present circumstances, let alone prevail.For all the fractures of present-day geopolitics, disaster relief is the last redoubt of concerted international action at its most salutary. Keeping it out only further delegitimizes the regime. [72]

East Asia

Japan offered US$ 11 million cyclone aid to Myanmar. This was in contrast with US$ 500 million Tokyo contributed in aid of tsunami victims. [73] China, which was also hit by a severe earthquake around the time Myanmar was devastated by cyclone Nargis, initially offered relief supplies worth US$ 4.3 million. Subsequently, at the 'International Pledging Conference', Beijing pledged US$ 10 million aid. [74]

India

India–sharing a long land border of 1670 km. with

Myanmar and with ties dating back to third century B.C. when Buddhism made inroads into Myanmar–was deeply concerned about the deadly cyclone that ripped into its immediate friendly neighbour. President, Prime Minister and Minister for External Affairs of India lost no time in conveying their deep distress to the government and people of Myanmar. They had also "conveyed India's readiness to provide immediate emergency relief assistance and to assist Myanmar in its rehabilitation efforts." [75]

India was one of the first parties to send relief supplies. On May 7, two IAF planes discharged relief supplies under "Operation Sahayata." India sent three more aircraft carrying relief supplies. Besides the Indian aircraft, two Indian Navy ships, which braved high velocity winds and other hazards, reached Yangon port where Myanmar's Minster for Social Welfare, Relief and Resettlement, Maung Maung Swe, was present to receive relief material that included clothing, blankets, medicines and food materials. [76] Gratifyingly, Indian Navy ships were the first to offload sea-borne aid supplies at the Yangon port. As *The Hindu* has pointed out, India fought shy of claiming credit for such a "humanitarian first." [77] The significance of India's offer of aid to Myanmar was that with a view to steer clear of any stand-off between the West and Myanmar, New Delhi preferred to go alone unlike at the time of the 2004 tsunami, when India had joined a 'core group' comprising members like the US, Australia and Japan, in reaching out to Indonesia. [78] Thanking India for its prompt aid, Myanmar's External Affairs Ministry spokesman said: "India's assistance has been spontaneous and immediate keeping in mind our close and good neighbourly relations with Myanmar." [79] Pleased with India's timely help, Myanmar, which refused to accept Western aid workers, requested India to send Indian doctors. India readily responded by despatching a team of 50 army medical personnel accompanied by four "bricks" of medicines weighing about five to six tons for treating about 4,000 patients. [80]

India also actively participated in 'International Pledging Conference' in Yangon on May 25, 2008. Addressing the Meeting, Jairam Ramesh, the Union Minister of State for Commerce and Power, pointed out that "India had already sent to Myanmar the much needed initial relief" besides deploying medical teams in the affected areas, "when many in the international community were still in the process of organizing themselves." Ramesh also promised that India would "assist Myanmar fully in (its) reconstruction phase" as in the relief and rehabilitation stages. He "saluted the people and the Government of Myanmar for their resilience and fortitude in facing (the) devastation" caused by cyclone Nargis. Ramesh also earnestly appealed to the global community to keep the process (of extending aid) apolitical...in the true humanitarian spirit." [81]

The military leaders of Myanmar, who were already pleased with India's "apolitical response" to the cyclone crisis in contrast to the "Western political game plan of fishing in the cyclone-stirred turbulent waters," were overwhelmed by Ramesh's words of comfort. Myanmar's premier Thein Sein, Foreign Minister Nyan Win and other leaders in their talks with Ramesh, expressed their "appreciation" of India's "apolitical" approach. [82] However, Ramesh's remarks, not unexpectedly, came under severe criticism in certain Western circles. Sam Zarifi, Asia-Pacific Director, Amnesty International, took strong exception to Ramesh's observations and said that it was Myanmar's leaders who "politicised" the aid effort of blocking humanitarian assistance and denying permission to aid experts to go to the affected Irrawaddy delta which, in his view, amounted to "a blatant violation of international human rights obligations". He, therefore, suggested that instead of "saluting" Myanmar's ruling 'State Peace and Development Council' (SPDC), India should have pressed the military government "to allow aid and expertise to reach those who need it most as soon as possible." [83] However, Ramesh's stand was vindicated by the joint statement Noeleen Heyzer, UN under Secretary-General of ESCAP, and Surin Pitsuwan, ASEAN's Secretary General, made after their visit to the Irrawaddy delta:

On the ground, we saw that while the relief phase is far from over and unmet humanitarian needs remain significant ... much has been accomplished to bring assistance to most villages in the delta and that some level of normalcy was starting to take shape...The resilience of the people could be seen in the face of the children and adults we spoke with. But the pain and trauma was also palpable...And yet, the determination of the local community to bounce back and carry on with their lives, amidst so much damage and suffering was encouraging and a testament to the will of the Myanmar people to rebuild their lives. [84]

The policy the junta adopted in accepting the offers of the aid wherein it betrayed its prejudices against the Western countries and its predilections for its Asian neighbours such as India and China came in for sharp criticism, particularly from the United States. Lamenting that the junta was highly forthcoming in accepting help from India and not from the US, America's First Lady Laura Bush said: "I think India can help. India is close on the border there. I think there are a lot of ways they could help and get help there quickly, may be the Burmese government would accept it more readily from the Indian government than they do from the US government... Certainly we hope that India, and other countries in the neighbourhood can step aid up if they won't accept aid from the US." Laura, however, urged India and other countries to "use their influence" to encourage a democratic "transition" in that country. [85]

US Secretary of State, Condoleezza Rice, urged India to prevail upon the junta to reverse its course and allow in large scale assistance as well as aid experts. [86] On May 12, 2008, India acted promptly on Rice's request to urge Myanmar to accept international relief supplies "to supplement their efforts". Reacting positively, Myanmar conveyed to India its "readiness to accept international relief and medical supplies." [87] The fact that an American aircraft landed at Yangon on May 12, 2008, testifies that India's benign intervention did yield positive results.

Referendum on Draft New Constitution Amid Cyclone Relief Operations

In response to the global community's demand for a democratic rule in Myanmar and as part of a seven step "road map to democracy" that was meant to lead to a multi-party election in 2010, the junta created a national convention to draft a new constitution which was completed in September 2007 after 14 years of off-and-on meetings. The principal opposition party–National League for Democracy (NLD)–led by Aung San Suu Kyi boycotted many of the meetings. [88] Nonetheless, the junta announced that the referendum on the draft Constitution would be held on May 10, 2008. On May 9, 2008, the state controlled daily, *The New Light of Myanmar*, urged voters to approve the draft Constitution: "To approve the State Constitution is the national duty of the entire people today. Let us all cast 'Yes' votes in the national interest." [89]

In view of the devastating cyclone, the international community called for the postponement of the referendum. On May 8, 2008, the UN Secretary General Ban Ki-moon asked Myanmar government to postpone its planned referendum "due to the scope of the disaster and to focus instead on mobilizing all available resources and capacity for the emergency response efforts." [90] On May 6, 2008, the US Congress passed a resolution condemning the new Constitution and referendum. [91] Aid groups urged the junta to pay full attention to save the victims of the cyclone rather than diverting critical resources toward the referendum. [92] On May 9, 2008, NLD called on the regime to defer referendum. [93] The Myanmar government also tuned down the UN proposal to allow independent observers to monitor the referendum and the offer of technical expertise for the referendum saying, that it had sufficient resources to hold the referendum on its own. [94] The junta was apprehensive of the outside world bringing "the contamination of foreign ideas and standards." [95]

Further, since the generals perceived that for sustaining their struggle for political power Constitution of their own making was essential, the holding of referendum at the earliest was on top of their agenda. The generals also seemed to have felt that if the referendum was postponed, it would be a victory for outside elements, who were trying to destabilise Myanmar. [96] However, as a sop to the global community, the military government decided to hold referendum as per schedule on May 10, 2008, in areas where cyclone's impact was least and on May 24, 2008, in storm-ravaged areas, including Yangon. After two rounds of balloting, the regime claimed the Constitution was approved by 92 percent of voters. [97]

The global community, which was already enraged by junta's closed door policy in the management of cyclone relief, was further alienated by the referendum and the new Constitution which was condemned on various grounds. At the outset, while the nation's generals have hailed the referendum as a key step toward democracy, the US and other critics firmly held that the regime would not loosen its 'white knuckle grip' on power in Myanmar. [98] Human rights activists and the pro-democracy activists of Myanmar decried referendum as a classical case of intimidation and rigging by the government. [99] Several features of the new Constitution were most outrageous to the junta's adversaries: 25 percent of the seats in Parliament were reserved for the military officers; Ministry of Home Affairs would be effectively controlled by the military; the provision, that anyone married to a non-Burmese would be debarred from running for public office, effectively sealed the political fate of Aung San Suu Kyi; and immunity was granted to members of the junta from legal prosecution. [100]

Conclusions

The cyclone Nargis was the worst ever storm to hit Myanmar. Therefore, the junta, which had declined any outside help on an earlier occasion, following the 2004 tsunami, sought international help. The global community which was deeply concerned about the victims of cyclone Nargis, readily responded. It became deplorable that the issue of cyclone relief should turn out to be a source of yet another threat to the already strained relations between the Western countries and the military regime of Myanmar with the former insisting on foreign aid experts being allowed to distribute the aid directly to the cyclone victims, and the latter already paranoid, barring the Western aid workers from entering the cyclone-affected areas. The efforts at mediation by the UN Chief and other Asian neighbours such as Thailand and India, were in vain as the generals stuck to their guns. On the other hand, the junta did not feel any constraint in approaching its Asian neighbours for assistance.

All said and done, Western countries as well as the military rulers of Myanmar missed a golden opportunity offered by the cyclone Nargis to narrow the gulf between the two parties through confidence building measures. Instead of heaping the military rulers with moral support and liberal funds, the West bungled the relief effort by wounding the vanity of the generals whose stranglehold on the power in Myanmar needed no special mention. Given the fact that the Generals were sitting pretty, the West should have taken the lead to mitigate the differences with the former. In other words, the best course was to initiate measures first to win the trust and confidence of the military regime by appearing to be accepting whatever they say and then try to bring the junta fall into the line with the international community. The junta, which did not have many defenders, could have been flexible on issues like allowing the Western assistance and deferring the referendum. However, in conclusion, it may be said that from the perspective of the victims of the cyclone Nargis,

West's aim of exploitation of the cyclone situation for promoting democracy in Myanmar was as unfortunate as the junta's unwarrantedly primary concern for referendum at a time, when the cyclone affected people were in dire need of aid. Thus, both the strategies, being untimely, had produced nothing but an adverse impact on the victims of the storm.

End Notes

1. http://www.upi.com/news/issueghtday/2008/05/06/Analysis_cyclone_ shows_natures_power/UPI-30741210113768.
2. http://en.wikipeida.org/wiki/1970_Bola_Cyclone.
3. http://en.wikipeida.org/wiki/Cyclone Nargis.
4. http://en.wikipeida.org/wiki/1991_Bangladesh_Cyclone.
5. http://en.wikipeida.org/wiki/CycloneNargis.
6. *Deccan Chronicle*, May 18, 2008.
7. *The Hindu,* May 22, 2008.
8. John Cherian, "Imperfect sympathy," *Frontline*, June 6, 2008, p. 51.
9. *The Hindu*, May 12, 2008.
10. *International Herald Tribune*, May 14, 2008.
11. http://disc.discovery.com/news/2008/05/05/cyclone-nargis_myanmar-02.html.
12. http://news.yahoo.com/s/csm/20080603/wl_csm/odwk_1.
13. *The Hindu*, May 11, 2008.
14. *Ibid.*
15. *Ibid.*
16. Cherian, n. 8.
17. *Deccan Chronicle*, May 8, 2008.
18. Cherian, n. 8.
19. http://www.whereamiwearing.com/travel/undemocratic_disasters_or_let percentE2 percent8 percent99s_invade_myanmar.html.
20. http://dis.discovery.com/news/2008/05/05 cyclone_nargis_myanmar_02.html.
21. *Deccan Chronicle*, May 9, 2008.
22. *Ibid,* May 10, 2008.
23. *Ibid,* May 19, 2008.
24. http;//www.democraticunderground.com/discuss/duboard.php?az_view_allxaddress=389x3278316.
25. *The Hindu*, May 23, 2008.

26. *Ibid*, May 24, 2008.
27. http://www.timesonline.co.uk/tol/news/world/artaicle4064609.
28. *Ibid.*
29. http://disc.discovery.com/news/20008/05/05cyclone.nargis_myanmar.02.html.
30. *Deccan Chronicle*, May 11, 2008.
31. *Los Angeles Times*, May 30, 2008.
32. http://www.timesonline.co.uk/tol/news/world/artaicle4064609.ec
33. Madeleine K. Albright, "Post-Iraq, World Wary of intervention in Burma," *Deccan Chronicle*, June 13, 2008.
34. http://www.usnews.com/articles/news/world/2008/05109/Myanmar_ilitary_dictators_obstruct_international_humanitarian_assistance.html.
35. *International Herald Tribune*, May 13, 2008.
36. Brahma Chellaney, "A forward-looking approach on Burma," *The Hindu*, May 14, 2008.
37. http://www.timesonline.co.uk, n.32
38. Cherian, n. 8.
39. *Deccan Chronicle*, May 22, 2008.
40. http://www.asianaffairs.com/page/asean/myanmar/diaster percent20relief percent20 aids percent20ready percent20to percent20p our percent20 in percent20as percent20toll percent20movements.
41. http://www.aseanaffairs.com/page/50276202.
42. *The New Indian Express*, May 7, 2008.
43. http://www.usatoday.com/news/topstories/2008-06-13_2019511721_x.htm.
44. Aung Hla Tun, "World fears for plight of Myanmar cyclone victims," *International Herald Tribune*, May 13, 2008.
45. Louis Charbonneau, "U.N. frustration grows at Myanmar's junta over aid," *Ibid.*
46. *Deccan Chronicle*, May 15, 2008.
47. *The New Light of Myanmar*, June 13, 2008.
48. http://www.latiems.com/news/printedition/front/la_fa_myanmar 7-2008 may07,0,2954009, full.stonp.
49. http://www.whereamiwearing.com, n.19.
50. http://www.usnews.com, n. 34.
51. Responsibility to Protect (R2P) is a 2005 UN resolution conceived to assist victims of genocide, war crimes and crimes against humanity but not natural disasters. Aung Hla Tun, n.44.

Also see Ramesh Thakur, "To involve or not to involve R2P in Burma," *The Hindu*, May 20, 2008.

52. http://www.usnews.com, n, 34.
53. See Srikanth Kondapalli, "China's 'Spring of Pearls' in the Indian Ocean," *World Focus*, No. 334, October 2007, p. 369; Bertil Lintner, "Rangoon's Rubicon: Infrastructure aid tightens Peking Controls," *Far Eastern Economic Review*, February 11, 1993, p. 28; Renaud Egreteau, *Wooing The Generals: India's New Burma Policy*, (Delhi, 2003).
54. *Deccan Chronicle*, May 18, 2008.
55. *The Sunday New Indian Express*, May 18, 2008.
56. *The New Indian Express*, May 20, 2008.
57. http://www.aseanaffairs.com, n. 41.
58. http://www.usatoday.com, n. 43.
59. Noeleen Heyzer and Surin Pitsuwan, "Step up response to Cyclone Nargis, "*The Hindu*, July 11, 2008.
60. http://www.mastersandcritics.com/news/asiapacific/news/article_1420877.php.
61. *The Hindu*, June 1, 2008.
62. http://www.mastersandcritics.com, n.60.
63. http://www.ctv.ca/servlet/ArticleNews/story/CTV News/20080606/burma_feature_080608/20080608?hub=TopStories.
64. http://en.wikipeida.org, n. 3.
65. http://www.asianaffairs.com, 40.
66. *Ibid.*
67. *The Hindu*, May 15, 2008.
68. http://www.nst.com.my/Current_News/NST/Saturday?NewsBreak/20080510160234/Article.
69. http://www.aseanaffairs.com/page/asean/myanmar disaster relief arf urges junta to speed up acceptance of disaster relief aids.
70. See http://www.aseanaffairs.com/page/asean-myanmar/diaster relief talks junta agrees to let neighbours in to help cyclone victims.
71. http://www.mastersandcritics.com, n. 60.
72. http://www.nst.com.my/currnt_News/NST/Friday/columns/2234784/Article/index_html.
73. *Ibid.*
74. *The New Indian Express*, May 24, 2008.
75. *Deccan Chronicle* & *The Hindu*, May 6, 2008.

76. *The Hindu,* May 9, 2008.
77. P.S. Suryanarayana, "Myanmar's Cyclone Crisis and India's aid." *The Hindu*, May 30, 2008.
78. P.S Suryanarayana, "A disaster and the politics of democracy," *The Hindu*, May 12, 2008.
79. *The New Indian Express*, May 13, 2008.
80. See *The Hindu*, *The New Indian Express* and *Deccan Chronicle*, May 16, 2008.
81. For the comments of Jairam Ramesh and the response of the military leaders of Myanmar, see Suryanarayana, n. 77.
82. *Ibid.*
83. *The Hindu*, June 7, 2008.
84. Noeleen and Surin, n. 59, *Ibid*, July 11, 2008.
85. *Deccan Chronicle*, "May 7, 2008. Also see Editorial, "Myanmar's hour of need," *The New Indian Express*, May 7, 2008.
86. *The Hindu*, May 11, 2008.
87. *The New Indian Express*, May 13, 2008.
88. *Los Angeles Times*, October 19, 2007.
89. *Deccan Chronicle*, May 10, 2008.
90. *The New Indian Express*, May 10, 2008.
91. http://en.wikipeida.org/wiki/Burmese_Constitutioanal_referendum_2008.
92. *The New Indian Express*, May 12, 2008.
93. *Deccan Chronicle*, May 10, 2008.
94. http://english.aljazeeraenet/news/asia-pacific/2008/03/20085251330241 80480.html.
95. Seth Mydans, "Constitutional referendum still the priority for Myanmar leaders," *International Herald Tribune*, May 9, 2008.
96. *Ibid.*
97. *The Hindu*, May 27, 2008.
98. http://www.latimes.com/news/printedition/front/la-fg-myanmar7-2008May 07,0,2954009, fine, story.
99. *Deccan Chronicle*, May16, 2008.
100. Editorial "Sham in Myanmar," *The Hindu*, April 18, 2008.

8

India-Myanmar Relations: Predicament and Prospects

Syed Ali Mujtaba

Introduction

India-Myanmar relation is really steeped in history certainly not couched in mystery. If only we delve deep into history, the historical facts emerge so glaringly that we are bound to get enlightened on various issues of immediate relevance. For instance, the moment we talk about Myanmar, it's all history that comes to our mind regardless of Myanmar being the mortal abode of the last Mughal King, Bhadur Shah Zafar, or the venue of the stories of the splendour of Indians who once flourished in Rangoon, or that of the hazardous trek of Indians in the wake of Japanese occupation of Burma during the Second World War…all these form part of Indian folklore. The last striking memory of Burma that remains encrypted on our minds, is the 1962 coup, following which, the Indians were ordered to leave that country empty handed. History seems to have frozen after that event as there has been hardly any news of India's Burma front.

The endeavour of this paper is to update the contemporary developments of India-Myanmar relations. The effort is to bring out the nuances of India's foreign policy towards Myanmar.

The executive summary of this paper is: India faces a moral dilemma whether to support the pro democracy forces in Myanmar or to adhere to the principals of real politics and get engaged with the military regime in its national interest. India's foreign policy makers are inclined to follow the mid path and have chosen to engage the military regime without abandoning its support to the pro democracy forces in Myanmar.

This paper highlights the history of India-Myanmar relations and talks about issues that surround Indo-Myanmar relations. The paper updates the particulars of the gas pipeline, developmental activities going on and touches the defence cooperation and the China factor. The entire discussion is crowned with a summary and a conclusion.

India-Burma Relations

India and Burma had enjoyed friendly relations from 1948 to 1962. Indian Prime Minister Jawaharlal Nehru and Burmese Prime Minister U Nu, were instrumental in cementing the initial political and diplomatic ties between two countries. India's commitment to a democratic Burma, began since then. India had provided military and economic assistance to Burma to strengthen its democratic forces.

However, the weak democratic setup in Burma could not hold on to its internal pressures and thus became vulnerable enough to lead to the military coup in 1962. General Ne Win who seized power, nationalized all private enterprises and many Indians became victims of this move. The worst part was that the new military ruler ordered the expulsion of all Indians from the Burmese soil empty handed. New Delhi had to arrange ferries and aircrafts to lift Indian people out of Burma. It's reported that by May 1964 over five lakh persons returned to India as refugees.

General Ne Win's idea of cocooning Burma from the rest of the world, further distanced Burma from India. During the India-China war of 1962, the military regime of Burma was prone to the Chinese side. All this had heavy repercussions on India-Burma relationship that totally got frozen after that.

During Indira Gandhi's rule, India avoided any contact with Burma especially as New Delhi remained critical of Burma for maintaining a poor human rights record and for the suppression of its democratic forces.

There was no change in India's Burma policy during Rajiv Gandhi's regime. New Delhi criticized the military takeover of Burma once again in 1988. India extended moral support to the pro democracy forces that rose up in an uprising in the same year in Burma. New Delhi provided "refugee status" to thousands of Burmese citizens that fled to India in the wake of military repression in Myanmar.

India's Policy of Engaging Myanmar

India-Myanmar relations saw a major shift during Narashima Rao's regime. There were three reasons stated for this paradigm shift in policy and for the first time that India decided to establish an all out contact with the military regime in Myanmar and it was also for the first time that India started looking at Southeast Asian countries and with this in view, formulated its Look East policy where in Myanmar played a central role. India also began seriously looking at the development of its northeast region that has been constantly plagued by insurgency, drug trafficking and smuggling and has close border with Myanmar. India's third objective to engage Myanmar was to contain the influence of China on the neighbouring country as it was becoming a cause of its security concerns.

So it's with these stated objectives, that India started to cultivate friendly relationship with Myanmar. India's then Foreign Secretary J.N. Dixit visited Yangon in March 1993 and signed bilateral agreement to control drug trafficking and border trade. India and Myanmar again held talks at Yangon in 1994. India assured that it would not interfere in the domestic affairs of Myanmar and Myanmar assured India that its proximity with China would not be directed against India. Both the countries signed a Memorandum of Understanding to maintain border tranquillity.

However, the new development in India-Myanmar relationship could not be maintained and it once again deteriorated in 1995, when New Delhi conferred Jawaharlal

Nehru Award on the pro democracy leader Aung San Suu Kyi, for promoting international understanding. The military junta of Myanmar reacted sharply to New Delhi's move to side with the democratic forces against the junta and suspended all the political and diplomatic channels that were established.

India slipped back to its old policy of supporting the pro democracy movement in Myanmar during National Front government headed by Prime Minister I.K. Gujral. At this time, India laid conditions on Myanmar like improving human rights records and restoration of democracy for improving the relationship between the two countries. Myanmar did not subscribe to either of the Indian views and once again the relationship between the two countries was put into deep freezer.

The real shift in India Myanmar relations came after the BJP led government assumed power in 1998. A new momentum was infused since then in the dormant Indo-Myanmar relationship. Fresh diplomatic engagement with Myanmar was made to achieve India's three stated objectives that were outlined during Narashima Rao's regime.

India's foreign secretary, K. Ragunath, who visited Myanmar in February 1998, discussed with his counterpart, certain issues like strategic cooperation on internal security, border management and modalities to enhance border trade. India- Myanmar foreign secretaries meeting was once again held in Yangon in August 2000, where effective border management and steps to curb drug trafficking and smuggling, were discussed. The two countries agreed to strengthen the infrastructure on the border and step up security, to promote border trade.

During Vajpayee era, India's foreign minister Jaswant Singh visited Myanmar and singed number of agreements there. During this time, India's chief of armed forces General VP Malik also visited Myanmar.

As a sequel to these visits made by the Indian dignitaries, Myanmar's foreign minister Win Aung visited India in January

2003. He was the first senior leader from Myanmar to visit India after more than 15 years. The two countries signed a protocol to establish regular bilateral ministerial consultations and agreed cooperation in projects related to infrastructure, energy and information technology.

Indo-Myanmar relationship peaked when, for the first time in 24 years, the head-of-state of Myanmar visited India in October 2004. General Than Shwe, during his visit to New Delhi, signed several agreements on issues like Tamanthi hydroelectric project, cultural exchanges and cooperation in non-traditional security issues. The two sides explored the possibilities to expand cooperation in areas like, industry, energy, rail transportation, communications, science and technology and health. India raised the issue of insurgency in its northeast region that had setup bases in Myanmar and the military ruler assured India to take necessary steps to flush out the rebels from its soil.

On the sidelines of 11th ASEAN Summit in Kuala Lumpur in December 2005, Prime Minister Manmohan Singh held talks with his Myanmarese counterpart Soe Win. The Indian Prime Minister raised the issue of insurgency in the northeast region of the country. He also expressed India's desire for the freedom of the opposition leader Aung San Suu Kyi.

India's pressure on Myanmar to curb insurgency in its northeast region bore results in January 2006, when both the countries jointly held military operation to flush out the rebels inside Myanmar's territory. It was for the first time that helicopters with guns were used in this anti-terror drive.

In the ongoing high-level exchanges between India and Myanmar, Indian President APJ Abdul Kalam visited Myanmar in April 2006. This was the first ever visit by an Indian President to Myanmar since independence of the country. During this visit, agreements on natural gas, satellite-based remote sensing and promotion of Buddhist studies were signed and new vistas of cooperation in IT, automobile, textiles, agro-based industries, river and land-based transportation system were explored. President Kalam also talked about democracy and assured India's help in the institution building process in Myanmar. The SPDC chief assured him to take India's help in implementing his proposed seven point plan for establishing democracy in Myanmar. The Indian President expressed concern over the welfare of Aung Sang Suu Kyi and requested for her early release and the SPDC chief offered to give a sympathetic consideration to this issue.

India's Foreign Secretary Shyam Saran followed up the exercise of engaging Myanmar and visited Yangon in June 2006. This was the seventh round of foreign office consultations between the two countries. The high point of Foreign Secretary Shyam's visit was the discussion on the India-Myanmar gas pipeline project. He discussed the issues of reconstruction of the Settwe port, Kaladan Multi-Modal transport project and Tamu-Kalewa-Kalemyo road project during his visit. The two sides took stock of the common security challenges posed by the insurgents in the northeast region.

When killer cyclone 'Nargis' struck Myanmar in May 2008, India was first to respond with relief and supplies. It pressed into service five aircrafts and two naval vessels laden with supplies and sent them to Myanmar along with a team of fifty doctors to help the victims of the deadly natural calamity. Myanmar praised India for its spontaneous and immediate help. India intervened in the US- Myanmar standoff on cyclone 'Nargis' that did not allow four US naval ships to berth and eventually nudged the military rulers towards allowing the US cargo aircraft to land in Yangon with supplies. Myanmar also allowed western aid workers and experts to help the cyclone victims on India's request.

India and Myanmar Gas Diplomacy

India has been evincing keen interest to procure gas from Myanmar to meet its energy needs. Myanmar supposedly has world's tenth-biggest gas reserves estimated to be more than 90 trillion cubic feet. India has bought 30 percent stakes in the exploration and production of gas in A1 and A3, off-shore blocks located in Sittwe area of the Arakan state in Myanmar. India's public sector undertaking, ONGC Videsh Ltd and Gas Authority of India Limited together hold the exploration and production rights in these gas fields.

There has been an intense negotiation going on between India and Myanmar for the procurement of the gas. A tri-nation pipeline project involving Myanmar, Bangladesh and India was mooted and the three countries signed an agreement on this project in Yangon in February 2005. Under this proposal, the 290 km. pipeline would run through the Arakan state in Myanmar via Indian state of Mizoram and Tripura, to cross over to Bangladesh, and to enter back into Indian state of West Bengal.

However, this project got entangled in a political row after Bangladesh sought other concessions from India to allow the passage of the pipeline through its territory. India rejected Bangladesh's demands and decided to search for an alternative route to bypass Bangladesh.

There had been an intense gas diplomacy going on between India and Myanmar since 2005. Several rounds of talks were held between the two countries on the pricing of the gas. When the row between India and Bangladesh broke out over the transportation of the gas, Myanmar started raising doubts over India's seriousness to transport gas from its gas fields. It gave an ultimatum to India that if the latter does not take quick decision, it might consider the selling of gas to some other countries.

So India came up with the alternative pipeline route that was 1,400-km long and would start from Myanmar's Sittwe area and run through Indian states of Mizoram, Tripura, Assam, and West Bengal to get linked with Jagdishpur-Haldia pipeline line in Bihar. Even though this route was almost three times the distance and cost wise three times more to the tri nation pipeline, India showed keen interest to go ahead with this alternative pipeline route. Parallel to it, !ndia also offered hard cash to buy Myanmar gas and import it through ship. India invited bids for long-term chartering service of a CNG ship for the transportation of the Myanmar gas.

Even as these negotiations were going on, Myanmar in March 2007 announced that it would prefer selling its gas to China. Its refusal came as a rude shock to India, and since then New Delhi has been engaged in intense discussions with Myanmar over this issue. It is hopeful of the import of gas from Burma and a final decision on the construction of an alternative gas pipeline to bring gas from Myanmar, would be based on the positive outcome of these negotiations. Meanwhile, a new twist has come in this story as now Bangladesh is ready to reconsider the Indian proposal for laying a pipeline through its territory to bring natural gas from Myanmar.

This high drama of gas diplomacy has still to unfold itself.

Infrastructure Development

There has been a flurry of activity going on in the field of infrastructure development between India and Myanmar. India has offered US$ 35million as financial assistance to Myanmar for its various developmental projects. This includes multi-modal transport system, road, and railways and telephone network.

Waterways: The Kaladan multi modal transport project between India and Myanmar is a combination of waterways and road highways. It's commissioned in the southern part of Mizoram with a total outlay of US$ 100 million. As a part of this project, India is rebuilding Myanmar's Sittwe port. The port situated on the mouth of the Kaladan River in Arakan connects to Assam's river in India and also link Mizoram to the Bengal Sea. India has agreed to rebuild the Sittwe port and hand it over to Myanmar. The two countries have come to an understanding about the transportation of gas and other natural resources from Arakan to India's northeast states.

Road: India is exploring a transport corridor through Myanmar, a potential gateway to East Asian countries, to form a free-trade region. The issue of building a 'trilateral highway' connecting India, Myanmar and Thailand is being discussed. The National Highway-39 that connects Manipur with Myanmar is considered as a gateway to ASEAN nations. Currently, a road from the border town of Moreh in Manipur to Kangla which is 110 kms. long, is operational. With plans to build another road via Mizoram, another gateway for a bilateral and regional trade promotion is in the offing. Another road connecting Zakhaotar in Mizoram with the Chin state of Myanmar is also being talked about. India's Border Roads Organization (BRO) has started the survey work of the 225 km. stretch road that would connect Mizoram with Tidium in Myanmar.

Rail: India is playing a big part in helping Myanmar to augment its rail infrastructure needs, by supplying rails and rolling stock and assisting in upgrading its rail network. This assistance is part of the ambitious Mekong-Ganga Cooperation (MGC) project that would link New Delhi with Hanoi. India has made available a line of credit of US$ 56 million to Myanmar to build a modern railway utility along the north-western and central flanks of its neighbour. India is also assisting in upgrading the Yangon-Mandalay sector of Myanmar railways. Indian Railways initiated the preliminary tasks to extend the broad-gauge track from Jiribam in southwest Manipur to Moreh scheduled to be completed by March 2010.

Issues around Indo-Myanmar Relations

India and Myanmar share 1,643 km. long common border. India's four states; Mizoram, Manipur, Nagaland and Arunachal Pradesh share the international border with Myanmar. Issues that surround Indo-Myanmar relations are; cross border insurgency, narcotics trade, border posts, border fencing, border trade etc.

Cross Border Militancy: India faces insurgency problem in its states of Nagaland, Manipur and parts of Mizoram across the Myanmar borders, whereas Myanmar faces insurgency from Naga (Khaplang group) from the Indian side. India-Myanmar Army has agreed to strengthen the mechanism to exchange intelligence along the international border to check cross border crimes. In January 2006, Myanmar and Indian Army conducted joint operation to flush out NSCN-K rebels where helicopter gun-ships were reportedly used.

Narcotics Trade: India faces the problem of narco-terrorism through the porous Myanmar border wherein drugs are smuggled to India and exchanged for arms and ammunition. The Indian army regularly seizes drugs worth crore of rupees in the international market from the Myanmar border. Myanmar remains the primary source of drugs problem in Manipur, Mizoram and Nagaland. Number of agreements have been signed between India and Myanmar since 1993 for collaboration to fight the drugs menace along their common border.

Border Post: India-Myanmar army is currently holding border post meetings at regular intervals at Moreh-Tamu in Manipur. The two countries have recently agreed to open four more border posts to facilitate army meetings. They are at Lungwa in Nagaland's Mon district, Bihang in Manipur's Churachandpur district and at Sapi and Zokawathar in Mizoram. Among the border posts, Zokwathar, Moreh and Lungwa are also international trade centres between the two countries.

Border Fencing: Border fencing is important to check narco-terrorism along India-Myanmar border. Recently, India has sanctioned to raise the iron fencing along Mizoram's 404-km border with Myanmar. It has also ordered the fencing of the 14 km. of the porous international boundary at Moreh in Manipur.

Citizenship for Indians living in Myanmar: The official

figure shows that as compared to over 20 lakh Indians residing in Burma in 1950, there were only three lakh and thirty thousand Indians living in Burma by 1980. Their number may have dwindled still further. These are fourth or fifth generation of the Indian Burmese who still do not have citizenship rights and therefore, have no franchise rights in Burma. They are still treated as Indian citizens. It's due to the delicate nature of India-Myanmar relationship, and India has never taken up this matter with the Military rulers in the course of its series of discussions. However, with Myanmar all set to go to polls in 2010, it is likely that the citizenship issue and the voting rights of the Indian-Burmese living for generations in Myanmar, will come up for discussions.

The China Factor

Any discussion on India- Myanmar relationship can not be concluded without any mention of the China factor. India and China both have strategic and security interests in Myanmar. Both seem to be competing with each other in view of their strategic considerations to extend their area of influence over Myanmar. Therefore, China is a key factor in India-Myanmar relationship. India's warming up relation with Myanmar, is to check China's growing influences in its neighbouring country. India's realization however, has come a bit late, as it has forfeited all its leverage over Myanmar by supporting the pro-democracy movement there, since 1960s. On the other hand, China has gained because of India's hands off policy with the military regime and its open support extended to pro-democracy, since 1962. Taking advantage of Myanmar's policy of splendid isolation with the rest of the world, China has developed a deep involvement in Myanmar. It has built its listening and weather posts on Myanmar's Coco Island.

The two countries have also agreed to establish a 30,000 square-mile offshore economic zone, to facilitate the exploitation of natural resources. This may have a bearing on India's maritime and economic interests in the Indian Ocean region. The growing Sino-Myanmar relationship brought about a sea change in India's strategic thinking and it decided to do business with the military regime and engage Myanmar by all means. Although a late starter, India is able to cover a lot of ground to extend its influence over Myanmar through an active cooperation with its military regime. A realization is dawning upon the military leadership of Myanmar that it cannot remain over dependent on China and therefore, Myanmar is showing keen interest to develop ties with India to counter-weigh China. Myanmar is aware of its strategic importance to both India and China and likes to develop considerable bargaining options with both these countries. The other reason is, since Myanmar remains isolated with the rest of the world, it wants to come closer to India to reduce its pariah status. The China factor is definitely providing a momentum to India-Myanmar relationship.

Defence Cooperation

Disregarding all international pressures, India made a major policy shift to neutralize China's burgeoning defence, diplomatic and economic ties with Yangon by starting arms supply to Myanmar. India reportedly supplied to Myanmar 75/24 Howitzers and 105-mm Indian field guns. According to sources, India supplied 98 truckloads of arms and ammunition to Myanmar as part of the agreement reached at the Home Secretary level talks in New Delhi. During his visit to Yangon, India's Defence Secretary Shekhar Dutt offered unspecified number of T-55 tanks that the Indian army is retiring, armoured personal carriers, 105-mm light artillery guns, mortars and the locally designed advanced light helicopters to Myanmar. Similarly, Indian Navy transferred two BN-2 'Defender' Islander maritime surveillance aircraft and deck-based air-defence guns and varied surveillance equipment to Myanmar. All this was part of the deal struck with the Burmese military junta to cooperate in flushing out militant groups operating from its soil in the northeast region of India.

It was also to neutralize Burma's dependence on Chinese arms.

India-Myanmar Naval Cooperation

The strategic importance of Myanmar in the Indian Ocean has made India initiate the naval cooperation with Myanmar. A number of Indian naval personnel have been making visits to Myanmar. Indian Navy chief Admiral Arun Prakash first visited Myanmar in 2003 and then again in January 2006 where he presented a consignment of communication equipment to his counterparts. His last visit became controversial because it was reportedly to discuss the sale of BN-2 Islander aircraft to Myanmar. This was objected to by Britain that had originally supplied it to India. The British High Commissioner to India, Sir Michael Arthur issued stern warning that if New Delhi went ahead with the sale, Britain would stop the supply of spares for Indian Navy's Islander aircraft. He added that Britain was bound by EU guidelines that no military dealings have to be done with Myanmar either directly or through third party.

India, however, did not care about such a warning and supplied the naval consignment to Myanmar. India and Myanmar engagement is also forging ahead in terms of naval cooperation. Two Indian warships, INS Ranjit and ISN Kuthar did joint naval manoeuvres with Mayanmar's navy in December 2005. The Indian warships' visit to Myanmar ports was the third of its kind in the recent past. In December 2002, an Indian naval fleet, comprising a submarine and two destroyers, berthed at the Yangon Port. Then in September 2003, two more Indian warships carried out four-day joint naval manoeuvres with the Myanmar navy. In exchange, a Burmese corvette was at Port Blair to take part in "Milan 2006." This was for the first time in four decades that a Myanmar ship visited a foreign port.

Conclusion

There are few salient features in the India-Myanmar relations. First, India faces a moral dilemma whether to side with the pro-democratic forces or engage the military government. The call of the conscience is to side with the democratic movement but the demand of the real politics is to discard the moral high ground and engage the military regime in Myanmar.

There are three key factors that are compelling India to develop a proactive relation with Myanmar. First, 'Look East Policy' to reach out to the ASEAN, second, coordinated effort with Myanmar to develop its northeast region and third, strategic policy to contain Chinese influence over Myanmar. In India's look east policy, the trilateral highway between India, Myanmar and Thailand plays a major role to reach the South East Asian countries. So is the Trans Asian railway that is to connect New Delhi with Hanoi.

A deep economic relationship with Myanmar, in India's view, would give a tremendous boost to the development of its northeast region. The planned infrastructure development of road, rail and waterways are all steps in this direction.

India sees China's involvement in Myanmar as having geo-strategic implications for the region and does not want to give it a free hand. It, therefore, would like to engage Myanmar through greater economic strategic cooperation.

Apart from bilateral relations, India is also engaging Myanmar through ASEAN and BIMSTEC. India's engagement with Myanmar through ASEAN began in 1997, when it was admitted as its full dialogue partner and in the same year, Myanmar became its full member. The Bay of Bengal Initiative for Multi-Sectoral Technical and Economic Cooperation (BIMSTEC) set up in 1997 is another forum through which India is engaging Myanmar.

It's not only India that is after Myanmar, it's also Myanmar that's after India. Facing sanctions from European Union and America, Myanmar wants to develop deep relations with India for economic reasons. India is one of Myanmar's major trading partners and fourth largest market for its goods. The most startling fact is that the bilateral trade between India and Myanmar has grown nearly eight-fold in recent years. In 2004-05, the bilateral trade has reached over US$ 500 million and the two sides have set a target of US$ 1 billion for the year 2006-2007.

India's policy of engaging Myanmar has definitely paid dividends even as the tug of war between the call of conscience and real politics continues.

9

Strategic Relations between India and Vietnam

C. Ravindranatha Reddy

India and Vietnam are strategically located in Asia and have been growing as economic and military giants in their respective zones of South Asia and Southeast Asia. Geo-strategic importance influenced India to evince keen interest in promoting its relations with Vietnam in the region. The emergence of communist China (1949) bordering both India and Vietnam added another dimension to India and Vietnam strategic cooperation. The fulcrum of Indochina strategic significance is the pivotal position of Vietnam in terms of its geographical size configuration and vicinal location in the regional frame work of Indochina states *vis-à-vis* China and Southeast Asia. The strategic and security cooperation between India and Vietnam, particularly against the background of Look East Policy, towards Southeast Asia, constituted an important dimension in India and Vietnam relations.

(A) Convergence of Interests

India and Vietnam share a wide area of convergence of interests on which solid strategic partnership was built. Though India and Vietnam are not immediate neighbours, they are not far away from each other. It is this geographical proximity that makes an imperative for India and Vietnam to attach paramount importance to each other in their foreign policy formulation. [1] India always desires stable, independent and non-aligned character of Indochina for its own security. The power which dominates Indochina could threaten the security of India also. This was proved during the

Second World War when Japan occupied Indochina and threatened India's north-eastern frontier through Burma (the present Myanmar). [2] Both India and Vietnam share disputed borders and have been subjected to military aggression by China. Vietnam is performing the role of a checkmate against Southward expansion of China thus, ensuring safety of other countries of Southeast Asia-a strategy which is vital to the security of India also. [3] Above all, the collapse of Soviet Union and the desire of China to emerge as Super power also made India and Vietnam to be cautious about their security which can be ensured among other things, by the strengthening of the strategic cooperation.

Vietnam is an important balancing force in East and Southeast Asia. It resisted the American efforts to dominate the region and subsequently, frustrated Chinese attempts to establish their hegemony. A strong Vietnam is an asset and contributes to peace and stability of Asia and the world and complements India's interests in the region. India knows for certain that Vietnam could play a crucial role in matters of regional security in Southeast Asia. Vietnam has been aware of India's crucial political support in the past and gives importance to India in regard to the strengthening of the strategic cooperation. Therefore, there is need for India to forge special relationship with Vietnam which would yield the strategic advantages in meeting the pressure of China.

In spite of changed international situation at the end of the cold war, Vietnam's admission into ASEAN, the Sino-Indian *detente*, Chinese regional influence, the Indo-Vietnam regional equations grew in scope and strength. [4] "Vietnam treats India with strategic importance", President Tran Duc Luong of Vietnam expressed thus to India's Foreign Minister, Jaswant Singh, in the course of the latter's visit to Vietnam, in November 2001. India and Vietnam enjoyed convergence of security interests which provided the basis for building and reinforcing strategic cooperation between the two countries. India in the past, had stood by Vietnam in opposing the US military intervention and this gesture was at the cost of Indo-US relations. [5] In this backdrop one may surmise, that there should be no impediment for India, to build up a strategic partnership with Vietnam.

Vietnam, a dominant country in Indochina, has land borders with Cambodia, Laos on the West and with China in the North. Vietnam strategically dominates not only North China Sea but also all the sea-lanes between pacific and the Indian Ocean and also provides a land and a sea challenge to China. Being a leading and the most powerful of the Indochinese countries, it has a major influence to exert in the capacity of the Southeast Asia's formidable military power.

Belonging to South Asia, India lies in the heart of Asia, the biggest continent. In keeping with the fact that India is the gateway of Southeast Asia and West Asia and is strategically located between major energy producers of West Asia and dynamic economies of East Asia. India's security and vital interests are closely knitted with peace and stability in the larger region of Asia. As such, India keeps close relations with regional powers including Vietnam. Several analysts pointed out, that India, along with China, would shape any future balance of power in Asia. In the emerging new world order after the end of the Cold War, India has sufficient space and pivotal role to play on the world stage. [6] India had argued that its security concerns in the post cold war years, would extend beyond the conventional geographical definition of South Asia. Given India's size, geography, trade links, security environment, its interest ranges from the Persian Gulf to the Straits of Malacca across the Indian Ocean, including the Central Asian region in the Northwest, China in the Northeast and Southeast Asia.

As India is a major military power in Asia, ASEAN expects India to play a useful and constructive role in the promotion of peace and stability. China is posing a major challenge to Southeast Asia. Given the growing indifference of the USA and Japan's reluctance to play any military role in

Southeast Asia, perhaps only India along with Vietnam, can counterbalance China and act as a psychological restraint. It generates a degree of commonality of interests in the foreign policy agendas of India and Vietnam and the US towards China with regard to Southeast Asia. [7] As Vietnam was liberated, India saw a strategic reason to consolidate its relations with Hanoi regime, through the Cold War years. The China factor, through the cold war to the current context of post–Cold War era, loomed large in connecting the bilateral equations, summed up by John Graver through the following observations:

Indira Gandhi realized that if India were to become a prominent power in Southeast Asia, it would have to prevent Chinese advance into Southeast Asia...a strong anti-Chinese Indo-China would guard the flank of the Indian sphere of influence in South Asia. There is thus a convergence of Vietnamese and India's views. Both were concerned with checking southern advance of Chinese power. [8]

China constitutes a common denominator in Indo-Vietnamese strategic calculus. Both enjoy convergence of strategic interest which could provide for building and reinforcing cooperation between the two countries. From New Delhi point of view, India's politico-strategic partnership with Vietnam would balance Sino-Pak strategic linkages. According to Indian analyst, K. Subramanyam, "India had large stake in ensuring that Chinese pressure and the Indochinese states were contained. That has been our basic policy from the fifties. The only country that can do this is Vietnam, the most capable nation of the region. That is where the strategic interests of India and Vietnam coincide." [9] Vajpayee's visit to Vietnam in January 2001 was a reaffirmation of strong links which had existed between the two countries and hence strategic partnership between India and Vietnam. Vajpayee recognized Vietnam as "pivotal for our Look East Policy" and a "Central element" in India's plans to forge strong ties with ASEAN. [10]

(B) India, Vietnam and Southeast Asia: Strategic Factor

After the collapse of the Soviet Union and the end of cold war, India began to revive its ties under Look East Policy with Southeast Asian countries, including Vietnam. The expansion of ASEAN to include Vietnam has also enhanced India's relations with ASEAN. [11] The economic and strategic potential of Vietnam, for all its being a communist country was duly recognized and Vietnam was incorporated as the seventh member of ASEAN group in July 1995. Earlier, the ASEAN countries were wary of Vietnam because of the presence of the Vietnamese troops in Cambodia and its bid to form all Indochina federation. With the withdrawal of troops and abandonment of any plans of federation, the way was paved for Vietnam to establish closer relations with ASEAN countries.

India was also integrated into ASEAN from sectoral dialogue partner in 1993, to summit mates in 2002. Meanwhile, India was also made part of ASEAN's Regional Forum (ARF) during 1996. [12] India believes that Vietnam's integration into ASEAN helped the strategic environment in Southeast Asia in favour of India. As India moved closer to ASEAN by its Look East policy, Vietnam maintained good political and strategic relations towards India. In addition to India's close relation with Vietnam, India's interaction with Southeast Asia received further boost once Vietnam became a member of ASEAN and a new strategic consensus emerged in the Asia Pacific region. India wanted to play a significant role as a major power in Southeast Asia to become a major world power. Therefore, India desired to develop political and economic relations with ASEAN, and use ASEAN as a bridge to connect itself to East Asia. [13]

Since India became ASEAN's full dialogue partner, India had strengthened cooperation with ASEAN both bilaterally and within the multilateral framework and actively participated in the regional, economic, political, security fora. This has given more possibilities for India and Vietnam to expand the mutual beneficial cooperation bilaterally and within the India-ASEAN dialogue mechanism. Vietnam as a member of ASEAN over reciprocated India by supporting every move of New Delhi, including its bid to keep Pakistan out of ARF. [14]

India and Southeast Asia in the post-Cold War years benefited considerably on the defence and strategic front in this region. The resolution of the decade long Cambodian crisis and a sea-change in ASEAN's outlook towards Vietnam as a potential ally rather than an enemy generated a fervent hope that the winds of peace would at last begin to blow over the entire Southeast Asia region. This favourable situation in the region and the scepticism of some countries regarding China, gave India an opportunity to enter the region. In fact, many Southeast Asian nations began to look upon New Delhi as a power for a kind of 'balancing role'. [15] Vietnam got integrated into the Pacific community and is well positioned to explain the virtues of India's importance at the forums like the APEC. India's position gets strengthened in Southeast Asia and Pacific community if it properly utilizes the services of Vietnam.

In turn, Vietnam gets assured of addressing its security concerns if India got involved in Asia-Pacific. [16] Given India's historical record of not being hegemonic in Southeast Asia, ASEAN welcomed India's strategic partnership. Within two years of its formation, India became a member of ARF in 1996, the only organ of the ASEAN which deals with the security matters of the region. India's security partnership with some of the countries like Vietnam was forged long-time ago. India and Vietnam strategic cooperation may be ascribed to the fact that both the countries perceived threat from China during 1970s and 1980s and professed solidarity with each other. The security of Southeast Asia is very much concerned with India's own security. [17]

The Vietnamese leadership through their past experience, views India as "a friend and neighbour" who does not force her views and prescribe solutions, but is ever ready to work together and address the common problems. Besides, India's entry into ARF brought New Delhi and Hanoi together in a multilateral security framework. The new status enabled India after 1998, to participate in the ARF, a multilateral security mechanism for Asia Pacific Region, and the Post-Ministerial Conferences (PMC) and to play a constructive and responsible role in promoting regional peace and security. This was indicated by the common stand India and ASEAN adopted on various regional and international issues including terrorism, integration with global economy, cooperation in diverse fields including science and technology, human resource development, trade and investment and transport and communication. [18]

ASEAN is willing to involve India in the security affairs of the region because it perceives India as a major economic and military power which could play a useful role. Close bilateral defence links would be a deterrent to a country like China. ASEAN looks at India from a different perspective. India could not only be a source of certain defence equipments but also be a major military power which could play a kind of balancing role. India's strategic objective would be to ensure that Southeast Asia remains peaceful and stable and does not come under the influence of any Asian major power or extra - regional power in the region. That is where ASEAN strategic aims coincide with both India and Vietnam. [19]

India's membership in the ARF facilitates an active cooperation of Vietnam in India's discussions with other members of the ARF on strategic and security issues. Perhaps the most important of the ARF deliberations from an Indian point of view were those that concerned the May 1998 nuclear tests. The initial reaction of some individual countries- Malaysia, Thailand and the Philippines to the nuclear tests was one of condemnation. Vietnam took slightly different position without endorsing the Indian tests. Vietnam strongly urged the nuclear weapon countries to take measures for disarmament. However, ASEAN as an organization was not committed to condemn India. Thus, India's membership enabled it to participate in regional security issues. The state of being a strategic ally enabled Vietnam help India to bail out of the situation following the nuclear explosion, in the ASEAN forum. The impact of India's decision to go nuclear, on the relations with Southeast Asia, has been minimal.

(C) China in India's Strategic Calculus

China has emerged as the new Asian giant. There is no Asian power that can match China which would be central to many new equations that might emerge in Asia-Pacific. Because of its nuclear power and economic potential, India could play a balancing role in the Asia Pacific. India's relation with China improved particularly because of the eased tensions on the border and the exhibition of greater sensibility by China towards India's concern *vis-à-vis* Pakistan. However, the concern would be, concerning the developments in Southeast Asia which, India presumes, would have security implications. China has been one of the most important factors in the overall evolution of India's foreign and security policies. The China factor has been critical in guiding India's ties with Southeast Asian countries including Vietnam. A strong Vietnam is an asset to both India and ASEAN to check the Chinese hegemony. The changing international security environment gradually exposed Russia which, having earlier stood by India and Vietnam for strategic needs, veered to the other extreme and got engaged in building up military might and help in the projection of the capabilities of China—a threat perception common to India and Vietnam. In such circumstances, while making all the efforts to keep China engaged in peace in Asia-Pacific, India and Vietnam worked together in building a partnership based on the convergence of interests. [20]

In the past, there was cold war divide between Indochina countries and ASEAN-6 for a very long time. It was China factor which had gradually moved India towards Vietnam, a dominant country in Indochina. India’s increasing solidarity with Vietnam, following its estrangement from China, witnessed India recognizing Vietnam as the latter installed Heng Samrin government in Cambodia. The attitude of India was partly guided by the larger policy of containing China's influence among the Indochina countries of Southeast Asia. During 1979, to show India's solidarity with Vietnam, Vajpayee, the Foreign Minister of India, cut short his maiden visit to China as China attacked Vietnam while he was still on the China's soil. When the Cambodian crisis continued, India, along with Vietnam and former Soviet Union, were together, trying to undermine the Chinese role in Southeast Asia, which was seen as the sole factor, guiding India's Southeast Asian Policy at that time. [21]

Though never stated officially, the common factor that has cemented India and Vietnam ties, was that of China. China had launched punitive military attack on both India (1962) and Vietnam (1979). China's perceived strategic concerns regarding India and Vietnam forced China to create strategic pressure points to destabilize these countries. In the case of India, China created Pakistan threat (nuclear and missile threat) and in the case of Vietnam, it posed as a proxy military challenge in Kampuchea, besides partaking of the direct force on both land and sea borders. [22] When George Fernandes, the Defence Minister of India, visited Hanoi in March 2000, he said that India must firm up strategic ties with key ASEAN and Asia - Pacific countries, including Vietnam. He added that the neglect of Vietnam would be at New Delhi's "own peril". [23]

ASEAN has strong apprehension over China's emergence as regional military power and this has been endorsed by the American military presence in the Asia-Pacific. China's future role, interests, capabilities and influence are major concerns to ASEAN as they are, to India. India sees itself as co-equal with China, as a nuclear power. In the international circles particularly in Asia, it is widely held that India could 'balance' China. In fact, it was this perception of ASEAN grouping that played a major role in ensuring invitation to India to join the East Asian grouping. [24]

India needs strategic relations with Vietnam and vice-versa. India could have given the kind of support to Vietnam that China gave to Pakistan. China used Pakistan as second front against India. China gave more military aid to Pakistan than the US did, and went on to provide critical aid to Islamabad in acquiring nuclear and ballistic missiles capability. [25] India's strategic aim is to assist in building Vietnam's armed forces to be militarily strong and self-reliant. If China could arm Pakistan with nuclear weapons and ICBMs, China should logically have no moral right to raise a hue and cry on this aspect. India will have to learn and to develop strategic pressure points against China, to counter what China has done and been doing all along so far on India's periphery. Vietnam has already declared that it viewed its relations towards India with 'strategic importance.' India should also reciprocate the same sentiment. [26] India would seriously get its long term strategic interests undermined, if it does not take cognizance of China's rapidly expanding economic and strategic profile in the eastern neighbourhood.

Both India and Vietnam have good reasons for China's figuring in their respective threat perceptions because of the previous record of China's aggression on both India and Vietnam. India and Vietnam, therefore, have a natural strategic congruence to restrain China from aggressive actions in future, and to handle the situation diplomatically. India's strategic and national security interests demand that Vietnam emerges as a strong state. Relatively, India is better placed to contribute towards the fulfilment of this aim in all fields, defence, and political cooperation, economic and technical assistance. [27]

The China factor weighs heavily and figures prominently in the respective calculus of both India and Vietnam. Indian Defence Minister George Fernandes was accurate when in 1999 he described China as a "major threat" to India. Indian Prime Minister Vajpayee had also in 1998 mentioned the

Chinese threat as an impulse for India's nuclear weaponization. [28] Recently, a Vietnamese foreign ministry official had remarked "we don't trust China". [29] In other words, Vietnam is suspicious of China and is scared of the Chinese intentions.

India desires to balance China with the collaboration of United States of America in Southeast Asia. Significantly, nothing has elevated India's strategic profile in Southeast Asia, more than the new relationship she has built with the United States of America. The new security convergence between USA and India is the perspective cooperation in maintaining the stable balance of power in the Indian and Pacific Ocean that is for countering emerging Chinese power. India's new alliance with the United States of America eased the path for building more intensive security links with ASEAN and has also created a space for a more self confident and mature engagement with China.

The US aim is to try and to bring India into the inner circles of the United States friends and allies in Asia. The US listed Japan, South Korea, Australia, Vietnam, the Philippines, Singapore and India as countries of prime relevance. Recent calls at Vietnamese ports by the US Navy ships projected as the first existing signs of Washington's military cooperation with Hanoi since the end of the Vietnam War. The US leaves out China with regard to the long term US military strategy in Asia. [30] India's improved ties with the USA, have also created the space for a more confident and constructive engagement with China in both strategic and economic terms. [31]

Whether in cooperative or confrontation mode, China in general, has been a major determining factor in moulding strategic ties with Southeast Asian countries. India's engagement with Vietnam has been visualized as an attempt to countervail China and its increasing influence in Southeast Asia. China factor has been the most persistent factor in determining the direction and nature of India's initiatives with Southeast Asian countries. At the official level, both sides continue to rebuff that their ties are being guided against any third power. However, the growing rapprochement between India and China has been welcomed in Southeast Asia, including Vietnam.

(D) Defence Cooperation

India has had a strategic understanding with Vietnam. Vietnam is in the process of reducing its military personnel quantitatively, replacing it with new equipment. But its military equipment almost supplied by the former Soviet Union, is outdated especially MIG 21 fighter air craft. The Vietnamese navy is also not strong. Given its claims for the islands in the South China Sea, both the air force and navy should receive attention in Vietnam. Vietnam is not in a position to replace its MIG-21 aircrafts or build a credible navy. It is there that India stepped in defence cooperation in Vietnam. [32]

New Delhi's defence relations with Hanoi developed slowly, in a limited manner, as part of an exchange of high level military delegations. The former Chief of General Staff of the Indian Army Gen. K V Krishna Rao visited Hanoi in May 1983, after Sino-Vietnam war of 1979. Lt. Gen. Nguyen Huy Van led a four member senior military delegation to India in July 1992, where they met the Chief of the Indian Army Staff Gen. Rodrigue as well as others. [33] In a similar move, the Director General of Military Intelligence of the Indian army, New Delhi, Lt. Gen. R L Sahney, visited Vietnam from November 10-13, 1998. The Chief of the Army Staff of India visited Vietnam from February 23-28, 1999. [34] As part of exchange of high level military delegations, the Vice Chief of the Indian Army Staff, Lt. Gen. Surendranath, visited Vietnam in 1994. A high level delegation headed by the Vietnamese Vice Minister of Defence and Chief of the General Staff, Gen. Dai Din Luyen visited India from May 3-11, 1995. The Director, Military Intelligence of Vietnam also visited India in September 1997. During the exchange of high level delegation of defence personnel, discussions were held for cooperation in ship repair, ship construction, hydrographics and other areas. [35]

When Prime Minister Narasimha Rao visited Vietnam in September 1994 India and Vietnam entered into a defence agreement which provided for the maintenance and upkeep of military equipment, mostly supplied by the Soviet Union. The stated mission of this agreement was to promote the bilateral cooperation between the defence establishments of the two countries and to ensure that it was not aimed against any third country. [36] Since then, India has been supplying ammunition, propellants, MIG tyres, spares and silver oxide aircraft batteries.

The most significant defence pact was signed in March 2000, during Defence Minister George Fernades visit to Hanoi, the first visit by an Indian Defence Minister to Vietnam. The wide ranging defence agreement paved the way for greater military-to-military cooperation, sale of advanced military light helicopters, assistance in repairs, overhaul of Hanoi's mainstay MIG fighters and raising of the level of military contacts between the two countries. The defence cooperation agreement also provides for framework for periodical talks between Defence Ministers of the two countries and cooperation between Indian Coast Guard and Vietnamese Sea Police in combating the growing menace of piracy in the eastern seas. [37] Bilateral agreement also provided for Joint naval training to combat piracy, jungle warfare and counter insurgency training, repair of MIG Aircrafts, pilot training and assistance on small and medium arms production. India also agreed to study Vietnam defence industry and to extend the technical know how by Indian Defence Research and Development Organisation (DRDO). [38] Fernades described the agreement as "most significant". [39]

In accordance with this defence pact Vietnam has offered to admit Indian Armed Forces personnel for training in the field of jungle warfare and to get this project underway speedily. The Vietnamese army has offered training in Vietnamese language to Indian officers selected for warfare course. Vietnam also agreed to study the catalogue of the ordnance factory board and to explore the possibilities of using the products and services, being offered by India's defence manufacturing industries. India also agreed to assist Vietnam in the process of setting up of its defence industry and also opened its door to the research, prosecuted by DRDO. [40]

There could also be immense advantages in commencing the sale of nuclear military hardware to Vietnam including some quality of Prithvi missiles with launchers under Govt. to Govt. soft loans. In future, the DRDO could provide technical know how to Vietnam's nascent armament industry. Vietnam has been seeking to upgrade the air force, availing cheaper Indian technology for refurbishing its ageing Russian Air Craft and to purchase military equipment. The enhanced military capabilities enabled India, not only to meet its own security concerns but also to project itself as a power to pursue the security affairs of the nations, whose peace and security was a matter of concern to India. [41]

Vietnam strongly voices the need for close relationship with India and so, New Delhi must respond to gain strategic depth in the region. Vietnam seeks modernization of its defence capacity and India can suitably play a partner for this purpose. Describing Hanoi as the most trusted friend and ally, Fernades said when India came in for a lot of flack from all over the world after 1998 nuclear tests, Vietnam "stood by us " because " they understand that if we went nuclear, there were good security reasons for it" [42] A strong partnership in the area of defence helps the two nations to get their relations reinforced, besides promoting stability, peace, prosperity in the region. Thus, the Indian Defence Minister's visit in March 2000 gave a fillip to the defence cooperation between the two countries. Vietnam has expressed some interest in the purchase of military equipment including the advanced light helicopters from and the repair and overhaul of its MIG aircraft fleet by

India. Though, India offered to modernize Vietnam's Army, Vietnam is currently plagued by shortage in spares and military hardware. Vietnam is not in a position to buy them since its priority is to rebuild its economy. But then, given its constraints of funds, India finds it difficult to underwrite this military assistance. [43]

Along with traditional and friendly relations, the Indo-Vietnamese relations and cooperation in defence areas have been gradually promoted, expanded and strengthened. In the process of development, the leaders of armed forces have paid attention to strengthening the cooperation between Vietnam People's Army and Indian Armed Services. Cooperation includes exchange of delegations, training programmes etc. After the visit of Fernandes, Indian Government drew a programme, in which Indian Army expressed an interest in the art of operations during the war. [44]

In respect of defence and security, India and Vietnam cooperate in education, training and information sharing. The Defence Ministers of both countries have also had frequent exchanges. Both shared information on the counter terrorism in the region. "Strength of defence links was reflected by the exchange of many high level visits and experience sharing between the two countries." said the Vietnamese Foreign Minister, Nguyen Dy Nien in the course of commenting on the strategic understanding between India and Vietnam. [45] Indian troops had been receiving training in the jungle warfare in Vietnam. Confirming this, A.B. Vajpayee said, when he visited Vietnam, "this is ongoing programme imparting of military training that has been going on since very long." Expanding Vajpayee's statement that Indians were being trained in the jungle warfare in Vietnam, Brajesh Mishra, the Security Advisor to Prime Minister of India, clarified that this exercise involved a few select officers and not combat troops in general. He said that the agreement was reached during the visit of Defence Minister in March 2000, to Vietnam. Brajesh Mishra also said that the Vietnamese officers received training at the National Defence College in India. [46]

Thus, the India-Vietnam defence co-operation has been going from strength to strength.

(E) Maritime Cooperation

India and Vietnam signed wide ranging agreements, which paved the way for greater maritime cooperation. The agreement signed at the conclusion of the visit of the Indian Defence Minister, George Fernandes, also provides a framework for a dialogue between the Defence Ministers and cooperation between the Indian Coast Guard and Vietnamese Sea Police in combating piracy in Eastern Seas. Under the new agreement, India would assist Vietnam in repairs and to upgrade and build warships and fast patrol crafts as well as trained technical personnel of the Vietnamese navy, sea police and pilots and technicians. India can also assist the Vietnamese Navy in terms of force modernization, communication, surveillance, systems integration, training and operational expertise. India's help can also improve the navy's capacity to counter non-traditional maritime security and to protect its off-shore oil platforms. In pursuance of the agreement, Vietnam also requested India for submarine training in October 2000. [47]

To curb China's growing military influence in Southeast Asia, India and selected ASEAN countries began holding joint military exercises. The Indian Navy has conducted joint exercises with Vietnam along with Singapore, Japan, South Korea, Indonesia and Malaysian navies to ensure the safety of the strategic water ways in the region such as Straits of Malacca and Isthmus Kra. Thus, India's Look East Policy launched in 1991, primarily because of economic concerns, has now assumed an added security dimension. [48] The joint exercises carried out by the Indian navy for nearly a decade with the Navies of Vietnam among others opened new possibilities for cooperation in anti piracy, disaster relief, rescue operations and security of sea lanes. [49]

The sea lanes in Southeast Asia are as important to India as they are to any other country. With regard to maritime cooperation, Brajesh Mishra said, "I would not look at relationship only from the angle of security or strategic concerns. There are commercial, economic and cultural components to this relationship which are important". Giving examples, Brajesh Mishra said, "If India wanted to import crude oil from Vietnam, then we want to provide security of sea lanes for it to reach us or any other country of that kind". [50]

Considering Vietnam's security problems in South China Sea, India's affirmation of help boosted Vietnam's confidence. India's three fleet tankers, which are capable of fuelling warships in the high seas, put the country into the reaches of the deep waters. A strong navy not only serves the security interests of India and Vietnam but also safeguards the sea lanes which are extremely important for commercial purpose. While commissioning a warship on April 14, 2000, the Indian Defence Minister George Fernandes said, "Our India's areas of interests extend from North Arabia Sea to South China Sea". [51] Further, there is ample scope for India to sell defence equipment to Vietnam on the basis of competitive price and quality.

China's maritime claims to waters deep inside Southeast Asia are also viewed with some anxiety by India. [52] They are seen by some, to be a factor in India's enhanced posture to the East. [53] The concern of India is the possibility that China might seek to develop relations with South Asian nations or Myanmar, in an attempt to encircle India. India's concern about China's naval involvement in the Indian Ocean, is closely related to encirclement. [54] A number of commentators argue, that India's development of naval base in the Andaman and Nicobar Islands is mainly a defensive measure, for blocking China's entrance into the Indian Ocean, should the need arise. [55]

The visit of George Fernandes in March 2000 provided an

added impetus to the maritime cooperation between India and Vietnam. During the visit, a fresh protocol was signed on defence cooperation to the effect that the naval exercises between India and Vietnam's navy and also those of coast guards of both the countries were incorporated. Accordingly, Indian coast guard ship, CGS Sangram, went on a good will visit to Ho Chi Minh City from June 7 to 9, 2001 and the Naval Chief Admiral Sushil Kumar visited Vietnam from September 17 to 20, 2001. It is important to note, that India and Vietnam are jointly combating the menace of piracy and cooperating with each other on areas of shipbuilding and hydrographical surveys. [56]

Under the new pact entered during the visit of George Fernandez to Vietnam, India would assist in the repair and upgradation and building of warships, fast patrol crafts as well as training of technical personnel of the Vietnamese navy, sea police and air force patrols and technicians. The pact paved the way for the visit of Indian naval ships to Vietnam's Ports and for the participation by the Vietnamese Navy and also for agreement to assist in the International Fleet review held in India in February 2001. [57] Accordingly, Indian Navy has sent three warships to visit Ho Chi Minh City. Vietnam Navy also sent a delegation to take part in the International Fleet review, held in Mumbai in March 2001. India displayed full commitment in repairing warships. [58] India stands ready to supply Vietnam with Patio-class boats for its navy. [59]

ASEAN members such as Indonesia, Malaysia and Singapore are able to counter piracy attacks with modern equipments, weaponry and trained personnel. But CMLV States such as Vietnam, suffer from the scarcity of resources in this area. The interest that India has shown in the sea lanes of Southeast Asia and its collaboration with its Vietnamese counterpart to fight piracy in the waters of the Indian Ocean to the South China Sea, should be seen in a positive light. [60] Apart from piracy, the ever expanding threat of terrorism has heightened the concern among the international maritime community, for the safety of cargo vessels, oil and gas tankers of Southeast Asia. [61] The maritime cooperation with Southeast Asia includes a joint operation to protect the sea lanes against piracy and drug trafficking and to wage an everlasting war against an ever growing terrorism. The military contacts and joint naval exercises that India had launched with ASEAN states in early 1990s are now expanding into full fledged defence cooperation. [62]

The defence pact signed with Vietnam within no time put into action by an Indian Navy Flotilla, exercising with Vietnam Naval Vessels in the South China Sea, is a potent warning to China that Beijing can no longer indulge in its usual undue liberties in India's backyard. [63] India has deliberately conducted high profile joint naval exercises in South China Sea, probably to indicate to Beijing, that New Delhi has the ability to impinge on China's traditional strategic area. [64] India has been getting its ties with Vietnam reinforced through naval exercises, goodwill visits and port visits. Three Indian naval ships paid a "goodwill visit" to Ho Chi Minh City from October 1-4, 1988. The aim of the visit was to strengthen the bonds of friendship that existed between the peoples of Vietnam and India to foster peace in the region. [65] India and Vietnam have also engaged themselves in the PASSEX Naval exercises and the Port calls to China were also initiated, in order to project a peaceful role in South China Sea. [66]

Vietnam has been seeking India's assistance to upgrade its navy. India sees such partnership as a counter weight against China. As part of Naval cooperation, Admiral V S Shekhawat, Chief of Indian Naval Staff, visited Vietnam from May 13-16, 1996. Three Indian naval ships, INS Rajput, INS Delhi and INS Kanpur, paid goodwill visits to Vietnam from October 1-4, 1998. Admiral Mai Xuan Vinh, Commander of the Vietnamese Navy, visited India from 5-11, September, 1999. Discussions were held for a possible cooperation in ship repairs, ship construction, hydrographics and other areas. [67]

Indian Coast Guard Ship “CGS Sangram” paid a goodwill visit to Ho Chi Minh City port from 29 September to 1 October 2003. The Indian Consul-General and Defence Attaché, attended the welcome as well as the send off ceremony of the ship. [68]

India's maritime objectives in the Asia-Pacific region were underlined by Defence Minister George Fernandes' assertion that Vietnam was emerging as Delhi’s strategic maritime partner. Thus, India's strategic plans stem from several important factors: anti piracy, protection of trade routes, balancing China and India’s desire to establish itself eventually as a regional power in Asia-Pacific. New Delhi's joint naval exercises, regularly held with Vietnam, along with other countries of Southeast Asia, are a manifestation of such a strategic reach. Thus, the convergence of strategic interests coupled with fast friendly ties, brought India and Vietnam closer. [69]

Both India and Vietnam are apprehensive about Chinese moves in the Indian Ocean and South China Sea respectively. China has successfully created strategic pressure over India by bringing Myanmar and Pakistan within its sphere of influence. A strategic partnership with Vietnam provided India to pressurize China. Thus, India and Vietnam together with other like minded countries can restrict Chinese ambitions to seek hegemonic role in future. [70]

China is of the view that India’s Southeast Asian diplomacy could complicate the Chinese-ASEAN relations, as the growing Indian-ASEAN naval cooperation is likely to impinge on the Chinese maritime interests, making a final resolution of the territorial disputes in the South China Sea, even more difficult. Indian-Vietnamese-Japanese defence cooperation under the aegis of the USA is also viewed with suspicion, given China’s unresolved territorial issues with every other country in the region. To China and India, which already have been encumbered with intractable territorial dispute and haunted by mutual suspicions, the potential for rivalry is added by the emerging India-USA-Australia Cooperation.

India is concerned about China's naval activities in the Indian Ocean. China would be equally worried about the Indian naval deployments in the South China Sea and the exercises it conducts with Japan. New Delhi is forging extensive defence and strategic links with most of the countries of Asia-Pacific in varying degrees, but the strategic partnership agreements with Tokyo, Jakarta and Hanoi acquired enormous importance. China is also trying to gain a strong foothold in other countries of South Asia, especially in Pakistan, Bangladesh, Myanmar and Sri Lanka. Thus, the management of maritime relations that India and China acquired, will be the key element in the Asia –Pacific security in the coming years. [71]

(F) Mekong-Ganga Cooperation (MGC)

India's attempt to establish sustained ties with Mekong riparian states, prompted by geographical proximity and strategic reasons, once again reactivated the Look East Policy from a different dimension of politico-strategic partnership with Indochina states, including Vietnam. Through Mekong Ganga Project, India strengthens its economic clout more in Southeast Asia and in Asia-Pacific and might balance the Sino-Pak strategic and security linkage, which in Yaswanth Sinha's view, is known as "India's Look-East Phase II". Thus, from New Delhi's point of view, India's politico-strategic partnership with Indochina seems vital. [72]

The signing of Mekong-Ganga Cooperation (MGC) agreement on November 10, 2000, in Vientiane, the capital of Laos, among the six neighbouring countries namely, Vietnam, Cambodia, Laos, India, Myanmar and Thailand, further accelerated the development of bilateral relations between India and Vietnam. By taking the advantage of Myanmar as a "gateway" to Southeast Asia, New Delhi believes to convert Northeast region of India from a security burden to a region of economic prosperity. Moreover, by improving the road route between India and Myanmar, via Northeast, New Delhi will eventually connect a section of Asian Highway. When completed, this entire Asian Highway project route will link Vietnam. [73]

Closer political relations of India with Mekong countries facilitate strategic access to the dynamic hub of Asia-Pacific rim. Such a relationship helps India within the ASEAN system, by adding weight to New Delhi. [74] It was Vietnam, Cambodia and Thailand which stood by India's candidature for the summit status with ASEAN. An India-MGC nexus could also help balance China's Look West Strategy to the Indian Ocean through its southern province of Yunnan, Myanmar and Bangladesh as a part of her "encirclement" policy of India, as some Indian observers argue. Myanmar has emerged as the Sino-Indian strategic sign post on either side of Malacca divide. Myanmar and India too have moved closer, as India, being concerned over the Chinese strategic incursions into Myanmar as well as the prospect of ASEAN membership to Myanmar, had shed for the time being, the initial boycott of the military junta. India had successfully completed the 135 kms. Kalemyo–Kalewa-Tamu road link which connects Manipur with Myanmar. [75]

Apart from direct relationship with individual ASEAN countries, the sub regional agreements were worked out with member countries, as the sub-regional plans confined to seven members of SAARC failed to gain consent. Subsequently, a sub-regional group outside its confines gained consensus leading to the establishment of BIMST-EC in 1997 and MGC in 2000. The shared histories and geo-contiguity of these Mekong basin countries with India and China, was complemented by politico, economic drive of "China accord", a new strategic value to the Mekong region. For both India and China Mekong countries provide a strategic accessibility, to reach the heartland of Asia-Pacific. Development assistance and transport linkages are the two key areas through which

India and China can constructively engage in the Mekong region. [76] Another strategic aspect of MGC has been the rail connectivity through Myanmar, Thailand, Cambodia to Vietnam. This would enhance the strategic cooperation between India and Vietnam, by the establishment of connectivity in Southeast Asia. Vajpayee, the Prime Minister of India declared, that India would cooperate with ASEAN to build a railway line from New Delhi to Hanoi that would pass through Myanmar, Thailand, Laos and Cambodia.

Both India and China formed separate sub-regional arrangement for the Mekong basin countries. In November 2000, India signed along with Cambodia, Laos, Myanmar, Thailand and Vietnam, the "Vientiane Declaration" in Laos, named Mekong - Ganga Cooperation. The new six nation sub-regional forum (MGC) deals with tourism, human resources, culture and transportation. Transportation assumes greater importance as signatories agreed to develop transport network which includes "East West Corridor" and "Asian Highway". [77] Thus, India and China are interlocked in a competitive game in the Mekong region. Both have joined separate regional groups and act independent of each other in devising strategies of cooperation with the countries of the region. Both the countries formed their respective Mekong groups in quick succession. China initialled "Agreement on Commercial Navigation on Lancang Mekong River" in April 2000 and India initiated Mekong Ganga Cooperation in November of the same year. [78]

In fact, the Chinese President was in Laos on the very next day, following the inauguration of MGC. Indian officials were at pains to dispel media's speculation that the latest Mekong venture was to counter China's growing influence in the region. Indian Foreign Minister Jaswant Singh, who had signed the Vientiane declaration in Laos, faced a query whether his country's MGC initiative which omitted China, was aimed at increasing India's influence. He laboured at length to say that the initiative was neither aimed at China nor deemed the means of increasing India's "Power projections". He continued: "This is a complete misinterpretation and misreading of the initiative. It is not the Mekong region alone. It is the grouping of the nations from Ganga to Mekong...It is an organization not directed at any one. It does not replace any other organization". [79]

If China, a Mekong country, is omitted from the MGC group while India is omitted from the other, it signalled the mutually divergent paths, the two Asian giants were charting in the same region. Politics is the determinant of Sino-Indian leadership in these two groups. China's exclusion from the MGC is seen as India's answer to Beijing's opposition to the enlargement of ASEAN plus 3 (China, Japan and Korea). Yet to interpret Sino-Indian engagement with the Mekong countries in strictly competitive sense could be an exaggerated perception. From the fact that China, the country of the origin of Mekong river was excluded from the MGC, one might entertain the suspicion that the project was intended for increasing India's influence in the region. India's path into Mekong region is in no way inviting rivalry between India and China. Further, China also welcomed the initiative, setting aside the misgivings, if any. [80]

The interesting dimension of India's Look East Policy is the new found interest in the regional multilateralism. Prominent among those, were BIMSTEC (Bay of Bengal Initiative for Multi-Sectoral Scientific, Technical and Economic Cooperation) in 1997 and MGC in 2000. India is striving hard to develop water, road and rail connectivity to the North east of India. [81] India's participation in the sub regional organization BIMSTEC and MGC ensured development and stability of its turbulent and strategically restive region of Northeast. [82] With an eye on China's growing influence in Southeast Asia, India has created an intriguing model of regional cooperation that plays on historical relations and cultural ties between India and Southeast Asia. More importantly the MGC lay out on the ambitious agenda, will serve to advance India's security agenda in the region. [83]

In the post cold war period, the foreign relations of India and China on one hand and Vietnam and China on the other hand, moved dynamically towards better understanding as never before. The 1990s witnessed an unprecedented goodwill gestures by India and China, Vietnam and China and India and Vietnam which had the impact on the stability, security and economic development of South, Southeast and East Asia. Yet, there is a continuation of mistrust and misunderstanding of India and Vietnam towards China. China's possession of nuclear weapon and support to Pakistan including the transfer of nuclear technology, heighten an awareness in New Delhi of the vulnerability of Chinese pressure. For their part, Chinese doubt India's support to the separatist movement in Tibet. In addition, the border problem continued to drag for several years. In spite of these problems, there had been a promotion of trade, technological and cultural relations among India, Vietnam and China. The prosperous India and China at peace with each other can only be a boon to the rest of Asia.

End Notes

1. A.K. Majumdar, *Southeast Asia in India's Foreign policy, a study of Indian relations with Southeast Asian Countries in 1947-1982*, (Calcutta, 1982).
2. Mohammed Ayoob, *India and Southeast Asia: Indian perception and policies*, (London, 1990) p. 8.
3. For details, see *Ibid.*
4. Subhash Kapila, "Indo-Vietnam Strategic Partnership: the convergence of interests," South Asian Analysis Group, p. 171, January 2, 2001.
5. J. N. Dixit, *Across Borders: 50 years of India*, (New Delhi, 1998) p. 91.
6. S. Bhat and V S Mani, *India on the threshold of 21st century: shape of things to come*, (New Delhi, 1991) p. 360.
7. Yogendra Singh, *Indo Vietnam relations; the road ahead,* (Institute of peace and conflict), Special Report No. 40, April 2007, pp. 1-514.

8. John W Garver, "Chinese-Indian rivalry In Indo china," *Asian Survey*, Vol. 27, No. 11, November, 1987, pp. 950-968.
9. K. Subramanyam, "Indochina strategic perspective," in T.N. Kaul, (ed.), *India and Indochina States: Perspective of Cooperation*, (New Delhi, 1984).
10. *The Hindu*, 10th January 2001.
11. Realising the economic and strategic potential of Vietnam, though a communist country, Vietnam was incorporated as the 7th member of ASEAN Group in July 1995. Earlier, the ASEAN countries were wary of Vietnam, because of the presence of Vietnamese troops in Cambodia and its bid to form an "Indo-china federation", withdrawal of troops and abandonment of any plans of federation the way was cleared for closure relations with Southeast Asian countries.
12. The ARF was set up in 1994 as a regional security dialogue platform with ASEAN as primary driving force. The ARF comprises of Australia, China, Canada, Russia, South Korea, North Korea, the USA and the 10 countries of ASEAN. The entry into ARF in 1996 puts India at par with western nations and China vis-à-vis Southeast Asian Regional Security and Economic and political arrangements.
13. Zho Hong, "India and China: Rivals or Partners in Southeast Asia", *Contemporary Southeast Asia*, Vol. 29, No. 1, January 2007, p. 128.
14. P.V. Rao, *India and ASEAN: Partners at Summit* (New Delhi, 1998) p. 37.
15. ARF, *Annual Security Outlook, 2001*, (ASEAN Secretariat, Jakarta, 2002).
16. K. Raja Reddy, "India, Vietnam and Asia-Pacific", *Proceedings of the Indian Association of Asia Pacific Studies,* (Sambalpur, 2004).
17. For details see, Swaran Singh, "China factor in India's ties with Southeast Asia", in Frederic Grave and Amitab Matto (eds), *India and ASEAN: Politics of Look East Policy,* (New Delhi, 2001), pp. 191-203.
18. Tridib Chakraborti, "From National Reconstruction to Market Economy: Space and .Time Analysis of India's Look East Policy", in P V Rao (ed.), *India and ASEAN: Partners at Summit*, p. 327.
19. For Details see, Naidu, GVC, *Post war Pacific ASEAN Security:*

Indian Perceptions and Options, (New Delhi, 1994).

20. K Raja Reddy, "India, Vietnam and Asia-Pacific", *Proceedings of the Indian Association of Asia Pacific Studies*, (Sambalpur, 2004).
21. For details see, Hemen Ray, *China's Vietnam War*, (New Delhi, 1983).
22. Swaran Singh, "China factor in India's ties with Southeast Asia" in Frederic Grave and Amitab Motto (eds) India and ASEAN, *The Politics of Look East Policy*, (New Delhi), p. 192.
23. Statement of George Fernandes, *Vietnam*, (New Delhi), April 2000.
24. P. S. Suryanarayana, "An ambiguous entity", *Frontline*, 13 January 2006, pp. 29-53.
25. VP Dutt, "Introduction", in V D Chopra (ed.) *Vietnam Today and Indo-Vietnam Relations* (New Delhi, 1999, pp. 15-16.
26. Subash Kapila, *India-Vietnam: Strategic Partnership*, 2 January 2001.
27. Prakash Nanda, *Rediscovery of Asia: Evolution of India's Look East Policy*, (New Delhi, 2003), p. 389.
28. J. N. Dixit, *Across Border: 50 years of India*, (New Delhi 1998), p. 408.
29. S Prasamrajan, "Ahoy Hanoi: with India and Vietnam reviving old bonds, the chances of strategic tie up becomes stronger", *India Today*, 20 November 2000, p. 50.
30. P.S. Suryanarayana, "Bush Puts India on Asia Pacific Map", *The Hindu*, 27 November 2006.
31. G.V.C. Naidu, *Post Cold-War Pacific Asian Security: Indian Perceptions and Options*, (New Delhi, 1994), p.82.
32. Ramesh Thakur and Carlyle A. Thayer, *Soviet Relations with India and Vietnam*, (Delhi, 1993), p. 254.
33. Prakash Nanda, *Rediscovery of Asia: Evolution of India's Look East Policy*, p. 390.
34. *Ibid.*
35. Tridib Chakraborti, "From National Reconstruction to market economy: Space and Time Analysis of India's Look East Policy," in P V Rao, *India and ASEAN: Partners at Summit*, (New Delhi, 2008), pp. 336-342.
36. *http://www.tribune.india.com/2000/20329/world.html.*
37. Tribid Chakraborti, n. 35, p. 328.
38. *The Hindu*, 29th March 2000.

39. *http://www.tribune.india.com/2000/20329/world.html.*
40. Thomas P. Thornton, "Indian Aircraft: the search for moulding a new world order," *Asian Survey,* Vol. 32, No.12, December 1992, pp. 1063-1077.
41. *The Hindu*, 28 March 2000.
42. Prakash Nanda, *Rediscovering Asia: evolution of India's Look East Policy*, p. 391.
43. Col. Nguyen Van Vui, "The national defence relationship between Vietnam and India in 30 years," *Vietnam*, January 2002, pp. 30-32.
44. P S Suryanarayana's interview with Foreign Minister of Vietnam, Nguyen Dy Nien, *The Hindu*, 22 November 2004.
45. Amit Baruah, "Consensus in ASEAN for Summit with India," *The Hindu*, 10 January 2001.
46. Yogindra Singh, "India Vietnam Relations: the road ahead," *Institute of Peace and conflict studies*, special report, No. 40, April 2007, p. 4.
47. C.S. Kuppuswamy, "India's policy; Looking Eastwards," *South Asian Analysis Group (India)*, No. 151, 29th April 2002.
48. Sudhir Davare, *India and Southeast Asia: towards security convergence*, (Singapore, 2006), p. 56.
49. Amit Barua, "Consensus in ASEAN for Summit with India," *The Hindu*, 10 January 2001.
50. *The Hindu*, 15 April 2000.
51. *Indian Defence Review*, January, 1988, p. 20.
52. G Jacob, "Chinese waves in South China Sea causing ripples in far off New Delhi," *Armed Force Journal International*, October 1990, pp. 40-41.
53. P Kaushik, "National Security Environment in 2000 A D," *Indian Defence Review*, July 1990, pp. 135-136.
54. Harrison, "India and the United States and Superpower rivalry in the Indian Ocean," in Harrison and Subramanyam (eds.), *Super Power Rivalry in the Indian Ocean*, (New York, 1989) p. 262.
55. Prakash Nanda, *Rediscovery of Asia: Evolution of India's Look East Policy,* p. 391.
56. *http://www.tribuneindia.com/2000/20329/world.html.*
57. Col. Nguyen Van Vui, "The National Defence Relationship between Vietnam and India in 30 years," *Vietnam,* January 2002, pp. 30-31.
58. Faizal Yahya, "India and Southeast Asia: Revisited,"

Contemporary Southeast Asia, Vol. 25, No.1, April 2003, pp. 79-103 (91).

59. John J Brandon, "Piracy on the high seas in big business," *International Herald Tribune*, (Washington DC), 28 December 2000.
60. Neela Benerji and Keith Bradsher, "A vulnerable time to be moving oil sea," *New York Times*, 19 October 2002.
61. Vallabhu Srilatha, "India-ASEAN maritime cooperation," in K Raja Reddy (ed.), *India-ASEAN problems and prospects*, (Tirupati, 1999), p. 188.
62. Bharat Karnad, "Counter poise to China: India as a Geo-strategic fulcrum", *The Times of India*, 6 September 2000, p. 4.
63. Waheguru Siddu and Co-authors, *China and India: Cooperation and Conflict*, (Boulder, 2003), p. 58.
64. "Indian naval ships pay good will visits to Vietnam," *Vietnam*, (New Delhi, 1998), p. 10.
65. Carlyle Thayer, "Vietnam's Naval Force", *Annual Defence and Diplomacy*, May 2001.
66. P. Limaye, "India's Relations with .Southeast Asia: Take a Wing," *Southeast Asian Affairs*, 2003, p. 49.
67. Ministry of External Affairs, *Annual Report, 2003-04,* (New Delhi, 2004).
68. Carlyle Thayer, "Vietnam's Naval Force", *Annual Defence and Diplomacy*, May 2001.
69. Tridib Chakraborti, "From national reconstruction to market economy," in P V Rao (ed.) *India and ASEAN*, pp. 326-327.
70. Yoginder Singh, *India and Vietnam Relations: the road ahead*, 2004, p. 4.
71. GVC Naidu, "Asian Great Power and Changing Maritime Security Environment in the Asia- Pacific," *Area Studies,* Vol. 1, No. 2, July 2007, pp. 15-30.
72. *The Week*, 28 January 2001.
73. Tridib Chakraborti, "Explaining the penumbra of Look East Policy," in K Raja Reddy, *India-ASEAN*, n. 61, p. 66.
74. For details See Y Yagama Reddy, "Mekong-Ganga Cooperation: A milestone in India-ASEAN partnership," *Indian Ocean Digest*, Vol. 19, No. 1, January-December, 2004, pp. 22-34.
75. For details see, P.V. Rao (ed.), *Indian Ocean in the twilights of millennium*, (New Delhi, 2003), p. 144.
76. Rodolfo, C Severino, *ASEAN rises to challenges,* (ASEAN

Secretariat, Jakarta, 1999), p. 209.

77. P.V. Rao, "Sub-regional Strategies of Cooperation in ASEAN: The Indian Approach," in K Raja Reddy (ed.), *India and ASEAN*, n. 61, p. 163.
78. *Ibid*, p. 166.
79. Amit Baruah, "Mekong initiatives not directed at China.: Jaswanth," *The Hindu*, 9 November 2000.
80. Amit Baruah, "Looking East," *Frontline*, 8 December 2000, pp. 49-50.
81. Prime Minister of India Mr A B Vajpayee address to the North East Business Summit in (New Delhi, 20th January 2003), *http.//pub.nic.in/release/release asp?* Relid plus 754.
82. Sonatomba Kanguyaw, "Trade, security and strategic concerns: India's Look East Policy and the suspect politics of ambivalence," *Alternative Frames*, Vol. 28, No. 2, April-June, 2004, p. 340.
83. For details see *http.//www.atimes.com/atimer/southasia/ FB11Df06.html.*

10

Towards East Asian Community in Asia-Pacific

Y. Yagama Reddy

Regionalization vis-à-vis Regionalism

Regional awareness, regional identity and regional consciousness are inherently imprecise and fuzzy notions; and hence the definitions of a region vary and are highly contested. Historically, nation and region have stood in much the same relationship to one another as actor and stage. The regions of the world, separated so much by history and culture as by physical geographical features, provided the political space. Religious, political, demographic and economic diversity of the region reinforces complexity that hardly offers common denominators in the regionalization. Regionalism was often analyzed in terms of geographical contiguity, social-cultural homogeneity (ethnicity, race, language, religion, culture, history, consciousness of a common heritage), economic interdependence (trade patterns and economic complementarity), political cohesiveness (regime type, ideology, i.e., similar political attitudes and behaviour), and organizational cohesiveness (existence of formal regional institutions). [1]

While regionalization implies the tendency or process to form regions, regionalism symbolizes the purposive proneness to create regional institutions and arrangements, although both find expression in the economic and security domains, including convergent motivations toward both political/security and economic forms of integration. [2] Regionalization, as a manifestation of globalization, presupposes one of the forms, viz., a component of globalization (convergent trend); a challenge or response to globalization (divergent trend); and or a parallel process to globalization (overlapping trend). [3] Regionalization is a process towards the end of integration. Globalization and regionalization are phenomena that form part of an historical process to the extent of shaping and enlivening the latter. The relationship between globalization and regionalization also offers distinction between *de facto* economic integration and *de jure* political institutionalization. [4]

Regionalism is emerging today as a potent force in the processes of globalization. If regionalism is understood as a component of globalization, the process of regional integration can be interpreted as part of the international (or global) economic order. Despite legitimate scepticism about the prospects of regionalism in many parts of the world, regionalism has been "a political movement based on the awareness of and loyalty to a region"; and thus, it is essentially "government-driven integration movement". [5] Inasmuch as a region connotes geographical relationship and mutual interdependence linking a limited number of states together, regionalism permits differential levels of integration and institutionalization in accordance with the degree of economic development and interdependence. Regionalism denoting "the idea of collective action at the regional level" [6] encompasses all such areas like free trade, economic integration, scientific and technical cooperation, and conflict management. Obviously, region-building has been central to many of the debates and a salient feature of the international system; and the regional organizations are thus regarded as a natural outgrowth of international cooperation.

Region-Building Process

Colonial masters undermined the regional character. The European-coined toponyms do testify to their indifference to the intrinsic realities. The Second World War betrayed the rationale in naming the theatres of War; and its consequences demolished the old European order and the regional agencies were subordinated to the pursuits of East-West conflict that manifested in bipolarity along the lines of ideological cleavages. Though region as a unit of analysis became important, Cold War tensions offered no scope for regional cooperation mechanisms. The collapse of the Soviet Union heralded in an era of reconfiguration of relations of economic and political power. The termination of ideological tensions provided a new interest in regional forms of international cooperation. The post-Cold War globalization, which is all about a reconfiguration of relations of economic and political power, has caused a spurt in forming the regions, with scant regard to the region forming factors and processes.

The post- Cold War new economic order, with focus on liberalization for the foreign capital and investment flows, is a multi-dimensional phenomenon of growing connectedness and interdependence encompassing economic, political, cultural, security and environmental relations across the borders. Geo-economic visions play up the importance of transnational flow of goods and services, capital and labour, and technology and ideas-a phenomenon popularly known as transnational liberalism or neo-liberalism. Contrary to the transnational liberalism are the viewpoints stressing the power of transnational geo-cultural blocs over neo-liberalism, as advocated by Huntington in his *Clash of Civilizations.* [7]

While the Cold War geopolitical views or discourses are re-specified, inclusion of the states in regional groupings toes the competition along the fault lines of geo-economics. Regional economic organizations/frameworks emerging out of complex interaction of factors have grossly ignored the economic divergence among the states concerned and further complicated the search for a common agenda. Economic regionalism focuses on the formation of preferential trading arrangements between groups of countries within geographic region. Thus, economic regionalism is discriminatory vis-à-vis the principle of non-discrimination which is the basis of multilateralism.

Multitude of regional cooperative mechanisms is looked upon as a prelude to the emergence of multi-polarity that is expected to foster global level stability. The inability to subsume the regional peculiarities tends to inhibit the much expected regional integration and constrain the efforts towards advanced types of regional economic cooperation. In several other cases, regional bodies hardly addressed the regional peculiarities that could inhibit the much expected regional integration. Mention may be made of Bay of Bengal Initiative for Multilateral Scientific and Technical Cooperation (BIMSTEC), Asia-Pacific Economic Cooperation (APEC), ASEAN-plus-Three (APT), Mekong-Ganga Cooperation (MGC), East Asia Summit (EAS) and Kunming Initiative which transcend the frontiers of the conventional regional bodies. Apart from these trans-regional organizations, there are regional security dialogue forums as, for instance, Australia-New Zealand-United States (ANZUS) Pact, Five Power Defence Arrangement (FPDA) and ASEAN Regional Forum (ARF) as well as the Summit meetings, like APT and ASEAN+l. A maze of proposals for regional groupings reminds us of the factors of mathematical equations or the compounds produced out of chemical reactions.

The plethora of regional arrangements bears testimony to *laizze faire* approach, what is to be known as hybridization of regions. As the quest for region-building tends to ignore the geographical limits, regionalism becomes diffused and unmanageable. Despite legitimate scepticism about the prospects of regionalism in many parts of the world, the call for strengthened regionalist arrangements has gained momentum in many parts of the world suggesting broad international forces are at work; and a single-region focus is inadequate. Evidently, many disciplinary fields through laying emphasis on multiple and coexistent forms of regional cooperation and integration have contributed to the development of New Regionalism Theory (NRT), which is thus closely linked to the phenomenon of globalization. In the light of the need for focusing on the *modus operandi* of the regional groupings, Saul B. Cohen, through his hierarchical regional model, pointed out:

Few communities are destined to have closer political, cultural and economic ties with some communities than with others (without geopolitical considerations). It is so, it is possible to delimit macro-regions (geostrategic regions) of the world which are united by a measure of complementarity in outlook/behaviour, or which have a potential for further integration. [8]

Regional Frameworks in Asia-Pacific

It is in this context that the debate on what is meant by Asia-Pacific in geographic terms assumes significance. It is somewhat perplexing to offer well-defined boundaries for a vast region like the Asia-Pacific region, as to be identified as an entity. In several instances, authors have either contextually or conveniently used the term, Asia-Pacific, with scant regard to the region forming factors and processes. In the absence of specific geographical limits, in many instances the boundaries transposed for the Asia Pacific region are seen defying the intrinsic realities. What would be the criterion for carving out Asia Pacific region as to be identified an entity *per se*? A cascade of questions has remained unanswered and baffled all those concerned with the relentless regionalization-pursuits in Asia Pacific.

Does the Asia Pacific region comprise the entire Asian continent and the entire Pacific Ocean?

Should the region constitute only that part of Asian landmass abetting the Pacific Ocean?

Should North and South Americas, just because of littoral status in the eastern rim of Pacific Ocean, be included as part of this region?

Shall India, an Indian Ocean littoral state and a member-state of South Asian Association for Regional Cooperation, find its place in the East Asian regional frame?

Should Australia, New Zealand and South Pacific island realm be also included in the mosaic of Asia, by defying asymmetry in geometry and physical make-up?

Asia-Pacific, typified by 'open' regionalism, is diverse, complex and geographically too expansive. Evidently, there has been confusion on the geographical dimension of the proposed regional framework and political ambiguity on the degree of inclusiveness and/or exclusiveness. On the face of it, Asia Pacific is to be reckoned as a geographical entity encompassing (i) the Asian land mass of East Asia and Southeast Asia on the Western Pacific Ocean front, (ii) the Pacific America (from Baring Straits in the north to the Straits of Magellan in the south) and the (iii) the Oceania. Again, there is ambiguity with respect to Russian Far East which is invariably a part of East Asia region; but the entire Russia, essentially Eurocentric country in historical and geographical considerations, hardly becomes part of East Asia.

Similarly, there is geographic distinction between East Asia and Southeast East Asia, insofar as East Asia is by and large known as Northeast Asia and Southeast Asia is reckoned as a separate entity. Without succumbing to arguments of whatsoever, Australia, India and New Zealand fall far beyond the realm of East Asia, given the fact that India is located in South Asia, while Australia and New Zealand are part of the Oceania. The geographical contiguity and functional rationale seem to justifiably offer a regional framework for 'Asia-Pacific' embracing the entire Asian landmass having frontage with the Pacific Ocean as well as the Pacific island realm abutting the Asian continent. India's emergent economic power rise and strategic capacity are vital as the Asia-Pacific region is replete with several traditional and non-traditional challenges. A host of factors including geography, economics, and historical ties are at the root of India's push toward the Pacific Ocean. This is reckoned as a logical proposition, as vindicated by the East Asia Summit of December 2005.

With the shift of the centre of gravity from the Atlantic to the Asia-Pacific, post-Cold War globalization has visualized the Asia-Pacific region as a key driver for technological innovation, notwithstanding the inherent diversities, differences and historical antagonisms. As the Asia-Pacific century evolves, there has arisen the need for an approach to regional economic and security cooperation. The political and economic interdependence, as Bruce Russett has observed, has made the nations in a region like Asia-Pacific so much closely linked as to accrue the benefits for mutual advantage. [9] Multilateral institutions in the Asia-Pacific, seen as mechanisms for a cohesive regional integration, have begun to come into existence in a prolific manner. Asia-Pacific emerges to the position of leading global liberalization through its 'open regionalism' that subscribes to regionalism-oriented-multilateralism, [10] having its focus on functional, action-oriented, and inclusive multilateralism. Though achieved success in cozy diplomatic relations that provides comfort to the political leadership of its members, Association of Southeast Asian Nations (ASEAN) has yet to establish itself as a popular concept and failed to elaborate its rhetoric to popular consciousness. [11]

Multi-lateral Institutions towards East Asian Community

ASEAN members consequently felt the need for a larger institutional framework within the "Asia Pacific" to address problems pertaining to the security and economic interdependence between Southeast Asia and Northeast Asia. This approach seeks to bring countries in the region together as equal partners to address challenges through voluntary and coordinated actions. ASEAN has thus taken the lead in building up an East Asian community, a model community into which countries in other regions might coalesce for a variety of reasons. [12] The development of East Asian regionalism has ensured the much needed regional cooperation in East Asia in a steadfast manner and thereby peace and security in the complex and dynamic region of Asia-Pacific. ASEAN has placed its strategic sights on steering East Asian regionalism, wanting to be a "winning gate to Asia" by securing linkages with the bigger Asian economies. Amitav Acharya considered "globalization and interdependence as tools of national security and regional order." [13]

ASEAN-based multilateral institutions, like ARF, APT and EAS have projected "East Asian regionalism" onto the centre stage of global interest. East Asian Community is a vision of Asian integration, developed by the East Asia Vision Group which envisaged that "the people of East Asia aspire to create an East Asian Community of peace, prosperity and progress based on the full development of all peoples in the region". [14] Being considered the first major step towards building an East Asian Community, EAS is viewed as the real beginning of the Pacific century. [15] Australia has advanced the rationale for an Asia-Pacific Community that there is no existing institution that covers the whole region (including India) and includes the different issue areas such as economy, security, and environment. East Asian member states also began constructing new regional frameworks of cooperation through APT arrangements; and much before APT came into existence East Asian counties participated in a number of regional fora/organizations—APEC, ARF, CSCAP, UNESCAP; and hence overlapping memberships.

East Asia Summit: New Regional Architecture of Cooperation

The 'Kuala Lumpur Declaration' (2005) outlined that "the EAS is intended to be an 'open, inclusive, transparent and outward-looking forum, with ASEAN as the driving force working in partnership with other participants of the EAS". [16] EAS was a transformation of APT into a more coherent and developed regional framework; and it thereby evolved as a more holistic regional concept in comparison to APT. [17] Thus, as locus of planned integration driven by national governments, EAS encompasses ASEAN+3 with India, Australia and New Zealand joining to make ASEAN+6, what is aptly termed as "Asia Major". [18] All the constituent nation-states enjoy access to the ocean, which serves as a unifying power. Expansion of the membership to include Russia and possibly other states might make the EAS more 'inclusive'; but it is feared that it would become less obviously 'East Asian' in focus. There are also certain contentious issues to be addressed: Whether ASEAN continues to provide effective leadership as the 'driving force' for the EAS, given the economic size of the three states (China, India and Japan) is exceedingly higher than that of any other ASEAN member state? Whether the character and climate of China-Japan relations facilitate/limit the progress in EAS? And whether the EAS develops a useful role alongside other regional bodies—APT and APEC?

Inclusion of the non-East Asian states into EAS has been contentious; and this cleavage persisted even up to the inaugural East Asia Summit of December 2005, when Malaysia (along with China) advocated a more distinctive and exclusive "East Asian" arrangement, while Indonesia and Singapore (along with Japan) pushed for a more open and inclusive grouping that incorporated Australia, India and New Zealand. [19]

Malaysia argued in favour of the 'core' APT member states as to be the main architects of the EAS process. At the inaugural meeting of EAS, hosting Malaysian Prime Minister Abdullah Badawi commented in relation to the grouping that:

You are talking about a community of East Asians. I don't know how the Australians could regard themselves as East Asians, or the New Zealanders for that matter. [20]

His predecessor, Mahathir Mohammed, also questioned why Australia and New Zealand, essentially Oceanic countries with limited socio-cultural linkages with East Asia, should be permitted to join the EAS. China was opposed to a broad 'extra-regional' EAS membership that would make the forum unwieldy and incoherent.

On the other, Singaporean Senior Minister Goh Chok Tong remarked during a speech:

How do we fold into the emerging East Asian architecture, just as we have melded Australia, India and New Zealand into East Asia Summit? An East Asian architecture that does not have the US as one of its pillars would be an unstable structure. [21]

In his Keynote Address, Singapore Prime Minister Lee Hsien Loong observed:

The changing economic patterns in East Asia will create a new regional architecture of cooperation ... a new framework of regional cooperation that reflects the growing intra-regional trade, investment and people linkages. One manifestation is the EAS. [22]

All said and done, EAS carries the stigma that it would serve merely as a 'forum' for 'dialogue'; if it is so, it will not develop into anything more than just a 'talk shop', and it will be neither as productive as APT nor as prestigious as APEC. The APT framework could remain the main vehicle for advancing regional economic cooperation and integration in East Asia, while the EAS framework offers a broader and more outward-looking dialogue forum for discussing a wide range of political, economic and other foreign policy-related issues. Though EAS is neither a substitute for the APT, nor a distinctly separate mechanism, it is generally held that EAS is to become counterweight to an increasingly ascendant China in an emerging East Asia grouping. [23]

Hopes and Uncertainties Co-exist

Even as addressing the complex and multidimensional problems of security in the Asia-Pacific region, there are challenges in the wake of building up defence capabilities by way of modernization and up-gradation of the armed forces and weapons so much as to escalate tensions belittling the spirit of interdependence. Though the security dialogues of various forms at different levels have also become imperative in the wake of security challenges by transnational crimes, this reminds the residual manifestations of the Cold War. Asia-Pacific region always contains the seeds of potential conflict at various levels, whose origins go beyond the Cold War. [24] Confidence-building measures are underway for promoting security cooperation mechanism, yet external threats warrant the participation of the concerned nations in a regional security framework outside the region. The more the engagement of external powers, the more the perception of threat to the regional stability. Collective responsibility to settle the disputes by peaceful means for the promotion of ASEAN 'regional resilience' thus seems to be elusive. Of much relevance to this context is the proliferation of terrorist activities in the region, portending an 'arc of instability' to the extent of undermining the spirit of the much professed 'arc of advantages'.

Though ASEAN seeks to secure linkages with the bigger Asian economies through the different FTAs, ASEAN's way of integration is alas confined to opening up regionally, and opening up some more to outside the region. While this strategy may satisfy ASEAN's desire to be integrated with its bigger neighbours, it does not capture the breadth of economic imperatives for the region. [25] FTAs may make the countries embroiled in a competitive bilateral process, which drives the FTA trend further forward to a stage what is referred as 'domino' effect. Proliferation of bilateral FTAs in the region is not consistent with the principles and goals of APEC which is a trans-pacific alliance between the US and East Asian countries. APEC too is preoccupied with the passive integration of commercial liberalization initiatives. The US remains as the major player in the Asia-Pacific region, [26] through a host of bilateral alliances, as for instance, with Japan, South Korea, Thailand and the Philippines. [27] Bilateral FTAs among APEC economies threatened APEC becoming irrelevant. EAEG (December 1990) plans to form a preferential trading arrangement between East Asian countries are considered to be rival or parallel to APEC. As *de facto* regionalization, Asia-Pacific region pursues trading relations without discrimination against outsiders; at *de jure* level it is supported by track-II organizations (PECC, CSCAP). Globalization in Asia-Pacific impels regionalization of both private (*de facto*) and public (*de jure*) in nature.

Though the region would not face a possible threat of external interference in the wake of *detente* among the regional powers, there is competition among the regional and external states for the economic and trade benefits, access to natural resources and markets of export goods and services as well as contest over political, cultural and other forms of influence. Further, the potential sea bed resources have made the littorals to stake unilateral claims on the extent of EEZs. All the littoral states would attach much importance to exploration of sea-bed resources, inviting foreign investment. This is nothing more than the involvement of the states/territorial entities in competition along the fault lines of geo-economics. The risk of competition gets aggravated through the involvement of private companies in the trade-and-investment-related quarrels. If it is so, geo-economics is identified with the weapons of commerce that may land regional-powers in military alliances. Geo-economic equations, which constitute a paradigm of globalization, are likely to ignite the geopolitical conflagrations. The geo-economics would neither become a substitute to geopolitics nor would it totally obliterate the latter. Thus, there has arisen need for focusing on the *modus operandi* of the regional groupings originated on account of compulsions and compromises testifying to *modus vivendi.*

End Notes

1. Bruce M. Russett, *International Regions and International Systems: a Study in Political Ecology*, Rand McNally, Chicago, 1967, p. 182.
2. Fawcett, Louise, "Regionalism in Historical Perspective" in Louise Fawcett and Andrew Hurrell (eds.), *Regionalism in*

World Politics, Oxford: Oxford University Press, 1995, 9-36.

3. Arie M. Kacowicz, Regionalization, Globalization, and Nationalism: Convergent, Divergent, or Overlapping? (Working Paper # 262: December 1998), Paper presented at the IPSA Study Group II: "New World Orders?" Workshop on "*Globalisms and Regionalisms,*" Centre for Development and the Environment, University of Oslo, Norway, 7 August 1998.
4. Higgottt, Richard, "The Political Economy of globalization in East Asia: The Salience of 'region building'", in Olds, Kris, Dicken, P., Kelly, Philip F., Kong, Lily and Yeung, Henry Wai-chung (eds.), *Globalization and the Asia-Pacific*, Routledge, London, 1999, p. 91.
5. Ellen L. Frost, *Asia's New Regionalism*, Lynne Rienner Publishers, Colorado, 2008, pp. 14-15.
6. Barti Chibber, *Regional Security and Cooperation: A Comparative Study of ASEAN and SAARC*, (Chapter 2), New Century Publications, New Delhi, 2004, p. 16.
7. Huntington, Samuel P., *The Clash of Civilizations and the Remaking of the World Order,* Simon and Schuster, New York, 1996.
8. Saul B. Cohen, *Geography and Politics in a Divided World*, (2nd edition), Oxford University Press, New York, 1973, p. 62.
9. Quoted in Palmer, Norman D., *The New Regionalism in Asia and the Pacific*, (chap.1), D.C. Heath & Co., Pennsylvania, 1991, p. 7.
10. Cae-One Kim, "Multilateralism and Regionalism in a Globalizing World: A Perspective from Asia Pacific Region", Keynote Speech at the *Third EUSA Asia-Pacific International Conference,* 8-10 December 2005, at http:// www.soc.nii.ac.jp/ eusa-japan/download/ eusa_ ap/keynote_Cae-OneKim.pdf.
11. Jenina Joy Chavez, "Building Community: The Search for Alternative Regionalism in Southeast Asia", in *Revisiting Southeast Asian Regionalism,* (Focus on the Global South, Chulalongkorn University Social Research Institute (CUSRI), Bangkok, December 2006 (at www.focusweb.org).
12. Yeo Lay Hwee, "Realism and Reactive Regionalism: Where is East Asian Regionalism Heading?" *UNISCI Discussion Papers*, May 2005.
13. Acharya, Amitav, "Globalization, Interdependence, and Regional Stability in the Asia-Pacific," (chap. III: pp. 41-66), in

Dewitt, David B. and Hernandez, Carolina G. (eds.), *Development and Security in Southeast Asia*, (vol. III: Globalization), Ashgate, Hampshire; 2003), pp. 42-46.

14. Ellen L. Frost, *Asia's New Regionalism*, n. 5.
15. Kishore Mahbubani, "Rising Unity in East Test for Global Trade", *New Zealand Herald,* 19 November 2005.
16. *Kuala Lumpur Declaration on the East Asia Summit*, Kuala Lumpur, December 14, 2005, available at www.aseansec.org.
17. Christopher M. Dent, *East Asian Regionalism,* Routledge, London and New York, 2009, p. 169.
18. Ellen L. Frost, *Asia's New Regionalism*, n.5, pp. 34-35.
19. *The Australian*, 6 April 2005.
20. *Japan Times*, 22 December 2005.
21. *Asia Society Conference*, Bangkok, 9 June 2005.
22. *5th International Institute for Strategic Studies "Asia Security Summit"*, (Shangri-La Dialogue), Singapore, 2 June 2006.
23. Christopher M. Dent, *East Asian Regionalism,* Routledge, n. 17, p. 169.
24. Djiwandono, J.S., "The strategic Dynamics of Post Cold War Southeast Asia," (chap. 11: pp. 170-180), in Roy, Denny (ed.), *The New Security Agenda in the Asia-Pacific Region*, (Macmillan Press, London: 1997), p. 171.
25. Jenina Joy Chavez, "Building Community: The Search for Alternative Regionalism in Southeast Asia", n. 11.
26. Desker, Barry, "New Security Dimensions in the Asia-Pacific," *Asia-Pacific Review*, 15(1), 2008, pp. 56-75.
27. Hara, Kimie, "Rethinking the 'Cold War" in the Asia-Pacific," *The Pacific Review*, 12 (4), 1999, pp. 515-536.

11

US and India in the Asia Pacific

G. V. C. Naidu

Much of the debate on East Asian security tends to focus on the rise of new power centres, in particular China, uncertain transition phase that the region has been witnessing, new assertive and growing roles of regional great powers, likely clash of interests among great powers and the resultant tensions, and the need for the creation of a new regional balance of power to address unforeseen challenges. Whereas these are some of the prominent issues that are expected to have considerable implications for whatever the new regional security order that might emerge in East Asia, a critical factor in any new matrix is the role of the U.S., notwithstanding the continued apprehensions about its commitment to and long-term involvement in the region. The paper proposes to deal with various shifts the U.S. has been effecting, which are fundamental and substantial to its erstwhile strategy of alliance-based security system with bilateral security arrangements and forward deployment of its troops constituting the centre piece.

The paper argues that, with India becoming an important player and a factor in East Asian security, the India-U.S. strategic partnership will become a critical element in the changing American strategy. In view of the uncertainties about the need and purpose of stationing large-scale military presence in one or two countries and relying exclusively on allies for military support, it may have become imperative for Washington to pursue a new policy comprising 'allies and friends' instead of 'allies only' to meet its strategic objectives. A significant element in the new strategy appears to be a special place that the U.S. is according to India.

Introduction

The 9/11 terrorist attacks and the consequent American military involvement (along with NATO forces) in Afghanistan and the American use of force to remove Saddam Hussein and install a more west-friendly regime in Baghdad are major landmarks in the contemporary international relations, that have ushered in a new era, an era that marks the end of the post-Cold War era and the beginning of a new, to use the Collin Powell phrase, 'post- post-Cold War era' and especially marks the start of a new global strategy, the U.S. is likely to pursue. What these developments portend is the uncertain future the alliance system the US has built so assiduously in the last five decades in Asia and Europe has been facing. While America's closest allies in Asia–Japan and South Korea–proved to be of little use in counter-terrorism efforts for that matter or the war in Iraq but for its being merely a symbolic contribution the other US-led European alliance, the North Atlantic Treaty Organisation (NATO), remained badly divided when Washington decided to dethrone Saddam Hussein. These developments in turn, have given rise to an animated debate about the viability and relevance of alliance-based policy either because of the lack of shared strategic interests, or because the traditional allies of the US are simply helpless when the latter needs their support most.

While one scholar dubbed the changes as "New Order: the End of Alliances," others have used the phrase, an "Age of Shifting Coalitions." [1] Are these such epochal changes that they would lead to an abrupt end of the era of alliances and begin a new era of less rigid, less institutionalized 'arrangements' and 'strategic relationships'? The following analysis tries to deal with the broad contours of the American Asia Pacific security policy and assesses its changing policies, especially the way it tries to grapple with emergent security challenges, evaluates the role of the American alliance system and forward deployment of troops in the coming years, and finally the implications for India. It is argued that the Asia Pacific region's strategic landscape remains complex because of the growing intra-regional economic cooperation and interdependence and hence a cause for concern. The rise of new power centres and the growing assertiveness of the Asian great powers are beginning to fundamentally alter the security order of the region. This is particularly so because, the regional security multilateralism (mainly the ASEAN Regional Forum-ARF), has failed to live up to its initial expectations. Undoubtedly, the region continues to be a major area of enormous importance to the US. Therefore, Washington would review the whole gamut of its policy, particularly with regard to its alliance system and troop deployment strategy. These developments are likely to enhance India's significance in the American policy calculations.

The US Factor

Amidst the complex maze of developments, a critical factor that needs greater attention is the nature of evolving the US policies in the region, within the larger framework of global unipolarity. The US-led unipolar movement is in the second decade and it is unlikely that this status will change in the next few decades despite economic rise of China, which is expected to overtake the US as the world's largest by 2040, according to many forecasts. Nonetheless, the American overall preponderance and its ability to influence developments across the global arena, are unlikely to be seriously challenged. Consider this: the defence expenditure of the US is more than the next ten countries put together; the dependence on the US market by the rest of the world is so great, that it is one of the largest trading partners for most countries around the world. Its control over global currency and capital is unparalleled. The US continues to be the single largest source of new and advanced technologies and no country is more attractive than the US to lure the best and brightest from all nooks and corners of the world. Former Soviet Union was the only country that came close to challenge the US military might.

The other power that appeared to threaten the American economic dominance for a brief while during the 1980s was Japan, but more than a decade of stagnation ensured, that it is no match. China may be fast emerging as a global power but its military power (notwithstanding its atomic weapons and intercontinental ballistic missiles that can reach parts of the American mainland) is no match to the greater might of the US. Moreover, even as China makes phenomenal progress economically, it is nowhere near the US either to generate capital or to develop technologies or to influence the global markets, let alone other aspects of soft power, which have come to play a vital part in augmenting a country's power. [2] No other country can boast of a Hollywood or a CNN with such a global reach, let alone Cola drinks, McDonalds, pop music, or its brand of democratic values. This is the reality that is likely to stay on for the foreseeable future.

It is against the above backdrop that the US policies in Asia are examined below because Asia has emerged as strategically and economically the most important region for Washington on the one hand, and, on the other, the US-led alliance system continues to be the mainstay of American policy, its presence the most pervasive and, by most perceptions it is the most influential power. To be sure, much before the 9/11 events and the American war against terrorism, Asia presented enormous opportunities as well as challenges to the US. If the US is the largest economy in the world, the next three largest economic powers belong to Asia-China, Japan and India—in PPP terms in that order. American trans-Pacific trade is 35 percent of its total in contrast to 19 percent with Europe. More than half-a-million Americans work in the Asia Pacific region and many more millions of jobs are dependent on trade with this region.

Some of the most dynamic, fastest growing and large

markets are part of this region. By any definition, no one can deny the rise of new power centres in the Asia Pacific with global ramifications. If Japan and the four Asian economic tigers earlier and now China represent the economic miracle in manufacturing with unprecedented growth rates, India's potential to emerge as the leader of new technologies are well recognized, especially in ICT, biotechnologies, pharmaceuticals etc. After being on the margins during much of the Cold War period, these Asian major powers are fast emerging as the lead players.

Moreover, the potential for an outbreak of a major conflict has also been probably the greatest in Asia. Aside from three known major flashpoints, Taiwan, South China Sea and Korea, this region is an abode of the largest number of territorial and maritime boundary disputes. Historical legacies and mutual suspicions particularly among great powers continue to persist, despite growing economic interdependence. There are a large number of small and weak states, which tend to be vulnerable to a variety of domestic and external pressures. Despite enormous progress, levels of economic bonds are still weak and the security linkages between two sub-regions, Northeast Asia and Southeast Asia, are tenuous. It is not necessary that Asia would have to go through the historical churning that went on in Europe before the stability occurred [3], but, notwithstanding the current peaceful transitory phase, no one can discount the possibility of clash of interest among the regional powers in the coming years.

Post-Cold Asia Pacific Security Setting

It becomes imperative to understand how the regional dynamics was taking shape in the aftermath of the Cold War in order to put recent developments in a perspective. It is well known that most of the bloodiest Cold War proxy battles were fought in the Asian theatre starting from the Korean War and reaching a crescendo in the early 1970s in Indochina. During the heady days, the US had committed more than half a million troops to this region, backed by a number of security arrangements and agreements. A major thrust of this policy was forward deployment of troops. The bilateral arrangements and troop presence were two solid pillars on which the American policy toward the Asia Pacific rested, known as the 'Francisco System'. And the primary objectives of this policy were containment of communism and to deter the Soviets and Chinese from spreading their influence to the rest of the region. After the end of the Indochina War in the mid-1970s, the Soviets managed a foothold in Vietnam, the first ever-military presence overseas.

What this meant was that firstly, the Asia Pacific security came to be dominated by the two Super Powers, and secondly, the regional great powers had very little role in shaping the regional security order. It needs to be mentioned here, that the arrangement the Americans had worked out, was not without its problems. This underwent considerable change once the Americans were defeated by the Vietnamese, and this led to complete withdrawal not just from Indochina but also from Thailand. The end of the Cold War later also put enormous pressure on the US to vacate its base facilities in the Philippines in 1992–the largest overseas bases that the US had, being the Clark Air Base and the Subic Bay Naval Base.

Gradually, pressure started mounting in the Northeast Asia too, especially by the Okinawans in Japan, to phase out the American troop presence. And more recently, especially the younger South Koreans have begun looking at American presence as an obstacle for peaceful reunification of the two Koreas. [4] What was regarded as growing irrelevance of the alliances and the stationing of troops in East Asia, certain events, in particular, the contest around the South China Sea dispute in the early 1990s, China's growing belligerence over Taiwan (the 1995 missile exercises), the North Korean nuclear crisis (1994), and economic matters undermining the political relationship between the US and Japan, compelled the US to undertake a re-look at the whole issue.

Yet another issue that played a significant role in infusing new dynamism into the alliances was the challenge a rising power like China posed. If history is any indication, rise of any new power centre tends to invariably affect the existing equilibrium. If recent perceived notions, especially in Tokyo and some Southeast Asian capitals that ASEAN has become more reverential to Beijing in every decision it has been taking are to be believed, China has emerged as an important factor. Although it is argued that China-Southeast Asian relations are mutually beneficial and that ASEAN's engagement is directly linked to China's behaviour, [5] the growing Chinese influence is undeniable. [6] The country that is likely to feel the change most, is Japan because, it is at its cost that China is seen to be enhancing its influence the unnerving effect of which is already seen in Tokyo.

Once it became clearer in the light of these developments that American presence was indispensable for the regional stability and to hedge against anything that is unexpected, attempts began to strengthen the alliances. The rationale advanced of course was, that these were not threat-based any more, but on the other hand, interest-based. Aside from the Revised Defence Guidelines agreement that was signed between Washington and Tokyo in 1997 (which goes far beyond the earlier one in terms of geographic scope and Japan's role), the US signed the Visiting Forces Agreement with the Philippines (1998), stationed over 1000-odd troops in Singapore, and entered into arrangements with a number of countries in Southeast Asia, Australia and India on ship visits, greater defence cooperation and security dialogues.

Importantly, much before the 9/11 events, one can see a marked shift in the Bush Administration's strategic focus moving away from Europe towards Asia. Richard Armitage, the Deputy Secretary of State said, "A lot more attention will be paid to Asia than was the case in the previous Administration." [7] He earlier co-authored an influential study, better known as *Nye-Armitage Report*, which had strongly argued in favour of re-strengthening the alliance with Japan as the cornerstone of the regional security because of the existence of potentially destabilizing tendencies. [8] The supposed conclusions of the Pentagon's strategic review, as leaked to the press, demanded redirection of the main military effort from Europe to Asia. Forces and weapons are to be designed or reconfigured to project power across the Pacific. George W. Bush certainly started looking at relations with China differently from the way Clinton described–as "strategic partnership". [9] Importantly, the Bush Administration has also started shedding more light on India, a self-proclaimed nuclear power. All these events suggest that the Asia Pacific region had already emerged as a prime area of US concern.

Although Washington was convinced of the need to continue to base its policy on the alliances, its most important ally Japan, did not appear to be as enthusiastic despite being concerned about the rise of China. Japan went out of its way to assuage the Chinese over the new Defence Guidelines, which obviously will make Tokyo a firm and active partner if American military involvement was warranted in the Taiwan Straits. Some Southeast Asian states were also concerned about creeping assertiveness and growing influence of China and hence wanted American presence, even symbolic, as an insurance policy. Every indication, thus, pointed that US alliances would be robust and remain the cornerstone of the American policy in the Asia Pacific.

Future of the Alliance System in Asia Pacific

As noted, the process of dispelling the uncertainties of the early 1990s and firming up of the US presence began in the later period of the Clinton Administration; however, the Bush Administration has been more forthcoming in recognising the destabilising tendencies that the Asia Pacific region is beset with much before 9/11. Rhetoric on China aside, there was a broad recognition that it was Asia, as opposed to Europe, that had become politically instable and hence will likely to pose many security challenges that might warrant American involvement/intervention. Though the attention was mostly rivetted to the dispute in the South China Sea, the Taiwan issue, and the Korean Peninsula, a host of other less serious problems such as Myanmar, narcotics, piracy, security of sealines of communication, proliferation of light weapons, etc., had been the major concerns. Condoleezza Rice's famous statement that: "Never again should an American president go to Beijing for nine days and refuse to stop in Tokyo or Seoul" [10] underscored the importance of these two allies. Simultaneously, attempts were also made to qualitatively improve relations with India [11] and interestingly, contrary to the past, for the first time Washington began to strategically locate India in the larger framework of Asia rather than just South Asia. [12]

Briefly, currently the US is bound to the Asia Pacific by five (of the seven worldwide) mutual defence treaties—US-Philippines (1952), ANZUS (1952), US-South Korea (1954), Southeast Asia Collective Defence (US, France, Australia, New Zealand, Thailand and the Philippines, 1954), and US-Japan (1960). On an average, the US Pacific Command participates in over 1500 military exercises and other engagements with the region. Among these, the most important ones are *Team Challenge*, which has come into being recently after merging three bilateral exercises into a regional one with Australia, the Philippines, Thailand and Singapore, *Keen Sword/Keen Edge* with Japanese Self-Defence Forces, and the *Rim of the Pacific* biennial large-scale power projection/sea control exercises with Canada, Australia, Japan, South Korea, Chile and the U.K. [13] With regard to the actual military strength that the US has deployed, it is about 47,000 and 37,500 military personnel respectively in Japan and South Korea. The US also stations about 1200 troops in Singapore as well as in the Philippines. In the case of the Philippines, American Special Forces troops were deployed in Basilan aimed to help the Filipino forces crush the Abu Sayyaf rebel group. Starting from about 160 in November 2002, the number has steadily gone up to over a thousand at present. It is believed that American presence has been very effective in curtailing the Abu Sayyaf's activities.

Although major pronouncements and a series of official documents on Asia Pacific both by the earlier administrations and the current ones prominently the *East Asia Strategy Initiative* (EASI), *East Asia Strategy Reports* (EASR), [14] *Quadrennial Defence Reviews* (QDRs) and the *National Security Strategy of the United States of America* of September 2002, have clearly underscored the crucial role of the alliances and the importance of multilateral initiatives, [15] it is however more recently that the talk of changing strategy has gained currency. The war in Afghanistan, the involvement in Iraq and the Filipino experience of fighting with the Muslim separatists have prompted the US administration to undertake a number of studies with a view to understand the kind of security problems that might arise and accordingly review the nature of American troop deployments in future. Much before the famous story that broke out in *The Los Angeles Times* on 29 May 2003, which gave some sketchy details, speculation had been rife especially in Japan that the US would invariably reduce its presence there.

What stirred the hornet's nest was the growing American perception that the nature of threats it faces has undergone a remarkable change. Although American troops in Japan could be quickly redeployed to Afghanistan, it has not been without problems especially because of long distance and weak logistical support system. Further, the inability of its traditional allies in fighting low-intensity wars is glaring; both Japanese and South Korean roles in regard to the US fight in Afghanistan or in Iraq have been very little. Second, there has been mounting opposition to the American troop presence from the local people. Roh Moo Hyun won the presidential election earlier on a wave of rising anti-Americanism in South Korea. Many Koreans feel that the State of Forces Agreement

(SOFA) is heavily in favour of the Americans and that the American troops are the biggest obstacle to unification with North Korea. [16]

It is much less emotional in Japan though, but for a variety of reasons, people of Okinawa (which accommodates 27 out of 47 thousand troops) have been opposed to the American bases. Japanese and South Korean enthusiastic support to the American effort in Afghanistan and Iraq despite strong popular opposition especially to the Iraq War, is because of the concern that their strategic significance to the US is waning. Fear has been mounting both in Japan and South Korea that the US might simply vacate its bases (or at least drastically reduce the numbers) as it did in the Philippines in 1992, which will force them to fend for themselves, which, in turn, will have its own political and economic ramifications.

The slogan 'Places not bases' has been heard quite frequently these days, in American think tanks and policy circles. A series of steps that Japan has taken, confirm its concerns about the alliance deployment of ships in the Indian Ocean for the first time, attempts to give greater role for the Defence Agency, moves to make bilateral security treaty with the US less one-sided, repeated assertions that Tokyo would increase its security role in the Asia Pacific, willingness to participate in the reconstruction of Afghanistan and Iraq, launching of military reconnaissance satellites, to take a decisive step on the deployment of missile defence forces starting from 2006, [17] and to undertake other measures to remove legal hurdles to facilitate greater deployment of troops abroad. It can be argued that, compared to South Korea, which bears about 40 percent of the cost of American troops, Japan's share is nearly 81 percent. While it is an advantage, in the American view, an alliance with Japan is not limited to protection of that country but also to check China's hegemonic designs, if any, and to ensure that the regional order remains in its favour. Incremental steps notwithstanding, Japan appears to be reticent to play the kind of larger role the US would want.

It is noteworthy that apart from their unwillingness (especially in the case of Japan) to take bold steps to countervail China's rise, there are serious limitations to both Japan and South Korea to contribute to the American future involvements in Afghanistan/Iraq like situations. Nor their support for a pre-emptive action in North Korea is warranted despite being extremely concerned about the danger its nuclear programme poses. And the recognition of this fact is reflected in the contents of a leak in *The L.A. Times*. According to this, which quotes extensively Douglas J. Feith, the then Undersecretary of Defence for Policy, and other unnamed senior Pentagon officials, sweeping changes are in the offing to realign American troops in Asia. Feith is reported to have said: "Everything is going to move everywhere. There is not going to be a place in the world where it is going to be the same as it used to be. We are going to rationalize our posture everywhere–in Korea, in Japan, everywhere." [18]

The changes in South Korea of moving the US troops away from the demilitarised zone and gradual handing over of the command of the troops to Koreans, have been underway already. Drastic reduction in troops may result if North Korea adheres to its promise of dismantling its nuclear weapons programme and bilateral relations between the two Koreas improve. Redeployment of forces to other regions, especially Central Asia and Southeast Asia, are viewed as potential launching pads for quick and clandestine movement of troops to future areas of conflict. What came as a surprise, was the restructuring and redeployment of the US troops in Japan. It is contended that "all but about 5000 (out of about 20,000) of the Marines (based on Okinawa) would move...." [19] This is in line with the thinking of Donald Rumsfeld who advocated the creation of a more agile, rapid force, to spread across several regions. [20] Expectedly, this has set off alarm bells ringing in Tokyo.

What is noteworthy is, that the earlier principal rationale to station troops in a particular country, was to protect that country from possible external threats–for South Korea from North Korea and for Japan from Soviet Union–is not valid any more. The situation in the Korean Peninsula continues to be fluid because of North Korea's intransigent attitude though an attack by the north is not seen to be imminent. It is widely believed that Pyongyang is using the only card it has, that is nuclear, to negotiate a deal. As anticipated, a solution to the nuclear issue is found breaking the earlier impasse although its eventual fruition is yet to be seen. Thus, American presence is perceived to be only so long as North Korea is seen to be posing a serious military threat to South Korea. Similarly, Japan does not face any threat of external aggression, and its prime security concerns would be taken care of if stability returns to Korea. Some presence with a qualitative improvement in weaponry may be required in Japan to deter China from embarking on any military adventure in Taiwan. Thus, the proposed realignment is likely to witness shifting of emphasis from Northeast Asia to Southeast Asia, [21] which has already been branded as terrorism's second front after Afghanistan. [22]

India and 'Allies and Friends'

In view of these developments, one could discern important adjustments to the American strategy in the Asia Pacific. What used to be basically limited to the alliance system and forward deployment strategy now seems to encompass 'friends' as well. India is considered as one of the friends of the US. India is probably the one Asian country that can counter-balance China almost in every sense. Hence, it makes a lot of strategic sense for Washington to befriend India especially because there is no direct clash of interest between the two after the nuclear issue has been no longer a hindrance. India's credentials as a responsible power, particularly with regard to the proliferation of WMD capabilities, are impeccable. Second, India has been in the forefront of fighting terrorism much before it got the global attention and hence the greater congruence of interests between New Delhi and Washington.

Third, India too is a rising power and is increasing its profile politically and economically in the Asia Pacific. Therefore, the realignment of forces that is taking place in the Asia Pacific, will make India an important partner and useful 'friend' because they share common concerns and interests, especially in Asia. US has gone out of its way to accommodate Indian interests by signing a nuclear cooperation agreement. The India-US 'strategic partnership' now encompasses a much larger canvass. Of the five most important dimensions of this relationship- nuclear energy cooperation, further strengthening of economic links, bilateral defence cooperation, global partner in addressing a range of issues, and a partner in building a balance of power that ensures stability and peace in East Asia and a countervailing power to a rising China. [23]

Not surprisingly, speculations have been many, given the recent bonhomie between the US and India and between India and Japan, that a new loose arrangement sans a treaty, called the 'Asian NATO', comprising the US, India, Japan, and Australia might be created. [24] The idea was apparently discussed in May 2003 when top Indian policymakers visited the Pentagon, which expectedly drew strong reactions from China. [25] The idea was also discussed at the senior officials' level on the sidelines of the ARF meeting in Manila in May 2007. The two high-profile military exercises that India conducted with Japan and the US for the first time near Japan in the Pacific and the much larger Malabar five-nation (Australia and Singapore are the other two) in September 2007 in the Bay of Bengal lent credence to the new American strategy.

Perhaps an equally important consideration that further increases India's strategic significance for the US is the Indian Ocean rim security. This region is increasingly emerging as the biggest source of global insecurity in a variety of ways. It is the epicentre of global terrorism whose tentacles spread to most parts of the world. Ethnic and sectarian strife is rampant in several parts and is the conduit for most of the world's illicit transfer of ballistic missile and weapons of mass destruction (WMD) equipment and technologies-the North Korea-Pakistan connection being the most prominent. The Indian Ocean rim region also is the largest source of a variety of non-traditional maritime security threats. India, with a navy that is the largest in the region and a geostrategic location, has a critical role to play in countering these threats and challenges, many of which are likely to become the preoccupations of the US.

Hence, it would not be surprising if Japan and India constitute two most important partners for the US in dealing with regional security. There are, of course, certain fundamental differences between Japan and India. The former is bound by a security treaty with the US and thus its role is quite different from that of India, which would be willing to join hands with the US in addressing certain common concerns and advancing common interests. There are many others, both alliance partners such as South Korea and Australia, and other friendly countries in Southeast Asia that would constitute important strategic partners.

Conclusion

Post-Second World War American strategy in the Asia Pacific has been largely based on bilateral alliance system and forward deployment with the twin objectives of containment and deterrence. In the aftermath of the Cold War, although the US was willing to endorse multilateral initiatives, it wanted them to supplement its existing policy. Since the end of the Cold War, the US has been faced with two sets of problems. While at the immediate level, the rise of terrorism, spread of WMD, and regional stability getting affected because of failed or failing states continued to engage the US, at the long-term level, issues such as threats to unipolar movement, rise of new power centres, regional and global balance of power, and sustenance of American preponderance in the Asia Pacific continued to loom large as part of its agenda. The US went to great lengths to dispel the post-Cold War uncertainties about its engagement with the region by reinvigorating the bilateral alliances and by repeatedly reiterating the commitment to station troops despite growing odds.

The 9/11 events and the war in Iraq appear to have compelled the US to fundamentally review its strategy of large concentration of troops stationed in Japan and South Korea. While this presence so far has been seen as a major stabilizing aspect, their usefulness to the US to face different kinds of contingencies is questioned. Prolonged involvement in Afghanistan and Iraq suggests that American strategy may undergo a major revamp. 'Arrangements or Coalitions' instead of 'Alliances', 'Places' instead of 'Bases', and small, agile, rapid forces spread across a more vast region than large concentration of troops in one or two countries, seem to be the new line of thinking. In this scenario, it is likely that India's strategic importance to the US will increase considerably.

Despite these changes, alliances are unlikely to disappear because the role they play in the American strategic calculus is different. It is expedient on their part to express their commitment to the region, and to ensure the regional balance and stability. America always followed a twin strategy of tackling immediate problems at one level and addressing long-term issues at another. The former warrants realignment of American troop presence while the latter insists on a robust alliance system. What shape the US policy is going to take in the coming years, will to a large extent determine the nature of regional security order in the Asia Pacific. In any case, by most indications, India's strategic importance as a 'friend' has increased remarkably. Thus, the US may extend a new strategy of 'allies' only to 'allies and friends' in realizing its objectives in the Asia-Pacific.

End Notes

1. Rajan Menon, "New Order: the End of Alliances", *Los Angeles Times*, March 2, 2003,

http://www.latimes.com/news/printedition/sunopinion/Jonathan Fenby, "Age of Shifting Coalitions", *The Japan Times*, March 29, 2003, http://www.japantimes.co.jp/cgi-bin/geted.pl5?eo20030329a2.htm, Robyn Lim, U.S.-RoK Alliance in Crisis, *The Japan Times,* March 29, 2003, http://www.japantimes.co.jp/cgi-bin/geted.pl5?eo20030329a1.htm.

2. Joseph Nye eloquently argues the significance of soft power in *The Paradox of American Power: Why the World's Only Superpower Can't Go it Alone*, 2002, (Oxford University Press; New York), pp. 8-12.
3. Aaron L. Friedberg, "Ripe for Rivalry: Prospects for Peace in a Multipolar Asia," *International Security*, 18 (3), winter 1993-94.
4. Rajan Menon, "The End of Alliances," *World Policy Journal*, XX (2) summer 2003, pp. 7-10.
5. Amitav Acharya, for instance, discusses the dynamics of Sino-Southeast Asian relations in Seeking Security in the Dragon's Shadow: China and Southeast Asia in the Emerging Asian Order, Working Paper No. 44, March 2003, (Institute of Defence and Strategic Studies; Singapore).
6. For an elaborate treatment of China's relations particularly with the recent member nations of ASEAN, see S.D. Muni, *China's Engagement with the New ASEAN*,(IDSS Monograph No. 2, 2002, IDSS; Singapore).
7. "Asia: The New U.S. Strategy," *International Business Week Online*-Asian Edition, May 28, 2001.
8. The United States and Japan: Advancing Toward a Mature Partnership, Institute for National Security Studies Special Report, National Defence University, http://www.ndu.edu/ndu/sr_japan.html.
9. More recently, the incident involving American spy plane, EP-3E Aires II signals intelligence (SIGINT) aircraft, making an emergency landing at a military base on Hainan island after a collision with a Chinese fighter jet in April 2001 and the prolonged standoff that ensued contributed to the straining of relations between the U.S. and China.
10. Condoleezza Rice, "Promoting National Interest," *Foreign Affairs*, 79(1) January-February 2000, p. 54.
11. The Bush administration sent out a number of clear signals that

it would remove sanctions on India, thus implicitly recognizing India's nuclear status.

12. Asst. Secretary of State, Christina Rocca, during her confirmation hearing of the Senate Foreign Relations Committee unambiguously stated that the administration's intention to lift the sanctions on India. *Times of India*, June 2, 2001. Richard Armitage, Deputy Secretary of State, also expressed similar opinion in an interview with the Hindu, *The Hindu*, June 18, 2001.
13. http://www.pacom.mil/about/pacom.shtml.
14. For a good overview of US policy initiatives during the Sr. Bush and Clinton Administrations, see William T. Tow, Asia-Pacific Strategic Relations: Seeking Convergent Security, 2002, Cambridge University Press; Cambridge, pp. 184-202.
15. See the Chapter III, "Strengthen Alliances to Defeat Global Terrorism and Work to Prevent Attacks Against Us and Our Friends," http://www.whitehouse.gov/nsc/nss.html.
16. Howard W. French, "North Korea Crisis Straining Washington's Asian Alliances", *International Herald Tribune* (online edition), February 25, 2003.
17. "Japan Plans to Deploy Missile Defence from 2006," *Japan Today* (online edition), May 31, 2003.
18. Esther Schrader, "U.S. to Realign Troops in Asia", *Los Angeles Times*, May 29, 2003, http://www.latimes.com/news/printedition/front/la-fg-asiamil29may29000425,1,2559437.story?coll=la percent2Dheadlines percent2Dfrontpage.
19. *Ibid.*
20. *Japan Today* (online edition), June 3, 2003.
21. Kurt M. Campbell and Yuki Tatsumi, "In the Aftermath of the Storm: US Foreign Policy in the wake of 9/11 and its Implications for the Asia Pacific Region," *Asia Pacific Review*, 19 (2), 2002, pp. 39-41.
22. John Gershman, "Is Southeast Asia the Second Front," *Foreign Affairs*, 81 (5) July-August 2002, pp. 60-74.
23. In a symbolic gesture, the US for the first time has deployed a nuclear-powered aircraft carrier, George Washington, in Japan at Yokosuka in September 2008.
24. Martin Walker, "U.S., India Discuss 'Asian NATO," *Washington Times*, May 30, 2003

http://www.washtimes.com/upi-breaking/20030529-030439-4513r.htm, Stephen Blank, "Inherent Dangers in an Asian NATO," *Asia Times*, September 19, 2003, http://www.atimes.com/atimes/South_Asia/EI19Df05.html.

25. "US Dreams of Asian NATO," *China Daily*, July 18, 2003, http://www1.chinadaily.com.cn/en/doc/2003-07/18/content_246030.htm.

12

Asia-Pacific Security Dynamics and India

S. Utham Kumar Jamadhagni

Before delving into the problems involved in India's interaction with the region of Asia Pacific, which is the focus of this article, a really fundamental issue is to be explained. Asia-Pacific region is understood as the region covering a wide area from Iran and Armenia in the west to French Polynesia in the east and from the Russian Federation and Japan in the north to New Zealand in the south. Being the largest regional grouping of its kind, it tends to inspire the specialists to view it as an unwieldy one. As aptly described by Professor P.V. Rao, "It is amorphous, least homogenous". [1] The construct of Asia Pacific as a region is fraught with doubts and scepticism. If by a region we mean, "a set of states which are located in geographical proximity to one another" [2] or a group of states marked by "contiguity of its component parts" [3] or the one that is linked by "shared characteristics, patterned interaction and shared perception", [4] then the Asia-Pacific region becomes a fluid region suffering from loose boundaries that seek to connect three continents–America, Europe and Asia–by stretching the very idea of regionness across the widest ocean on the planet, to make it an "uncertain and contested" [5] concept. It consists of countries at various rungs of the economic and political spectrum. Yet the region holds great promise as the vanguard of the world's political and economic future.

It is in this context of flux and prospect that the security dynamics in relation to India, are examined and the associated hurdles identified.

Excluding India

The ideational difficulty of Asia-Pacific adds to the challenge posed by India's interaction. The next issue is the fact that India has been recognized as a player only recently and that too only partially. In fact, the exclusion of India from the Asia Pacific community has been a major hurdle in the increased interaction with this region. Time and again, the membership or actually the non-membership of India in APEC appears on the international radar. Member-economies as the countries are termed, could be part of APEC, provided they exhibit geographical location, maintain extensive and sizeable economic relations with other members and possess market-oriented economy. India's export to the APEC countries has accounted for almost half of India's global exports. Countries of the APEC have invested independently in India. Thus, from an economic perspective alone, "a strong case for greater cooperation between India and APEC", could be made. [6]

The membership of the APEC could be the best means to enhance India's contribution to the world economy. India has attempted to gain an entry into the APEC since 1989. At first, India was not even seen as part of Asia-Pacific and later, its economy was not "liberalized enough" [7] for the economic integration that APEC has been aiming at. However, in 1997, there was a ten year moratorium on new membership. The 2007 summit decided against taking up the matter of new membership but decided in favour of taking steps to "consolidate its existing work". [8] New members need the consensus of all the existing members for admission. [9] Countries like Australia, though not openly opposing India's place, have been demurring, indicating less convincing reasons like lack of consensus while in reality the problem has been about tilting the balance in favour of Asia in the multilateral forum. [10]

As India stands to benefit from the regional grouping, the APEC too can derive benefit by networking with a "major emerging economy like India". [11] There are many experts and practitioners in favour of India being included as a member of APEC and leaders like India's former Prime Minister Atal Bihari Vajpayee opined, that formal membership is not required for recognition or sustenance of the fact that India is part of Asia Pacific. [12] But all is not lost for India which is now a part of the ASEAN Regional Forum (ARF). The success in gaining membership into the ARF, the only security related multilateral mechanism in Asia Pacific indicates, that India's Look East policy is right on target.

Asia-Pacific Security

First, it is pertinent to examine the security situation of Asia-Pacific and estimate India's stake in the region. The question of Taiwan, the unresolved conflict of the Korean peninsula coupled with the danger of nuclear weapons proliferation, the territorial disputes in the South China Sea [13] (Spratly and Paracel islands) and those between Japan and Russia (Kurile Islands) [14] tend to plague the Asia-Pacific.

While China treats Taiwan as an integral part, the Taiwan Island on its own, has declared independence. Being actively assisted by the US in its defence capabilities Taiwan represents the "biggest immediate threat" [15] to peace and stability of the Asia-Pacific region. Any effort by China to deal with Taiwan militarily, entails huge economic, political and social costs as well as a possible direct confrontation with the United States that could even involve nuclear weapons. [16]

The Spratly islands in the South China Sea, are a small group of islands that have multiple claimants for its vast natural resources in oil, natural gas, minerals and seafood. China, the Philippines, Vietnam, Taiwan, Malaysia and Brunei have staked sovereignty claims over all or part of the island group. China, by citing historical links, claims all the islands. The United States and Japan companies are involved in the off-shore exploration. The Paracel islands were captured by the Chinese forces from Vietnam on January 19, 1974. [17] In 1988, the Chinese and Vietnamese navies clashed and this resulted in the Chinese occupation of all of the Paracel islands. [18]

These challenges have sustained the US interest in the region. The Korean peninsula with a nuclear capable nation in North Korea and its animosity towards its southern neighbour, retains great power interest in the region. The tensions across the demilitarized zone in the Korean peninsula, are continuing amid the latent danger of the nuclear proliferation. [19] However, the issues of the danger of instability in the Korean peninsula and the territorial disputes of East Asia, which occupy much of the Asia-Pacific security rhetoric, can't be identified by India. But, the danger of nuclear weapons development and the possible proliferation from the Korean peninsula to other volatile parts of the world are of profound concern to countries like India which have an impeccable record on non proliferation. Apart from these, the problems of non traditional nature like drug trafficking, transnational crime, the environmental degradation, and terrorism, are also of deep concern.

The region houses the infamous golden triangle and crescent, the world's top opium producing regions. Unluckily for itself, India is sandwiched between the two regions and serves as a convenient conduit, what with a vast porous border because of land topography and a long coastline. Replete with many islands and seas, along with some of the busiest trade routes, the Asia Pacific region is vulnerable to piracy, maritime terrorism and trafficking of humans and narcotics. The countries of the region abound in natural resources and are credited with growing economies.

As a result of anthropogenic interference, there has been an unduly excessive exploitation of nature's bounties that have led to a large scale destruction of pristine forests and habitats, making the environmental degradation, one of the most important challenges in the years to come. These issues of non-military nature are identifiable for the benefit of countries like India.

Asia-Pacific in India's Eyes

The importance of Asia-Pacific to India, is mainly ascribed to the fact, that three (Japan, USA and Singapore) of India's top 5 foreign equity investing countries belong to this region. [20] The 'Look East policy'–India's foreign policy strategy to focus more keenly on countries lying to the east of the country–has broadened and deepened India's economic and strategic linkages with Southeast Asia in particular, and Asia-Pacific, in general. Economically, there has been a ten-fold increase in the merchandise trade and almost half of India's exports and imports are to and from this pan-region. While a more integrated new regional organization, termed by Australian Prime Minister Kevin Rudd as the "Asia-Pacific community" [21] might be far fetched, the existing organizations hold promise. Strategically, the manifold increase in India's naval interaction with almost all countries of the region, points to the significance of the Asia-Pacific, to India's security radar.

Also, the rise of China and the involvement of the USA in the region, are bound to impact upon the security of the Asia-Pacific. [22] The countries of China and India are gaining in the economic prosperity and in turn, in the political significance that have the potential to affect international relations. These "rising powers" and their interaction with other powers like the US, could impact on the existing Asia-Pacific security. This warrants a close watch over regional occurrences by India which is now being acknowledged not only as a regional power but also as a potential super power. Especially, the economic strengthening of China and its repercussions for the region's security, require careful evaluation.

Re-enter the Dragon

The phenomenal rise of the Chinese economic power to catapult this ancient civilization into a global power could alter the international order forever. The dominance of China as an economic giant, raises lot of concern regarding the implication of this development for not only the economic, but more importantly for political and security relations with its Asia-Pacific neighbours. The successful rejuvenation of China has also meant the harking back to the "Middle kingdom complex" which had regarded China as the epicentre and all other entities as vassals and peripheral states. [23] Chinese strategies derive from Deng Xiaoping's four notional axioms: "Avoid conflict; Build comprehensive national power; advance incrementally; and maintain stability, defend sovereignty, achieve pre-eminence and pursue parity". China has relentlessly followed these principles.

China's economic growth has been impressive in the last two decades. During 2000-2008, China has steadily maintained a GDP growth of over 9 percent. [24] Though the export competitiveness, labour laws or the lack of them and the ability to attract foreign investment tend to give China the edge, the neighbouring countries would be looking for some kind of impetus by catering to China's growing demands for products and services.

Together with a growing economy, there has been a long-term attempt to transform a peasant army into a leaner and meaner machine. This is in keeping with China's aspirations to "emerge as a key global power by 2050". [25] The means has been to upgrade and modernize the outdated weapons and systems systematically, mostly through indigenous development, but also by an outright purchase from countries like Russia or by an adopt back engineering, as was done with the Australian aircraft carrier *Melbourne,* purchased as scrap and split asunder, piece by piece. It is also reported that the Chinese have built a replica of the flight deck, for practicing carrier take-offs and landing. [26]

Since China had the security environment in the Asia-Pacific, this modernization is noted with some concern for its tremendous "psychological influence". [27] The modernization of PLA "could lead to a Chinese threat to the region". [28]

However, China stresses that military modernization is in line with its peaceful rise in the world. [29] Countries in the region like India and Japan are deeply concerned. China's forays into the Indian Ocean by the acquisition of port facilities in countries around India including Bangladesh, Myanmar, Pakistan and Sri Lanka, ostensibly to secure its energy sea lanes seem to fuel to the 'string of pearls' theory. According to this theory, China's strategy is towards a virtual encirclement of India. India's attempt to engage major powers in naval and maritime related exercises are seen as a reactionary measure to the above developments.

China has not only strengthened its economy and military might but also used it as a leverage to modify relations with ASEAN countries. It is becoming a major trade partner and this will soon augment its political influence too. The development of greater autonomous capabilities could accompany the expansion of sphere of influence. In the case of Asia Pacific, such exercises are being undertaken not only by China, but by Japan and India too. This would certainly "entail a clash of their interests". [30] China's increasing power and influence will affect not just countries like India but more so, the United States the sole superpower, whose position is under threat, if not at present, in near future at least.

Superpower Stakes

The Asia Pacific causes profound concern to the United States which still looks at it, as a region of uncertainties, tensions, and large concentrations of military forces. The Cold War problem of the two Koreas continues. The Korean peninsula poses the threat of spread of weapons of mass destruction. North Korea conducted its second nuclear test on May 25, 2009. The explosion is another reminder of the threat of nuclear proliferation in the Asia-Pacific. This was preceded by its test-firing of a rocket carrying a satellite on April 5, which is viewed "as a cover for a missile test". [31] It is claimed that the aim of the North Korean moves is, to "realize strategic technological achievements rather gaining tactical negotiating leverage". [32] With China, the big power support for North Korea, uninterested in bringing real pressure on the regime, the US has to calibrate an appropriate response, if it aims to keep peace in the region. Apart from the regional security situation, there are fears that missiles like the recently tested Taepodong with intercontinental range potential, along with nukes, will be offered to anti-American actors. [33]

Neighbouring countries like South Korea and Japan, have been Cold War allies of the US. The United States, having extended the Cold War alliances views them as the "bedrock of the regional security policy" [34] in the Asia Pacific. The continued enhancement of alliances with countries like Japan and Australia and the promotion of a stable relationship with China, have been the strategies, adopted.

In spite of debates on whether the US is a declining power in the wake of the rise of countries like India and China, scholars like Fareed Zakaria argue that "new points of tension will emerge" providing the United States "a window of opportunity" in playing a large and a constructive role in the coming global order. The influence might wane but the interest is bound to continue. United States wants and attempts to promote a "security community" in the Asia-Pacific, which in Karl Deutsch's definition makes up a group of states that "share dependable expectations of peaceful change". [35] This region is also expected to move from measuring differences to measuring progress. America's forward military presence in this region is, perhaps an important determinant of its security. Apart from the bilateral arrangements to enhance the security of the region, attempts are also on, to create multilateral structures that calibrate response to the question of security situation, as a principal aim in the Asia Pacific.

Japan

Yet another regional player, whose ties with its neighbours had been turbulent in the past and who possesses the power potential for the present and future, is Japan. Outstanding disputes with major regional powers like China, Russia and Koreas, are worrisome problems for this island nation. Japan could assume a more active role in the region's economic and security calculus. However, even when the politics and economy have greatly changed worldwide as a result of the end of Cold War and the advances of globalization, Japan's security policy, being rooted in this period accounts for Japan's inability to shed the dependence on the US, true to this period. The Japan-US Security Treaty, signed in 1952, that ensures Japan's security and the Article 9 of the Constitution that severely limits the functions of the 'self defence forces', have been hotly debated in this Asian country. Only as recently as in 2005, have the Japanese officially termed their defence forces as "military" and in 2006, elevated the defence agency to the ministry.

The question of the re-evaluation of its security policy arises because of the changes in the Asia Pacific region and its effect on Japanese relations. Now, in view of the Korean issues, there are recommendations for augmenting the force and for arming it further. [36] The Japanese offshore deployment of forces began with Gulf war. The decision to send troops to foreign countries is being viewed upon with suspicion. An assertive Japan, together with the rise of "latent militarism", along with the possibility of the US disengagement, is seen as providing a conveniently ripe environment for a reversal of the old Japanese security policy. [37] Ironically till date, in spite of efforts to increase its international responsibility Japan has for long made only financial contributions, and refrained from getting directly involved in the political and military engagement what is termed, a cheque book diplomacy. [38]

Japan has a lot of stake in the security of the Asia Pacific region. The historical baggage of animosity with neighbours like China and Korea, still dogs this otherwise advanced nation. Precisely because Japan and China are neighbouring countries, there tend to be historical issues between them that are irksome and difficult to address. Now, the economies of Japan and China are becoming increasingly closely intertwined. For Japan, China is the second largest trade partner, next to the US. For China, Japan is the largest trade partner. China is in the process of expanding its political and economic power, and hence Japan must cultivate a healthy and friendly relationship with it, which is similar to that it had courted with the US. The complicated shifts in the relationships between Japan, the US, and China, and the resulting delicate changes in the Japan-US alliance, do not seem to have been properly recognized. [39] Thus, to foster a more congenial regional environment, Japan has to forge closer ties with the Asia Pacific. [40] The massive aid offered to countries to recover from the financial crisis in East Asia and the spearheading of campaigns to form organizations like APEC have really augured well.

Multilateral Mechanisms

The multilateral security mechanisms are available at both official and non governmental levels in the Asia Pacific region. Foremost among the official mechanisms, is the ARF which displays a regional commitment to multilateralism as an approach to ensure greater security. [41] ARF is one of the first region-wide groupings "unambiguously dedicated to facilitating a security dialogue and enhancing regional stability". [42] There are also organizations other than government based ones like Council for Security Cooperation in the Asia-Pacific (CSCAP) and NEACD (Northeast Asian Cooperation Dialogue) and the Shangri La Dialogue, an international conference organized yearly by the International Institute of Strategic Studies, London, which are termed 'track two' organizations. The achievement has been modest at best. With an array of organizations competing for influence and authority, the effectiveness of each separate entity needs study. Some of the other organizations include the Conference on

Interaction and Confidence Building Measures in Asia (CICA), CSCAP, Korean Peninsula Energy Development Organization (KEDO), Trilateral Coordination and Oversight Group (TCOG), and the six-party talks aimed at tackling the Korean issue.

The Shanghai Cooperation Organisation is a confidence building mechanism aimed at peaceful resolution of the bilateral disputes between Russia, China, Kazakhstan, Kyrgyzstan, Tajikistan and Uzbekistan. It has an explicit mandate to address terrorism. The Shangri La dialogue is seen as a regular dialogue forum among regional defence officials and officials like ministers from East, Southeast and South Asia along with the US and the UK that allows frank discussion of a wide range of security issues including terrorism, cross-strait relations, piracy, narcotics, arms control and disarmament. [43]

The ARF attempts to replicate the ASEAN experience in functioning as a platform for discussing mutual problems, generating confidence to quell mutual suspicion and anger and anything that leads to internecine warfare and to achieve cooperative behaviour. The CSCAP was formed to augment the diplomatic resources of the ARF by using working groups on confidence and security building measures, comprehensive security, maritime security and transnational crime. In spite of a plethora of institutions, they are not equipped to meet all the challenges faced by Asia. None of the initiatives are a thorough-going representative of the entire Asia.

Conclusion

The Asia-Pacific region is one of the most complex yet amorphous regional frameworks in the world. Major powers like the US, China and Japan are significant players in this area. India has only recently been recognized as part of this region. Even now, India hardly figures in security literature pertaining to this region. Recently, India's stature has grown considerably and operations like the 2006 Tsunami relief work, launched throughout the region, have begun to exude confidence. After great deal of effort, India has been able to find a place in the multilateral fora, especially the cooperative ventures in energy, climate change, and such others. While cooperation is improving, competition also becomes evident. India is even seen as a threat.

Significantly, India is a member of many of the organizations mentioned above. However, lack of comprehensive results, warrants the seeking of membership in more and more organizations. Besides this, India has pursued the path of bilateral relationships even on pan regional issues like maritime security. The wide ranging naval interaction with almost all countries of this region to shore up maritime security, is an apt example. The naval exercises designed to shore up straits security have also been of a multilateral nature. However, most initiatives have not been able to explore the path of multilateralism.

Unless there is concrete effort towards addressing pressing security issues in a concerted fashion, these multilateral initiatives will remain mere paper tigers. Though it might be said that India requires greater engagement, the ground realities and the complexities of the security dynamics of the region, are so different that they administer a stern measure of caution to countries like India, before venturing to join organizations of the Asia-Pacific region.

End Notes

1. P.V. Rao, "Engaging Asia: India's strategies," Conference paper presented at the 4th India-ASEAN International Seminar, February 12-13, 2007.
2. Craig Snyder, "Regional security structures", in Craig A. Snyder (ed.), *Contemporary Security and Strategy*, (Taylor & Francis, 1999), p. 102.
3. Barry Buzan, "Asia Pacific – What sort of a region in what sort of a world," in Anthony G. McGrew, Chris Brook, (eds.), *Asia-Pacific in the New World Order*, (Routledge, 1998), p. 84.
4. *Ibid.*
5. Mark Beeson, *Institutions of the Asia-Pacific: ASEAN, APEC,*

and Beyond, (Taylor & Francis, 2008), p. 4.

6. K K Modi, "India: APEC's Missing Piece?," *CACCI Journal*, Vol. 1, 2008, p.4 http://www.cacci.org.tw/Journal/2008 percent20Vol percent201/Modi-Speech.pdf.
7. India may not get APEC membership, India news online, September 10, 2007 http://news.indiamart.com/news-analysis/india-may-not-get-ap-16698.html.
8. No room for India as APEC shuts door on hopefuls, AFP, http://afp.google.com/article/ALeqM5hwNnrKa6v_ylnfqt_BwWyoYyhSdg.
9. APEC Ministerial Statement On Membership, November 1997, http://www.apec.org/etc/medialib/apec_media_library/downloads/sec/pdf.Par.0008.File.v1.1.
10. For a report see, No APEC membership for India, *South Asia Times*, Vol. 5, No.2, Septemer 2007.
11. India and APEC, *The Hindu*, January 13, 2007.
12. India's Perspective on ASEAN and the Asia Pacific Region, Address by H.E. Shri Atal Bihari Vajpayee, Prime Minister of India Annual Singapore Lecture, 9 April 2002, http://www.aseansec.org/2787.htm Also see Bikky Khosla, APEC membership—how much will India benefit?,http://www.tradeindia.com/newsletters/archive/newsletter_11_sep_2007_29.html.
13. For details refer Scott Snyder, The South China Sea Dispute: Prospects for Preventive Diplomacy, Special Report No. 18, August 1996, United States Institute of Peace, http://www.usip.org/pubs/specialreports/early/snyder/south_china_sea1.html.
14. The BBC report on "Japan's island row with Russia", August 16, 2006 gives a brief introduction to this dispute. http://news.bbc.co.uk/2/hi/asia-pacific/4797701.stm.
15. As cited in Rajeswari Pillai Rajagopalan, "Understanding China's Military Strategy," *Strategic Analysis*, Vol. 32, Issue. 6, November 2008, p. 1015.
16. *Ibid*, p. 1018.
17. http://www.globalsecurity.org/military/world/war/spratly.htm.
18. http://paracelspratlyislands.blogspot.com/2008/01/american-role-in-south-china-sea.html.
19. Patrick M. Cronin, Michael J. Green, *Redefining the U.S.-Japan Alliance: Tokyos National Defence Program*, (DIANE

Publishing, 1994), p. 28.
20. Fact Sheet on FDI, http://dipp.nic.in/fdi_statistics/india_FDI_March2009.pdf.
21. Possible free trade deal for Asia-Pacific?, http://www.bilaterals.org/article.php3?id_article=12347 http://www.bilaterals.org/article.php3?id_article=12347.
22. Evelyn Goh, "US strategic relations with a rising China," in Kevin Cooney: Y, Kevin J. Cooney, Yoichiro Sato, (eds), *The Rise of China and International Security: America and East Asia Respond to the Rising Power*, (Taylor & Francis, 2008), p. 59.
23. W. Lawrence Prabhakar, "China's strategic Culture and current international dynamics: A perspective from India," in V.P. Malik and Jorg Schultz eds., *Rise of China: Perspectives from Asia and Europe*, (Pentagon Press, Delhi, 2008), p. 38.
24. Calculated from the US China Business Council website, http://www.usc,"hina.org/statistics/economy.html.
25. Subhash Kapila, China's Military Modernization: Major Thrust Areas
http://www.southasiaanalysis.org/papers23\paper2228.html.
26. China: Rusting Carriers May Prove Tea Leaves for Naval Future http://www.stratfor.com/analysis/china_rusting_carriers_may_prove_tea_leaves_naval_future.
27. G.V.C. Naidu, "Asian Great Powers and changing maritime Security environment in the Asia Pacific," *Area Studies: A Journal of International Studies and Analyses*, Vol 1, No. 2, July-December 2007, p. 19.
28. Michael Chambers, "Rising China: A threat to its neighbours?" in Carolyn Wilson Pumphrey," *The Rise of China in Asia: Security Implications: Security Implications*, (Army War College Strategic Studies Inst Carlisle Barracks PA, Diane Publishing, 2002).
29. Jayshree Bijoria, *Countering China's Military Modernization*, http://www.cfr.org/publication/9052/#1.
30. G.V.C. Naidu, n. 27, p. 29.
31. North Korea conducts nuclear test, *BBC News*, May 25, 2009, http://news.bbc.co.uk/2/hi/asia-pacific/8066615.stm accessed June 11, 2009.
32. Bruce Klingner, North Korea's Nuclear Defiance, webmemo http://www.heritage.org/Research/AsiaandthePacific/wm2457.cfm accessed June 11, 2009.

33. Peter Brookes, "North Korean Nukes: O's Kick in the Teeth," http://www.heritage.org/Press/Commentary/ed052809a.cfm accessed June 11, 2009.
34. http://www.eastwestcenter.org/fileadmin/stored/pdfs/seniorpolicyseminar2008_1.pdf.
35. As cited in Blair, Hanley, "From Wheels to Webs: Reconstructing Asia-Pacific Security Arrangements," *Washington Quarterly*, 24:1, Winter 2001, p. 8.
36. http://www.worldbulletin.net/news_detail.php?id=43685.
37. For a detailed discussion refer Thomas L. Wilborn, Japan's Self-Defense Forces: What Dangers to Northeast Asia?, 1994. http://www.strategicstudiesinstitute.army.mil/pdffiles/pub102.pdf.
38. Purnendra Jain, "Japan's interest in the Indian ocean," *Journal of Indian Ocean Studies*, Vol. 11, No. 1, April 2003, p. 11.
39. Taniguchi Makoto, Some Proposals for Japan's Foreign Policy http://www.iwanami.co.jp/jpworld/text/ForeignPolicy01.html.
40. Mike Mochizui's Japan and the Strategic Quadrangle, in Michael Mandelbaum ed., *The Strategic Quadrangle*, (Council on Foreign Relations, New York, Japan, 1995), p. 149.
41. Ralph A. Cossa, *Major Powers in Northeast Asian Security*, (DIANE Publishing, 1996), p. 11.
42. Mark Beeson, n.5, p. 56.
43. Satish Kumar, "Recent security initiatives in Asia," in K. Santhanam and Srikanth Kondapally (eds.), *Asian Security and China, 2000-2010*, (IDSA, New Delhi, 2004). p. 46.

13

Emerging Indo-US Strategic Relations: Impact on Asia-Pacific

Sudhir Singh

Indo-US relations have taken a new lease of life especially, after the end of the Cold War. In the Cold War era, both countries were considered almost as poles apart, and the cordial relationship having remained formal failed to blossom into anything like a sweet romance. Although the US had supported India during 1962 Chinese war, after the 1971 Indo-Soviet treaty, the relations were not at all conducive to anything like a consistent growth. The declassified American documents revealed the apprehensions entertained by President Nixon against Prime Minister Indira Gandhi during the Bangladesh War of 1971. Despite this harsh aspect of the past, the relations remained at least sustainable, during 1980's. The post Cold War twist in the relationship introduced a new flavour to the relations between the two.

A variety of factors compelled both the countries to come closer in due course. To mention first of all, the end of the Cold War led to changes in the strategic calculations in the entire Asia in general and in South-South West Asia in particular. It is also pertinent to mention here that, with the new power equations in the contemporary world system, one has to see that the Indo-US relations have local as well as global dynamics. The simple algebra of the foreign policy right from the Kautilaya to Morgenthau, reminds us that the foreign policy is guided by the commonality of interests and that the idealism has no practical value. The changing contours of international politics have put both India and the US on the same platform where there is a variety of convergence of interests. Although there are certain pockets of divergences of interest, convergences of interest are more powerful than the divergences and therefore, the ongoing relations are increasing rapidly and seem to emerge stronger in foreseeable future.

In strategic area, both the countries have travelled a long way and have launched number of joint operations. The ongoing chemistry between India and the US, has alarmed China too and therefore, China has also adopted the policy of engaging India instead of continuing its traditional policy of encircling India within South Asia in particular and in Asia in general. This was vindicated by the Chinese stand during Kargil Crisis [1999]. Both Prime Minister Nawaz Sharif and COAS Pervez Musharraf went to Beijing and requested Chinese to extend support. Instead of extending support, the Chinese advised the Pakistani leaders to settle the dispute with India in an amicable manner at the bilateral level. This shift in the traditional Chinese policy about India is ascribed to the growing Indo-US relations. This cementing of the bonhomie between both the countries has compelled the Chinese to adopt the engagement process with India. The Chinese accelerated the process of economic engagements with India. The volume of bilateral Indo-Chinese trade reached up to 38.6 US$ billion in the FY of 2007-2008 and slated to cross 60 US$ billion in 2010. [1] However, despite several rounds of high profile negotiations, there is hardly any progress in settling thorny boundary dispute between both these traditional rivals. In fact, the development in the relations between both the countries followed the historic high profile visit after many years, by the Indian Prime Minister Rajiv Gandhi, in 1988.

This vindicates that mere excellent economic relationship between the rival countries like India and China, is not enough because, the issues of strategic and political relations must be settled first. However, Kargil episode also became a paradigm shift of the bi-lateral relationship between India and the United States. It is pertinent to mention here, that since the independence, the US had been one of the most ardent supporters of Pakistan on account of various compulsions on the chess board of the international system. Kargil issue is important because the US during this crisis, began to toe the traditional policy of dealing on the basis of equality to India and Pakistan. It was the last year of the second term of President Bill Clinton's tenure when Clinton facilitated a deal between India and Pakistan. When Pakistan had violated the ceasefire line, Clinton prevailed on Islamabad to withdraw its army back to the former place of peaceful time. Through this peace initiative, the US could prevent a dangerous situation in South Asia.

Even the first four years of President Clinton become significant when his junior Minister for State, Rabin Raphel had meaningfully termed Kashmir as a nuclear flash point and hence a dangerous place for the world. Given these facts as forming the background, the Kargil initiative by the US may be deemed a Himalayan shift in the traditional American policy in South Asia. Interestingly enough, it was the situation when just few months before the US had imposed a gamut of sanctions on India in the wake of its ambitious atomic bomb blast at Pokhran in May 1998.

During President George W. Bush period (2000-2008), the bilateral relations between the US and India improved in an unprecedented manner. Barring progress at several fronts, the Bush administration at least conferred the status of a strategic partner on India and participated in several combined military exercises both at bi-lateral and at the multi-lateral level. Finally, in the last leg of his regime, President Bush clinched a nuclear deal with India and provided a special status to India within the global order. This deal is not merely confined to the energy sector but is slated to expand the canvass of bi-lateral relations in the wide gamut of other important areas, including the strategic relationship. One more important area of common concern between the US and India, has been counter terror.

The US faced the tentacles of terror on its land in

September 2001, while India has been struggling with the incidence of terror over years since 1990, till the ghastly Mumbai episode (November 2008), deemed for the time being, as the last one to challenge the very authority of the Indian state on adequate security measures to prevent untoward incidents of the kind. Southeast Asia has been struggling with the menace of terror since many years and now it has spread into some unconventional places like southern Thailand. It is already an issue of concern in Indonesia and the Philippines and slated to extend its tentacles into the remaining countries of Southeast Asia. All the three, the US, Southeast Asian countries and India, with Japan and Australia, could take effective steps in eliminating the menace of terror.

This bonhomie between India and US tended to reformulate many important bilateral relations in Asia in particular and in the entire world in general. The so-called *Arc of Democracy* which includes U.S, India, South Korea, Japan, Singapore and Australia has the potential to make an impact of the power configuration of Asia-Pacific. Since the end of the Cold War the concept of rising China has been extremely popular, gaining ground at least for finding an answer to the relevant issue of the maintenance of balance of power within Asia. The entire international relations concerning Asia were viewed by harbingers of the international politics through that prism and the concept of the balance of power and the theory of Prisoner's Dilemma were used to score points on their rivals by way of ensuring their individual dominance within the context of Asia. The territorial disputes between China and Japan, India, Malaysia, Vietnam, the Philippines and Brunei, coupled with the tension prevailing in the Taiwan Straits, provided an opportunity to the uni-polar power, namely, the US, to play the game safely by pitting one country against another, as all countries have been psychologically obsessed with the burden of history since centuries.

In *Strategic Appraisal, 1996,* the RAND Corporation recommended that the US government should reinforce its alliance with Japan and Republic of Korea (South Korea), improve its cooperation with ASEAN, and support the defence of Taiwan and ASEAN, in order to contain China. [2] The most significant example of the US using the security dilemma theory to contain China, is the issue of Taiwan. [3] In April 2000, the newly elected President George Bush had declared that the US would assist the self defence of Taiwan at all costs and sent a clear message to all the parties concerned, that the policy goal of the US was to prolong the "no war, no independence, and no unification situation indefinitely." In January 2009, President Bush completed his second tenure and the US thus, having been successful in maintaining the status quo could put the Chinese under the prisoner's dilemma.

The arms race and the security dilemma have provided a proper excuse for the American military presence within Asia-Pacific. The rising China started posing a threat to the US dominance over Asia-Pacific gradually, after the downfall of the USSR, either from the idealistic perspectives of values (Western Democracies and Human Rights etc,) or from the realistic perspectives of the national interests. In December 2000, the US National Intelligence Commission released a report on the world in 2015 saying "if China becomes stronger, it will then seek favourable rearrangement of power in the Asia-Pacific and may engage in conflicts with its neighbours and some outside forces." As a rising power, China will keep on expanding its own influence without considering the US interests. [4] In the last week of September 2008, the NSG passed the resolution of India's entry into the elite nuclear club and both the houses of the US Congress (House of Representatives and the Senate) also approved it and the much debated 123 Treaty thus became the reality. [5]

Much has been debated on this issue in domestic as well as international media and considering the way, the Chinese have done the last minute sabotage in Vienna to this NSG waiver, it is vindicated that the Chinese have remained utmost concerned with the fallout of this deal because, according to their interpretation, this deal has not been confined to the issue of the cooperation of nuclear energy but will be extended into the realm of the strategic relationship too. If the US wants to play the stopper like the British Empire did in the 19th Century, it will need to entrap other regional powers i.e. Japan, India and Russia into confrontational or strategic, competing relations with China. The American scholar, Huntington had said, "Theoretically speaking, the US could contain China by playing a balancing role if other powers would like to balance China as well." [6] Since Russia has become friendly with China following the settlement of their old boundary disputes and more significantly that of the 2008 conflicts between Russian and Georgian forces over the dispute of South Ossetia, there is hardly any possibility of Russia being friendly with the US, despite the former's weak economic status.

In this situation, the US could hope that only Japan and India could play this role. Since the end of World War-II, US and Japan have had excellent security relationship. The discord between China and Japan has been historical in the sense, it originated in their age-old rivalry for dominance in Asia. In 1894-95, Japan had defeated China and again between the First and the Second World Wars (1914-1945), Japan, having invaded China, killed thousands of the Chinese. This rivalry still manifests itself in the conflict of Taiwan and North Korean nuclear issue. China, India and Japan, the three major Asian powers, are now engaged in power struggle that has the potential of shaping the future of international relations as significantly, it is not confined to Asia. [7] Of course, China has an edge among these three but Japan as an old power with the US as a trusted ally, wields enormous power.

India is an emerging power in Asia and has already shed its masculine shy to be active in international politics. The Japan-US bi-lateral relationship has been extremely important for the power structure of Asia. In the context of growing India-U.S bonhomie in recent years, it is pertinent to note that India-Japan bilateral ties have also increased by many folds.

Japan's changing perception of India's growing profile at the regional and the international level has been significantly noticed since the August 2000 visit to India by the Japanese Prime-Minister Mori Yoshiro. The first of its kind in a decade by a Japanese Prime Minister, Mori's visit was a major turning point in India-Japan relations. Mori prepared the ground for treating India as an important regional ally by declaring that "Japan and India are global partners." [8] India's foreign policy approach toward China and other major powers in the Asia-Pacific, is marked by strategic flexibility.

Although India is a participant in the China-Russia-India trilateral dialogue, it has also endorsed the strategic idea forwarded by former Japanese Prime Minister Abe in his book, *Utsukushi Kunie* (Toward a beautiful country) about the quadrilateral dialogue involving India, Japan, the U.S and Australia. The initial nod to the Abe's idea came from Indian Prime Minister Manmohan Singh in December 2006, when an Indo-Japanese joint statement stated that, "the two leaders share the view on the usefulness of having dialogue among Japan, India and other like minded countries in the Asia-Pacific region on themes of mutual interest". [9] This quadrilateral dialogue was formally initiated in Manila on the sidelines of ARF meeting on May 25, 2007. The four countries also participated in joint naval exercises in the Bay of Bengal in September 2007, demonstrating their willingness to engage in multi-lateral defence diplomacy as a *"quartet of democracies"* in the Asia-Pacific region. [10]

India-China relationship has also been marred by several disputes which include Tibet question, all weather China-Pakistan friendship, expansion of India's nuclear weapon programme and Chinese overt policy of *Encircling India* within South Asian region and other impeding incidents in the close neighbourhood. Since the landmark visit of the Indian Prime Minister Rajiv Gandhi to Beijing in 1988, both China and India had improved their bi-lateral relationship in a big way particularly, in the economic area and cultural arena. The bi-lateral economic relationship was accelerated in a phenomenal way. The volume of bi-lateral trade between India and China which was below US$ 5 billion in early 1990s had crossed US$ 38.6 billion in the FY 2007-08 and slated to cross US$ 60 billion by the FY 2009-10.

There are other areas where both the countries together have achieved improvement. But the crucial issue of boundary has remained unresolved till now, despite several rounds of high voltage negotiations between both the traditional rivals since Prime Minister A.B. Vajpayee's Beijing visit of June 2003. Chinese staunch opposition to the NSG waiver in Vienna (September 2008), is an ample proof of the Chinese mindset continuing to entertain misgivings about the growing Indo-US relationship. The Sino-Indian relationship today is "Just like an unsunken, unrotten but static boat. [11] China and India fought an open war in 1962 and China still holds thousands of square km. of the Indian territory under its occupation and stakes claims on more than one thousand square km. of the Indian territory, which is, by all means, an integral part of India. The Indian Parliament had passed a unanimous resolution that it is a national duty of India to recapture every inch of land daringly and illegally occupied by China during 1962 War.

The stagnant Sino-Indian relations opened the door for the US, to attempt to rope in India, to contain China. The unhappy experience with China in the past and the current suspicion of Beijing made New Delhi an ideal partner in Asia for the US for purposes of implementing a containment strategy against China. [12] This entire exercise comes under the aegis of balance of power within the scenario of the international politics. Power transition theory was originally advanced as a rival to the balance of power theory. The idea that power parity leads to war, is in sharp contrast to the classical realist theory of Hans Morgenthau, Henry Kissinger, and Kenneth Waltz, which argues that major war is likely once one state is preponderant and unlikely, when great powers are relatively equal. A balance of power keeps the peace by convincing the potential aggressor that war will entail both high cost and a low probability of success. A direct challenge to the classic realism and the balance of power theory and power transition theory, views the international system certainly not as anarchic, but as a hierarchically organized order in which actors accept their position based on relative power distribution. [13]

The growing Indian profile in the international system has provided an opportunity for the US, to put India to balance China. To repeat what I have stated earlier, both have enough reasons to be suspicious of each other and in the foreseeable future, there is hardly any possibility that both the countries would be able to settle their thorny border conflicts.

Impact on Asia-Pacific

The growing Indian profile in Asia-Pacific has gained paramount significance in the post Cold War scenario. With the end of the Cold War, the strategic and political divide between the two countries became less important. The structural changes in Asia's security environment gave India and Japan much more strategic manoeuvrability compared to their status in the Cold War period. For instance, the collapse of the bio-polar security architecture in Asia was followed by the restructuring of the troops' strength by the U.S., including the closure of America's largest overseas military base located in the Philippines in 1992. The reduction of the U.S troops affected the strategic balance in Asia, induced Japan to venture a search for like- minded strategic partners. In this context, the growing bonhomie between India and the U.S also influenced Japan's perception of India as a potential like minded partner in Asia. This is really relevant to the prevailing reality that the U.S, in its utter preoccupation with the problems of Iraq and Afghanistan, has been unable to pay adequate attention to the entire Asia-Pacific.

The growing China-ASEAN relationship, particularly the

economic relationship vindicates a kind of lack of will on the part of the US, to pay adequate attention towards this currently most important arena of the world. However, since the last two centuries Japan has been one of the dominant Asian powers with aspirations at the global level. However, after the tragic atomic attack on its cities during the Second World War by the US, Japan kept a low profile in the international system as well as in the Asia-Pacific. The ongoing global recession has been predicted as an example of declining US global dominance. What kind of impact it will have on Asia remains a question. Interestingly, all the three leading countries of Asia, China, Japan and India, are growing very smoothly as well as simultaneously on economic front. Since the end of the Second World War, the US had been trying to dominate Asia but till the end of the Cold War, the USSR's resistance was acting as a counter balance. The surprising engagement of Chinese by the US during 1970s, was indeed an attempt to weaken the Soviet bloc. This diplomatic initiative of the US paid the dramatic dividend, when in 1979, the Chinese supported Mujaheeden resistance war against the invading red army in Afghanistan.

It is pertinent to mention here, that both China and the Soviet Union were harbingers of the communist movement during the Cold War era but in the case of Afghanistan, China opposed the Soviet Union. This became a classic example to prove that only convergences of interest are the basic foundations of foreign policy and that the commonality of ideology need not matter on all occasions. After the end of the Cold War, the US remained dominant in Asia by engaging maximum important countries within Asia through military alliances and by fostering trade and other linkages. Japan, a close ally of the US thus far, has shown signs of playing an independent global role. The recent and sustainable rise of China has further strengthened Japan's desire to be a dominant power. In this context, the growing India-Japan relationship served as a push factor for their positive relationship with the US within the power structure of the Asia-Pacific. This is the secret of the rapidly growing bi-lateral relationship between Japan and India since last few years, despite the fact that their bilateral trade stood at merely around 25 percent of the entire Sino-Indian bilateral trade.

Asia-Pacific has been one of the emerging regions of the world. Australia has been one of the important countries within Asia-Pacific, though not directly. Australia had been intimately close to the western powers ever since it came into existence and after the Second World War, it had begun playing a second fiddle to the US within Asia-Pacific. Australia has been one of the durable democratic countries within Asia-Pacific and both the U.S. and India have been engaged with Australia on many fronts to ensure order within Asia-Pacific region particularly, during the post-Cold War and in the post-9/11 scenario. However, the decade long government of Prime Minster Howard, had been defeated and replaced by the labour government with Kevin Rudd as Prime-Minister at the fag end of 2007. Australia has been considered as the traditional comrade in arms of the US for a long time in Asia in particular and in the entire world in general. Australia has been engaged in Iraq as well as in Afghanistan, with the US led operations.

The new Prime Minster has announced that he would withdraw Australian forces from Iraq and would not follow American dictates in the pursuit of foreign policy. The new Prime Minister, who is fluent in Mandarin, seems to change the contours of trilateral relations among India, US and Australia. But given the prevailing circumstances at the international level, there is a strong possibility that the bilateral relations between India and Australia will be stronger in foreseeable future too. There are number of convergences of interests like terror, maritime security, global warming, economic relations, science and technology, tourism, and Diaspora etc. Needless to say, that the convergence of interests has also compelled both the countries to sail in the same boat. Despite Rudd Government's slight inclination towards China,

Australia has been sustaining excellent bilateral relationship with Japan and India in all important sectors. Australia, United States, India, Singapore and Japan have undertaken several joint naval exercises in the Indian Ocean Region and elsewhere. Foreign policy of any country is not guided by any particular choice but it is decided according to the national interest of the particular country.

Australia did not dare develop adverse relationship with the US, Japan, India and Singapore to appease China. However, India and Australia avail themselves of a better relationship. However, after the 1986 Rajiv Gandhi's visit to Australia no Indian Prime Minister visited Australia. It is relevant to mention here, that during this interregnum, many Australian Prime Ministerial visits had been paid to India. In recent years, the major discord between India and Australia has been the issue of the sale of the uranium by Australia to India. Australia sold it to China freely, but unwilling to sell the same to India. Recently, France has decided to sell huge quantity of uranium to India and deal has been done. Despite these small irritants, Australia and India kept engaged to each other and it is the same case with Australia and Japan and Singapore.

The emerging international strategic environment in Asia-Pacific in general and in the post Cold War and the post-9/11 scenario in particular, has compelled America and India to cement their bilateral cooperation. The same logic applies in the case of India-Australia relationship. Therefore, commonality of interest is increasing between India and America. By and large, Australia and India also share this commonality. Therefore, Australia being a country close to Asia, must realize that the growing strategic relationship between India and America is in their interest too and must promote and protect bilateral relations on both the sides. The same logic works for a better and robust bi-lateral relationship between Japan and India. The prevailing scenario in the Southeast Asian region has also compelled Australia, which is only a next door neighbour to it, to contribute its mite to this ongoing bonhomie. China is seeking a uni-polar Asia under her towering leadership and contrary to that Japan, India and the US want multi-polar Asia to flourish.

In the larger context, it is in the larger canvass of the Australian national interest also. The growing Indo-American strategic relations will act as the push factor of Australian interest particularly, in Asia-Pacific. Therefore, the growing Indo-US strategic relationship has more positive impact on Australia. The tentacles of terror have been in upward trends for the past many years within Asia-Pacific. Likewise, the incidence of the violation of maritime security has remained a big factor of concern for the entire world in general and the U.S, India, Australia and Japan in particular. Therefore, despite challenges ahead, the U.S, India, Japan and Australia need to work together to ensure peace and order within Asia-Pacific. The US has already been working for the tri-lateral dialogues involving Japan and India and another one with Japan and Australia. The United States and Japan with tacit understanding with India and Australia, must cooperate fully with ASEAN members.

In recent years, Indo-Japan relations increased by many folds. In a broader policy decision, Japan decided in post-Cold War scenario, to expand the contours of its foreign policy preferences in Asia in conformity with changing balance of power in Asia-Pacific. While Japanese foreign policy still holds utmost importance for its relationship with the U.S, its desire to forge a "strategic" relationship with India, clearly indicated that Tokyo started to strike a wider and more active diplomatic course in the 21st century. There is hardly any reason that U.S. would be suspicious about the growing bonhomie between India and Japan. Instead, the U.S. should be happy that two great democracies of Asia with convergences of interest with the U.S are coming closer. In recent years, the U.S. has been preoccupied with its ongoing assignments in the Middle East and so, the Asia-Pacific region seems to have taken a back seat in its list of priorities. The U.S. view is that closer trilateral relation among Japan, India and Australia is a stabilizing regional force. This growing relationship will serve two purposes of the U.S foreign policy; first it will become a natural containment of China and secondly it will work as a balancer in Asia-Pacific region, given the reason that it is an old policy of the U.S. not to allow any single power to dominate Asia-Pacific, even as the second fiddle. The convergences of interests of Japan, India and Australia will work as a push factor to cooperate within this framework, in the foreseeable future.

The American presidential doctrine outlined in *The National Security Strategy of the United States of America* has stated about Asian security order that "given the situation, the United States will, if necessary, act pre-emptively. The United States will not use force in all cases to pre-empt emerging threats, no nations should use pre-emption as a pretext for aggression. Yet in the age where the enemies of civilization openly and actively seek the world's most destructive technologies, the United States cannot remain idle while dangers gather. [14]

The American presidential doctrine outlined in The National Security Strategy of the United States of America, has significant implications for the Asian security order. [15] Unlike some past presidential doctrines such as the Nixon Doctrine, the Bush Doctrine (2000-2008) was not specifically oriented towards Asia. Its target was a global threat, although this threat is very much present within Asia. After Bush, Obama has taken over as the new president and it is widely debated that either he will pursue the Bush doctrine in the realm of foreign policy or he will change it. Given the past experiences of American foreign policy, every President has to pursue national interest and whatever Bush has done was very much in the national interest of the U.S. Therefore, there is little possibility of the radical change within the contours of foreign policy by newly elected President Obama

Administration. A number of pundits of the international system have predicted that there would be no major changes in the US policy towards Asia-Pacific which is the power house of the international system in the 21st Century. It is in the larger US interest to ensure multi-polar Asia, while allowing the uni-polar system at the global level to sustain. In contrast, the Chinese seek uni-polar Asia dominated by itself and multi-polar world with China as an important power. In this prevailing situation the US would prefer multi-lateral power structure within the Asia-Pacific.

According to one school of thought, the U.S. and China could not sustain the present state of bi-lateral relationship. They are cooperating on several fronts and still, their economic relationship has almost reached its nadir. Cooperation and conflict form a stable phenomenon in this age of globalization. However, this school of argument is not anything new as it came into being in the late 1950s. Ever since A.F.K Organski first formulated it as a competing theory to counter traditional balance of power theory, power transition theory has undergone various modifications and expansions. The original basic statement of the power transition perspective is found in Organski's world Politics (1958), with extensions to the nuclear era in the second edition (1968). [16] There are common areas of concern where both China and the US could cooperate. It is all a matter of counter terror and global warming. But given the development of both the countries, the level of cooperation between the two countries, has not been satisfactory. They believe in the old theory of balance of power. Therefore, they indulge in this game despite massive cooperation in many important sectors including economic relationship.

To ensure wider perspectives of peace and development within Asia-Pacific, this engagement needs to be particularly extended to Indonesia, a country which has the largest majority of Muslims of the world and touches the borders of the Strait of Malacca, Asia's most strategically crucial trade route. [17]

Indonesia's stability and its treatment as a significant regional power will be crucial to peace and security in the Asia-Pacific region. The post-Cold War strategic environment is in a dramatic flux, as evident from the changing power equations, as well as the formation of new strategic partnerships and military arrangements; it is coupled with the post-9/11 scenario. In this fluid and uncertain scenario, the Asia-Pacific region is at the threshold of the unprecedented developments. This region, as Kurt M. Campbell argues, is on the cusp of major changes in its strategic environment. [18]

This is also in the larger interest of the common masses of the region to sustain a healthy balance of power within the region. The growing Indo-US relationship after the much debated nuclear deal, has reached a very healthy level. There are some concerns that the newly elected Obama Administration may change Indian policy from the level President Bush had fixed. These sceptics forget the simple fact that, when the nuclear deal came for voting in the American Senate and both Obama and his rival John McCain voted in favour of the deal. The foreign policy of the US is based on national interest and the growing nice relationship with India is in the U.S. interest too. Therefore, despite one irritant statement about Kashmir from Rice, the UN representative of Obama the ongoing relationship seems to be sustainable in foreseeable future. It has persuaded Japan to have a better relationship with India and the way Indo-Japan relationship has grown up within the last one decade, is path breaking. These changing relationships which will sustain at least for the immediate future will have benign impact on peace, security and human security developments, within Asia-Pacific.

End Notes

1. *The Hindu*,(New Delhi), 17 July 2008.
2. Zalmay Khalizad, "U.S Grand Strategy; Implications for the United States and the World," *Strategic Appraisa*l, *1996*, (RAND, 1996), pp. 23-34.
3. Although Taiwan is a small state, we could still apply the

security dilemma theory to the case, given the fact that Taiwan is publicly engaged in military confrontation with the mainland.

4. Lee Kuan Yew, "How will Bush Administration Maintain Stability in East Asia?," *The Strait Times*, April 13, 2001.
5. *The Times of India*, (New Delhi), October 3, 2008.
6. Samuel Huntington , *Cultural Conflicts and the Restructuring of the World Order*, www.shuku.net.
7. Emmott, Bill, Rivals, *How the Power Struggle Between China, India, and Japan Will Shape Our Next Decade*, (Harcourt, 2008), p. 13.
8. Ministry of Foreign Affairs of Japan, "Japan-India Summit Meeting [Summary], August 2000, http;www.mofa.go.jp/region/asia-paci/pmvooo8/India_s.html.
9. *Joint Statement toward Japan-India Strategic and Global Partnership*, 15 December 2006.
10. "India, Japan, U.S. Hold Naval Drills," *Times of India*, (New Delhi), 16 September 2007.
11. Ms. Mira Sinha Bhattacharya's (Co-Chairman, Institute for Chinese Studies, India) speech at the seminar on the status quo and prospects on the Sino-Indian Relations sponsored by China review (A Hong Kong based Magazine) *China Review*, 2001. 3., p. 61.
12. *Washington Quarterly*, Winter 2000.
13. Zhu, Zhiqun, *US- China Relations in the 21st Century*, (Rutledge, London, 2006), p. 15.
14. Gurtov, Mel and Peter Van Nees (ed.) *Confronting Bush Doctrine; Critical views from the Asia-Pacific*, (Rutledge, London, 2005), p. 204.
15. For the full text of the Bush Doctrine, see, "*President Bush Delivers Graduation Speech at West Point*," The White House , Office of the Press Secretary, June 1, 2002, online at www.whitehouse.gov/news/releases/2002/06/200220601-3.html.
16. *Ibid*, p. 167.
17. Funabashi, Yoichi, "Keeping up With Asia," *Foreign Affairs*, September/ October, 2008, p.122.
18. Campbell, Kurt, M, "Energizing the U.S-Japan Security Partnership," *Washington Quarterly*, Autumn, 2000, p. 128.

14

Asia-Pacific: India's Perception

C. Sheela Reddy and N. Amareswaran

As the world has been increasingly acknowledging India's rising power status, India has begun adapting its foreign policy, to meet the international challenges of the 21st Century and to increase its global influence and status. For many years, India took pride in its role as the leader of the Non-Aligned Movement (NAM) and viewed itself as the chief defender of the rights of the less developed countries. In the past few years, New Delhi subjected its strategic vision to enlargement most noticeably in Asia, and allowed the definition of its security interests to get broadened.

The 21st Century is being touted as the Asian age, primarily belonging to China and India. The end of the Cold War and the growing impacts of globalization are inspiring India to redefine its position and its role, both at the regional and at the global level. Since the economic liberalization of 1990s, which had led to the growth rates of 6-7 percent per annum, India's global presence has been steadily visible. Two issues have been shaping India's rise-the political dividend it has garnered as the world's largest democracy and its growing economic status, which, according to projections, will cause it to emerge, along with China, as a key economic driver of the future. India, the acknowledged leader of the South, is transcending that role to play a larger role at the global level. Post-Cold War global politics have been witnessing changes in power equations between and among states. [1]

Foreign Policy and Economy of India

India's Foreign Policy covers vital issues of development,

peace and stability. The principles of India's foreign policy are:

- Fostering cordial relations with other countries,
- Solving conflicts by peaceful means,
- Maintaining the Sovereignty and equality of all nations,
- Independence of thought and action as per the principles of NAM, and
- Equality in conducting international relations.

India has a long history of collaboration with several countries and is considered as a leader of the developing world. India was one of the founding members of several international organizations, most notably the United Nations, the Non-Aligned Movement, the Asian Development Bank and the G20 industrial nations. India has also been playing an important and influential role in other international organizations and regional organizations like East Asia Summit, World Trade Organization, IMF, G8+5, IBSA, SAARC and BIMSTEC. [2]

The economy of India, measured in USD exchange-rate terms, is the twelfth largest in the world, with a GDP of around US$ 1 trillion (2008). It recorded a GDP growth rate of 9.1 percent for the fiscal year 2007-2008, which makes it the second fastest big emerging economy after China, in the world. In view of this rate of sustained growth, many economists forecast that India would, over the coming decades, have a more pronounced economic effect on the world stage. Being the world's fourth largest armed forces, and fourth largest economy (in PPP terms), India is regarded as a regional power and as a potential superpower. It is India's growing international influence that increasingly gives it a prominent voice in global affairs. [3]

India's Southeast Asian Connections

India followed a socialist-inspired approach for the most part of its post-independence history, with strict government control over private sector participation, foreign trade, and foreign direct investment. However, since the early 1990s,

India has gradually opened up its markets through economic reforms by reducing government controls on foreign trade and investment. The privatisation of publicly owned industries and the opening up of certain sectors to private and foreign interests, have proceeded slowly amid political debate. India launched 'Look East' policy in the early 1990s, following its adoptions of economic reforms and the end of Cold War.

Up to 1991, it might have been said that India's Asia connections were more formal than close, with a limited economic content; the political content was equally modest. Under Prime Minister Rajiv Gandhi (1984-89), an effort had been made to improve relations with individual states in Southeast Asia, but this did not attain fruition. Visits by Indian leaders to Southeast Asia were few and far between. Indira Gandhi visited Jakarta and Manila in 1981, the first by an Indian premier in well over a decade, was of 24-hour duration. Rajiv Gandhi travelled to Bangkok in 1986, for a 17-hour stay. [4]

India did not pursue any structural mechanisms with ASEAN; APEC had bypassed India. For all its cordial political ties with the individual countries in Asia, India remained a non-member of any regional entity that covered Southeast Asia, other than the 1975 Bangkok Agreement and of course, the UN regional body on Economic and Social Commission for Asia and the Pacific (ESCAP). The Bangkok Agreement of 1975 provides for limited trade preferences among its member developing countries (Bangladesh, India, Lao PDR, South Korea and Sri Lanka; China joined in 2000). The preferences margins were not deep enough, and the Bangkok Agreement fell far short of a real Preferential Trade Agreement (PTA).

The creation of the Asia Pacific Economic Community (APEC) in 1989 was preceded by a 'Pacific Community Seminar' convened by Australia and Japan in 1980, which led to the creation of the Pacific Economic Cooperation Council (PECC). At that time, India was perceived to be indifferent to these developments, and by the time India openly evinced an interest in membership in the early 1990s, it found the door closed. In 1997, APEC suspended further membership applications for 10 years, but even in 2007, there was no sign, as yet, of that door, being kept open, for India.

The question as to whether India is part of the Asia Pacific, seems disingenuous. By any definition, India lies either within, or on the periphery, assuming that the geography principle is to apply strictly. For instance, the southernmost territory of India, the Andaman Archipelago, lies a scant 80 miles from Indonesia. It also virtually abuts on the Malacca Straits. In reality, both by its size and by its current and potential politico-economic role as a mainstream Asian state, India amply qualifies itself for membership.

ASEAN-India relations grew rapidly after 1991. In 1992, India became a sectoral dialogue partner (the sectors covered, being trade, investment, tourism and science and technology); in 1995, India joined China, Japan and South Korea as a full dialogue partner of ASEAN. In 1996, it joined the ASEAN Regional Forum (ARF); in 2002, it became a summit partner of ASEAN (ASEAN+1). In 2005, together with Australia and New Zealand, India joined the annual East Asia Summit (EAS) process, in what has become 'ASEAN+3+3'. EAS is of particular significance to India, because it conferred on India, a role in the emerging regional architecture. India has much to contribute to and to gain from a Comprehensive Economic Partnership of East Asia (CEPEA), evolved within the framework of EAS. [5]

India's trade with ASEAN countries rose from US$ 9.7 billion in 2002-2003, to more than US$ 30.64 billion in 2006-07. The 2010 trade target of US$ 50 billion (set at the November 2007 6th India-ASEAN summit), certainly appears modest, given the present dynamism in India's foreign trade, which has produced a doubling in India's share of world trade between 1992 and 2006, albeit on a very modest starting base. As for Foreign Direct Investment (FDI), India is both an increasingly attractive destination, and a dynamic foreign investor in its own right, in Southeast and elsewhere. This, combined with the managerial talent and entrepreneurship that operates across the world market, adds to India's economic strength and attractiveness. [6]

Studies by RIS (Research and Information Systems for Developing countries), New Delhi, show that India's integration into East Asian systems (ASEAN, China, Japan and South Korea) would show sizable welfare gains for all, including India, in various permutations and combinations. BIMSTEC is another emerging regional cooperation mechanism that engages India in Southeast Asia. Launched in 1997 as a link between South and Southeast Asia, BIMSTEC was originally extended to Bangladesh, India, Myanmar, Sri Lanka and Thailand, which gave this group its name, with the addition of the phrase 'economic cooperation'. After Bhutan and Nepal joined the group in 2003, it has taken the name The Bay of Bengal initiative for Multi-Sectoral Technical and Economic Cooperation. BIMSTEC is engaged in an ambitious programme of activities.

India maintained bilateral political relations with virtually all the ASEAN states, with a matching elevation in the economic and other exchanges. Ground reality showed that India's 'Look East' posture was not an empty promise. In the mid-1990, Singapore Premier Goh Chok Tong likened China and India to the two wings of the ASEAN aircraft fuselage.

India is integral to Asia, by history, culture and in relation to the future of this continent. A dynamic, resurgent India is an essential component in the renaissance of Asia, offering partnerships to the other states and drawing from them the cooperation that would work to the mutual benefit of all the countries and make Asia an even more powerful locomotive of world growth. [7]

Rising Asia-Pacific

Asia has many players and contenders to be its leader both regionally and globally. From within the region China, India and Japan are the key actors, while the US is the most dominant outside stakeholder in the region, followed by Russia.

A former editor of '*The Economist*' wrote recently: "For the first time the Asia-Pacific region has three powerful countries-China, India and Japan-at the same time. The peace and prosperity of the world will increasingly be shaped whether the rivalry between these three powers turns out to be constructive or destructive."

The UN Economic and Social Commission for Asia and the Pacific (ESCAP) while celebrating its 60th anniversary in March 2007, suggested that the 21st Century would be the "Asia-Pacific century". On January 9, 2008, ESCAP published its latest annual report in Bangkok. The report forecast that the economic growth rate for the region in 2008, would be 7.8 percent, which is only slightly lower than the 8.2 percent of 2007, and still the highest in the world. The most important reason for the economy of the Asia-Pacific to maintain vitality, is the high economic growth in China and India. [8]

Asia-Pacific is attracting more and more attention the world over. Many of the much-talked about new emerging economies such as BRICs, VISTA countries, N-11, are located in the Asia-Pacific. Countries that had their economic take-off earlier, such as China, India, ROK, Singapore, and Malaysia, have continued to maintain sound economic performances. More and more countries, such as Indonesia, Vietnam, the Philippines, Turkey, and Iran, are speeding up their economic development with spectacular results. Economic integration and regional and sub-regional economic cooperation have also scored great achievements. Various FTAs are shaping themselves with steady steps forward. Trade and investment with each other among the countries within the region, have seen marked growth. The Asia-Pacific, including the new emerging economies in it, has become the most important driving force for the entire world economy. [9]

Politically, the influence and impact of the Asia-Pacific are also growing enormously and distinctly. Unlike some other parts of the world, the region has, on the whole, maintained peace and stability for decades. There have been no hot wars or armed conflicts between Asia-Pacific countries for thirty years and more. ASEAN celebrated its 40th anniversary last year, and its membership has expanded and its role, enhanced. The "10+3" (ASEAN plus China, Japan and ROK) have entered the second decade of cooperation. ARF, APEC, ACD (Asia Cooperation Dialogue) and EAS have all played an important and effective role in promoting stability, cooperation and development. Generally speaking, in spite of the ups and downs, the relations among the major countries in the region have been stable, and the interdependence among all the countries in the region, has improved markedly. Recently, the cooperation between China and India has made rapid and fruitful progress, and the relationship between China and Japan has also been an important turn for the better.

The Asia-Pacific region is the venue where the Five Principles of Peaceful Coexistence of 1954 and the Ten Principles of the Bandung Conference of 1955, were initiated. In recent years, the Asia-Pacific region has actively promoted and disseminated the new concept of security which is adapted to the ongoing global developments and is based on mutual trust, mutual benefit, equality and cooperation. In so doing, the Asia-Pacific region has also played a major positive role in international security. Such principles as those respecting each other's sovereignty, building up mutual trust and treating each other as equals, settling disputes through peaceful and diplomatic means, seeking common interests, while duly addressing other countries' concerns, are being established as the consensus among most of the countries in the region. All this has helped the region, to play an increasingly constructive and important role in the international affairs.

As a rapidly rising region, the Asia-Pacific should certainly join hands with all the other parts of the world and strive hard together with them to promote the common security and prosperity in our global village. [10]

India and Asia-Pacific Community

It is almost a conventional wisdom now, that the centre of gravity of global politics has shifted from Europe to the Asia-Pacific in recent years especially with the rise of China and India, the gradual assertion by Japan of its military profile, and a significant shift in the US global force posture in favour of the Asia-Pacific. The debate now is, whether Asia-Pacific will witness rising tensions and conflicts in the coming years as a result of various powers jockeying for influence in the region or whether the forces of economic globalization and multilateralism will lead to peace and stability. It is, of course, difficult to predict or to perceive as to when exactly the major powers in Asia-Pacific such as China, India and Japan would rise and grapple with a plethora of issues that confront any rising power in the international system. But what is clear is, that all major powers are now re-evaluating their policy options *vis-à-vis* the Pacific.

The Australian Prime Minister, Kevin Rudd's proposal dated 4 June 2008, for the establishment of an Asia-Pacific Community (APC) by 2020, besides giving further momentum to the growing demand for a new regional architecture in the Asia-Pacific, befits the region's changing geo-political reality in the 21st century and has evoked mixed response. The proposal comes at a time, when the Asia-Pacific is already struggling to manage and to sustain the existing frameworks of cooperation–ARF, APEC, and EAS. The proposed APC has raised various questions, whose answers will also bring forth the objectives and implications of such a proposal. What are the issues in the Asia-Pacific, which require to be addressed in such a grouping? Why should the region have another institution, when there are already a number of institutions operating in the region? What does the proposed APC seek to achieve that is utterly different from the declared objectives of the existing regional institutions? How does India figure in the proposed framework and is it likely to address its interests?

The economic landscape of the Asia-Pacific is rapidly changing and the single-most important change is the rise of Asia as the global economic powerhouse. The Asia-Pacific, which represents roughly half of the global population, contributes around 37 percent of global GDP, in terms of Purchasing Power Parity (PPP). Approximately, 40 percent of the global growth in 2007 came from Asia. It is expected that Asia will constitute about 45 percent of the global GDP, one-third of the global trade and 25 percent of the global military spending, by 2020.

The noticeable feature in the Asia-Pacific is the simultaneous growth of cooperative engagements between different countries or groups of countries. The region has witnessed a sudden upsurge in the efforts directed towards bilateral, sub-regional and multilateral economic integration. Almost every country in the Asia-Pacific is engaged in FTA negotiations with other countries. The formation of the EAS, is an important highlight of the pan-Asia- Pacific engagement process. The emergence of new power centres in Asia, necessitates their greater representation in the global politico-strategic deliberations and the greater global attention towards Asian affairs.

There are three existing mechanisms–APEC, ARF and EAS–which claim to offer an overarching platform for dealing with different sets of challenges facing the Asia-Pacific region. The APEC, formed in 1989, seeks to promote economic cooperation among the countries of the Asia-Pacific and to regulate the economic affairs of the region. It excludes India and has recently decided against keeping itself open to additional members in the near future. However, it has not been very effective over the years, because of the reduced Australian influence in the Asia-Pacific. The ARF, formed in 1994, aims to address security challenges facing the region, through transparency and confidence building measures. However, the institution has proved to be a mere talk-shop and failed to deliver the goods practically on every issue.

Finally, the EAS, formed in 2005, is relatively new and its mandate has remained limited to the issues of energy, culture, economic cooperation and so on. USA is not a member of the EAS. Further, the organization faces the spectre of being sidelined by the ASEAN+3 frameworks, involving ten countries of ASEAN, China, Japan and South Korea. Now the question arises that if the three above mentioned institutions have not been able to deliver the goods, what is the guarantee that the fourth one will be successful? Can we not modify or reform the existing structures rather than adding another one to the list of non-performing institutions? These questions bring us to examine different aspects of the proposed Asia-Pacific Community (APC).

First, all major powers in the region need to be accommodated in a single architecture, which can best represent the changing strategic equations in the Asia-Pacific. In terms of membership, while APEC excludes India and the EAS excludes USA, the APC brings both of them together. In other words, the APC recognizes India as an important player in the Asia-Pacific, and calls for continued US presence in the strategic deliberations of the Asia-Pacific. Second, instead of each organisation deliberating on different issues, the region needs to look at the challenges holistically to be able to deliberate effectively on all types of issues, such as traditional and non-traditional security issues, economic and political issues. The APC combines the security-exclusive functions of ARF, economic objectives of the APEC, and new emerging issues, such as, climate change and energy, as discussed under the EAS. In other words, the APC offers a comprehensive package, proposing to deliberate on significant political, security and economic issues on a single platform. Third, the Asia-Pacific needs to learn to function in the way, the European Union does. In other words, the APC will function as a building block towards the formation of a European Union model, in the region.

India's relationship with the multilateral cooperative frameworks in the Asia-Pacific has been a mixed baggage. India has not found any entry into the APEC. India's membership of EAS received contestation from different quarters, and its contribution to the security discourses in the ARF has remained minimal. Ever since its inception, the EAS has been sidelined by the ASEAN+3 grouping, which incorporates ASEAN-10 and three East Asian countries–China, Japan and South Korea.

The large-scale effort towards economic integration in the Asia-Pacific has remained confined to the ASEAN+3 frameworks, rendering the participation of India, Australia and New Zealand under the EAS, merely symbolic in nature. At the same time, India has been able to develop a long-term and wide-ranging cooperation with ASEAN, which now occupies an important place in India's politico-strategic calculations in the Asia- Pacific. In fact, ASEAN is the only multilateral platform, in which India has participated effectively, which, in turn, has facilitated India's representation in the ARF and EAS. India's participation in any new multilateral framework, should not be seen as a factor diluting the strategic importance of ASEAN in the Asia-Pacific.

Therefore, India should welcome any new regional framework in the Asia-Pacific, which aims at broadening the geographical scope of efforts towards integration. Given the nature of strategic partnership with ASEAN, India's competition with China for strategic space in Asia and Africa, and its growing relations with the US, India should support any such proposal that seeks the continued presence of the US in the Asia Pacific, taking every care to see, that the latter does not adversely affect India's relationship with ASEAN. The proposed APC, in its current form, ensures both the strategic imperatives of India.

There are profound changes taking place in the Asia-Pacific, which have begun influencing global affairs and will continue to do so in the near future. Therefore, the region needs a new framework, which is all inclusive and efficient enough to represent the region thoroughly. The proposed APC does not offer anything exceptional and can be viewed as an addition of USA to the EAS. Again, it is the same old framework, with some difference in packaging. Whether it is a combination of the EAS and USA, or a revised fusion of APEC and India, it should be beneficial to India's strategic presence in the Asia-Pacific. [11]

Conclusion

The Asia-Pacific is the most dynamic and promising region in the context of global economy. It is a region with worthwhile potential and is full of hope especially as peace, development and cooperation remain actively associated with it, to form its general trend. As long as all the parties concerned act in the spirit of setting aside their differences to allow the common ground to expand enough to accommodate their combined efforts to seek peaceful and negotiated solutions to the otherwise still-vexed historical issues and to the current disputes of interest, Asia-Pacific will surely be able to enhance mutual trust, achieve win-win progress through cooperation and usher in an era of radiant future in the region. The choices that nations in the region opt for or make, will affect the way the events take shape in Asia. The habit of making right choices would enable the nations to move from potential though internecine confrontation to fruitful and genuine collaboration and serene cohabitation, even as the elements of healthy competition will be allowed to make the impact of their legitimate presence felt, in terms of yielding the desired results from time to time.

End Notes

1. Ummu Salma Bava, "India's Role in Emerging World Order," *FES*, New Delhi, March 2007.
2. www.mofa.go.jp/region/asia-paci.
3. www.en.wikipedia.org/wiki/economy_of_india.
4. Takenori, "The World as India Sees It," p. 6.

5. *India Quarterly*, Vol. I, January-March 2006.
6. Naidu, G.V.C., "Whither the Look East Policy: India and Southeast Asia," *Strategic Analysis*, Vol. 28, No. 2 (April-June 2004).
7. Lica Curtis "India's Expanding Role in Asia: Adapting to Raising Power Status," *Back grounder*, (February 20, 2007); Published by Heritage Foundation.
8. Subash Kapila, "Russia-India-China Strategic Triangle Contours Emerge," *South Asia Analysis Group paper. No. 1424*, 21 June 2005.
9. www.saarc-sec.org.
10. Stephen J. Blank, *Natural Allies? Regional Security in Asia and Prospects for Indo-American Strategic Cooperation*, p. 66.
11. Vibhanshu Shekar; "Asia-Pacific Community Options and Opportunities for India," *IPCS*, New Delhi, No. 74, June 2008.

15

Asian Approach to Economic Development: The Case of East Asia's Four Tigers

B. Srinivasulu and V. Ramesh Babu

Among other things, renaissance implies innovative application of culture, learning and skills. This is happening in an unprecedented way in East Asia. It has brought about profound consequences for the region and for the world.

Ong Keng Yong
Secretary-General of ASEAN

The Four Asian Tigers (Hong Kong, Singapore, South Korea and Taiwan) pursued an export-driven model of economic development. These countries and territories focused on developing goods for export to highly-industrialized nations. Domestic consumption was discouraged through government policies such as high tariffs. Perceiving education as a means of improving productivity, the Four Asian Tigers focused on improving the education system at all levels and placed heavy emphasis on ensuring that all children attended elementary education and compulsory high school education. [1] Money was also spent on improving the college and university systems.

Since the Four Asian Tigers were relatively poor during the 1960s they had an abundance of cheap labour. Coupled with educational reform, they were able to leverage this combination into a cheap, yet productive workforce. The Four Asian Tigers committed to egalitarianism in the form of land reform, to promote property rights and to ensure that agricultural workers would not become disgruntled. Also, policies of agricultural subsidies and tariffs on agricultural products were implemented. The common characteristics of the Four Asian Tigers are: focus on exports to richer industrialized nations; trade surplus with aforementioned countries; sustained rate of double-digit growth for decades; non-democratic and relatively authoritarian political systems during the early years; and high savings rate. [2]

Table 15.1 shows the ranks of GDP (by nominal) of South Korea, Taiwan, Hong Kong and Singapore given by International Monetary Fund (IMF) and the World Bank (WB) in 2006. According to the IMF, the ranks are 12th (South Korea), 22nd (Taiwan), 36th (Hong Kong) and 44th (Singapore).

Table 15.1: List of Countries by GDP (nominal)

2006 List by the IMF			2006 List by the WB		
Rank	Country	**GDP (Millions of US $)**	**Rank**	**Country**	**GDP (Millions of US $)**
-	Gross world product	48,144,466	-	Gross world product	48,244,879
1	USA	13,244,550	1	USA	13,201,819
2.	Japan	4,367,459	2.	Japan	4,340,133
3.	Germany	4,367,459	3.	Germany	2,906,681
4.	China	2,360,113	4.	China	2,668,071
5.	UK	2,373,685	5.	UK	2,345,015
6.	France	2,231,631	6.	France	2,230,721
7.	Italy	1,852,585	7.	Italy	1,844,749
8.	Canada	1,269,096	8.	Canada	1,251,463
9.	Spain	1,225,750	9.	Spain	1,223,988
10.	Brazil	1,067,706	10.	Brazil	1,067,962
11.	Russia	979,048	11.	Russia	986,940
12.	South Korea	888,267	12.	India	906,268
13.	India	886,867	13.	South Korea	888,024
15.	Australia	754,816	15.	Australia	768,178
22.	Taiwan	355,708	22.	Poland	338,733
36.	Hong Kong	189,538	35.	Hong Kong	189,798
39.	Malaysia	150,923	37.	Malaysia	148,940
44.	Singapore	132,155	40.	Singapore	132,158
58.	Vietnam	60,995	57.	Vietnam	60,884
121.	Cambodia	7,096	119.	Cambodia	7,193
143.	Fiji	2,977	141.	Fiji	2,822

Sources: 1. International Monetary Fund, World Economic Outlook Database, April 2007: Countries, World and EU, Data for the year 2006. 2. World Bank-July 2007, Data for the year 2006.

Miraculous Growth

The growth and development in many East Asian countries were hailed as an economic miracle. The standouts included the 4-Asian Tigers' growth rates of real per capita gross domestic product from 1960 to 1995 were around 6 percent per year, right behind were Indonesia, Malaysia, Thailand, and China. These performances placed this East Asian group at the top of the world's growth list.

The Asian reputation has suffered recently because of financial crises and recessions. These crises did highlight some policy shortcomings, such as unwise credit subsidies and deficient regulation of financial markets. But the negative reaction has been sharply overdone. In comparison with typical developing countries, government policies in most of the East Asian countries have been fiscally responsible, pro-market, and, hence, reasonable. Yet, even before the recent setbacks, the 4-Tigers' economic record was challenged in two well-known studies by Alwyn Young. [3]

Alwyn Young argued that the high rates of economic growth reflected very little technological progress. Growth occurred mainly because of extraordinary rates of capital accumulation, some in the form of education (human capital), but most in machines and buildings. The lack of technological progress was surprising because, even if these countries were inventing little, they should have been benefiting from the superior techniques they were imitating from the world's most advanced countries. Historically, long-term economic growth has been sustained by significant increases in productivity due to technological and organizational change. The accumulation of huge amounts of capital and labour can work for a time, but ultimately must be backed by improvements in technology. [4]

In Singapore, Alwyn's analysis suggests that rapid growth was supported almost entirely by physical and human capital accumulation. In fact, investment was so high that the rate of measured productivity growth was actually negative. To Young, the high rate of investment persisted only because of the government's policies of forced saving and implicit subsidies to foreign capital. Alwyn's thesis was popularized and misinterpreted by economic journalists who even compared some Asian economic policies to the high-investment programs of Stalin's Soviet Union.

A study by Chang-Tai Hsieh [5] published by the University of California at Berkeley challenges key parts of Alwyn's conclusions on productivity growth. The most dramatic revisions apply to Singapore, where Hsieh notes that observed rates of return on investment have been roughly stable since the mid-1970s, not declining as Alwyn's calculations would imply. Combine that fact with Singapore's robust growth in real wages, and Hsieh shows that measured productivity growth had to be positive-an estimated 2.2 percent per year-rather than the 0.7 percent reported by Alwyn. According to Hsieh, Alwyn's analysis went wrong because of its reliance on Singapore's government national account statistics, which dramatically overstated the growth of the capital stock. Hsieh also found that Taiwan's productivity growth was better than that previously assessed by Young (3.7 percent vs. 2.1 percent), but got less dramatic results for South Korea (1.5 percent vs. 1.7 percent) and Hong Kong (2.7 percent vs. 2.3 percent). [6]

Even these higher estimates on productivity growth for Singapore and Taiwan understate the contribution of technological progress to economic growth. Improvements in technology raise the demand for physical capital (machines and buildings) and human capital (highly educated workers). But the resulting expansions of capital input are filtered out in the usual calculations of productivity growth. A full explanation of these countries' growth would attribute more to the contribution of technology than Alwyn's original thesis. It is improvements in technology that explain why so much capital accumulation could have occurred, especially in Singapore, without encountering diminishing returns. Thus, overall, we continue to have ample grounds to view the East

Asian growth and technological performances as miraculous.

The slower pace of output growth in several East Asian economies has been accompanied by much more pronounced differences in investment spending across economies. While investment spending growth in China has continued running at double digit rates, in many of the other middle and high income economies of the region the recovery of investment after the 1997-98 crisis and the 2001 slowdown has often been weak and erratic. This has led to very different policy concerns around the region. Unlike policy makers in China, who are concerned to ensure that the present investment boom there does not lead to overheating, policy makers in many of the NIEs (Newly Industrializing Economies) and middle income Southeast Asian economies are concerned about the causes of continued relative weak investment. [7] Table 15.2 shows the real fixed investment growth of Southeast Asian countries and also 4-tigers.

Table 15.2: East Asia Real Fixed Investment Growth

Country	1980-89	1990-96	1997-01	2002-06
China	8.2	15.2	9.9	12.4
South East Asia				
Indonesia	8.9	11.5	-5.9	6.3
Malaysia	7.0	17.7	-6.6	3.3
Philippines	0.4	5.3	0.2	1.0
Thailand	8.5	12.3	-14.5	7.7
Asian 4-Tigers				
Hong Kong, China	5.3	9.3	-0.2	2.5
South Korea	8.6	11.5	-1.8	2.1
Singapore	6.3	13.1	0.6	3.0
Taiwan (China)	7.4	9.2	1.7	1.4

Source: World Bank (2008): World Development Report 2008, Compound annual average growth.

Re-Assessing the Health of the Asian Tigers

Until mid-1997, the rapid growth of the East Asian

economies was widely regarded as a miracle. This growth had propelled Asia to such heightened importance in the world economy that some already anointed the next millennium 'The Pacific Century'. The Asian 'Tigers' economies and the 'Tiger Cubs' (Indonesia, Malaysia, Thailand and the Philippines) are boasted phenomenal rates of economic growth. The impact reverberated around the world. Because of the global nature of the economy, the cost of supplies, of labour, and the prices of competitive products were affected for many businesses throughout the world. The deflation in East Asia helped keep inflation low in the US. Now, with the East Asian recovery apparently underway, the dynamics will change. Interest rates, prices, and competition all may be different. Business people everywhere need to keep informed about these changes and plan accordingly.

When the Thai government was forced to abandon the peg of the baht to the dollar on July 2, 1997, it sounded an alarm throughout the region. Investor sentiment changed overnight. Within days, speculators attacked the currencies of Malaysia, Indonesia, and the Philippines. Not even the grown-up East Asian economic tigers, Hong Kong and Korea, were spared from the attack. [8] The currency crisis spread rapidly throughout the region and beyond and finally grew to include much of the emerging market arena.

While the countries which were mostly affected by the crisis differed in important respects, they also shared some important characteristics. They generally had policies fostering low levels of inflation and fiscal discipline by the government, and all had experienced rapid economic growth in the previous years. The openness of their economies, and high savings rates, combined with the low cost of production, encouraged foreign investment. In the early 1990's, what had been a reasonably modest inflow of capital increased more than six-fold. In the early 1990's, the Federal Reserve set the US interest rate artificially low to stimulate the American economy. Given that the exchange rate of the Tigers was tied to the dollar, and the growth rate of their economies was strong, they looked very attractive. More money flowed in than could be profitably used at modest risk. Much of the investment moved into ill-conceived real estate projects. These projects, in turn, became the collateral for a great deal of debt.

When the dollar began to recover in mid-1995, the exports of the tigers became less competitive. Pressures on their currencies grew because their underlying economies were not growing in tandem with the dollar's rise. The pace of capital inflows slowed and investors had difficulty in obtaining credit. Local exporters, who might have increased their sales abroad in a period of devaluation, faced fierce competition from the same region in which they had tried to export their way out of the crisis. Furthermore, with the entire region under pressure, exporters from several countries were competing with each other to try to export their way out of the crisis. The shift in perceived future investment risk impacted the stock markets of these countries, and pressure mounted even further, especially on countries with large current account deficits. Then the real estate bubbles burst, and the drop in real estate values left banks holding huge portfolios of bad property loans. The risk of default sparked a wider financial crisis.

There were, however, some key domestic factors that also contributed significantly to East Asia's financial crisis. These included inherent weaknesses in the financial systems of these countries: little regulation and lax supervision, little reporting of financial data that would allow outsiders to evaluate a business, poor management of risk, and continuous lending to politically well-connected firms, sometimes at the government's direct behest. There was often little due diligence regarding the creditworthiness of the borrower or the economic merit of the project for politically-favoured enterprises. Particularly in Korea, domestic enterprises were dominated by poorly-managed, but politically well connected, conglomerates that were highly financed by debt. These conglomerates soaked up most of the available credit, leaving little left for small businesses, thus creating an unbalanced industrial structure that found itself in competition with both the low-wage economies in the region and with Japan. [9]

Prognosis

In one sense it could be easy to renew one's faith in Asian miracles when observing the rate of economic recovery in these economies over the past year. Factories are scrambling to keep up with soaring export orders and increasing domestic demand. Stores are jammed and corporate earnings are surging. The Institute of Developing Economies forecast in mid-December of 1999 that, excluding Japan, East Asia's ten biggest economies would expand 6.5 percent in 2000, up from 1 percent in 1998, when six of the economies actually contracted. Table 15.3 provides an overview of growth rates of real of ASEAN nations.

Table 15.3: Growth Rates of Real GDP (Percent)

Country	2000	2001	2002	2003	2004	2005	2006	2007
India	4.4	5.8	3.8	8.5	7.5	9.4	9.6	8.7
South East Asia								
Brunei	2.8	2.7	3.9	2.9	0.5	0.4	4.4	0.6
Cambodia	8.4	7.7	7.0	8.5	10.3	13.3	10.8	10.2
Indonesia	4.9	3.8	4.3	4.8	5.0	5.7	5.5	6.3
Lao PDR	5.8	5.8	5.9	5.8	6.9	7.3	8.3	7.5
Malaysia	8.9	0.5	5.4	5.8	6.8	5.0	5.9	6.3
Myanmar	13.8	11.3	12.0	13.8	13.6	13.6	12.7	-
Philippines	4.4	1.8	4.4	4.9	6.4	5.0	5.4	7.2
Thailand	4.8	2.2	5.3	7.1	6.3	4.5	5.1	4.8
Viet Nam	6.8	6.9	7.1	7.3	7.8	8.4	8.2	8.5
Asian 4-Tigers								
Hong Kong	8.0	0.5	1.8	3.0	8.5	7.1	7.0	6.4
South Korea	8.5	3.8	7.0	3.1	4.7	4.2	5.1	5.0
Singapore	10.1	-2.3	4.0	3.5	9.0	7.3	8.2	7.7
Taiwan	5.8	-2.2	4.6	3.5	6.2	4.2	4.9	5.7

Source: Asian Development Bank (2008): Key Indicators for the Asia and Pacific, Manila.

Yet, while the worst part of the crisis seems to be over, the risk of setbacks cannot be excluded. Some fundamental problems remain. The region is still suffering from the collapse in asset prices. While the smaller companies are recovering, the large conglomerates still have excess capacity. There is an escalation of corporate bankruptcies, and even the overall rate of growth has slowed down from its peak in mid-summer, 1999. Much will depend on the global scenario. The young Tigers cannot grow themselves out of recession domestically. They do not have sufficient aggregate demand. The credit crunch will hamper their attempts to keep themselves out of recession, but the key issue is whether there will be a slowdown in the US economy and, if so, whether the economies of Japan and Europe can sustain enough growth to compensate. The rise in global oil prices could also make inflation a major concern. [10]

In the longer term, the key issue is whether these countries are willing to make the difficult, but crucial reforms in their financial and political systems. There is widespread agreement that there must be much more transparency in their banking systems. Adopting generally accepted accounting standards is part of that. Crony capitalism, where loans are made on the basis of political connections rather than on the merits of the project, will have to give way to much better risk management. New regulations are needed along with a legal infrastructure that will enforce them. Finally, there must be openness to competition in the banking industry. Foreign banks can bring new technology and people experienced in data management, risk control, internal oversight, and external supervision. Prior to the crisis, most of the countries in the region restricted the entry of foreign-owned banks. That has begun to change.

South Korea is now actively promoting small and medium-sized businesses. The newly elected government in Indonesia is redirecting economic resources from capital-intensive industries such as aerospace and automobiles to labour-intensive manufacturing and agribusiness. At the same time it is investing more in education. And Thailand has been lowering barriers to foreign investment in retail and consumer finance.

Structural reforms are painful. They involve loss to people who have benefited under the previous system, especially the politically well connected. On the other end of the economic scale, they often translate into unemployment and social pain that may cause social upheaval and rioting. Yet, unless progress is made on structural reforms, foreign capital will not flow into the region. It will require political resources and courage to stick with these reforms. [11]

One of the real problems of a quick partial recovery is that the impetus for structural reform could be sidetracked. For those countries willing to make the changes-or which are forced by events they cannot control to make such changes-the prospects are positive. Some important macroeconomic fundamentals are in place. The region has a high savings rate. The labour force is young, well educated, hard working, and disciplined. Real estate prices have dropped to realistic level. Asia is still a cheap export base as well as home turf to a burgeoning consumer class. Most of the governments are pursuing free market policies, and democratic movements are getting stronger.

The question is whether the tigers will decide to stay in the arena and compete in the free market or will be tempted to crawl back into their dens and hope for a different kind of miracle. The answer to that question will affect not only businesses in those countries, but those around the world.

General Conclusion

The Four Asian Tigers were strongly affected by the 1997 Asian financial crisis, which impacted each Tiger to varying degrees. While Taiwan was not as strongly affected, South Korea was badly battered by the crisis. However, South Korea rose up to become the 9th largest economy in the world (2007 standard) and Taiwan remained as the 23rd largest economy in the world. Because of the focus on export-driven growth, many countries were caught in a game of currency devaluation. The current criticism of the Four Asian Tigers is that these economies focus exclusively on export-demand, at the cost of import-demand. Thus, these economies are heavily reliant on the economic health of their targeted export nations.

In addition, these nations have met difficulties after they lost their initial competitive edge, cheap productive labour. India and China have now emerged as fast-growing economies based on cheap labour, largely replacing the Tigers. Some economies were becoming overheated, stock prices were overvalued, property prices were sky-high and investors were jittery and nervous. Because of the structural weaknesses in the regulatory framework, once capital flight began, the stock market nosedived and the major Asian currencies depreciated significantly. This caused social unrest, political instability, regime change and financial bailing out by the International Monetary Fund (IMF). This also gave impetus to some Asian governments to impose capital controls to restrict currency outflows and maintain monetary and financial stability. Taiwan created legislation requiring all outgoing capital transfers to be declared. However, there were no direct restrictions.

Since the beginning of the crisis, most of the Tiger economies have become financially stable with resilient institutions and companies and regulatory frameworks in place to prevent another crisis. This has also shown many Asian governments that the easy and predictable prosperity of export-led growth and cheap labour costs won't last forever. To better compete with the emerging manufacturing giants like China and India, they will have to create new industries, move up the value-add chain and create stronger service sectors in their economies.

End Notes

1. Collins, Susan M. and Bosworth, Barry "Economic Growth in East Asia: Accumulation versus Assimilation," Brookings

Papers on Economic Activity, (1996).

2. Krugman, Paul, "The Myth of Asia's Miracle," *Foreign Affairs*, Vol. 73, No. 6, November/December 1994.
3. Alwyn Young, "The Tyranny of Numbers: Confronting the Statistical Realities of the East Asian Growth Experience", *Quarterly Journal of Economics*, No. 110, August 1995.
4. *Ibid.*
5. Chang-Tai Hsieh "What Explains the Industrial Revolution in East Asia? Evidence from the Factor Markets," *American Economic Review*, (Pittsburgh, PA), June 2002.
6. *Ibid.*
7. Ermisch, John F. and Huff, W. G., "Hyper growth in an East Asian NIC: Public Policy and Capital Accumulation in Singapore," *World Development*, Vol. 27, No. 1, January 1999.
8. Adams F.G., "The East Asian Development Ladder: Virtuous Circles and Linkages in East Asian Economic Development," in F. G. Adams and Sh. Ichimura (eds), *East Asian Development: Will the East Asian Growth Miracle Survive*, Westport (Conn.), Praeger, London, 1998).
9. Kim, Jong-Il and Lau, Lawrence, "The Sources of Economic Growth of the East Asian Newly Industrialized Countries," *Journal of the Japanese and International Economics*, (Tokyo), September, Vol. 8, No. 3, 1994.
10. Ito T., "Growth, Crisis, and the Future of Economic Recovery in East Asia," in J. E. Stiglitz and Sh. Yusuf (eds.): *Rethinking the East Asian Miracle*, (Oxford University Press, Oxford, (2001).
11. World Bank, *The East Asian Miracle: Economic Growth and Public Policy*, (World Bank with Oxford University Press, Oxford, 1993).

16

Kevin Rudd and His Security Architecture Proposal for the Asia Pacific

Rajaram Panda

Background

Regionalism in the Asia Pacific region as a concept is not a recent phenomenon as it dates back to the early 1980s. Dr. Okita Saburo, the architect of Japan's Income Doubling Plan of the 1960s, and Sir John Crawford of Australia, the architect for opening up of Australia's trade with Japan in the late 1950s, were two major visionaries whose contribution to foster regional economic cooperation in the Asia Pacific region remains unparalleled. Masayoshi Ohira, the then Prime Minister of Japan, a product of Hitotsubashi University, was the first Japanese leader who saw some merit in the idea of a Pacific regional economic grouping and was influenced by Okita's idea. Ohira sent Prof. Kiyoshi Kojima of Hitotsubashi University to travel to the countries in the Asia Pacific region, to sell this idea.

It was around this time that Okita Saburo and Sir John Crawford forged a fruitful friendship with this common interest. In fact, Crawford was thinking and writing about the need in these terms in the 1930s. Together with Okita, he inspired the Pacific Economic Cooperation Council in 1980 (PECC), which eventually paved the way for Asia Pacific Economic Council by 1989. Since then, Prof. Peter Drysdale and Prof. Ross Garnaut of the Australian National University have been pursuing the idea and have been providing intellectual inputs on the idea of institution formation in the Asia Pacific region.

Ever since other valuable forums and institutions have also

emerged, some cantered on ASEAN. The way they are all related to each other, is not yet clear. There is a fresh idea on this line of thinking that has emerged from Australia after the Labour party captured power during the November 2007 election and the following accession of Kevin Rudd to the office of prime minister. Rudd is of the view that none of the existing organisations in the region addresses all the political dimensions of cooperation. Several of them do not span the Pacific and many do not include a new emerging economic giant, India. Therefore, on 4 June 2008, Rudd declared that it was the time to build an Asia Pacific Community and in doing so, he was only following the footsteps of many, as mentioned earlier, who have been striving to build such a community for quite sometime. The purpose of this paper is to describe Rudd's proposal and to examine its feasibility. It will also be examined as to how and whether the proposal will be received in the countries in the region. First of all, it is necessary to highlight the challenges that Rudd faces in the short run.

Rudd's Challenges

Australian foreign policy has suddenly reached a stage in the Asia Pacific region after the Labour Party headed by Kevin Rudd staged a sort of coup when he defeated during the elections held in November 2007, the conservative coalition headed by John Howard who had governed Australia for over a decade. Even before the results were declared, pundits in Canberra were debating whether the Rudd government stays clear of the exciting promises of past Labour high-flyers Gough Whitlam, Bob Hawke and Paul Keating or if Rudd would try to copy the conservative's line that has given Australia an unprecedented prosperity.

Though Rudd sold his policy of economic conservatism to the voters perfectly well and obtained the voters' approval to rule the country, his foreign policy assumed a strong Asia-Pacific focus. While Howard was a veteran globe-trotter, Rudd was a successful former diplomat. Both supported the long-term alliances with the United States and Japan, upbeat trade with prospering China and India, armed support against terrorism in Afghanistan and Iraq and the material aid in the Asia Pacific. While most Australians remained in two minds, whether to stick to the tried and proven or to back an incompletely delineated change, it was the swing voters that determined the outcome in favour of the Labour. After four terms in Canberra, prompted by the prospect of a fair chance of securing a fifth term, the Conservative banked on its record to regain the office, albeit with a starkly reduced majority. But, that was not to be the final count.

Having assumed office, Rudd faced the issue of critical choices. His real challenge has been on the foreign policy front, in particular, how to deal with the contentious nuclear issue. In the wake of impending Indo-US civil nuclear cooperation agreement and the pending clearance by the 45-member Nuclear Suppliers' Group (NSG), Australia's vote will be critical. The NSG coordinates export controls on sensitive nuclear and dual-use of equipment, materials and technology to ensure their use for maintenance of peace as well.. NSG guidelines ensure that apart from the five "declared" nuclear powers, such materials are provided only to signatories of the Nuclear Non-Proliferation Treaty (NPT).

The US is seeking an exemption for India in the NSG, even though India is not a signatory to the discriminatory NPT. On the NSG, Australia's vote is critical. Australia is one of the strongest supporters of the NPT regime, and has 40 percent of the world's proven uranium reserves. Rudd has taken the stand that Australia would not sell uranium to any country that is not an NPT signatory and therefore India may become ineligible to import uranium under the Labour government in Canberra. No sooner Rudd came to power, than he overturned Howard government's commitment to supply uranium to India, a decision Rudd might regret as Australia might not be able to enjoy its comparative advantage in uranium exports for long in a world hungry for nuclear power to replace fossil fuels.

Having worked before in China as a consultant for the global financial advisory firm KPMG and being fluent in the Mandarin, Rudd is aware of the fact that riding the resources boom is essential if Australia is to ensure continued prosperity. But going by the argument that Australia will have no hesitation to sell uranium to a totalitarian, potentially unstable China (an NPT signatory) but will refuse to sell it to a democratic, stable India, whose rapid industrialization needs access to efficient low-carbon forms of energy, would seem contradictory to Australian foreign policy under Rudd. Australia still feels that the draft India waiver circulated among the NSG members considering exemption for India, carries amendments that are cosmetic and not as per its demands. New Delhi believes that the changes made in the draft should address the concerns the sceptic countries have entertained.

Viewed from a different perspective, Australia would share the US line in viewing India as a strategic partner and a reliable ally in America's growing strategic competition with China. Rudd ought to be also aware that the NPT regime is already breaking down. For example, in defiance of the so-called international community, North Korea has already tested the nuclear weapons, and Iran is intent on acquiring them. And, if Iran does really acquire nuclear weapons, it is plausible to believe that Saudi Arabia, Egypt and Turkey will soon follow suit.

The changing international environment and the change in priorities on resource economics in the wake of heightening global demand for essential raw materials and energy to sustain uninterrupted economic growth in emerging economies, may put Australia in a difficult situation in which a policy review on the issue of nuclear security may become inevitable and inescapable. Not that Australia has lost faith in the US as an ally, but a close ally such as Japan is openly questioning whether it should continue to rely on the US for its nuclear security. Closer home, Indonesia might find confronted by a rising China and a rising India, both armed with nuclear weapons. Therefore, the possible revival of a Gaullist approach reminiscent of conservative Prime Minister John Gorton days (1969-1971) which believed that Australia could not afford to entrust its nuclear security to the allies who might prove unreliable in a crisis, may not be unthinkable.

Notwithstanding the stand that Australia has taken on the nuclear issue, Rudd wants to be projected as a visionary in the Asia Pacific region and as an architect of institution building. The paramount issue that Rudd has placed on the table for the future of regional cooperation in Asia and in the Pacific, is the issue of how to build a political and security framework beyond the framework of economic cooperation that the existing architecture however incomplete helps to secure. [1]

Rudd's Proposal for the Asia Pacific

Rudd put forward a concept during a speech addressed to the Asia Society AustralAsia Centre on 4 June 2008, just days before he had left on a week-long visit to Japan and Indonesia. In his lecture entitled as "It's Time to Build an Asia Pacific Community", Rudd proposed a regional architecture for the wider Asia Pacific region. He argued that there is a need for a strong and effective regional institution to "underpin an open, peaceful, stable, prosperous and sustainable region". He stressed the importance of the regional institutions in addressing collective challenges that no country could address alone.

Rudd's vision for an Asia Pacific Community embraces "a regional institution which spans the entire Asia Pacific region–including the US, Japan, China, India, Indonesia and the other states of the region" and "a regional institution which is able to engage in the full spectrum of dialogue, cooperation and action on economic and political matters and future challenges related to security". Rudd appointed the foreign affairs secretary and a one-time ambassador to Indonesia Richard Woolcott, as Australia's envoy to visit the capitals of the wider region and to discuss his proposal.

This is the beginning of a serious intellectual discussion of what the necessary elements of this might be for a region whose defining characteristic is pluralism–pluralism of political systems of intuitions, religions, and of course, stages of economic development. Thirty years ago, the economists concerned about securing politically the growing economic integration within a pluralist East Asia and Pacific economy, struggled with the same issues from this perspective. [2]

The earlier debate about economic cooperation arrangements can usefully inform the current debate about constructing a stronger political and security architecture to reinforce what it is there in the economic front. Rudd's initiative should be seen as an invitation to other leaders, policy makers, and thinkers in the region, to join in a serious discussion about how best the Asia Pacific region could be organized. Had Rudd come up with a fully-baked proposal, the exercise could be self-defeating. Evolving regionalism in Asia Pacific requires that all parties concerned, should have an active part in the process, especially in the shaping of a new vision in the region. In fact, Indonesia should support Rudd's initiative and the process of deliberations that will follow from it. [3]

The new architecture can be built on two main pillars. The one pillar is that of a revitalized APEC with a strong ASEAN Plus Three (APT) as its core East Asia. This forms the economic pillar of the regional architecture. The immediate question is how to involve India in this process. The other pillar of the political security is that of a transformed East Asia Summit (EAS) that is supported by the ASEAN Regional Forum (ARF) at the working level. The EAS is already proclaimed as a leaders-led forum to discuss strategic issues.

The central issue is whether it is possible to construct a concert including the new powers in Asia to get engaged with the established power cantered on the United States, as the structure of regional power undergoes dramatic change. This is important to the future of regional political stability in the intrinsically unstable process of transition in the balance of regional political power.

Critics in Australia, not only from the Opposition but also the former Prime Ministers Bob Hawke and Paul Keating, were quick in pointing out that Rudd's vision has not been well thought out. Opposition's foreign affairs spokesman Andrew Robb said that the plan was presumptuous. He said Rudd's first job is not to make series of pronouncements about a grand architecture for the region, telling China, Indonesia, Japan and India how they will be organized as a region by Australia in the next 20 years. However, criticism apart, it seems too early to come to a definite conclusion about the feasibility of the proposal before making an in-depth study. In a globalizing world and with the integration of economies of more countries with the global economy, the proposal may not fall short of merit.

Rudd's proposal is not the first one. Since 2006, the PECC has embarked on a study on the Regional Institutional Architecture (RIA) for the Asia Pacific and has begun discussing this in a number of regional forums. It is significant that Rudd's initiative will help elevate the discussion to the highest level of policy making in the region. It is also significant that Rudd is prepared to organize a process towards a new consensus in the region, to further advance the one that was reached in 1989 with the creation of APEC. Woolcott's visit to the capitals of the region to sell the idea might lead to a high-level conference of government and non-government representatives to advance the proposal. Woolcott was instrumental in drafting the 1989 consensus. Rudd is hopeful that Woolcott will complete the work he began on Prime Minister Bob Hawke's behalf, 20 years ago.

What are the main ideas in Rudd's proposal? His first premise is that global economic and strategic weight is shifting to Asia. With this, the changes and challenges for Asia will also be great. The challenges as described by Rudd include:

enhancing a sense of security community; developing a capacity to deal with terrorism, natural disasters and disease; enhancing non-discriminatory and open trading regimes across the region in support of global institutions; and providing long term energy, resource and food security. The second premise is that none of the existing regional mechanisms (APEC, ARF, the ASEAN Plus Three, and the East Asia Summit) "as currently configured are capable of achieving these purposes". Hence, there is a dire need for a new regional architecture. The proposed Asia Pacific Community is not envisioned to be an economic union, not a monetary union, not even a custom union and certainly not a political union.

Rudd believes that the existing regional mechanisms may continue in their own right or embody the building blocks of an Asia Pacific Community. However, he has identified two additional building blocks. First is the Six Party Talks, which could be transformed into a wider regional body to discuss confidence and security building measures in North East Asia and beyond. Second is the development of a Free Trade Area of the Asia Pacific (FTAAP).

Appraisal

The essential preconditions for an effective security institution-building do not as yet exist in Asia. It is where Rudd's proposal might hit major road blocks. Major powers can cooperate on individual issues like North Korea, but they cannot yet hold a sensible discussion about the future power structure in Asia, because they continue to stay in fundamentally incompatible positions, and none of them is yet convinced that those differences are not worth fighting for. Until there is some movement on those fundamentals, efforts to build new forums to bring them together may only entrench and amplify competitive attitudes but not assuage them. Therefore, some analysts, argue that if Rudd really wants to help build a peaceful Asian Century, he needs to start by talking to each of the major powers about the attitude of one to the other, and to leave the organization of new forums until there is a better chance of their agreeing on fundamentals.

The Six-Party Talks are tailor-made for resolving the problem on the Korean Peninsula, and as the name indicates, they only involve six countries. Expanding the membership would amount to duplicating the existing multilateral ARF. A more feasible approach seems to be to strengthen this multilateral forum and to turn it into a full-fledged regional forum that is no longer ASEAN driven. The FTAAP could be the dreadful kiss of death for the Asia Pacific Community albeit it has strong proponents in certain quarters. This discriminatory arrangement is a totally misguided proposal as it goes against the grain of regionalism in Asia Pacific, which as Rudd himself proclaimed "must be an open region".

However, does the above argument on Rudd's proposal make a correct starting point? From the experience in building regional cooperation on economic and political affairs in East Asia and the Pacific, Peter Drysdale has a different perspective. According to him, the trick to be used in Asia and the Pacific is not to start from trying to secure an agreement on principles across a complex plurality of economic, political and security interests in the region, but to get engaged in the process of developing rules that are acceptable to the key players–even the simplest rules for an engagement in dialogue on these issues–and not to attempt to impose a comprehensive common set of principles or values. The reality is that the latter course dooms the enterprise before it starts.

It is therefore correct that Rudd and other leaders in Japan, Indonesia and elsewhere are right to start talking about the processes which can help define a rules-based, not principles-based, Asia Pacific Community that includes discussion of not only economic but also political and security affairs. It is important to remember the difference between securing agreement on common principles and establishing processes of engagement and rules of behaviour in critical areas of regional and international affairs. As Drysdale opined that respect for the plurality of the Asia Pacific Community and community building through functional processes would proactively deal with the practical problems of common concern. [4]

It is hard to imagine that all the potential building blocks could become elements of a new single "regional institution" for the Asia Pacific. An EU-type process may be attractive, but cannot be created in the Asia Pacific. Instead, it is plausible to think of having an Asia Pacific regional architecture that consists of several institutions. What needs to be attempted is to reform and restructure the existing mechanisms so that they become key elements of a more coherent and consolidated regional process. It needs a high-level understanding, readiness and decision to be able to reform and restructure those mechanisms.

The shaping of the new architecture for the Asia Pacific region is not simply by adding to the APEC process and by adding the US to the EAS process. It will take much more than that, and should begin with the restructuring of the existing processes. It is worth saying that the APEC has the main ingredients as a strong pillar of the regional architecture. The EAS continues to be groping for the best method of serving the region. As it is still in its formative stage, it can easily be redirected. The region already has some of the ingredients for creating a meaningful regional architecture, but it needs progressive thinking and purposeful actions to capitalize on them.

Ever since Rudd floated the idea of an Asia Pacific Community in June 2008, the concept has been mostly derided. Some critics are now predicting that Rudd will quietly drop the idea soon. One of the most common criticisms concerns the meaning of proposal and the mode of its functioning. Rudd and his foreign minister Stephen Smith keep on using the word architecture, saying that the target is that by 2020, the key players will be able to sit down together and talk about both economics and strategic matters. While acknowledging the relevance of the existing organizations, they feel that the shift in power and influence requires something more.

It is to be noted that ASEAN started off in the mid-1960s with half a dozen of nations. No one probably envisaged then that ASEAN will be what we see today: the ARF, the East Asia Summit, India, Australia and other nations being dialogue partners. Therefore, in the new era there is a growing strategic need for the evolution of a new architecture, emerging either from the restructuring process of the existing architecture or a new piece of architecture emerging out of the continuing dialogue process.

It is also argued that the new body, when emerges, would not necessarily solve the problems of the region. There are issues in the region that are still difficult and sensitive. There are issues which some of the major powers do not want to be dealt with by others in a multilateral framework. For example, some of the territorial issues between Japan and South Korea, Japan and China are sensitive ones. Again, China may be reluctant to discuss the Taiwan issue with others.

Opinions differ on Rudd's idea even within the Labour Party. Former Australian Prime Ministers Paul Keating and Bob Hawke, both members of Rudd's centre-left Labour Party, have criticized the Asia Pacific Community proposal, saying an EU-style model was inappropriate for Asia. This undermines Rudd's "open dialogue and discussion" observation. Shadow Minister for Trade Ian Macfarlane was blunt in reacting to Rudd's proposal as empty, thought bubble policy, mentioning that it was an evidence of the dangers of Rudd's arrogant, non-consultative style. ASEAN nations are wary of the possible direct impact that Rudd's proposal may have on their own regional architecture. For example, Malaysia will not proceed with a free trade agreement with Australia until a wider deal is struck with New Zealand and ASEAN.

Opposition Liberal Party foreign affairs spokesperson Andrew Robb said it was "presumptuous" of Rudd to lecture the region on the need for unity and to offer himself as the helmsman of an Asian counterpart to the European Union. Robb said: "His first job is not to be making pronouncements about grand architecture for the region, telling China, Indonesia and Japan and India how they will be organized as a region by Australia in the next 20 years." [5]

It is not clear how India will manage its foreign affairs in the Asia Pacific region under Rudd's architecture. Though his marketing manager for the Asian Union campaign, Richard Woolcott, the right-hand man of Bob Hawke, who put together the APEC forum in 1989 is the appropriate person for the job, it might be borne in mind that APEC, which has 21 members and meets in a member country once in a year, includes all the region's big powers except India. Rudd's Asian Union initiative includes India, but Rudd is yet to visit as Prime Minister. However, India has expressed concern that Rudd is too close to China and dismissive of India's potential. [6] Woolcott argues that Australia as a middle power is appropriately positioned to suggest the idea because had countries like the US or China or Japan or some other big power suggested it, other nations would have expressed apprehension.

Rudd does not want the EU as a model, but feels that lesson can be learnt from it, which in the 1950s had been seen by sceptics as unrealistic. Following criticism from his predecessors Rudd has played down comparisons with the EU. Liberal MP Dennis Jensen says an EU-style arrangement with Asian nations should not be considered now. He reasons that once one gets into this, one will get into other complexities of unified currency and so on. [7]

Other critics at home view Rudd's proposal differently. They say Rudd's announcement that its neighbours need Australia (under his leadership) to steer them into a new Asia Pacific Community, was designed to distract attention from mounting domestic crises. They recognized the fact that the global power and influence is shifting towards the Asia Pacific region and that this directly affects Australia along with other neighbouring countries. But to suggest that Australia should take charge of organising a community response to this end is a different matter altogether. [8] Having let the cat (Australia's initiative) out of the bag publicly, Rudd may find insurmountable obstructions on the road to success through backdoor diplomacy. Other criticisms include that it is unthinkable that China will enter into an alliance with Japan and the US in the next 50 years.

Rationale

The manner in which Rudd is pursuing his idea of a grand scheme for an Asia Pacific Community, has attracted serious academic scrutiny. Ever since Rudd first came up with the idea in June, he has travelled through China, Japan, Indonesia, Singapore and other nations in the region to sell the idea, apart from sending his marketing manager Woolcott on the same mission.

Delivering the 29th Singapore Lecture on 12 August 2008, Rudd spoke on "Building on ASEAN's Success–Towards an Asia Pacific Community", and stressed that the transnational scope of the challenge is huge. Dealing with the challenges of a more integrated world means understanding both the limitations of the state and the limitations of markets–and embracing cooperative solutions to global challenges. Challenges lie beyond the reach of any single nation state, however powerful. For example, climate change is the consequence of the failure of free markets to account for pollution externalities adequately. Similarly, the recent international financial turbulence was precipitated by not altogether effective regulations. The gathering challenges of energy, water and food security reveal the need for a long term management of these critical global resources.

One of the major security threats of the 21st Century thus far– terrorism–has revealed itself to be diffuse, elusive and absolutely no respect for national boundaries and largely immune to the polarized geopolitics of the Cold War era. None of the major contemporary global challenges can be addressed by anytime like a retreat into isolationism or unilateralism. Thus, today's global challenges derive from a diverse mix of market failures, ineffective regulation, and inadequate international institutional frameworks to deal with the global public good.

What are the drivers of Global Change? The world is experiencing a rapid change of an order of magnitude, rarely experienced in human history. These challenges are complex, intricately interconnected, and global and therefore tend to defy exclusively any kind of national response. These changes thus demand that every nation review and renew its national objectives, its participation in regional and global institutions, and its place in a dynamic world. And nowhere is the pace of change greater than in the Asia Pacific region.

It is estimated that by 2020, Asia will account for around 45 percent of the global GDP, one third of global trade and nearly one quarter of global military spending. The region's population is continuing to grow to reach 4.6 billion by 2020 out of a total global population of 7.7 billion. Rapid population growth, combined with rapid urbanization, will place an increasing pressure on resources, particularly in relation to energy. Asia's energy consumption could grow by around 40 percent by 2020, or to put it in another way, more than half of the increase in global energy consumption by 2020 will come from Asia. The rise of India and China is a significant part of this shifting pattern of global economic and strategic weight towards the Asia Pacific region.

This rise will be among the key defining developments of the 21st Century. The rise of China in particular, represents the great unfolding drama of this new century. How China responds to the new challenges will be keenly watched. Beyond this shift in geopolitical power, a further factor driving global strategic change is the future course of economic globalization. The freer movement of goods, services, people and capital across borders has brought many fruitful benefits. It has generated high rates of global growth. In has enhanced the prospects, in particular, of developing countries which have kept themselves exposed to the international economy. The economic liberalization of recent decades has also liberated numerous people around the world out of poverty, expeditiously than at any other point of time in history. The challenges of economic liberalization, however, also need to surface and their strategic consequences need to be addressed. The illegal movement of people, drugs, weapons and capital across the borders, is accelerating.

There is a growing sense of grievance among some who believe that they have not had full access to the benefits of globalization, or that their condition is becoming worse, as a result of globalization. Even in states which have benefited unambiguously from globalization, there is often a backlash against it when economic times get tough. These economic realities entail important strategic consequences.

A third major international change is the evolution of the concept of 'national security'. The traditional concept of the term endures the security of one nation in relation to another. But the concept is broadened enough to include the threats to international and national security posed by non-state actors who facilitate the global reach of terrorism. National security is broadening even further in the outlook of some states to include food security, water security and energy security as well as security from the threat of health pandemics. Climate change will lead to changed rainfall pattern and, therefore, to changes in agricultural production that will have an impact on food security. Competition for increasingly scarce energy resources will make it more important than ever for nations to manage territorial disputes. These are all evolving concepts of national security that have significant strategic consequences. Can the existing international organizations produce real results in all these areas–from human rights to trade liberalization and climate change?

What the nations, therefore, require is, to craft policy responses to this rapidly changing region and the world. Australia is committed to an activist diplomacy aimed at enhancing the regional security and an open global economy enhanced by effective institutional and regulatory arrangements. Nations, however, must act in concert with other states, both regionally and globally.

At the regional level, the example of ASEAN stands prominent among regional institutions around the world. Having been born at the height of the Cold War 41 years ago, the organisation's most impressive achievement has been the building up of a sense of regional identity, a sense of community and a sense of neighbourhood. Though the member countries have diverse histories, political systems, religious beliefs, social systems and cultural backgrounds, they have forged a real sense of community with historically few substantive ties. ASEAN represents an outstanding essay in the institutional success and has paved the way for a wider regional architecture including the EAS and ARF.

Like the ASEAN, the APEC is another instance of a success story in the region. APEC has shown that its model of cooperation and dialogue can deliver practical results across the wider region. APEC's day-to-day work on harmonization of customs regulations, for example, may not shape the global terrain but they do make a practical difference to business. They make it easier to conduct business across international boundaries and that helps drive the economic growth by the lowering of the costs of transactions. If APEC's idea for a Free Trade Area of the Asia Pacific, as recommended by the US, is taken forward, it would be a significant boost to the regional prosperity.

APEC also works in the important area of regional disaster response, a field in which the ARF also plays a role. The cost of natural disasters in the region over the past decade has been staggering. According to the Red Cross, last year alone, 241 disasters across Asia resulted in more than 15,000 deaths. In

2008, one is reminded of the cyclone in Burma and the earthquake in China in which more than 150,000 had lost their lives and hundreds of thousands more were seriously affected. Such incidents raise the need to respond quickly. It is beyond the power of even one largest state to respond to large-scale natural disaster, when it occurs. Therefore, there is a need for regional mechanism that would facilitate quick response as the first 24, 48 or 72 hours are critical.

In the perspective of the above argument, it transpires that the evolution of a regional architecture is an evolving, not static, process. It has changed perceptibly since the first steps were taken to establish ASEAN 41 years ago. In view of the events that keep on unfolding, the existing regional institutions such as ASEAN, APEC and EAS may not be adequate and therefore a larger Asian Pacific Community that is open-ended can be envisioned. Rudd wants all major players–the US, Japan, China, Korea, Indonesia, Malaysia, Singapore, Australia, India and others–to get engaged in an open conversation about the region's future.

Rudd is concerned that, without a strong sense of shared interests, there remains a risk of succumbing to the perception that future conflicts within the region may somehow be inevitable. Indeed, issues such as an access to scarce materials like raw materials, energy and fresh water, pose risk of conflict and Rudd calls for a regional institution which spans the entire Asia Pacific region to be able to get engaged in a full spectrum of dialogue, cooperation and action on economic and political matters.

Is it Feasible?

Are the various potential dimensions and features of community-building necessary, feasible or desirable? There are already many plurilateral forums in the Asia Pacific competing with each other for attention and for very scarce policy-making resources. There may be merit in seeking to collapse these into one, but which one should give way to the other? If there is to be a single institution what will be its nature?

Western Europe has opted for the EU, a treaty based organization, with strong supra-national authority which has required members to cede very substantial sovereignty. Membership has expanded from 6 to 27, but those wishing to join need to adopt a vast body of legislation and social norms designed by the existing members. The EU's existing approach to economic cooperation is quite explicitly discriminatory and the EU is notorious for its opposition to WTO-wide genuine free trade in agricultural products and other labour-intensive products vital to the ability of the poorest to trade their way towards prosperity. In contrast, experience has shown that successful cooperation in the Asia Pacific, including the ASEAN, needs to be based on principles of openness, equality and evolution.

The EU has achieved a lot, but does not yet have a common security policy, energy policy or even free trade in services. In the Asia Pacific context, the capacity to set achievable objective depends on the scope of cooperation. One can wish for institutions which cover all aspects of regional cooperation ranging from security, economic and cultural cooperation and include as many participants as possible. But it is hard to reconcile cooperation by many on many things with achieving meaningful depth of cooperation on any issue. If, besides APEC's salutary experience its membership has expanded from 12 to 21 to embrace India, one wonders if it is feasible to stop there. It seems to be more realistic to hold regular meetings of Asia Pacific leaders and ministers to oversee the work of the existing and possibly the new forums and institutions which are sufficiently specialized and cohesive to set and achieve realistic targets. [9]

At the moment, Rudd's concept of a regional architecture in the Asia Pacific seems wooly without any lucid details, though Rudd justifies it as a long term aspiration goal. For some, it does not make sense to have another regional organization when there are quite a good number already in existence, with the APEC, more or less, in a similar role. It would make more sense to re-energise APEC, and to include India in it, than to start all over again with another organization to transcend the existing one. [10]

Position of Russia

In the evolution of a regional architecture, where does Russia stand? America's preoccupation with and involvement in the Iraq and Afghanistan wars have significantly undermined its influence in the Asia-Pacific region. China's power projection objectives make it an appropriate candidate to fill the American void in the Asia Pacific and to reconfigure the region's geopolitical architecture. [11] In this changing geopolitical landscape, Russia has been slowly repositioning itself in the region through arms sales, participation in regional venues like the Six-Party Talks cantering round North Korea's nuclear program, and energy exports. Though Russia's military presence in East Asia has declined, Asia watchers are witnessing an aggressive Russian campaign to dominate regional defence technology sales. [12]

According to a 2006 Congressional Research Service report, between 1998 and 2005, Russia inked more than US$ 29 billion in arms sales to Asian countries. India and China have been key drivers for Russia's arms sales, but Moscow is counting on new clients. In 2007, Russia and Indonesia agreed to go in for a US$ 1 billion arms sales package deal that includes Kilo-class submarines. Russia's "arms diplomacy" is designed by strategic design, which creates a strong client base that can later be transformed into a larger relationship. Mostly, the analysis today focuses on the rise of China and India and the almost inevitable reconfiguration of the Asia-Pacific security architecture but with Russia floating on a sea of resource wealth, this analysis no longer holds good. Clearly, Russia is attempting to reconstitute itself in certain ways that likely will challenge the US influence in the region even while the US remains engaged in the region through its defence alliance with Japan and South Korea and increasing links with China.

From Russian perspective, maintaining stability in the Asia Pacific region is of utmost priority. But when one takes note of some recent Russian actions, including its announcement that it will restart patrols of the 37th Air Army (Russia's strategic missile and bomber force) over Arctic, Atlantic, and Pacific Oceans, and the recent incident whereby Russian TU-95 Bears flew provocatively close to American military bases in Guam, one cannot miss the fact of Russia being intent on its presence in the region as well as its impact. Russia will not certainly rejoice in the Western expansion into its old sphere (read the NATO expansion to the proposed installation of missile defence systems in Poland and the Czech Republic) and therefore will spare no effort to check the spread of American influence. The formation of the Shanghai Cooperation Organisation (SCO) helped Russia maintain "stability" in Central Asia to the exclusion of the US. SCO norms are distinctly Russian and Chinese and are not necessarily in line with America's geo-strategic objectives in the Asia pacific. That Russia wants to use the SCO as a balance against the Western maritime coalitions and be the guardian of the greater Eurasia is much too evident to miss one's notice. [13]

Besides its arms sales to India, China and Indonesia, Russia also has a captive market for selling its arms in the Middle East. In mid-August 2008, Syrian President spent two days in the Russian capital with a shopping list of sophisticated weapons. If the conflict in Georgia ushers in a sustained period of renewed animosity between Russia and the West, Washington fears that a newly emboldened but estranged Moscow could use its influence, money, energy resource, UN Security Council veto and its arms industry to undermine American interests around the world. In these circumstances, Rudd's proposal for a regional architecture may hit a new road block as the otherwise accommodative Russia may turn out to be a challenge.

India's FTA with ASEAN

Ever since India's Look East policy was adopted by Narasimha Rao government, there has been steady strengthening of India's position in the region. The conclusion of India-ASEAN FTA after four years of negotiations in Singapore at the ASEAN Economic Ministers meeting in the first week of September 2008 and later to be formally accepted by the leaders at the Bangkok summit scheduled for December 2008 has been a watershed agreement for India's economic engagement in the Asia Pacific region. This will facilitate India's playing its dual role in emerging broader regional architecture in the region. [14]

As a result of the FTA, the trade between India and ASEAN, which is now US$ 38 billion, is expected to surge to US$ 50 billion by 2010. India has already slashed most of its tariff lines, but the hitch was on the relatively large number of items on the "sensitive list". [15] Though Indian industry and trade tend to be sceptical about the FTAs because they generally happened to put the other side at a greater advantage, it was a demonstration of New Delhi's commitment to regional cooperation and freer trade. The truism, however, is that the FTA should further strengthen India's ties not only with ASEAN, but also with the whole of East Asian region. It marks another milestone on New Delhi's "Look East" policy. [16] The new trade pact can also be seen as the triumph of India's economic diplomacy with a political focus.

As already mentioned, experts on both the sides fear that either of the parties has caved in for the sake of striking the deal. Neither of the parties termed the pact as "a win-win deal" but the win-win approach has become a standard formula for political and other negotiations in the post Cold-War period. Outwardly, the ASEAN will stand to gain more from this deal than India, at least to begin with.

India has agreed to reduce substantially and progressively its import tariff on a few items of utmost export-importance to some key ASEAN states such as Malaysia, Indonesia and Vietnam. These items are palm oil, coffee, tea, and pepper. As for the petroleum products, Brunei's export lifeline, India has been equally accommodative. Similarly, the ASEAN countries have also committed themselves to giving greater market access than available now in respect of Indian exports. On balance, the new trade pact which will create a free trade area of 1.7 billion people and US$ 2.3 trillion GDP as of now, can be seen as the triumph of economic diplomacy with a political focus. [17] Both India and the 10-member ASEAN nations are no longer viewing the regional and global political issues through the prism of Cold War perspective that defined bilateral relations but in the light of reconfiguration of power equations that has been determining international politics in which the actors aspire for a win-win situation. International relations no longer are being defined as a zero-cum-sum game.

India-ASEAN FTA needs to be seen in the broader context of global trends and longer-term strategic interests of the country. Regional or bilateral free trade arrangements have become important aspects of any country's trade policy. Over 350 RTAs/FTAs are currently in different stages of negotiations and the bulk of world trade is now conducted within the FTAs. Indeed, India-ASEAN FTA is a part of the trend of ASEAN concluding FTAs with all its dialogue partners. China was the first dialogue partner to complete FTA negotiations with ASEAN. South Korea and Japan too concluded similar agreements subsequently. With India, Australia and New Zealand concluding negotiations, a new trade framework has emerged in which regional and bilateral trade could be conducted smoothly. Seen from the perspective of the EAS summit and the 10+3+3 perspective, we clearly see the evolution of a broader regional architecture in the Asia-Pacific region. In the light of this, Rudd's proposal, though too ambitious, can be examined objectively.

How Does Australia View India?

There has been no irritant in India-Australia relations, though differences on some sensitive issues remain. These, however, do not threaten to derail the healthy economic relations that remain between the two countries. The strategic interests of both the countries in the broader Asia Pacific region match quite well. For the Indian students, Australia has emerged as a major destination for higher education. Indian IT professionals have commanded respect in software companies in Australia. After the assumption of office by Rudd, certain issues threatened to derail India-Australia relations somehow. Rudd's bias towards China because of his knowledge of Mandarin and long stay in China, threatened to overshadow Australia's relations with India. While Japan and Indonesia also appeared in Rudd's Asian diplomatic radar, India placed into the sidelines in Rudd's foreign affairs framework.

Though Rudd showed diplomatic insensitivity towards Japan and Indonesia by overlooking these two countries and by choosing China as the first country to visit after assuming the office, he corrected himself soon after facing criticism by pledging to work with them both bilaterally and on regional issues. As regards India, Rudd did include India in his Asia Pacific Community framework but by reversing the decision of Howard government to sell uranium, he seemed to distance himself from India. [18] Further, by announcing in haste Australia's withdrawal from the Japan-sponsored quadrilateral (comprising US, India, Australia and Japan as members), Rudd seemed to please Beijing. Selling uranium to authoritarian China and a known proliferator of nuclear materials, and not to democratic and non-proliferator India, seems ethically wrong.

True, China is Australia's largest trading partner with bilateral trade touching AUS$ 53 billion mark in 2007, as compared to India-Australia bilateral trade, which is in the vicinity of US$ 10 billion. Also, the Chinese are by far the largest migrant community from Asia in Australia as compared to Indians, who constitute a one-third of the Chinese in

Australia. Prime ministerial visits between India and Australia are ludicrously low as compared to that between Australia and China. While Prime Minister Bob Hawke in 1989 and Prime Minister Howard in 2000 and 2006 visited India, no Indian Prime Minister since Rajiv Gandhi (1986) visited Australia. This demonstrates India's lack of political interests in Australia. Prof. Purnendra Jain of Adelaide University and a keen watcher of India-Australia relations lucidly explains as follows: "Chanting the mantra of Commonwealth, English and Cricket links will not be enough if India seriously wants to be a political player Down Under. While arguments that Australia's uranium policy is discriminatory and Canberra's cosying up with then Chinese authoritarian regime at the expense of democratic India smacks of hypocrisy have made some public intellectuals and media commentators receptive to India's views, it will be difficult for India to compete with the influence that China commands in Australia. For that to happen, India needs to engage Australia systematically and strategically with major government and public diplomacy initiatives." [19]

It is possible that Rudd is constrained by domestic political compulsions and his own softness towards China, which makes Rudd to overlook China's tainted proliferation record and to allow China to have an easy access to Australia's uranium. But Canberra should understand the strategic compulsions that require New Delhi to maintain a minimum deterrence capability. China's proliferation, vertical and horizontal, in this volatile neighbourhood, is not a reality, India can simply ignore. India would not like to see Australia being uneven in its friendship towards Asia's two giant neighbours.[20] Rudd's government can ill afford to ignore India in its search for a regional security architecture and both the countries should try to correct the historical deficit in their overall relationship. The uranium issue must not, therefore, be allowed to come in the way of sculpting a healthy bilateral relationship in many fronts between the two countries. [21]

The highly influential daily the *Australian* has been a leading critic of the Rudd government's uranium policy. It argues that Australia must sell to India to promote both closer economic relations and to help reduce global warming. Once the nuclear deal with the US goes through the US Congress and the international trade with India in nuclear technology and materials begins, the Rudd government may be left with no option but to allow sales of yellow cake to India.

Conclusion

Rudd's idea seems grand but at the moment does not appear achievable. His handling of Australia's foreign policy does not please all the countries in the region. Rudd has planned to hold a conference in 2009 to discuss the proposal for a new Asia Pacific Community. Indonesian President Susilo Bambang Yusdhoyono has also a novel idea. He is proposing to hold Democracy Forum (not much heard before) late this year (2008) in Bali, and has asked Rudd to co-chair with him. Rudd's trip to Indonesia was relatively uncomplicated. It was a bit tricky.

A few days before the Labour Party trounced the centre-right government of John Howard in November 2007, Howard had signed a landmark agreement, affirming Australia as Japan's second-ever formal ally, after the United Sates. That agreement seemed to be a useful bulwark against a rising China. But Rudd being fluent in mandarin and a former diplomat, felt towards China's insatiable demand for Australian coal and iron ore and seemed to have placed Australia's relationship with the dictatorial China over and above Australia's relationship with free Japan, or that is how his policy is being perceived by watchers of his foreign policy in the Asia Pacific.

To make matters worse, Rudd took office just as Japan's annual whaling trip to the southern ocean was generating a great deal of bad publicity in Australia, threat to get the Australians' largely positive image of Japan tarnished. Then, as if to confirm Japan's worst insecurities, in April 2008, Rudd made his first pompous Asian trip as Prime Minister to China, but not to Japan. Rudd used his knowledge of the Mandarin so skilfully that even while pointedly disagreeing over China's trampling on Tibetans' rights, he did not annoy the Chinese but on the other hand pleased them by denouncing those in Europe who were calling for boycotting Beijing's Olympic games.

In dealing with Japan, Rudd defined Australia's foreign policy by reaffirming Australia's relationship with Japan as "a comprehensive strategic, security and economic partnership", and pointed out the "brittleness" that hangs on bilateral relations. However, Tokyo was not impressed that Rudd had ditched the quadrilateral security dialogue between the US, Japan, India and Australia. Both Japan and Australia have close relationship, which has remained overwhelmingly and predominantly economic. Both by being major trading partners and by virtue of their security alliance with the US, Japan found it hard to interpret that it has been relegated to a secondary position in Australia's foreign policy calculation under Rudd. Though Rudd had to do some fancy diplomatic work to assuage Japan's hurt feelings during his visit to Japan, he clearly did not like being kept waiting for a meeting with the Japanese Prime Minister, Yasuo Fukuda. But his unfortunate waiting for meeting Ysuo Kauda was inevitable considering the fact that the latter was preoccupied with his domestic political problems, arising from a no-confidence motion against him in the Upper House of the Diet. True, the aim of Rudd's Japan visit is to make amends for the dent in their relationship caused by his perceived bias towards China. Still, Japan remains sensitive about Australia's new romance with China, under Rudd.

End Notes

1. Peter Drysdale, "The Asia-Pacific Community Idea," *http://eastasiaforum.org/2008/06/19.*
2. *Ibid.*

3. Hadi Soesastro, "Kevin Rudd's Architecture for the Asia-Pacific," *http://eastasiaforum.org/208/06/09.*
4. Drysdale, n.1. Also, see P.S. Suryanarayana, "New 'Security' Ideas in East Asia," *The Hindu*, 22 August 2008.
5. "Rudd's Asian Union Idea Draws Flak," Asia-Pacific News, 5 June 2008, *http://www.monstersandcritics.com/news/asiapacific/news.*
6. *The Australian*, 19 August 2008.
7. *Ibid.*
8. Malcolm Calless, "Asia in Club Kevin?," *The Australian*, 22 August 2008.
9. Andrew Elek, "Kevin Rudd's Vision for Asia Pacific institution-building,"*http://eastasiaforum.org/2008/06/12.*
10. S.P. Seth, "Rudd catches up with Indonesia and Japan," *The Jakarta Post*, 7 August 2008.
11. *The Economist*, 11 June 2008.
12. Nirav Patel and Vikram Singh, "Washington Should Pay Attention to Russian moves in the Asia-Pacific," *http://www.worldpoliticsreview.com/article7/28/2008.*
13. Peter Baker, "US sees much to fear in a hostile Russia," *International Herald Tribune,* 21 August 2008.
14. Nagesh Kumar, Emerging Regional Architecture in Asia," *Business Standard,* 6 September 2008.
15. Editorial, *The Hindu*, 1 September 2008.
16. *Ibid.*
17. P.S. Suryanarayana, "A free trade area within Asian," *The Hindu*, 6 September 2008. See also, *The Hindu*, 29 August 2008.
18. Purnendra Jain, "Do not let Rudd Sideline India in the Asian game," *The Asian Age,* 24 June 2008.
19. *Ibid.* See also, *The Hindu*, 24 June 2008.
20. Editorial, *The Times of India*, 11 September 2008.
21. Purnendra Jain, "Pushing Aussies too hard for uranium will not help much," *The Asian Age*, 12 September 2008.

17

Sino-Indian Relations: Dead Weight of Old Mindsets or Opening of New Vistas?

Rabindra Sen

If we examine the history of India-China relations, we notice that the relationship has gone through a tortuous process. [1] Friendship there was initially, but it was followed by confrontation. The two countries became engaged in an armed conflict the memory of which even after more than four decades is yet to be completely wiped out. Confrontation was followed by detente which in turn was followed by normalization of relations. Ambassadorial relations were restored in 1976. From 1981 the two countries have been engaged in border talks. [2] But in spite of protracted negotiations which have been going on for more than a quarter century, India and China have not been able to settle the problem. Some progress may have been made in these negotiations, but a resolution of the problem still seems quite far off.

This paper discusses the flurry of diplomatic exchanges and visits undertaken by the leaders of the two countries, especially in recent times, which appear to have added a fresh momentum and given rise to hopes about giving the relationship a new direction. The question is whether these visits have ushered in a new era of hope and consolidation in bilateral relations or is it that the change that appears to have set in is more apparent than real. One way of examining the Sino-Indian relationship, especially from the Indian standpoint, is to analyse and understand the Chinese perspective vis-à-vis issues of great importance to India. It is important to see how the Chinese perception influences its policies with regard to those issues. This paper seeks to study the Sino-Indian relationship by highlighting the Chinese stand on two such issues, namely India's aspiration for permanent membership of the UN Security Council and the highly controversial Indo-US Nuclear Deal. [3]

India had set up diplomatic relations with the People's Republic of China on April 1, 1950 becoming the first non-communist country to do so. Chinese Premier Zhou Enlai and Indian Prime Minister Jawaharlal Nehru exchanged visits in 1954. China and India jointly initiated and proposed the Five Principles of Peaceful Co-existence. Friendship, however, gave way to confrontation and the two countries found themselves involved in a war in 1962. However, after Atal Behari Vajpayee's (then Minister of External Affairs) visit to China in 1979, China agreed to end assistance to the secessionist groups in India's North-East and keep peace along the Line of Actual Control (LAC). [4] Indian Prime Minister Rajiv Gandhi visited China in 1988 and this visit has gone down as the well-acclaimed landmark in the history of Sino-Indian relations. C.V. Ranganathan, a former Indian Ambassador to China, aptly remarked, "It was a symbolic, yet tangible signal at the highest political level that India-China relations would no longer be mired in the past and that the two Governments would be forward looking and impart a momentum to an all round development of relations." [5] In 1991, Chinese Premier Li Peng visited India and then in 1993 Prime Minister Narasimha Rao went to the People's Republic of China. Chinese President Jiang Zemin's visit to India in 1996 was another landmark event in Sino-Indian relations. It was the first visit by a Chinese Head of State to India after the establishment of diplomatic ties. During this visit the two countries agreed to build a constructive and cooperative relationship oriented to the twenty-first century on the basis of the five principles of peaceful co-existence.

Dark clouds gathered on the Sino-Indian horizon in 1988 after India carried out nuclear tests especially because the then

Prime Minister A.B. Vajpayee cited the Chinese threat as one of the reasons behind the tests. China took the lead in drafting the UN Security Council Resolution 1172 which, *inter alia*, condemned the tests. In June 1999, however, tension abated as Indian External Affairs Minister Jaswant Singh paid a visit to China and the two sides affirmed that both the countries should refrain from regarding each other as a threat. Both the countries realised that it was this that was the pre-requisite for the growth of Indian-China relations. In March 2000, the two countries held the first round of security dialogue. In May the same year, a crucial visit to China was undertaken by President K.R. Narayanan. In July 2000, Chinese Foreign Minister Tang Jiaxuan came to India. Tang Jiaxuan was the first high ranking Chinese official to visit India after the May 1998 nuclear tests. [6] Chinese Premier Zhu Rongji visited India in January 2002 and the two countries reaffirmed that they did not pose a threat to each other. The next year was marked by visits to China by A.B. Vajpayee and George Fernandes.

Sino-Indian relations have been developing at a fast pace since the historic visit of Chinese Premier Wen Jiabao to India in April 2005 and the upgrading of bilateral ties to a strategic level. The Chinese premier's visit actually coincided with the fifty-fifth anniversary celebrations of the establishment of diplomatic relations between India and China. "The two sides believed that premier Wen Jiabao's highly successful state visit...marked a new level of India-China relationship and opened a new chapter in the friendly relations and co-operation between the two countries," said the joint statement signed by the two sides. [7] Emphasising the importance of the visit, Wen Jiabao said that the visit produced three major results. The first was the joint statement announcing the establishment of a strategic and cooperative partnership for peace and prosperity. The second result, Wen said, was the signing of an agreement on the political guiding principles for the settlement of the boundary question. And the third major result was the adoption of a five-year plan for all-round cooperation and trade between the two countries. [8] The then Indian Foreign Secretary, Shyam Saran, hailed Wen's landmark India visit, saying, "It was an extraordinarily successful visit." [9]

2006 was celebrated as the India-China Friendship Year. The then Indian Defence Minister Pranab Mukherjee's visit to China in May 2006 was a major highlight of the activities jointly undertaken by the Indian and Chinese governments to mark 2006 as the 'Year of India-China Friendship.' The visit was to enhance Sino-Indian military ties with a view to boosting mutual trust and adding more content to the nascent strategic relations between the two sides. During the highly successful visit a Memorandum of Understanding on defence cooperation was signed. Pranab Mukherjee told his Chinese counterpart that India did not regard China as a threat. China should not consider India a threat either, he said. [10] 2006 also witnessed the historic agreement between India and China to reopen the Nathu La border trade point. The Himalayan pass, which was a part of the famed Silk Road, was closed after the 1962 war. [11] The decision to restore trans-border trade across Nathu La was considered a pragmatic move to enhance mutual trust and bilateral cooperation. [12]

Chinese President Hu Jintao's visit to India in November 2006 marked the culmination of the Year of Friendship celebrations. President Hu's visit came after ten years of his predecessor's and gave a definite boost to the economic, political and strategic relations between New Delhi and Beijing. The agreements signed between the two countries during President Hu's visit reflected the consolidation of their bilateral bonds. [13] During his visit the Chinese leader talked of "building trust through trade" and also declared that the two countries were "not rivals or competitors but partners for mutual benefit." President Hu concluded his visit stating that his purpose was to enhance mutual trust and raise strategic partnership to new heights. [14] The visit was successful in putting in place mechanisms and institutional linkages to lead to greater engagement between India and China in various areas including a move to increase trans-border connectivity.[15] President Hu described the outcome of the talks as positive and said that the Sino-Indian relationship ceased to be confined to bilateral and regional dimensions and attained global significance. [16] The Chinese head of state proposed a four-point strategy for strengthening the Sino-Indian relationship. [17] This included increasing mutual trust, enhancing business cooperation, increasing cultural and social exchanges and stepping up friendly consultation for an early settlement of the boundary issue. India and China also agreed to expand their economic cooperation. China has as a matter of fact overtaken the United States as India's largest trade partner. The two countries managed to meet the US$ 20 billion target set for 2008 by October 2006. [18] India and China decided to broaden their cultural ties by celebrating 2007 as the "Year of Friendship" through tourism. Also a hotline has been set up between the foreign ministers of the two countries for the enhancement of bilateral ties. The visit by Sonia Gandhi in late 2007 and one undertaken by Prime Minister Manmohan Singh in early 2008 too have been important events.

Any discussion of Sino Indian relations will entail some consideration of the vexed boundary issue that has been nagging the relations for decades. We will not discuss the details of the positions of the two sides on the issue and the complexity of the problem. But what is worth commenting on is the current state of affairs so far as the ongoing negotiations on the sensitive issue are considered.

The two sides formed the Special Representatives mechanism in June 2003 during the visit of the then Indian Prime Minister Atal Behari Vajpayee to China. The Special Representatives were appointed to explore the framework for a boundary settlement from the political perspective of the overall bilateral relationship. India and China committed themselves to arriving at a "package settlement" of the boundary question in a spirit of mutual respect and mutual understanding. [19] The Special Representatives' work is essentially divided into three phases, and the first phase was successfully completed with the signing in April 2005 during the Chinese Premier Wen Jiabao's visit to India of the Agreement on the Political Parameters and Guiding Principles for the Settlement of the India-China Boundary Question. [20]

After the ground breaking political principles crafted before Wen Jiabao's visit in April 2005, there has been precious little progress in the talks between India and China. Nevertheless, in the joint declaration issued on November 21, 2006 during the visit of President Hu Jintao to India, both sides reiterated that an early settlement of the boundary question would advance the basic interest of the two countries and would, therefore, be pursued as a strategic objective.

Setting the thorny issue is a difficult task, but the two countries have taken "good initiatives" in developing confidence building measures along the Line of Actual Control. Both sides have already come to recognise the importance of going beyond claims and counter-claims. [21] "Both countries recognise that they are neighbours and that it is better to live in peace than in tension," said Pranab Mukherjee after his three nation tour to China, Japan and Singapore in 2006. [22] In an interview echoing the same sentiment Chinese Ambassador to India Sun Yuxi had said in 2005, "the most important point is to keep the border area peaceful while we develop border trade and friendly exchanges between New Delhi and Beijing. The border issue should not stand in the way of all round development and our bilateral relations." [23] During his visit to India in late 2006 President Hu Jintao too laid emphasis on the need to maintain peace and tranquillity in the border areas till the final settlement of the boundary question. [24]

It is noteworthy in this context that representatives of the Indian and Chinese Armies get together in Border Personnel Meetings (BPMs) on the Line of Actual Control. These meetings are held four times every year: by the Chinese in

February and June and by the Indians on 15 August and 20 October. Two of the meetings are formal and the others celebrate the Chinese Spring Festival and India's Independence Day. Apart from setting up a joint working group, the two countries signed the Peace and Tranquillity Agreement (1993) and agreed on Confidence Building Measures (1996) when former Chinese President Jiang Zemin came to India. [25]

In recent years especially, Sino-Indian relations have been warming with a flurry of official exchanges, covering issues from border disputes to enhanced trade and closer political ties. V.K. Nambiar, former Ambassador to China and then the United Nations has said that relations between India and China have improved greatly in the past few years and have retained their momentum. [26] Indeed, developments over the last few years, as Alka Acharya observes, have undoubtedly taken bilateral relations between India and China on the verge of a qualitatively new phase of understanding. [27]

Developing friendly relations with China is an important priority of the Government of India. [28] Speaking at the Shanghai Institute of International Studies on January 11, 2006, the then Indian Foreign Secretary observed, "our relationship with China is a key component of our "Look East" policy. There is a strong consensus in India on improving and developing our relations with China." [29] China's strong position in the hierarchy of nations makes it an imperative that we continue to steadfastly address ourselves to the task of developing good-neighbourly, friendly and cooperative relations with Beijing. China too recognises India's growing importance and now attaches considerable importance to ties with New Delhi.

Although both China and India want to put their relationship on an even keel, at the same time the two sides have had to grapple with problems in their relationship. While it is certainly true there has been a forward movement in bilateral relations, discordant voices pointing to doubts, apprehensions and anxieties about each other's intentions and actions have continued to resonate. Although, therefore, even if one may emphatically mention that there is now a better atmosphere of understanding between the two countries, one has to admit that unfortunately "this understanding is bogged in a quagmire of mutual suspicions and mistrust, which at times tends to far outweigh the positive dimensions. [30] It will suffice to quote from the writing by a well-known former Indian diplomat G. Parthasarathy who has observed, "… China remains the most destabilising factor for Indian national security. It has consistently sought to undermine India's influence in Asia and indeed across the world." [31]

Opinion on the question as to whether the above assessment is an entirely correct and acceptable reading of China's mind, deeds and intentions with regard to India is bound to vary. No one would argue that there are no thorny issues affecting Sino-Indian relations. The long-standing territorial disputes clearly are major stumbling blocks that have remained unresolved for more than forty years. India has its concerns and anxieties vis-à-vis China. For example, India is wary of China's special relationship with Pakistan, albeit not perhaps to the same extent as in the past. China too has its own concerns and is suspicious of New Delhi's strategic partnership with the United States and its implications for China's security. The two Asian giants also carry the burden of mutual historical mistrusts and misgivings. As former national security advisor Brajesh Mishra has said, a feeling of distrust still encompasses Sino-Indian relations. [32]

Let us now turn to India's bid for permanent membership of the UN Security Council and the Indo-US nuclear deal as test cases for explaining Sino-Indian relations in terms of their mutual perceptions. So far as the first issue is concerned, China has not directly, openly and unequivocally supported India's candidature for permanent membership of the United Nations Security Council. In 2006, Pranab Mukherjee did in fact admit that China had not extended any support to India's campaign for permanent membership of the UN Security Council. [33] On this question Beijing sticks to Chinese Premier Wen Jiabao's declared line that China welcomes a greater role for India in international affairs and in the United Nations. At a press conference at the end of his visit to India in 2005, Wen said, "we fully understand and support the Indian aspiration to play an even bigger role in international affairs and in the UN." China attaches "great importance" to India's role in both international and regional affairs, Wen said, adding that "India is a very populous developing country and also a very important developing country." [34]

If Wen's remarks could be interpreted as a tacit recognition of and support for India's case and claim to find a place in an expanded and reformed Security Council, so were the observations of former Chinese Ambassador to India Sun Yuxi who in an interview to the *Times of India* had said, "Generally speaking, China supports the reform plan of the UN. The UN was formed 60 years ago and the world situation has changed a lot. It has to adapt and restructure to address the present needs. We attach more importance to expanding the membership and the role of developing countries in the UN and UNSC. That's where we stand. India, apart from China is the largest developing country and our position is clear on that." [35]

Two points emerge from a close look at the above statements. First, China does feel the need for a reform of the UN Security Council as part of a general reform of the UN. Second, China also supports the demand for a greater voice of the developing countries in the United Nations and the UN Security Council. Juxtaposed with the Chinese acknowledgement of India's position as an important, populous, and large developing country, what logically follows is a recognition of India's desire for a permanent seat in the UN Security Council as fully justified. Still the fact is that China has not given an unequivocal support to India on the issue. What has prevented China from doing so? Is it

Pakistan's active opposition to India's move to get into the UN Security Council? Is it also China's strong and openly stated opposition to Japan's attempt to become a permanent member of the UN Security Council? Opposition in the case of India, though not openly stated, might thus be to a greater or lesser extent because of Japan's inclusion in the G-4 (India, Japan, Germany and Brazil).

China has made known its displeasure about India teaming up with Japan for permanent membership of the UN Security Council. Howsoever important the above factors may have been in influencing Beijing's stand, a more plausible interpretation would be that China wants to play safe and wait for a consensus to emerge on the vexed issue. It remains to be seen if a wide and overwhelming acceptance of India's entry into the UN Security Council as a permanent member would bring about a change in China' policy with regard to this question. As of now India, it seems, too is prepared to wait and rightly so. As Pranab Mukherjee said addressing a press conference after his three-nation tour to China, Japan and Singapore in 2006, this issue did not come up during his visit to China. [36]

The gap in mutual understanding, the apprehension on one side about what the other might be up to, explains the Chinese response to the Indo-US nuclear deal, The tug of war between the government and its critics especially the Left parties over the much talked about Indo - US nuclear deal led to intense speculation about the future of the deal and the implications for the country. Being an eye-catcher for a considerable period of time, the matter was greatly important not just for this country. Other countries, especially those which are in the IAEA Board of Governors and the Nuclear Suppliers Group, closely observed the unfolding drama in the Indian capital cantering round questions over the fate of the Indian government. Among these countries was India's largest neighbour China. As the IAEA route for India - specific safeguards and most importantly the NSG approval were the sine qua non for operationalising the nuclear deal prior to its final approval by the US Congress, a question before China watchers in this country, and perhaps elsewhere too, was what stand China would take at the IAEA and subsequently the NSG. The question was important because China's position on the nuclear deal was non-committal and ambiguous. China till the last moment kept India guessing by playing its cards close to its chest.

Russia, U.K. and France backed the deal without reservations. It was even reported that in spite of the political uncertainties prevailing in India, the United States, France, Russia and Great Britain were working overtime to secure passage of the nuclear deal through IAEA and NSG. It was also in the air that the IAEA and the NSG might both be seized of the matter simultaneously for beating the clock. Of the member countries of the NSG, some were convinced that waiver should be given to India. France, for example, strongly backed India's case. France viewed India as a responsible country and said that grant of waiver to it by the NSG would strengthen the global non-proliferation regime, instead of weakening the system as apprehended by some quarters. "It is in the interest of the NPT regime if India has a relationship with the international community. The net benefit is for the NPT system, besides that for India," said a senior official of the French Atomic Energy Commission. [37] He said the July 18, 2005 understanding between India and the United States was a "positive step" as it made it clear that New Delhi wanted to be with the international community [38] Also some countries softened their stand and came around to make room for the exemption to enable trade in nuclear material and technology with India. But some countries were not convinced. [39]

Beijing reacted cautiously to the Indo-US civilian nuclear agreement hoping that the cooperation of "relevant countries... conform to the regulations of the international non-proliferation regime and their own international obligations.

[40] While making obvious their lack of enthusiasm for the Indo-US agreement, which according to Zhang Lijun of the China Institute of International Studies marked a total change in Washington's nuclear policy towards India, [41] the Chinese government spokespersons avoided outspoken comments on the agreement. The government controlled media in China, however, did not observe any such restraint. For example, *the People's Daily*, the mouthpiece of the ruling Communist Party of China (CPC), wrote on November 4, 2005: "This would be a hard blow on America's leading role in the global proliferation prevention system as well as the system itself. This will bring about a series of negative impacts. Now that the US buys another country in with nuclear technologies in defiance of international treaty, other nuclear powers also have their own partners of interest as well as good reasons to copy what the US did. A domino effect of nuclear proliferation, once turned into reality, will definitely lead to global nuclear proliferation and competition." [42]

The state-run Xinhua news agency said, "While many blame the Democratic People's Republic of Korea and Iran for frustrating international efforts on nuclear non-proliferation, double standards adopted by some western countries on nuclear issues could also be said to add to the problem, for their stance has undermined the authority of the Nuclear Non-proliferation Treaty (NPT)." "The double standards are manifested in another case–India, a country which has detonated nuclear bombs but refused to sign the NPT", the 2006 Xinhua year-ender on non-proliferation noted. [43] Beijing sought to justify its lack of enthusiasm on the ground that such a special waiver to India could weaken the global non-proliferation architecture. [44]

Before the US President George W. Bush's visit to India in February 2006, then Chinese Ambassador to India Sun Yuxi, while responding to a question about Beijing's reaction to the Indo-US civil nuclear deal, told media persons in New Delhi nonchalantly, 'We are very happy. Every Government has the right to develop its energy. Given that India is a rising country, in the developing world, we fully understand your energy needs." [45] Similarly, in an interview ahead of the maiden India visit by the Chinese President Hu Jintao later in the same year the Chinese Ambassador said, "Every country has the right to develop energy in any form, including nuclear, to meet its development needs." [46] But what is important is that Sun Yuxi at the same time emphasised that the objectives of non-proliferation should also be respected and strengthened. [47] Also, ahead of President Hu's visit to India, Assistant Chinese Foreign Minister Cui Tiankai said that while countries could carry out peaceful nuclear energy co-operation, it should be conducive to the maintenance of the non-proliferation regime in the international community. [48]

The goal of non-proliferation, howsoever important it may have been as a factor, was only the tip of the iceberg. Chinese reservations and uneasiness about the Indo-US nuclear deal should actually be viewed in the overall perspective of the marked improvement in Indo-US ties and also the Sino-US mutual perceptions. Beijing's own perceptions of the US game plans were no doubt a vital factor. While Beijing and Washington seek a "constructive" and "cooperative" engagement, beneath the surface there is an undercurrent of tension resulting from the mutual perceptions. Beijing suspects that the US is looking for the possibility of a new alignment of forces in the Asia Pacific region. [49] Commenting on the defence cooperation agreement signed by India and the United States on June 28, 2005, for example, the state-run *Global Times* in an article expressed apprehension that the agreement might be part of Washington's scheme of things to form an affiance network to guard against China. [50] Not surprisingly, the Indo-US nuclear deal has been a subject of debate among Chinese scholars, some candidly expressing apprehensions that the United States is pressing India to contain China. In an article in *Beijing Review* after President George W. Bush's visits to India and Pakistan, Zhang Lijun wrote, "India is the best bet to restrict a future strong China, as per US regional strategy in Asia." [51]

The Chinese concern can by no means be said to have been unfounded. Writing in the journal *Foreign Affairs* in 2000, Condoleezza Rice, then an academic, had observed, "China is not a status quo power but one that would like to alter Asia's balance of power in its favour. That alone makes it a strategic competitor, not the strategic partner the Clinton administration once called it." "The US must block China's rise," she continued, "by courting other regional powers, including India and weld them into an anti-China alliance." [52] After becoming the main security and foreign policy figure in the Bush White House, Rice strongly pushed the policy of "containing" China. [53] In this context one may also refer to the views expressed by Ashley J. Tellis, one of the influential American analysts, who too opined that the United States should build up India as a countervailing power in Asia against potential Chinese threats. [54]

Also worth noting in this connection is the US Defence Department's Third Quadrennial Defence Review (QDR) released in February 2006 which mentioned India as a key strategic partner while projecting China as a potential rival.[55] The Chinese Foreign Ministry quite naturally issued a statement characterising the QDR as a 'serious misrepresentation' of facts. Chinese officials said that the American Defence Department document only reinforced the view that the US wanted to retain its hegemonic influence in world politics at all costs. [56]

India has been tying to reassure Beijing that the mutual containment theory as regards India and China is untenable. Indian Prime Minister Manmohan Singh has said that strengthening of ties with the US would not be at the cost of a relationship with China. But China does not appear to have been convinced.

India needed Chinese support at the Nuclear Suppliers Group of which China is an important member. Beijing opened the door for nuclear energy cooperation with India, but of course without saying that it endorsed the Indo-US nuclear deal and without committing to push India's case in the NSG. In a significant statement a day before Chinese President Hu Jintao reached New Delhi in November 2006, the Chinese foreign office spokesperson Jiang Yu, said that Beijing would adopt a 'responsible' position with regard to the Indo-US deal at the NSG, but she also said that China wanted a few 'clarifications' over the deal. [57] China thus continued to harbour misgivings with regard to the issue.

From the above discussion it clearly emerges that China viewed the Indo-US nuclear deal as one that would undermine the non-proliferation regime. Since China in the past harped on the need for guarding against any weakening of the non-proliferation regime and repeatedly mentioned it even in the context of the Indo-US nuclear deal the conclusion is inescapable.

China initially had suggested that the NSG should consider a 'criteria-based' approach instead of a country-specific exemption, which many thought was perhaps intended to keep the door open for its long time ally Pakistan in the future. [58] Pakistan itself wanted a similar deal from the United States, but the latter refused to oblige.

China has supported India's civilian nuclear aspirations and agreed to promote bilateral cooperation in the area. The mention of this in the joint document released in Beijing in January 2008 after talks between the prime ministers of the two countries was taken in some circles as a softening of the Chinese stand on the nuclear issue and a boost for India. [59] There was, however, no clear cut mention in the joint statement of China giving India support in the NSG. [60]

We all know how China behaved in the final rounds of the negotiations at the NSG. China had to factor in several considerations. If China did not oppose the Indo-US deal, it would not have gone down well with Islamabad. But no matter how important the Pakistan factor was, it would have been undiplomatic on China's part to disturb the process of improvement in Sino-Indian relations by blocking the deal all by itself. Faced with this dilemma China would have been happy to point to a lack of consensus on the issue to save itself the embarrassment of having to openly say no to India. In fact, in September 2007 Chinese foreign ministry spokesperson Jiang Yu had said that there were still "different opinions" among the NSG countries on allowing India to join the nuclear club and easing restrictions for international nuclear trade. [61] China no doubt was likely to express its reservations, but the question was whether it was going to be a high-pitch criticism or a muted one. It seemed unlikely that China would take the lead in speaking against the nuclear deal and it appeared that it rather would prefer allowing others to be more vocal. [62] If a consensus did not emerge so much the better, but if it did it seemed unlikely that Beijing would balk at it. But circumstances were such that the Chinese ultimately were forced to show their cards fully.

Towards the end of the negotiations in the NSG Beijing decided to make its dissent open. China seemed to threaten the entire process, stating its national position that essentially urged countries to strive for a balance between non-proliferation and promoting civil nuclear energy cooperation. It also hoped the NSG would address "aspirations" of all parties seeking peaceful use of nuclear power. [63] China delivered a surprise even by threatening to leave, objecting to the manner in which the United States was "forcing" a consensus. [64] Ultimately after US President George W. Bush contacted his Chinese counterpart Hu Jintao asking him not to block the waiver, [65] China decided to retrace its steps and fall in line. The Chinese move at the last minute came as a surprise to India. "We were a little surprised about China," said National Security Advisor M.K. Narayanan pointing out that Chinese President Hu Jintao and Prime Minister Wen Jiabao had told Prime Minister Manmohan Singh that they would never be a part of the problem and never create difficulties for India. [66]

China is important to India in more ways than one. In the new millennium China's importance and international standing is bound to increase and so will India's. The two countries, therefore, need each other and have to work hand in hand. Both sides have everything to gain from improved bilateral ties. Friendship with China will be a bargaining chip in dealing with threats to our security. If, however, China and India want to move towards a further blossoming of their relationship, the two countries have to first of all try and promote mutual trust and understanding.

The Chinese Ambassador to India Zhang Yan has rightly pointed out, "Mutual understanding and trust between the two countries need to be further strengthened." [67] Both sides need to extricate themselves the vicious circle of the old mindsets that have conditioned and given rise to mutual perceptions which in turn have governed relations between the two countries. The question from the Indian perspective is whether we are strategizing for "security from China" or for "security with China." [68]

At this stage, both the elements are visible on the face of India's diplomacy vis-à-vis China. [69] Is not the same true of Chinese diplomacy towards India as well?

End Notes

1. C.V. Ranganathan, "India and China : Asia's giants", *The Hindu* (Special Independence Day Volume), August 15, 1997, p. 132.
2. For the first seven years the negotiations were labelled "senior level talks." In 1988, the tag was changed to "joint working group" and then to "special representatives' talks" – a process that was initiated in June, 2003.
3. For a brief discussion of Sino-Indian relations in the context of these two issues see the author's paper in S.D. Muni and Suranjan Das (eds.), *India and China: the Next Decade*, New Delhi, Rupa. Co., 2009, pp. 60-65.
4. Snehalata Panda, "Sino-Indian Relations in a New Perspective," *Strategic Analysis*, Vol. 27, No.1, January-March 2003, p. 125.
5. Ranganathan, *op. cit.*, p. 133.

6. C. Uday Bhaskar, "A Small Step Forward: Measured Approach towards China," *The Times of India* (New Delhi), August 3, 2000.
7. *News from China* (Embassy of the People's Republic of China, New Delhi), Vol. XVII, No.4, April 2005, p. 18.
8. *Ibid.*, p. 11.
9. *Ibid.*, p. 18. For a detailed study of the importance of the visit of Premier Wen Jiabao, see, *Premier Wen Jiabao's Visit to India : Prospect and Retrospect*, Occasional Study No.7, 2005, Institute of Chinese Studies (Delhi).
10. *The Times of India*, June 1, 2006. Not long ago, while addressing a gathering at Mumbai, Pranab Mukherjee had stressed the importance of our not forgetting in our policy-making that India had once been invaded by China. The Chinese Consul-General in Mumbai, who was present at that meeting, strongly objected to the remarks. And yet, Pranab Mukherjee himself presented a totally positive projection of China both during his visit to China and on his return. See, B. Raman, "See no evil, hear no evil...", *The Pioneer* (New Delhi), June 28, 2006.
11. The decision to resume trade between India and China through Nathu La was first taken in 2003 during the historic visit of former Indian Prime Minister Atal Behari Vajpayee to Beijing. New Delhi had interpreted Nathu La's acceptance as the India trade point to be Beijing's first step towards fully recognising Sikkim as an integral part of India. Later in 2003, during the ASEAN (Association of South East Asian Nations) Summit in Bali, Beijing had informed India about Sikkim's removal from the Chinese foreign ministry's website. *Strategic Digest* (Institute for Defence Studies and Analyses, New Delhi), Vol. 36, No.5, May 2006, p. 663.
12. Zhang Lijun, "Path to Prosperity", *Beijing Review*, Vol. 49, No. 29, July 20, 2006, p. 12.
13. *The Asian Age* editorial, November 23, 2006.
14. C.P. Bhambri, "Alter the pro-US prism", *The Pioneer*, December 4, 2006.
15. *The Economic Times*, November 24, 2006.
16. *The Asian Age*, November 23, 2006.
17. *Ibid.*
18. According to a study undertaken by the Associated Chambers of

Commerce and Industry of India (Assocham). Sino-Indian bilateral trade will touch $ 50 billion by 2010 and both the countries may jointly dominate world trade completely. *The Statesman* (Kolkata), November 20, 2006.

19. *The Pioneer*, June 26, 2006.
20. *Ibid.*
21. P.S. Suryanarayana, 'A new entente', *Frontline*, February 24, 2006, p. 50.
22. *The Asian Age*, June 14, 2006.
23. *The Times of India*, April 7, 2005.
24. *The Asian Age*, November 23, 2006.
25. *The Statesman*, October 20, 2006.
26. Hong Hu, "Building Bridges", *Beijing Review*, vol. 48, no.14, April 7, 2005, p. 24.
27. Alka Acharya, "Climbing Down", *The Economic Times*, November 17, 2006.
28. See, *News from China*, vol. XVIII, no.3, March 2006, pp. 13-14.
29. *Strategic Digest*, vol. 36, no.2, February 2006, p. 161.
30. Acharya, *op. cit.*
31. G. Parthasarathy, "Strategic partner or threat", *The Pioneer*, June 29, 2006.
32. *The Times of India*, September 11, 2006.
33. *The Asian Age*, June 14, 2006.
34. *News from China, op. cit.*, p. 13.
35. *The Times of India*, April 7, 2005.
36. *The Asian Age*, June 14, 2006.
37. *The Statesman*, October 1, 2007.
38. *Ibid.*
39. One may in this connection refer to the reservations expressed by the six holdout countries–Austria, Netherlands, Norway, Ireland, New Zealand and Switzerland. Ireland, Austria and New Zealand especially stuck to their positions till the last moment.
40. *The Pioneer*, Marh 6, 2006.
41. Zhang Lijun, "A Passage to South Asia", *Beijing Review*, vol. 49, no.11, March 16, 2006, p. 14.
42. B. Raman, "Who gained from Hu's visit?", *The Pioneer*, December 5, 2006. The editorial appeared after a meeting of the Nuclear Suppliers Group (NSG) members on the Indo-US deal. *Ibid.*
43. *The Economic Times*, December 8, 2006.

44. Raman, "Who gained from Hu's visit?", *op.cit.*
45. *The Pioneer*, February 17, 2006.
46. *The Statesman*, November 20, 2006.
47. *Ibid.*
48. Anil K. Joseph, "China quiet on deal passage", *The Asian Age*, November 18, 2006.
49. Suryanarayana, "A new entente", *op.cit.*
50. *The Pioneer*, July 21, 2005.
51. Lijun, "A Passage to South Asia", *op.cit.*
52. Tatiana Shaumian, "Hu cares about oil", *The Pioneer*, April 30, 2006.
53. *Ibid.*
54. See, Ashley J. Tellis, "Testing Waters", *The Statesman*, July 19, 2005.
55. John Cherian, "The China factor", *Frontline*, March 10, 2006, p. 16.
56. *Ibid.*
57. *The Times of India*, November 27, 2006.
58. Indrani Bagchi, "Beijing softens stand as talks begin at IAEA", *The Times of India*, November 22, 2007.
59. *The Economic Times*, January 15, 2008.
60. *Ibid.* In any case, Chinese stand on the importance of the precondition of abiding by the international non-proliferation mechanism with regard to cooperation on the peaceful use of nuclear energy remained unchanged. In September 2007 Chinese foreign ministry spokesperson Jiang Yu had said, "We believe that all countries can carry out cooperation on the peaceful use of nuclear energy under the precondition of abiding by the international obligations. The relevant cooperation should be conducive to maintaining and strengthening the principles and validity of the international non-proliferation mechanism". *The Economic Times*, September 17, 2007.
61. *The Economic Times*, September 17, 2007.
62. Rabindra Sen, "Chinese Chequers", *The Telegraph*, July 17, 2008.
63. Pranab Dhal Samanta, *Indian Express*, Posted online: Sunday, September 07, 2008 at 0557 hrs. (Internet source).
64. *Ibid.*
65. *Ibid.*
66. Indian Express, Posted online: September 07, 2008 at 0120 hrs.

(Internet source:
http://www.indianexpress.com/story_print.php?storyid=358283).

67. See, *News from China*, vol. XXI, no.4, April 2009, p. 10.
68. Rabindra Sen, "Rhetoric and Reality', *The Telegraph*, April 8, 2009.
69. *Ibid.*

18

China and Regional Security Architecture

D.S. Rajan

A debate among major Asia-Pacific nations on what exactly should be the ultimate regional security architecture is now in progress at a time, when fast-growing trade linkages and deepening cooperation through various integration mechanisms have already been transforming the region's economic and political landscape. The debate itself certainly looks like a response to the rising impact on the region from a combination of traditional and non-traditional security threats; its objective is also becoming clear - progressing towards evolving a new security mechanism for the whole region, supplanting the existing various sub-regional groupings. In this process, the centrality, which the People's Republic of China (PRC), a fast rising regional and global player, would occupy, may not be difficult to imagine. Beijing's emerging views of a regional architecture as expected, are closely linked to its own security perceptions and at the same time, it cannot be denied that the same is the case with other key Asia-Pacific powers, like Japan, ASEAN, Australia, the US and India. As views vary, the intra-regional differences on the subject being noticed appear normal. However, the final picture likely to emerge becomes important. In the ensuing paragraphs, an attempt has been made to trace various positions and to analyse their likely implications for the evolution of a regional security mechanism, acceptable to all nations concerned.

China's Vision

Beijing's stated vision is to establish 'harmony' in Asia-Pacific region; to achieve this, it has proposed a regional security cooperation concept featuring 'equality, mutual benefit, openness and practicality', according 'due role' to ASEAN Regional Forum (ARF) Security Policy Conferences. In its view, in parallel to the pursuit of such a co-operation, the existing regional and sub-regional cooperation mechanisms need to be developed. [1] By way of seeking to explain its 'harmony' goal in strategic terms, the PRC thinks that ' peace is a product of parity, balance of power and offensive and defensive strengths' and that no sacrificing of the security interest of one country need be involved in helping other nations achieve security. In this context, it believes that there should be no expansion of military alliances and deployment of missile defence system in the region; 'missile defence partnership in some areas would be detrimental to the interests of strategic balance, confidence building and regional stability'. [2]

China also stresses the connectivity between regional security and its 'new thinking' on security, based on 'mutual trust, mutual benefit, equality and coordination'. [3] It believes in the 'non-exclusive' nature of regional cooperation and in drawing on the development practices of other regions. [4]

Japan's Position

Japan's official position is to accept the need for a 'multilateral collective defence security mechanism' in the Asia-Pacific region, similar to the North Atlantic Treaty Organisation (NATO) in Europe. Tokyo, at the same time, admits problems in this regard due to the existing 'diversity in the region's political and economic systems, cultures and ethnicities'. In these circumstances, Japan seems to prefer a short-term approach aimed at 'strengthening the existing multi-layer frameworks for bilateral and multilateral dialogue, while securing the presence and engagement of the US in the region'. [5] It lays emphasis on the 'synergy between Japan-US Security alliance and Tokyo's Asian diplomacy'. Japan also feels that the 'balance of power' factor could be significant in the changing regional security environment, but what is essential in this regard is the countries concerned, reaching 'mutual understanding'. Tokyo does not treat China as a threat to Japan, but wants Beijing to enhance the transparency of its military capabilities and their true purpose. [6] Some scholars in Japan have been more specific than the government on regional security mechanism. They have stressed the need for an "East Asia Security Forum" consisting of core states (ASEAN plus 6 including India, along with the US).

The Forum, in their view, should reflect the principle of 'inclusive multilateralism' and 'cooperative security'. Concerning China, they recommend a 'cautious' Japanese engagement with that country, 'predicated on traditional balance of power approach' and for this purpose, foresee a 'consolidation of strategic links between the four largest democratic states—Japan, India, Australia and the US. [7]

ASEAN

The ASEAN views itself as the 'centre' of the regional security architecture. [8] It visualizes the roles of a 'facilitator' and 'honest broker' to itself for the architecture, citing the reason that ASEAN nations enjoy the distinction of being in a 'pivotal geographic position', that enables it to provide a 'neutral ground where powers with intersecting interests meet'. It hopes that the architecture could be shaped as the existing various structures like the East Asia Summits, Shangrila Dialogue and ASEAN Defence Ministers meetings, continue to evolve. The ASEAN identifies "three principles" to guide the development of an effective architecture namely, 1) the regional security is a matter of collective responsibility of all the countries that have a stake in the region's security, 2) the architecture should be 'open and inclusive', and 3) the regional cooperation should be based on mutual respect and is in accordance with international law. [9]

Australia

Australia stands for a creation of an 'Asia-Pacific Community' by 2020, a body similar to the European Union, to span the entire region including itself, the US, Japan, China, India, Indonesia and other regional powers and visualizes a charter for such a Community to get engaged in 'a full spectrum of dialogue, cooperation and action in economic and political matters and future challenges relating to security'. Canberra's concept has evolved from two premises—the global economic and strategic weight is shifting to Asia and the existing fora like ASEAN were not designed to promote cooperation across the entire region, in view of the 'greater diversity' in the region's political systems and the economic structures. [10] A remedy to the situation is readily found in the proposed Community which could 'enhance the region's "fragmented" security and political cooperation as well as help resolve a number of regional conflicts that tantamount to raging controversies on Taiwan, Kashmir and North Korea. [11] China promptly welcomed the proposal by saying that the latter idea is in line with its hope for joint efforts in the region to 'enhance exchanges and mutual political trust as well as deepen mutually beneficial cooperation, for achieving common development'. [12]

The US

The US acknowledges the 'provisional' nature of efforts to find a new Asia-Pacific security architecture and welcomes the ASEAN leadership in this search. It assures continued commitment to the region as a 'resident' power as certain as its 'sovereign' territory stretches from the Aleutian Islands to Guam in the Western Pacific. While discussions on a new security architecture progress further, Washington in the interim would like to get various existing forums institutionalized deal with the 'region-specific' problems and to depend on its 'time-tested' architecture involving 'alliances' (with Japan, South Korea, Philippines and Thailand) and "partner-nation capacity building" (with India and Vietnam), the latter being described as a 'new thinking in US overall defence strategy'.

As per the declared US benchmarks for building new security architecture, that process should not be a 'zero sum game' and anything like an exclusion of a single country would mean ignoring the reality of Asia's security today. Besides, 'the entire region should be treated as a single entity and that there should be no separate East Asian order'. [13]

India

In New Delhi's formulations, Asian security cannot be viewed in isolation from the region's broader political and economic aspects. To accommodate Asia's 'diversity', a 'pluralistic security order' based on a 'cooperative' approach, is indispensable. Under such 'polycentric' security, each participant will have 'equal stake and responsibility'. India believes that the order must be 'open and inclusive' and must take into account the conditions prevailing in Asia. There should be no transplant of ideas from other parts of the world and any sub-regional security arrangements that are narrow and ultimately ineffective, should not be created. The building blocks for the new framework could be the dialogue forums like ARF, Comprehensive International Cooperative Association (CICA) and Shanghai Cooperation Organization (SCO). [14]

Positional Analysis

A comparative analysis of the positions of major Asia-Pacific players on the regional security architecture reveals divisions among themselves on the following issues:

1. **Participation of the US:** If the phrase 'open and inclusive' is missing in Chinese formulations it would imply the Chinese being cautious about the US participation in the architecture which, despite Beijing's support albeit on at its own terms, is to be ascribed finally

to the Australian proposal that includes the US by all means. On the other hand, a near-unanimity prevails among other nations on the US role. The US itself is against 'any zero sum game' and exclusion of any country in the region. It may not be happy about its existing exclusion from the regional bodies like the East Asia Summit, Shanghai Cooperation Organization and India-China-Russia trilateral dialogue. Japan, on its own part, is firm in backing the US 'presence and engagement' in the region. ASEAN, by insisting on 'collective responsibility of all states that have a stake in the region's security', has indicated its approval of the US involvement. India's formula of an 'open and inclusive' architecture also reflects a stand welcoming the US.

2. **US Alliances in Asia:** The US and Japan on one side and China on the other, are clearly at odds with each other on the issue of American alliances in Asia. Washington's emphasis on its 'tested alliances' in the region and Japan's vision of 'synergy between US-Japan alliance and Tokyo's Asian diplomacy' stand in contrast to Beijing's perception that the US-led alliance in Asia is detrimental to the interests of the 'strategic balance' in the region.
3. **Who Should Lead the Architecture?:** On this issue, India and Japan seem to be on the same side; India's 'polycentric' approach matches with Japan's line to set up a 'multilateral collective security mechanism'. In comparison, ASEAN tends to stress its own 'centrality' in the architecture. The Chinese formulations are silent on the subject. However, their mention of 'parity', 'equality' and 'balance of power' and prescription that the security of one nation should not be sacrificed while ensuring the security of others, reveal Beijing's mind on the security order that the PRC should play a central role. Beijing and Tokyo desire a 'balance of power', but their interpretations are utterly different from each other. The PRC's intention to play a 'pre-eminent' role is already manifest in its

declaration of support extended to the leadership of the ASEAN plus three (including the PRC) in matters of ASEAN Regional community but with Beijing giving 'long term and strategic guidance'.

4. **Learning from other Models:** Sino-Indian divergence is apparent on this subject. In matters of regional cooperation, China is in favour of learning from outside powers; India's stand on the other hand, is to build an architecture by taking into account only the conditions in Asia, without resorting to any transplant of ideas from other parts of the world.
5. **Sub-regional Security Arrangements:** India is against the creation of any 'ineffective sub-regional security arrangements' lest New Delhi's attitude towards the ASEAN's goal of forming a Regional Community by 2015, which has a security component should be questioned. Also, India, China, Japan and the US approve in varying degrees, the development of the existing sub-regional organizations, till a regional architecture emerges. Still, Australia seems to display a subtle difference in its attitude on this issue. Canberra considers such organisations as the ARF, as incapable of addressing the problems of the region in their entirety and on this basis, opts for a regional mechanism.

Concerns: Vision Connectivity

Differences of opinions are bound to surface in a debate. However, the security concerns of each country should be correlated with its respective positions on the regional security architecture. Taking the case of Japan first, its perception of the US alliance as a key to face threats from China (caused mainly by the military modernization and resource development in East China Sea), from Russia (created by unsettled territorial issue) and from North Korea (because of the nuclear weapon programme) provides an underpinning to its vision of a regional order with the US involvement.

ASEAN too, sees in the US a security guarantor against the impact from China-related potential conflicts (South China Sea territorial disputes) and a balancing factor to China's rise. This, along with the threats from extremism and the contradiction between Islam and modernization in Southeast Asia, have been influencing the ASEAN view of a regional security order. In regional forums, where the US is not represented, ASEAN has been careful in opposing the Chinese proposals which are likely to harm the US interests. For example, it did not accept Beijing's offer to join the Southeast Asia Nuclear Free Zone, which excludes the US.

For Australia, the priority for the new government led by Prime Minister Kevin Rudd is to act as a balancer of relations with China and the West and accordingly, his "Asia-Pacific Community" concept is being regarded as an effort to create an institution providing checks and balances between major powers. While an alliance with the US continues to be important for it, Canberra is increasingly eyeing the economic benefits coming out of cementing relations with Beijing. China has become important for Australia for mining and agriculture exports and it has emerged as Australia's second largest trading partner. Japan and ASEAN, on their parts remain cool to Rudd's idea. Prime Minister Fukuda took no notice of the idea during Rudd's visit to his country. Instead, he chose to emphasize the significant roles of Japan and ASEAN in the context of the Asia-Pacific. ASEAN is of the view that Rudd has deviated from the principles of his predecessor over regional integration. The re-assurance later of Prime Minister Rudd that ASEAN would continue to be the 'core' of existing regional architecture, [15] did not suffice to clear the air.

The US perceptions of a global and regional security order are also linked with its views on the emerging world and the Asia-Pacific security scenarios. In this regard, the challenges being perceived by Washington concern Iran, Iraq, Afghanistan and Russia globally and China, Myanmar and North Korea regionally. The 2008 'US National Defence

Strategy' identifies terrorism (Iraq and Afghanistan) as the main global threat and as a shift from the strategy adopted so far to deal with that, has begun to give focus to the use of both 'hard' and 'soft' power. China and Russia have been listed as powers which have 'potentials' to challenge the US-led international order. The US will strive to establish partnership with the two. But Washington will 'hedge against Beijing's growing military modernization and impact of its strategic choices on international security'. US interaction with China will be for a long term and multidimensional. [16] In Asia-Pacific, the US stated goal is to form "a new Asia-Pacific Democratic Partnership". [17]

India's profile in the Asia-Pacific region is increasing as a result of its Look East Policy the scope of which now stands extended to wider East Asia and Pacific basin. New Delhi feels that this, coupled with growing inter-dependence between the nations, have widened the scope of India's responsibility in the region. In its view, the nature and scope of trans-border threats are rising and issues relating to climatic change and food and energy security, are also becoming important. [18] To meet the main challenges of the border, maritime security and energy security, India is building its own leverages in the region; it is taking active steps like holding talks on border issue with China, conducting active maritime diplomacy and carrying out energy cooperation. The fact that India has become a significant factor in the Asia-Pacific balance of power, cannot be disputed; however, a rivalry between New Delhi and Beijing seems implicit in this process. Herein lies the real meaning of New Delhi's 'polycentric' approach to regional security architecture.

China's role will be the key to setting up of a regional architecture. The current picture points to a situation of 'Beijing versus the rest'. It is because of the significant differences between its stand and that of other nations. China's regional security concerns, as can be seen from various official documents and pronouncements, relate to 'still not properly solved territorial and maritime disputes', Taiwan issue, the 'three evils' of terrorism, ethnic separatism and religious extremism and threats to sea lanes of communication. Beijing also discerns challenges in the US alliances and deployment of missile systems in the region, weaponisation of outer space and nuclear proliferation. It views with strong suspicions the US role in the region, particularly its ties with Japan and India as reflecting attempts to 'contain' China. The quadrilateral concept of 'alliance of democracies' (Japan, Australia, US and India) and the joint 'Malabar' military exercises by these nations, have been the principal Chinese targets. Beijing also thinks that the Indo-US civil nuclear cooperation agreement is against the interests of the international non-proliferation regime and that India's nuclear programme is a security threat for China.

Signs of China's hesitation to give a leading role to India in regional integration, are not difficult to see. For instance, India's regional cooperation policy is being criticised by China for its alleged aim to control the Malacca Straits. [19] In the formation of the proposed ASEAN Regional Community also, Beijing visualises no role for India. [20] Instead, it wants to play a 'guiding' role to ASEAN plus 3 in this regard. Regarding East Asia summits, the PRC is only willing to accept India (and also Australia and New Zealand) as an 'outsider' member. The Chinese actual attitude to India runs contrary to what President Hu Jintao had said in India (November 2006), "Both China and India positively view each others' participation in Asian inter- regional, regional and sub-regional cooperation process". It is not at all surprising that the concerns of Beijing as mentioned above, are finding an echo in the Chinese vision for a regional architecture.

Conclusion

The PRC appears to believe that its concerns can effectively be dealt with only by a security order led by it; this is, despite its 'rhetoric' on 'equality and parity' in the order.

Beijing, in this regard, sees the US as principal challenger and this imposes on China the necessity to have an Asia-Pacific strategy aimed at limiting the US power and exerting influence in the region thereby to rise as a dominant regional power. Japan and the nations in Southeast Asia (especially Malaysia, Singapore, Thailand and the Philippines, which have increased their military ties with the US) are, on the other hand, looking at the US, for balancing China's rise and for getting the regional security stabilized. India, on its part, is giving equal importance to confidence building with China and strengthening of the partnership with the US, besides getting closer to other regional powers which carry a clout, like Japan, ASEAN etc. Especially, it does not want to be seen as one belonging to any anti-China grouping but still, Beijing suspects New Delhi's pro-US tilt. What is being witnessed ultimately is a Sino-US competition threatening to complicate the regional geo-politics. Suffice it to conclude that it is the bounden responsibility of all the major powers involved, the US, China, Japan and India to create the much-needed regional security architecture, acceptable to one and all.

End Notes

1. Speech of Chen Ziaogong, Assistant Chief of PLA General Staff at ARF Security Policy Conference, Singapore, *Xinhua*, May 8, 2008.
2. Speech of Lt Gen Ma Xiaotian, Deputy Chief of PLA General Staff at the 7th International IISS Shangrila Dialogue, Singapore, May 31, 2008.
3. President Hu Jintao's speech at Boao Forum, Hainan, 12 April 2008, *Xinhua*, April 13, 2008.
4. *Ibid.*
5. *Japan Diplomatic Blue Book*, 2008.
6. Speech of Japanese Defence Minister Shigeru Ishiba at the 7th IISS Security Summit, Shangrila Dialogue, Singapore, May 31, 2008.
7. Hitoshi Tanaka, "East Asia Community Building: Toward an East Asia Security Forum," *East Asia Insights*, Vol. 2, April 2, 2007.

8. *China Daily*, August 13, 2008, quoting from a June 2008 statement of the ASEAN rotating Presidency.
9. "ASEAN and Asia's Regional security Architecture," Speech of Singapore Defence Minister Teo Chee Hean, at the Munich Conference of Security Policy, February 10, 2008.
10. Australian Prime Minister Kevin Rudd's speech at Asia Society Australasia Centre, Sydney, June 5, 2008.
11. *The China Post*, quoting Australian Prime Minister Rudd, June 6, 2008.
12. *Ibid*, quoting PRC Foreign Ministry spokesperson Qin Gang.
13. Speech of the US Defence Secretary Robert Gates at the IISS Shangrila Dialogue, Singapore, May 31, 2008.
14. Speech of Mr Pranab Mukherjee, India's Minister for External Affairs, at Peking University, June 6, 2008, http://www.indianembassy.org.cn/Press/20080611-3.htm.
15. *China Daily*, August 13, 2008.
16. US Department of Defence website, also *Peoples Daily*, August 6, 2008.
17. White House Press Secretary, August 7, 2008.
18. Dr Manmohan Singh's speech at the Combined Commanders Conference, New Delhi, October 24, 2007.
19. Prof. James Holmes, US–China Economic and Security Review Commission, US Naval War College, June 14, 2007.
20. ASEAN Secretary-General Ong Ken Yong, *Bloomburg*, November 20, 2007.

19

India-Australia Relations: Possible Avenues of Energy Co-operation

G. Jayachandra Reddy

Energy has a critical place in the Trade and Economic Framework because India is the world's sixth largest energy consumer and its energy needs are growing. Australia, meanwhile, is a net energy exporter. So a neat fit is emerging.
– Warren Truss, Minister for Trade, Australia

Energy is a key element of national economic development and is therefore an essential component of national security. [1] Energy, in general is conceived as a resource for many a service in day-to-day activities along with other resources. Befittingly, it can be described as a source for igniting complementarities as well as conflicts; rise and downfall of economies; victory and defeat of a war; tradition and modernity of society; dependence and subsistence; obligatory and dictatory and energy, environment and development, eventually, which can dictate the road map of geopolitics as well the world order of the day. Geopolitical significance of a region/country can be determined through its demand and supply equations of energy. For instance, Dennis Rumley and Sanjay Chaturvedi view that the India Ocean Region has become increasingly important to any discussion of energy security, not only because of the critical importance of regional states as energy suppliers, but also because of the essential role of the Ocean as an energy route. [2] It is a well-known fact that of all global seaborne trade, the maximum tonnage moves through the Indian Ocean in any year. Unlike the other major oceans of the world where littoral trade accounts for nearly 70 percent of the volume, in the Indian Ocean, only 20 percent is intra-regional, the rest is being accounted for countries external to the region. [3]

In view of the burgeoning economy of Asian countries and emerging as one of the major world markets, Indian Ocean, obviously, has been attached much strategic significance, by both external powers as well as littoral states. Because of its huge economy, population and size apart from its location, comparatively India's concerns over India Ocean is very much significant. The Indian Ocean littorals are also privy to 65 percent of the world's total oil reserves and 35 percent of its natural gas. [4] India's dependency on Indian Ocean for its seaborne trade, especially crude oil and natural gas requirements will be growing for ever, which emphasizes that India can't ignore the strategic significance of Indian Ocean security and to resolve enduring India's energy security. India's relations with Australia are nothing but extending the strategic energy cooperation in line with the strategic security of Indian Ocean. In view of the growing importance of the energy in general and Ocean waters as routes as well as sources of energy playing another significant role, being a pivot, Indian Ocean has been crucial in terms of energy security.

With this background India and Australia are expected to make a platform to promote bilateral cooperation towards energy security. India and Australia are exposing two exclusive characteristics of energy security; greater demand and energy crisis, and leading exporter of energy and exceptionally handling the energy crisis management systems respectively. With certain multidimensional strategic, economic and energy significance of bilateral cooperation, an attempt is made to conduct a study with a scope of identifying possible areas of energy cooperation between India and Australia.

Energy Demand Dynamics

Thanks to industrial revolution, its implications are

experienced over energy sector, unusual expansion of markets and proportionate enhancement of production of goods and services. In certain situations the access between producer and consumer becomes detrimental and leads to global financial crisis that simply means what we have been experiencing since few months. Evidently, inflation rates are reaching the peak and affecting the life of a common man, specifically unimaginable from third world countries. Of course, such incidents are temporary and its impact may be low but permanent.

Energy is another criterion to bring a division between countries like producing and consuming. Though, many developed countries are endowed with limited energy resources, they are capable of managing their requirements with large scale investments in the developing countries–directly or indirectly. This is only a short gap. On the other side the developing nations basically creating larger markets, obviously, generate new opportunities for investment in producing goods and services of their own. This situation gradually comes to peak and demands energy equally with developed countries, within a couple of decades.

During the last quarter of 20th Century (1980-2006), primary energy consumption increased by about 64 percent (from 6.64 BT to 10.89 BT); oil by 31 percent (from 2.96 BT to 3.89 BT); gas by a spectacular 98 percent (1.45 TCM to 2.87 TCM), primarily driven by the growing demand from developing world. [5] World primary energy consumption increased by 2.4 percent in 2007, down from 2.7 percent in 2006 but still the fifth consecutive year it is of above average growth. The Asia-Pacific region accounted for two-thirds of global energy consumption growth, rising by an above average 5 percent, even though consumption in Japan declined by 0.9 percent. North American consumption rebounded after a weak year in 2006, raising by 1.6 percent doubling the ten years average. Chinese growth of 7.7 percent was the weakest since 2002, still it is above the ten years average (as was China's economic growth). China again accounted for half of global energy consumption growth. Indian consumption grew by 6.8 percent, the third largest volumetric increment after China and the US. EU energy consumption declined by 2.2 percent, with Germany registering the world's largest decline in energy consumption. [6]

Table 19.1: Consumption by Fuel Type (Quadrillion BTU and percentages)

Category of Energy	1980	1990	2002
Petroleum	131 (46)	136 (39)	159 (39)
Natural Gas	54 (19)	75 (22)	95 (23)
Coal	71 (25)	90 (26)	98 (24)
Hydroeletronic	18 (6)	23 (7)	27 (7)
Nuclear	8 (3)	20 (6)	27 (7)
Total	285 (100)	348 (100)	411 (100)

Source: EIA, *also see* Energy Security Issues, *The World Bank Group*, 2005, No. 36110.

Altogether, the data explicitly indicates that the demand for energy will be very much promised. This is the high time for any country to concentrate and improve the capacity of their energy production. Recent events in oil and other markets have brought the issue of energy security to the forefront. High and volatile price rise affects short term risks to economic growth and long term energy security. Although it will mean different things to different countries, there is a strong common interest that ensures the world can produce and use energy at reasonable costs and in a sustainable way to ensure the quality of life of the world's peoples. [7]

Undoubtedly, energy security has become a prime agenda before independent economies and at global level, irrespective of size and quality of economic character of a nation. At this situation diversity of resource base, demography, demand, production and the scientific treatment of the energy security should be taken into consideration.

Poverty reduction and economic growth are the prime objectives of national policy, but this formula seems to be very difficult in the Indian context. An analysis considering endowment base, population and access to energy provides a glaring energy security of India. Per capita energy consumption in India is less than 500 kgoe, compared to the global average of nearly 1,800 kgoe. [8] India is currently known to hold 0.5 percent of the world's oil reserve (BP 2007). Most of the fields are in declining stage and around 80 percent of oil being produced today comes from field discovered before 1974. India's share in world oil production is 1 percent, with ONGC contributing almost 82 percent of it. However, India is the 6th largest consumer of oil, consuming 3.1 percent (over 120 million tones) of the world oil share and 70 percent of which is being imported. India's gas reserve is also only 0.5 percent of the world's reserve. Its production share stands at 1.1 percent, with ONGC contributing 79 percent of it.

The key to self sufficiency in the energy sector depends not only on the resources, but on many other factors–generation, distribution, efficiency in usage, reduction of losses in transmission and storage. The development of environmental friendly technologies is imperative for public acceptance of high power systems. Higher fuel prices and emphasis on 'return on capital' are the two major considerations that demand construction of plants, capable of running with minimal maintenance over extended lifetimes. Simultaneously, there is a need to reduce particulate and pollutant emissions and eliminate generation of greenhouse gases. Transmission systems must be reconfigured to operate in a more distributed fashion; high energy density storage devices should be developed. All these stages need innovative inputs from both science and engineering disciplines. [9]

Energy Situation in India and Australia

Recent oil (and other commodity) price rises, and

continued rapid industrialization in China and India, have raised concerns about longer term energy security. Almost all mainstream energy forecasters predict growing global demand growth, underpinned by developing country growth and continued, albeit much slower, growth in demand in the industrialized economies. For example, the latest forecasts of the International Energy Agency (IEA) show total global energy demand increasing by more than 50 percent by 2030. [10] This study requires comparative analysis of the basic components of energy of India and Australia. Such analytical framework provides a platform where the important potentials and weaknesses of both the countries can be easily understood. Of course, the analysis of entire spectrum of energy components is certainly difficult in view of the availability of data. Presently few major components—oil, coal and natural gas—have been considered for analysis.

Oil is one of the most important components of energy. It also involves many processes to get the end product for consumption. Analysis of the significance of oil production, consumption and refinery certainly provides clarity in between the supply and demand ratio and the efficiency of refining of oil. In fact, many other issues–oil reserves, per capita consumption, production and refinery–have not been included, due to certain limitations. There is coordination between production, consumption and refinery in Australia, whereas in Indian context, oil production has not been changed over a decade (1997-2007) but consumption growth has become mandatory due to its larger population growth and escalating demand for oil. Just because of this reason India largely depends on crude oil imports and so domestic refinery activities are increasing. It is necessary for India to learn from Australia, how the balance is possible between consumption and production oil.

Coal plays significant role in guiding any country's economic growth and development. When India and Australia are taken into consideration for comparison, lot more interesting identical and contrary observations are possible. In view of explosive population and lack of alternative approaches towards other non-conventional energy resources, obviously, demand for coal may be very high. On the other hand, Australia's demand for coal and its consumption is consistent over a period of eleven years (1997-2007). It is mainly because of optimum population growth that provides an opportunity to have surplus production and export of coal. India's absolute production is higher than Australia's total coal production but inverse relationship between production and demand of coal is observed. Less production and more consumption is the character of India's dependency for coal imports as against to Australia's exportable surplus through more production and less consumption.

Technically natural gas is another important aspect of energy. Analysis of demand and supply ratios of natural gas is no way different from coal distribution and reflects similar characteristics in the case of the distribution of natural gas and its demand and supply ratios. Moreover, India is inferior to Australia in its absolute production and in recent times India is also missing its balance between production and consumption. Surprisingly, India's consumption has been multiplying since 2004 and against stagnation in its production. Such trend is significantly alarming the rate of demand for natural gas. To answer this question, either India should try to accelerate domestic production or efforts must be on the lines to go for international strategic gas pipelines, which certainly support to meet the long run demands of natural gas in India.

Enhancing energy security will require a far sighted and cooperative approach internationally, as well as a variety of specific initiatives and interventions at the national and international level. [11] The analytical summary clearly exhibits that India and Australia are abundantly producing fossil fuels like, coal, oil and natural gas. The fundamental difference lies with the per capita production and consumption. On the other hand Australia has proved its advancement in other areas of energy (energy conservation methods).

Complementarities between India and Australia

Australia and India relations have significantly grown in the post cold war period encompassing greater political, economic, defence and scientific fields, and people-to-people cooperation. In the recent past India's relations with the United States also improved tremendously and resulted in the form of nuclear deal. Obviously, it would become a testimony in favour of India in dealing the nuclear deal with other countries.

Australian Foreign Affairs Minister, Downer, on the occasion of ASEAN 40 Ministerial Meeting and 14th Regional Forum in Manila, hailed the successful completion of negotiations between India and the United States as a 'very positive and historic development...which is very much in Australia's interest.' and also emphasized that the relationship between Australia and India has never been stronger. As economic partners and on security and strategic issues, Australia and India are collaborating at a level not seen before. [12]

Australia's uranium supply to India can be looked at a triangular issue–request from China and India for the same, the influence of the United States and the national interests of Australia. India's External Affairs Minister, Mukherjee replying to a question said that it was not appropriate "to compare (India) with China. Because, China is a nuclear-weapon state, which India is not (under the Nuclear Non-Proliferation Treaty)". [13]

Mukherjee, in an another meeting with his Australian counterpart Stephen Smith has agreed to take the level of relations to a 'strategic partnership' and work towards the objective...and also welcomed the ongoing work to develop strategy papers under the Joint Working Group on Energy and Resource, to further enhance Australia-India cooperation. [14]

In 2004, nuclear power met approximately 3 percent of India's electricity demands. India has 15 power reactors in operation with a total generating capacity of 3,310 megawatts electrical (MWe). India has plans for a major expansion of nuclear electricity generation. Seven reactors are under construction with a planned capacity of 3,920 MWe. A further 19 are proposed. India plans to generate 25 percent of its electricity with 20,000 MWe of nuclear capacity by 2020. [15] Geoscience Australia stated that India's prospectivity for major uranium deposits is low. India has reasonably assured resources of 42,568 tonnes of uranium recoverable at less than US$ 130/kg., compared to Australia's resources of 701,000 tonnes recoverable at less than US$ 40/kg. [16]

Cebu Declaration on East Asian Energy Security, 15 January 2007 addresses three major issues–to increase energy efficiency, to reduce excessive dependency on fossil fuels by developing alternative energies and to guarantee a stable energy supply, especially in countries which have become more dependent on imports. [17]

For this purpose, in Cebu Japan announced a cooperation initiative, worth US$ 2 billion, to promote energy savings and to spread the use of clean energy in the rest of the Asia-Pacific region. Further more, the East Asia Summit agreed to create a working group on energy cooperation, which will deliver a report at the next summit, as well as arrange a system of periodical meetings between Energy Ministers (already in place in ASEAN and the ASEAN+3 process, known as AMEM and AMEM+3, respectively). [18]

Australia has a longstanding policy of selling uranium only to those countries that are party to the Nuclear Non-Proliferation Treaty and which have a bilateral safeguard agreement in place with Australia. Under this policy Australia is currently unable to sell uranium to India. There are no automatic implications for Canberra's policy from the nuclear cooperation agreement between the US and India. [19]

The third meeting of the India-Australia Joint Working Group on Energy and Minerals was held in Canberra on 29-30, January, 2003. The meeting of the Joint Working Group reviewed the Protocol of the 1st and 2nd Meetings and also identified new project proposals in the fields of Mining, Coal, Power, Petroleum & Natural Gas and Non-Conventional Energy Sources and decided to work together to develop the collaborative projects discussed during the meeting.

India also accounted for 6 percent of Australia's energy exports in 2005-06, from 5 percent in 1995-96. [20] The Australian Bureau of Agricultural and Resource Economics (ABARE), expects that Indian LNG imports will increase to 8.1 million tonnes per annum (mtpa) by 2010 and 11.2 mtpa by 2015. This will involve an expansion at the existing import terminals and/or new LNG terminal projects. [21]

Ravi Kastia, Group Executive President and Business Head of the Aditya Birla Group and Chairman of CII's National Committee on Mining, giving his perception on mining industry and India and Australia relations, said that an India-Australia Joint Working Group (JWG) on Energy and Minerals was established in 2000 for enhancing bilateral co-operation in the energy and mineral sectors. Organisations such as the Geological Survey of India (GSI), Indian Bureau of Mines (IBM), and the Mineral Exploration Corporation Limited (MECL) have shown interest in collaborating with their Australian counterparts on state-of-the-art technology for exploration and exploitation of minerals. The Federation of Indian Mineral Industries (FIMI) and the Minerals Council of Australia (MCA) have undertaken a joint scoping study focused on trade and investment barriers in the India-Australia mining sectors, with a view to promoting bilateral mineral trade and investment. [22]

Conclusion

Present study provides a summary to draw certain conclusions at macro level of energy security like; (i) India and Australia are exclusively different in terms of energy demand and dynamics, which lays a platform to establish bilateral cooperation in general; (ii) Though both the countries have more or less same quantities of fossil fuels–coal, oil and natural gas, India depends not only on imports of raw materials pertaining to energy but wider possibilities in terms of science and technology in production, supply and consumption are inevitable to improve sustainability and conservation of fossil energy resources. India should also possibly depend on Australia in the process of exploring the science and technology concerned with generating alternative energy sources.

India should also continue and intensify the current trend in making use of different multilateral platforms in achieving the appreciation of ongoing nuclear deals with many countries. In this direction the cooperation from Australia has been much important, in view of its active role in ASEAN and East Asia Summit, wherein India also actively engaged. In view of the greater possibilities of energy cooperation, this study is strongly recommending, conducting a detailed micro level study to meet the needs of exploring the cost benefit analysis and further establishing bilateral energy cooperation between India and Australia.

End Notes

1. Keith, R.C., ed. 1986, *Energy, Security and Economic Development in East Asia*, (New York, St Martin's Press).
2. Dennis Rumley and Sanjay Chatuvedi, 2005, *Energy Security and the Indian Ocean Region*, (South Asian Publishers Pvt. Ltd., New Delhi), p. 2.
3. Das, P.S., Indian Ocean in India's Security Calculus, *Journal of Indian Ocean Studies*, Vol. 9, No. 3, pp. 316-317.
4. Arvind Kumar, India and Nuclear Weapons in the Indian Ocean, *Journal of Indian Ocean Studies*, Vol. 12, No. 3, 2004, pp. 390-403.
5. BP Statistical Review of World Energy, 2007.
6. BP Statistical Review of World Energy, 2008, p. 2.
7. Energy Security Issues, The World Bank Group, 5 December 2005, No. 36110.
8. *India: Addressing Energy Security and Climate Change*, Ministry of Environment & Forests, Ministry of Power and Bureau of Energy Efficiency, Govt. of India, October, 2007, pp.

1-11.

9. Baldev Raj, 2006, Energy Security for India-A Challenge to Materials Scientists and Technologists, *IGC News Letter*, Vol. 68, pp. 1-8.
10. Energy Security Issues, The World Bank Group, 5 December 2005, No. 36110.
11. *Ibid.*
12. Suryanarana, P.S., Australia Assures Cooperation in Civil Nuclear Energy Sector, *The Hindu*, 1 August 2007, see www.thehindu.com/2007/08/01/stories/2007080159931400.htm
13. *Ibid.*
14. India, Australia Agree to Work Towards a Strategic Partnership, Andhra News, 12 September 2008, see at www.andhranews.net/India/2008/September/12-India-Australia-agree-63646.asp.
15. Australian Department of Industry Tourism and Resources, submitted a report on 'Inquiry into Australia's Relationship with India as an Emerging World Power', to the Joint Standing Committee on Foreign Affairs, Defence and Trade, Submission No. 37. p. 9.
16. *Ibid.*
17. Pablo Bustelo, The East Asian Summit and Energy Security, Fundacion Real Instituto Elcano, Madrid, 2007, see at www.realinstitutoelcano.org/analisis/imprimir/1105imp.asp.
18. *Ibid.*
19. Australian Department of Industry Tourism and Resources, submitted a report on 'Inquiry into Australia's Relationship with India as an Emerging World Power', to the Joint Standing Committee on Foreign Affairs, Defence and Trade, Submission No. 37. p. 10.
20. ABARE Australian Commodities, September Quarter, 2006 www.abare.gov.au.
21. Australian Department of Industry Tourism and Resources, submitted a report on 'Inquiry into Australia's Relationship with India as an Emerging World Power', to the Joint Standing Committee on Foreign Affairs, Defence and Trade, Submission No. 37. p. 8.
22. Australia India Business, 2008, p. 147.

20

Nation Building in Fiji: Need for India's Sustainable Linkages

P. Munirathnam Reddy and
E. Subbarama Krishnaiah

If the attainment of national unity and harmonious living of ethnically or racially diverse populations of a state is considered an ultimate object of nation building, then the process of nation building in Fiji is still an unfinished task. It has been posing a challenge to the social scientists, political proponents and constitutional experts to work out a viable model of democratic instrument of nation building in Fiji. The rise of ethno nationalism and intensification of ethnic or racial conflicts and ethnicization of politics and politicization of ethnic or racial communities, are a regular feature in Fiji.

Fiji is a multiracial and multicultural sovereign democratic nation-state in the South Pacific region, wherein the two opposing racial groups—indigenous Fijians (54.3 percent) and Fiji Indians (38.2 percent) have been destined to live together along with the minor ethnic groups of Chinese, Japanese, Europeans, Tongans and other Pacific Islanders (7.5 percent) in a total population of 8,40,201. [1] Racial conflicts are a recurrent feature over power sharing in the governance of Fiji. The indigenous Fijians, out of fear of domination of Fiji Indians, frequently get the constitution amended in their favour with brute force and invariably relegated Fiji Indians to the receiving end as second class citizens.

The British as a colonizing power had brought Indians as indentured labourers to work in the sugarcane fields of Fiji, during the period from 1879 to 1916, the year that the indenture system was abolished in Fiji. After their indentures expired most of the Indians stayed back, settled and made Fiji their home. Most of the present Fiji Indians, over 98 percent, are the descendants of the majority of those indentured Indians, not integrated fully into the Fijian society and maintain a separate cultural identity, being advanced in economic status and education, without whom Fiji cannot thrive. On the other hand Indigenous Fijians, who were left alienated by the colonizing power, but vested with inalienable rights over more than 83 percent of Fijian land, lived in their traditional economy distancing themselves from the mainstream modern economy for a long-time. The British 'divide and rule' policy kept the indigenous Fijians and Fiji Indians as opposing groups throughout the colonial rule and separated them physically and culturally until it introduced communal politics and racial constitution on the lines of Westminster style parliamentary democracy at the dawn of Fiji's Independence in 1970.

The political parties—Alliance Party (AP) patronized by the Fijian traditional chiefs and National Federation Party (NFP) dominated by the Fiji Indians-- though professed non-racial and non-communal, were very much communal in practice. A new political outfit Fiji Labour Party (FLP) founded in 1985 as a non-racial and non-communal party, captured power in coalition with NFP and formed Fiji Indian-dominated government in 1987. Within a month of its existence, the Fiji military, instigated by the traditional chiefs dislodged this government by orchestrating two coups, declared Fiji a republic, and severed links with the Commonwealth by replacing the British monarch with a Fijian chief nominated by the Fijian Council of Chiefs as sovereign head of state.

The newly promulgated paternalistic constitution of 1990 gave over representation to indigenous Fijians and legality to the Fijian Council of Chiefs (Great Council of Chiefs) in the Westminster style parliamentary democracy. Even this constitution had not worked out on its own terms. Fiji economy deteriorated as a result of the exodus of skilled Fiji Indian professionals to other developed countries which continued since 1987 because of insecurity and racial strife. The two General Election results of 1992 and 1994 invariably forced the Indigenous Fijian politic to seek the support of the Fiji Indians to run the governments. Succumbed to the pressures of Fiji Indian political parties and international organizations in 1995, the indigenous Fijian-dominated government under the leadership of Sitiveni Rabuka (the perpetrator of 1987 coups) compromised to realities and appointed a Constitutional Review Committee to review and amend the 1990 racial constitution.

The resultant 1997 constitution, which replaced 1990 constitution, was a correctional measure. Even though the new constitution remained more progressive and broadly more representative of Fiji communities in the political governance arrangements and the clause that the prime ministership was exclusively for indigenous Fijian was removed, it still maintained emphasis on the communal in forming the parliament and put in place structures that perpetuated racial division in the Fiji society. The Fiji Indian-dominated government headed by Mahendra Choudhry, elected in 1999 based on 1997 constitution, was overthrown after a year in existence by a civilian-led coup of indigenous Fijian George Speight.

The subsequent military-installed interim civilian government and the following elected governments in 2001 and 2006, the political governance dominated by the indigenous Fijians under the leadership of Laisenia Qarase and his policies didn't instil confidence in Fiji Indians that they would be fairly treated and protected. As a result, the Fiji Indian exodus continued and the Fiji Indian population dropped from 51 percent (1966) to 48.8 percent (1986) to 38.2 percent (2004). The latest military coup in December 2006 was entirely a different one. An indigenous Fijian military commander Frank Bainimarama replaced the indigenous Fijian dominated Laisenia Qarase democratically elected government accusing over the politicization of prison services and criminal justice system, pervasive corruption, serious economic decline, deterioration of law and order and deepening racial schism. The deposed Prime Minister Qarase accused the Fiji Indians and described the coup as 'Indian coup', [2] with Mahendra Choudhry, the Machiavelli behind Bainimarama.

The current crisis has its origins in the Fiji coup of 2000. The coup of 2000 was aimed at the multi-ethnic government led by Mahendra Choudhry. The proponents of the coup were an armed faction not closely associated with the military, who opposed their actions. After Bainimarama declared martial law and resolved the crisis by force, an interim government was sworn in headed by Bainimarama picked candidate Laisenia Qarase. He managed to get elected in 2001 and 2006, and has since begun to take actions that have provoked the displeasure of the military.

Three contentious bills brought by Qarase before the parliament—the Reconciliation Tolerance and Unity Bill (RTU Bill) that gives amnesty to 2000 coup perpetrators, the Qoli Qoli Bill which proposed to have control of sea bed resources to the indigenous Fijians and the Land Tribunal Bill that also favoured Indigenous Fijians were considered objectionable to Military as well as Fiji Indians. The Military insisted Qarase to drop the bills in the interest of the nation and to resign. As Qarase did not heed to the military call, the military commandant Bainimarama deposed the Qarase government.

The interim civilian government installed by the Military, with Bainimarama himself as Prime Minister, initiated "People's Charter for Building a Better Fiji for All", with the objective to rebuild Fiji into non-racial, culturally vibrant and united, well governed, truly democratic that sought progress and prosperity through-merit based equality of opportunity and peace. Commander Bainimarama asserted that "the military is the only entity that can bring change. No other entity that has an influence with the Fijians is professional and apolitical like us." [3]

The Impediments to Nation Building in Fiji

The recurring coup culture infers that the nation building in Fiji is still elusive and it could be achieved only when the two major competing racial groups, indigenous Fijians and Fiji Indians, shed their present mind set and work together not only in political adjustments but also in cultural integration to know each other and honour each other for their mutual benefit. To understand the intricacies in the nation building, the commonly cited factors or determinants by the social scientists are analysed below:

Inalienable Land Rights to Indigenous Fijians over 83 percent of Fijian Land: The King of Fiji Seru Cakobau ceded Fiji to Britain in 1874 for protection of Fijian race from the onslaught of settled Europeans in Fiji. Arthur Gordon, the first Governor of Fiji, under instruction from the British Queen for the protection of Fijian race, entrusted 83.4 percent of Fijian land [4] that was available at that time (leaving crown land and free hold) to the Fijians and granted inalienable rights over it and the ordinance of 1880 barred them to sell the lands to any non-Fijian. Governor Gordon believed that this act would protect the Fijian race to continue their traditional life and traditional economy. Further, Governor Gordon invited the Fijian Council of Chiefs for friendly encounters to take their advice in all policies affecting the Fijian race. He introduced dual administration, one for native Fijians and the other for Europeans and other immigrant population. The institution of traditional Fijian Council of Chiefs was well nurtured by the colonial government and the native Fijian administration was put under their control. National Land Trust Board (NLTB) which was established in 1940 by the colonial government, mainly to look after the interests of the Fijian landowners, extended lands with the consent of the Fijian landowners for cultivation to the Indian farmers for leases for a considerable period.

After Fiji's Independence, the Agricultural Land Lord and Tenants Act (ALTA) was enforced in 1976 and accordingly the NLTB fixed leases of 30 years period to the Fiji Indian farmers for cultivation of sugar cane. The 1997 NLTB report revealed that over 80 percent of Fijian landowners wanted their lands back when the leases expired. As many as 1995 such leases expired in the year 2000 and 2080 expired in 2005 and there was no hope of further extension of leases. [5] With the result, the displaced Fiji Indian farming families migrated to urban centres in search of jobs or employment that posed a major problem to the Fijian government for resettlement.

Fiji Indian Cultural Persistence and Their Self-imposed Apartheid: The contagious disease measles contracted from the Europeans took a heavy toll of the native Fijians and nearly one fourth of its population downsized in 1875 at the time of annexation of Fiji by Britain. The Europeans in Fiji owned 8.45 percent of cultivable fertile land (freehold) which was purchased from the Fijian chiefs before annexation of Fiji during the period 1860 to 1875. The Europeans used the land for commercial plantation of cotton and sugarcane which was carried at the beginning with the help of local Fijians. Sensing that they were unfit for the hard work, alternatively the Europeans engaged labourers of neighbouring Melanesian islands supplied by the European sailors by 'black-birding'. As this system was banned by the British government as an inhuman slave trade, Governor Gordon, had before him the onerous task of meeting the demand of the European plantation owners for labour. With his experience he gained in Mauritius and Trinidad as Governor before, Governor Gordon decided to bring Indians as indentured labour to overcome the labour problem of the budding British crown colony.

Indenture system, through which the Fiji government recruited Indians for a maximum period of 10 years on contract basis on agreed wages to work in the commercial plantations in Fiji and free return voyage was promised on government exchequer after the indentures expired. To meet the growing demand for labour, the colonial government of Fiji allowed the willing migrant Indians to stay without any repatriation. Indian labour migrants from various parts of India—mainly from North India (Bihar, Uttar Pradesh and Rajasthan) were indentured and carried through Calcutta port from 1879 to 1902 to a tune of 45, 439 and the rest from Madras port to a tune of 15526 from South India mainly from Arcot and Chengalpat districts of Tamil Nadu and Coastal districts of Andhra from 1903 to 1916 when the indenture system was finally abolished. Nearly 45,000 Indians settled in Fiji after the indentures were over in 1921. Free emigrants from Gujarat and Punjab to a tune of nearly 2500 were settled in Fiji during the period 1901 to 1930s as trading community by establishing businesses in urban and rural sectors. Most of the present Fiji Indians are the fourth and fifth generation descendants of those migrated Indians in Fiji.

The Indo-business community who trace their ancestry to Gujarat and Punjab only maintain business and family links with India and the other Fiji Indians, the descendents of indentured Indians, totally lost their roots in India. The language, religion and traditions and even personal names of Indian origin are still continued and maintained by the Fiji Indians though caste system of India lost its relevance after crossing the ocean. The indentured labourers who worked in sugar cane and other commercial plantations settled in isolated villages based on language and region they came from India and rarely mixed with indigenous Fijians in their day to day life. The dual administration of colonial government put them apart of any inter-mix until late 1960s. All groups from the beginning explicitly desired to retain their cultural identity. Indians, whether their heritage was founded on Hinduism or Islam, wanted to protect and perpetuate it. [6] Arya Samaj, Ramakrishna Mutt and other Hindu religious organisations of India stepped in and constructed Hindu temples and established schools in the Indian dominated villages and continued to refresh Indian culture among the Fiji Indians and contributed for 'Little India' in Fiji.

According to 1956 Fiji Census, the number of Fiji Indian households were 26,031 and were classified in accordance with the languages spoken within them Hindustani 17164, Hindi 3644, Tamil 1498, Urdu 1223, Gujarati 830,Telugu 797, Gurmukhi 468, Malayalam 134, and not stated 273. Less than one sixth of those were Muslims, the remainder were Hindus with a small fraction of Christians and Sikhs. It was also estimated that 92 percent of Fiji Indians were born in Fiji. [7] The distancing of indigenous Fijians and Fiji Indians for a long time by the colonial government to live in their own worlds as watertight compartments [8] until the self-rule was granted to Fiji in 1966 when the double administration of the colonial government was replaced with an elected legislative council on communal lines comprising representatives from indigenous Fijians, Fiji Indians, and Europeans and other non-Fijian ethnic groups (General Electors) was introduced to run the government on Westminster type democracy. For the first time national roll was introduced on communal lines by which a voter was expected to caste his vote not only to his communal representative but also to the representatives in other communal categories. At the same time, steps were initiated to encourage the indigenous Fijians and Fiji Indians to interact with each other and understand each other.

Fiji Indian Economic Ascendancy and Empowered Social Status: Arthur Gordon's paramountcy of Fijian interests—where the indigenous Fijians were left to their traditional life and Chiefly System lingering to traditional economy were continued undisturbed alienated completely the indigenous Fijians from commercial modern economy. The Indians who settled in Fiji after their indentures were over, took lands (10 acre plots) for lease from the Europeans and the Australian-owned CSR company, cultivated sugarcane and sold the same to sugar mills and thus earned hard money. The

NLTB which was constituted by the Fijian administration through a government statute in 1940 to look after the indigenous Fijian lands also extended lands for lease to Indians for cultivation of sugarcane on behalf of indigenous Fijian landowners. The Fiji Indians deprived of the right of acquiring any landed property, began to invest their capital in business and children education.

They monopolized the surface transport, settled as artisans and petty shopkeepers, hoteliers in urban centres and enhanced their social status on par with the Europeans. Fiji Indians monopolized the sugar industry, market economy and continuously contributed for Fiji's economic prosperity. To quote Ahmed Ali, the Fiji Indian academic, education was the highest priority for Fiji Indian parents. Indians were a majority among skilled tradesmen and technicians in various enterprises; big and small. In 1968, of the 643 Fiji university graduates, Indians comprised 464, and of these 115 were working overseas. By comparison there were only 77 Fijian graduates, 63 Chinese and 39 others. The utilization of Western education to Indian advantage became apparent consequently. The Fiji Indians dominated the professions such as medicine, law, accountancy, civil services and university academics and became an indispensable community in Fiji adopting the European way of lifestyle in urban areas. [9] The widening economic disparity between Fiji Indians and indigenous Fijians and the economic ascendancy of Fiji Indians set a jealous eye of the indigenous Fijians. The treating of indigenous Fijians by the Fiji Indians as uncivilized and 'jungle' further aggravated their anger over Fiji Indians.

Rising Demographic Profile of Fiji Indians: By 1921, when the indentures of Indians expired, the total Indian migrants at that time recorded 60,634 (38.6 percent) of the total Fiji population. The other racial groups, the indigenous Fijians 84,475 (53.7 percent) and Europeans and other minor ethnic groups 12,157 (7.7 percent) accounted for the rest of the population of Fiji. The Indians, after choosing Fiji as their home, prospered well by choosing sugarcane cultivation and by becoming part of the export economy. Their demographic profile steadily increased and overcame the indigenous Fijians by 1946 where Fiji Indian population constituted 46.2 percent and the indigenous Fijians stood at 45.3 percent. The 1966 census of Fiji recorded the highest percentage of Fiji Indians 50.5 percent against the indigenous Fijians of 42.4 percent. With the establishment of self-rule and subsequent proclamation of Fiji Independence in 1970 and the dominant rule established by the indigenous Fijian leadership through parliamentary democracy witnessed a gradual decrease of Fiji Indians to 49.8 percent in 1976 and 48.8 percent in 1986 as against 44.2 percent and 46.0 percent respectively of the indigenous Fijians.

The 'Nationalists' who formed a splinter group in 1974, broke away from the Alliance Party to lead 'Touki Movement' composed of the extremist elements of ethnicity, floating the slogan 'Fiji for Fijians and Indians and others set out'. They moved an unsuccessful resolution in parliament in 1975 for repatriation of Fiji Indians at the British expenses. [10] The revival of 'Touki Movement' in 1987 and the subsequent two coups orchestrated by the Fiji Military in 1987 and the 2000 coup by George Speight, and the ethnically assertive indigenous Fijian governments led by Laisenia Qarase, which mainly targeted Fiji Indians and their domination in politics and economy, forced the emigration of Fiji Indians. As a result, the Fiji Indian population was downsized to 38.2 percent as against 54 percent of indigenous Fijians; a reversal of the 1921 Census!

Fiji's Chiefly System or Bose Levuvakaturaga (Great Council of Chiefs): The Fijian Council of Chiefs also known as Great Council of Chiefs is the highest assembly of Fijian chiefs. It consists not only of traditional chiefs but of commoner Fijians as well. At present it consists of 55 members, 3 each from 14 traditional Fijian provinces and 3 from traditional Rotuma Council and six members nominated by the Minister for Fijian Affairs. Prime Minister, President and Vice-president of the Republic of Fiji are the automatic members of GCC in addition to the former Prime Minister Sitiveni Rabuka who is a permanent GCC member. The GCC is given a significant role in national politics. The Council appoints the President, who is required to be of Chiefly rank and the Vice-President of the Republic of Fiji besides nominating 15 out of 32 senators in the upper house of the Fiji parliament with a mandate to protect indigenous Fijian interests. Earlier days this Council had the power to pass laws and regulations binding Fijians in colonial period. It is a time-honoured traditional institution that embraces the entire indigenous Fijian people. It is at the heart of the Fijian political and socio-economic systems. It derives its strength and cohesiveness from a well defined hierarchy of groups and subgroups (vanua, yuvasa, mataqali and i-tokatoka) with clearly specified roles.

The relationships of groups and sub-groups are governed by adherence to recognized codes of protocol and customs. Each group and sub-group has a leader or chief, normally chosen from its members. These leaders know their responsibilities with respect to members of the sub-groups as defined in custom and tradition. In traditional Fijian thinking, which remains a potent force in politics today, there is a preference in higher levels of leadership for a strong representation of those who by tradition, birth and experience have been assigned the role of leadership. Fijians cannot normally be sacked from their leadership positions within their clan or tribe. They hold their position until death. The land is possibly the strongest unifying factor amongst the Fijian people. Land translates into the Fijian language as Vanua. This word can mean 'my piece of land' or 'my birth place' or 'my home land' or 'my province' or 'my country'. It's meanings are many, and its implications overriding! These things bind them together in a psychological way that can be a powerful cohesive force. Fijian Chiefly system is by tradition the social and political apex of the Fijian polity and is an important stabilizing factor in Fiji's polity. [11]

Indigenous Fijian Dominated Fiji Military: Fijian chiefs in pre-colonial period were always at war and maintained their armies with European recruits to assist and help. Seru Cakobau of Bau province emerged as Tuiviti, the king of Fiji with aggressive army. After the annexation of Fiji in 1875, the British colonial government used the armed force created by Seru Cakobau to fight tribal war fares in the interior of Vitilevu and other parts of Fiji. The disbanded constabulary was continued to perform police functions. At the out-break of First World War, the Fijian Battalion was formed recruiting able bodied indigenous Fijians to serve British Empire's interests in France and Italy. The Fiji Indians missed an opportunity to join the army when the offer came to them during Second World War. Since then, the Fiji Military remained exclusively indigenous Fijians consisting of 3527 soldiers at present. Only 15 Fiji Indians found their place in the army. [12] Fiji Military earned world reputation in UN peace keeping mission work and nearly one fourth of military is recruited to such work. The rest of the force is used to look after the national security and law and order problem in Fiji. The section 112 of 1997 constitution of Fiji states that "it shall be the overall responsibility of the Republic of Fiji Military Forces (RFMF) to ensure at all times the security, defence and well being of Fiji and its people".

However, it earned reputation that it abused several times of its power to topple the democratically elected governments to fulfil the aspirations of knave politicians or power hungry military officers using the rhetoric of racial schism. To quote Brij V. Lal: "Fijian Army was a great symbol of power, the ultimate guarantor of Fijian rights which might be called upon to intervene in the political arena in the event of political change that was unacceptable to the Fijian establishment." He further observed: "Fiji coups were the culmination of a convergence of various wounded egos and aggrieved interests within the Fijian society". [13]

Intra-Fijian Conflicts: Consisting of 14 Fijian (Tribal) provinces represented by traditional Fijian Chiefs, Fiji is organized into 3 traditional confederacies, kubusa, Burebasaga, and Tavuta, each with a paramount Chief. The Chiefs of the eastern region of Fiji dominate these confederacies and well entrenched and dominated the Fiji politics and governance. George Cakobau, Ganilau and Kamisese Mara belonged to this category. The provinces of Western Vitilevu, though comparatively rich in resources, were not adequately represented in Fiji politics in 1970s and 1980s. Some Chiefs of these provinces such as Butadroka, Osea Gavidi and Apisai Tora raised their voice for the fourth confederacy. Disgruntled with the attitudes of the Eastern Chiefs they even started Nationalist Movements, such as Touki Movement.

Exposed to the Parliamentary democracy and modern commercial market economy, the Fijian commoners (middle-class) who got educated and employed in various government jobs and commercial enterprises, began to assert themselves and got elevated their status to compete with the Chiefs under the label 'meritorious chiefs'. Timoci Bavadra and Col. Sitiveni Rabuka come under this category. Rabuka expressed his personal antipathy to Mara whom he compared to a pampered banyan tree under which nothing grew. He further invoked the Melanesian model of leadership, asking that distinctions be made between meritorious chiefs, such as himself, who achieved power and status through his own efforts without the advantage of privileged birth, and of the traditional chiefs of the more traditional kind. Rabuka even proclaimed that "the dominance of customary chiefs (traditional chiefs) in government is coming to an end." [14]

Teaiwa, a Fijian analyst, observed that Fijian nationalism and the associated conflict between Fijian and Indian cannot be the source of the country's difficulties because a Fijian nation does not exist and has never existed. The country's problems are intra-Fijian, stemming from the clash between chiefs and commoners, the emergence of a *nou veau riche* Fijian middle class and Fijian intellectuals demanding a place at the decision-making table, all set in a context of intense provincial (tribal) rivalry and splits in the Fijian army. [15] Similarly Brij Lal argues referring to Fiji Coup of 2000: "Race has been portrayed in the media and popular commentary as the main issue behind the present turbulence. It is an issue, but there is more to the story than meets the eye. Speight has trained his sights on the Indians, but he is also leading a middle-class revolution against the Fijian establishment". [16]

Racially Polarized Political Parties: At the beginning, the evolution of party system to contest and represent in the parliamentary democracy was based largely on divided racial groups, indigenous Fijians (Alliance Party), Fiji Indians (National Federation Party) and other racial minority groups (General Voter's Party). The Indigenous Fijian Alliance Party (A.P) dominated in politics and ruled Fiji under the Fijian Chief Sir Kamisese Mara from 1966 to 1987, the NFP opted for opposition. Multiracial Fiji Labour Party (FLP) which was formed in 1985 aligned itself with NFP in a coalition and came to power in 1987 defeating A.P. Within a month of its existence, the FLP and NFP coalition government was dethroned by a military coup and the Alliance Party was blamed for its behind the screen role. In 1990s, the multiracial FLP has gradually become Fiji Indian dominated party when Mahendra Choudhry became its President. The Great Council of Chiefs-sponsored Fiji Political Party, 'Soqosoqoni Vaka vulewa ni Toaki (SVT)' governed Fiji from 1992 to 1999 under the leadership of Sitiveni Rabuka. 'Soqosoqo Duata in Lewinivanua (SDL)' governed Fiji from 2001 to 2006 in coalition with conservative alliance (CAMV), a nationalistic party that broke away from the SVT.

The General Voters Party (GVP), the rump of a once significant party that mostly merged into what is now the United Peoples Party in the late 1990s enjoying the support of the Europeans, Chinese and other minorities led by Dan Johns. The other minor parties which represent indigenous Fijians are: Fijian Association Party (FAP) founded by Josefata kamikamica to oppose Rabuka; Dodonu ni Touki (DNT), ethnic Fijian party led by Dr. Fereti S. Dewa; National Alliance Party of Fiji (NAPF) founded by Ratu Epeli Ganilau as the successor to the defunct Alliance Party (AP); Nationalist Vanua Tako Lavo Party (NVTLP) and a new nationalist party, a splinter from NVTLP; Party of National Unity (PANU), which was founded as multiracial in 1998 but was subsequently transformed into ethnic Fijian. All the parties in Fiji in one way or other exploded racial emotions during election campaigns by their race targeted speeches and steadfastly contributed to the widening racial divide to perpetuate.

Language Policy and Education System: Fijian, Hindustani (Fijian Hindi) and English are the official languages of Fiji, which were conferred equal status by 1997 Fiji constitution. Preponderance is also given to English as official language of the Parliament as well as media of educational instruction from primary education (IV Grade) to tertiary education although English is spoken natively by probably no more than 1 to 3 percent of Fijian population. The other two languages, Fijian and Fijian Hindi, are predominantly spoken by 95 percent of the population who are diametrically placed to grow up in separate enclaves and uncultured as such with little intermix. [17] There is no national language to know each other and to understand each other's cultures. The education system which was developed akin to New Zealand education system by the colonial masters continued to this day without any drastic changes. Besides English as second language, the languages of the respective ethnic groups (Fijian in the case of indigenous Fijians and Fijian Hindi in case of Fiji-Indians) have been taught in school curriculum as first language to impart their respective cultures and there is no third language learning in school curriculum as most of the schools have been managed by either religious organizations or committees constituted by the respective communities and the Government's role in establishing schools is very minimal (of 154 high schools in Fiji, only 12 are managed by the State (Fiji Ministry of Education) [18]

Fiji Indians with different language groups—Hindi, Gujarati, Punjabi, Tamil, Telugu, Malayalam etc., developed over a time during sugarcane plantations a common lingua franca, the Fijian Hindi, popularly known as 'Fijibat' (Fijitalk). Likewise, the indigenous Fijian tribal groups who were and have been with distinct tribal languages and dialects--got converted to Christianity and adopted 'Bau' tribal language as Fijian language (to which the Bible was translated) as 'lingua franca' in the later part of the 19th Century. At least primary and secondary education system in Fiji needs to be thoroughly overhauled to suit the local conditions with an inter-mix of indigenous Fijian and Fiji Indian students at school level. Alternatively the learning of the language of the other ethnic group (e.g. the Fiji Indian students should learn the Fijian language and vice verse) should be made compulsory in the school curriculum.

Political Accommodation of Multiracial Groups through Constitutional Arrangements

The 1987 Fiji military coup exploded the myth that the racial parity and the nation-building achieved through political accommodation of racial groups in parliamentary democracy through 1970 Constitution would last long. The nationalist and toukei movements of indigenous Fijians in 1975 and 1987 aimed at Fiji Indians succumbed to destabilizing the nation by bringing the concepts, Toukei (host) referring to indigenous Fijian and Vulgai (guest) referring to Fiji Indian. The most powerful and exclusively indigenous Fijian politicized army in a bloodless coup has overthrown the elected government, abrogated the 1970 Constitution, whipped up racial emotions and perpetrated ethnocentrism of indigenous Fijians in the name of Fijian Nationalism. Its slogan was "Fiji for Fijians (indigenous Fijians) and the guest (Fiji Indian) has ought to leave the country". The ethnicity of the Fiji military-dictated Interim Government forced the Fiji Indian emigration. A look into the statements of that time by the political leaders reveals the hapless conditions of Fiji Indians and the heightened ethnicity of indigenous Fijians.

- Jairam Reddy, NFP leader and former minister in 1987 FLP/NFP coalition government referring to the apathy of Fiji Indians at the strike of 1987 coup said, "We know no other country; we have no other home". [19]
- Adi Finau Tabakaucoro, the Interim Government Minister referring the Fiji Indians said, "This is not their country. They still speak Hindi. They still eat curry. They are not Christians". [20]
- Major General Sitiveni Rabuka, the 1987 coup perpetrator averred, "We are trying to make this place perfect for Fiji people, and if it's not perfect for others, then that's too bad. They will have to go". [21]

The mind and philosophy of indigenous Fijians and the haplessness of Fiji Indians clearly demonstrate that the nation building is of much more complex in multi-racial and multicultural Fiji. The political accommodation (constitutional arrangement for political representation of racial groups) alone would not do. Cultural accommodation or integration and cross-cultural nationalism, obedience to Fiji Nation State are much more essential for enduring national unity and racial harmony. The period after the 1987 coups of Sitiveni Rabuka, nothing is resolved except the Fijian desire to prevail. The Fijian leaders say, Indians can stay in Fiji but on Fijian terms. Their skills are needed as also their money but not their voice in political life of the country. In effect, they want to create a second girmit for the Indian Community: a life of service and servitude, lived on the sufferance of the Fijian people and vulugis, guests. [22]

The political developments in 1990s proved that 'the race'

is not the root cause for racial conflicts but the other extraneous causes including, intra-Fijian conflicts between traditional chiefly confederacies, widening gap between chiefs and commoners and their economic disparity (class-conflict), levels of education attainments, employment avenues, modernization of society, changing family structure from extended families to nuclear families, aspiration for individual social status. During this period the Fiji Indian politicians emerged as 'king-makers'. Ironically, Col. Rabuka who perpetrated the coups of 1987 sought the support of FLP and NFP (Fiji Indian dominated political parties) for forming government in 1992 and for the survival of his government in 1995. In view of the conditions imposed by the NFP and FLP, the pressures of international organizations and the ground economic realities faced by the country, Rabuka decided to amend the 1990 Racial Constitution for fair representation of racial groups.

The resultant 1997 Constitution involved a complex compromise between Fiji's Indian political leaders and Fiji's indigenous Chiefs and politicians. This constitution has been considered the most viable perfect political accommodation of racial groups that ever achieved in Fiji and it survived the successive Fiji coups of 2000 and 2006. Although Fiji's Great Council of Chiefs retained considerable powers over the selection of Fiji's Head of state, and over the nominees for the Senate and effectively exercised their veto powers over further constitutional changes, Fiji's Prime Minister needs no longer be an ethnic Fijian. Number of reserved 'Indian' and 'Fijian' seats have been brought closer to respective weights in the population. For the first time, open seats have been introduced, where all parties may compete for the votes of the entire electorate'. In addition, a multiparty cabinet, a provision in which the victors of the election offer positions in the cabinet to parties who secure at least 10 percent of the vote, or 8 or more seats in the election. [23]

While arguments in Fiji's Court of Appeal in Chandrika

Prasad vs. Fiji Government case, the London-based Australian lawyer Geofrey Robertson has told Fiji's Court of Appeal that the Country's 1997 Constitution is one of the finest in the world in safeguarding indigenous Fijian rights. [24] The other high point is the virtual impossibility of legally altering the 1997 Constitution. The amendment to the constitution requires the consent of two-thirds of both houses of parliament. Fiji Indian politicians will never vote to change a document that gave them more than many even asked for. [25] Above all, the Great Council of Chiefs ratified the instrument as the supreme law of the land. Jairam Reddy, the opposition leader and the lawyer turned NFP politician who was instrumental in drafting this non-racial constitution, was conferred Fiji's highest honour, the Companion of the order of Fiji in recognition of his services to Fiji. [26]

Cultural Integration and Cross-cultural Nationalism

In Fiji there are three major ethnic groups which exhibit many differences of physiognomy, language, cultures, values and religion. These are of lesser degree between indigenous Fijians and Europeans who have some proximity as far as Christian religion is concerned. The European missionaries led by William Cross and David Cargil started the process of Christianising the indigenous Fijian population between 1835 to 1860. Some sort of cultural assimilation and integration is seen between Europeans and indigenous Fijians and the same is expressed in inter-ethnic marriages. But among the majority of the people, there is hardly any dialogue and many are not even neighbours. They live apart in different situations both social and spatial. The majority of Europeans and Fiji Indians live in towns and plantations with fences around them and prohibition notices on the gates. Most indigenous Fijians live in rural villages, and most of them who live in towns, live in low cost housing areas. [27] If ethnicity differentiates the people of Fiji, there is also ethnic loyalty.

Ethnic loyalty involves privileges for one's ethnic group

and denial or reduction of rights to others. If racial politics and racial political parties serve as a means to achieve racial equality, then there is a place for them in the affairs of Fiji. Equity in crucial areas, such as income and levels of achievement is a pre-requisite of racial harmony and of national unity. Once equality is achieved, society is less subject to stresses and strains and harmony is more likely to be the result. [28] To understand the meaning of racial equality it is important to understand the core values of the various groups. It is important that the characteristics of the major ethnic groups be understood and accepted or respected by each other.

Once these are understood, there is a better chance of isolating the root causes of certain problems. [29] For racial equity to be achieved and for the sake of nation building, it is imperative that each ethnic group living in Fiji must face boldly the pain of self-examination, admit wrongs, and accept that the cure lies in the rejection of some practices and concepts no matter how dear to the heart they may be. Apart from knowing well one's own culture, ethnic groups must also educate their people to know other peoples' cultures, their value systems, and in particular their language and attitudes to live in order to know how to deal squarely with them and on equal terms. Without full awareness of ethnic differences, and appropriate provisions for them, no realistic form of democracy will be achieved in Fiji. The School system must consciously strive to do this as a first step towards the effort of nation-building.

Unless the racial groups in Fiji understand well each other's cultures and accept them for what they are, in selecting and assimilating those elements into their own cultures in order to enhance racial equality, harmony, and nation building for the future are going to be very difficult and the attainment of true racial harmony will be a mirage. [30] Nationalism, cross-cultural in nature and allegiance to the state of Fiji are to be developed by all races rather than ethnic loyalties or ethno-nationalism exhibited by the indigenous Fijians. Indigenous Fijians must reconcile that the other racial groups, who have settled in Fiji by historic accident during colonial period made Fiji their home, would live along with them and share the resources of the country. It is very apt to recall the speech made by Jairam Reddy, the NFP politician and opposition leader in Sitiveni Rabuka government, in 1992 addressing the parliamentarians: "Top-level accommodation between political elites was deemed necessary precisely because of the resilience of racial tensions in Fiji". He added:

Mr. Speaker, Sir, you can have multiculturalism in two ways. You can...have multi racial parties...That kind of multiracialism is, may be, a bit premature for Fiji, perhaps we are not ready for it...The communal pools (sic-pulls?) are extremely strong...we are locked into a situation where we will continue to look into the indefinite future in terms of race...There is another kind of multiculturalism...Let us each be in our separate racial compartment...Let communal solidarity prevail...Let every one be united, but from our respective positions of unity, let us accept that we must co-exist and work together...It may be...that that is a more realistic approach. [31]

Fiji Indians in South Pacific Countries

Fiji has become a beacon light to the development activities and the process of growth in the entire Pacific Ocean. It is the most focal country in the Pacific. It is at the hub of the main communication networks and provided with widest range of facilities. Large numbers from other pacific islands come for education. University of South Pacific, Pacific Regional Telecommunications College, South Pacific Commission Home Economics Training Centre, Pacific Theological College, Pacific Regional Seminary, Fiji School of Medicine and various other colleges admit students from South Pacific Countries, but majority students admitted to these colleges are the children of Fiji Indians in view of the high priority given to education by Fiji Indian parents.

Academic and technical training can be viewed by the Fiji Indians as a kind of property, one which is portable and stays with the individual. [32] "The Fiji Indians have not merely developed the country, Fiji, but they have taken a hand in developing a new regional entity in the Pacific which they call the Pacific way of life i.e. to live by consensus by discussion and never by confrontation" [33] to quote Bhagavan Singh, the former Indian Envoy to Fiji. Many Fiji Indians provide essential technical services to other Pacific countries by short visits from Suva base. Many Fiji Indian lawyers travel to neighbouring Pacific countries to serve clients there, as do some accountants and others. A number of Fiji Indian wholesalers have their sales-men constantly on the move through out the region. Most Pacific regional organizations are based in Fiji. Fiji Indians are the greatest potential beneficiaries from these organizations. USA, Canada, Britain, Australia, New Zealand have accepted growing number of Fiji Indians, especially professionals and tradesmen.

Discussion and Conclusion

Nation Building in Fiji is still elusive and is a very difficult process unless the main two racial groups, Indigenous Fijians and Fiji Indians, shed their present mindset and rapproach each other for their mutual benefit; not only political rapprochement but also cultural one including the attitudinal changes. The South Pacific countries consider Fiji as their heart and through cultural proximity and primordial relationship. They always supported indigenous Fijians, the fact that evidenced during the coups of Sitiveni Rebuka in 1987 and George Speight in 2000. The Fiji Indians didn't get the wider support for their distress among the nations of the South Pacific.

However, Fiji Indians are respected for their ingenuity and professional skills and are regarded as an indispensable major migrant community in South Pacific. The rapprochement between these two racial groups politically and culturally immensely benefit India to forge economic linkages with the South Pacific countries, which have been endowed with vast resources, using Fiji as a springboard. India was accorded the status of Dialogue Partner in the 16-member Pacific Islands Forum in 2002 in which Australia and New Zealand have also been members along with the South Pacific nations. At the beginning of 1980s, the Indian population in South Pacific countries was estimated at 12 percent and of which more than 90 percent belong to Fiji Indians. At present Australia and New Zealand have considerable Fiji Indian Population (more than 40,000 in Australia and more than 12,000 in New Zealand) settled in jobs, business and pursuing higher education.

The linkages of India with Fiji continued since late 1870s starting with indenture system. Indian Trade goods, Indian cinemas are important components of imports of Fiji. Following Fiji military coups of 1987 diplomatic ties were severed between India and Fiji and New Delhi was cut off from the entire Pacific region. [34] However, relations between Fiji and India have been revived [35] with renewed interest after India had become 'Dialogue Partner' in Pacific Islands Forum (PIF) in 2003. Earlier in 2000, the Islands nations supported India in getting elected to a non-permanent seat on the UN Security Council. India's small aid program to the Pacific region is mainly scholarships, rural technology and health care. In 2000, the Indian government initiated a new scholarship program attracting growing numbers of students from through out the region. [36]

In 2005 Nauru, the smallest South Pacific country sought the help of Indian Government to rectify the hardware problem of its computer systems. In 2006, India gave US$ 1,00,000 to each of the 14 Forum Island countries and expanded assistance with training. In recent times, Micronesia has also sought the help of India in establishing the coconut oil extraction factory and mention may be made of India's gesture to Kiribati with a desalination plant. The Indian government which had extended a soft loan of US$ 5.4 million in 2007 for the rehabilitation of Fiji's ailing sugar industry, has been actively considering proposals for assistance in the infrastructure and rural development sectors [37] India also offered to give Fiji voting machines for its elections in 2009(now postponed to 2014) following the military coup of 2006.

For India's outreach in the South Pacific countries, the fair image of Fiji Indians would immensely benefit India and hence promotion of nation building in Fiji is an imperative need for India in the years to come.

End Notes

1. www.Fiji.gov.fj/uploads/FToday2006-2007.doc>accessed20July 2009.
2. Rumblings of a Revolution, *The Sunday Morning Herald*, October 27, 2007, http://www.smh.com.au/cgi-bin/common/popupPrintArticle.pl?path=/articles/2007/10/26 accessed28/3/2008> also see http://www.smh.com.au/articles/2007/10/26/1192941338637.htm"Commander RFMF-Public Declaration of Military Takeover," (http://www.fiji.gov.fj/publish/page_8092.shtml), Fiji government website in which Commander Bainimarama said that "Qarase has already conducted a 'Silent Coup' through bribery, corruption and introduction of controversial bill. (……); also see "2006 Fijian Coup d'etat" (http://www.en.wikipedia.org/wiki/2006_Fijian_Coup_d' percentc3 percentA9tat..... Retrieved 28/3/2008).
3. "Rumblings of a Revolution," *The Sunday Morning Herald*, October 27, 2007.
4. Sir Alan Burns, 1963, Fiji, London: Her Majesty's Stationary Office, p. 205.
5. *Peace Initiatives* (Editorial) Vol. VI, Nos. I-III (January-June 2000), p. VII.
6. Ahmed Ali, 1981, "Fiji: The Fiji Indian Achievement", Pacific Indians, Suva Institute of South Pacific Studies, University of South Pacific, p. 28.
7. Sir Alan Burns, n. 4, p. 111.
8. In colonial times, non-Fijians were forbidden by law from

settling in Fijian villages, while, conversely, Fijians (indigenous Fijians) could be forced back to their villages if found in urban areas(Henry Srebrnik," Indo-Fijians: Marooned without Land and Power in a South Pacific Archipelago?" in Parvathi Raghuram, AjayKumar Sahoo et. al (eds.), Tracing an Indian Diaspora, (Sage publications India Pvt.Ltd , New Delhi, 2008), pp. 90-91.

9. Ahmed Ali, n. 6, p. 27.
10. Stephanie Lawson, 1991, The Failure of Democratic Politics in Fiji, (New York), p. 205.
11. Filipe Bole, "Fiji's Chiefly System and its Pattern of Political Self-reliance", in Ron Crocombe et. al (eds.) Culture and Democracy in South Pacific, (1992,Suva,Institute of Pacific Studies, University of South Pacific), pp.72-79.
12. Rumblings of a Revolution, n. 2.
13. Brij V. Lal, 1998, Power and Prejudice: The Making of Fiji Crisis, (Wellington: New Zealand Institute of International Affairs), pp. 55 and 58.
14. Brij V. Lal, "Rhetoric and Reality: The Dilemmas of Contemporary Fiji Politics", n. 10, p. 106.
15. Teresia Teaiwa, "An Analysis of Current Political Crisis in Fiji", *Peace Initiatives*, Vol. VI, Nos. I-III, January-June 2000, pp. 35-38; John E. Davies, "Ethnic Competition and the Forging of the Nation-State of Fiji", *The Round Table*, Vol. 94, No. 1, January 2005, p. 63.
16. John E. Davies, "Ethnic Competition and the Forging of the Nation-State of Fiji," *The Round Table*, Vol. 94, No. 1, January 2005, p. 63.
17. Fijian (indigenous Fijian) and Indian (Fiji Indian) children attended separate schools, even in areas of mixed population (Henry Srebrnik,2008, "Indo-Fijians: Marooned without Land and Power in a South Pacific archipelago?," n. 8, p. 91.
18. Jan Prosser, "Seeking the Good Life in Fiji: Managing the Educational Transitions," *Journal of Human Ecology*, Vol. 19, No. 3, March 2006, p. 229.
19. Nicholas D. Kristoff, 1987, "In a South Seas Eden, a First Taste of Race Strife," *New York Times*, 1 May 1987; Brij V. Lal, 1989, "Fiji Indians and the Politics of Exclusion", see n. 20.
20. *Ibid.*
21. Henry Kamm, 1988, "Fijians Fretting Under One-Man Rule,"

New York Times, 22 July 1988; Brij V. Lal, 1989, "Fiji Indians and the Politics of Exclusion, see n. 20.

22. Brij V. Lal, 1989, "Fiji Indians and the Politics of Exclusion," *Foreign Affairs Reports,* Vol. XXXVIII, Nos. 7and 8 (July-August 1989), p. 109.
23. Jon Fraenkel, 2000, "The Triumph of the Non-Idealist Intellectuals? An Investigation of Fiji's 1999 Election Results," *Australian Journal of Politics and History*, Vol.46, No.1, 2000, pp. 103 and 105.
24. Pacific Nius Media Release, 21 February 2001; "Ethnic Competition and the Forging of the Nation-State of Fiji," *The Round Table*, Vol. 94, No. 1, January 2005, p. 63.
25. Hindi Accorded the Status of Official Language, "Ethnic Competition and the Forging of the Nation-State of Fiji," n. 22, pp. 68-69.
26. http://en.wikipedia.org/wiki/Jai_Ram_Reddy retrieved 24/7/2009
27. Asesela Ravuvu, 1992, "Culture and Tradtions: Implications for Modern Nation Building," Culture and Democracy in the South Pacific, Suva, Institute of Pacific Studies, University of South Pacific, p. 60.
28. *Ibid*, pp. 61-62.
29. *Ibid*, p. 63.
30. *Ibid*, p. 64 and 65.
31. Jon Fraenkel, 2000, n. 21, pp. 102 and 103.
32. Donald Brenneis, "A Comparative View of Overseas Indian Communities," Pacific Indians, 1981, Suva, Institute of South Pacific Studies, University of South Pacific, p. 225.
33. Bhagawan Singh, "Indians in the Pacific," in Vidya Sagar and Manohar Puri (eds), Mother India Children Abroad, (New Delhi, International Publishers n.d.), p. 28.
34. Sharan observed, "In spite of good beginning made by India in laying foundations of friendship and cooperation with South Pacific Island countries, the relations could not take a firm root in the region and by the 1990s, India's links with the Island countries ceased to exist" because India had little to offer, (Ron Crocombe, 2007, Asia in The Pacific Islands: Replacing the West, Suva, Fiji: IPS Publications, University of South Pacific, pp. 273 and 274; Sharan,Tripurari, 1997, "India's policy Interests towards South Pacific: A Study in Interests and Objectives," Ph.D thesis, University of Delhi).

35. After adopting 1997 Constitution, Fiji was readmitted to the Commonwealth in 1999. Immediately diplomatic relations were restored between India and Fiji. Further India improved relations with the neighbouring countries of Pacific steadily, and this was attributed to the diplomatic skill of India. Fiji opened its High Commission in Delhi in 2005 (Ron Crocombe, n. 32,p. 274).
36. India offers four programs, mainly to civil servants. The Technical and Economic cooperation program funds 25 officials from Fiji and 15 from all other Islands nations together for one- to six-month courses in information technology, business development etc. From 2004, an extra 30 scholarships annually have been shared among member countries of the Pacific Islands Forum. The Indian Council for Cultural relations gives Scholarships 25 (three-or four-year scholarships) at Indian Universities. In 2005, over 100 Islands students were in India at Indian government expense (Crocombe, n. 32, p. 420; Subha Singh, "Reaching Out to the South Pacific", *Frontline*, Vol. 19, Issue 20, October 12-25, 2002).
37. Subha Singh, "Hesitant Steps," *Frontline*, June 29, 2007, pp. 86-88; Ron Crocombe, 2007, Asia in The Pacific Islands: Replacing the West, Suva, Fiji: IPS Publications, University of South Pacific, p. 275.

21

Indians in New Zealand

G. Vijay Kumar Reddy and M. Prayaga

Background

Almost all the nations in the world today are characterised by cultural and ethnic plurality. New Zealand is no exception. Multi ethnicity has come to stay in the nations of the world despite inter ethnic, cultural and religious tensions. Immigration of different ethnic and cultural groups into Europe U.S.A. and Pacific nations has been taking place since long time. New Zealand of late is receiving large number of immigrants from Asian nations. Asian immigrants are fastest growing immigrants. Today Asian immigrants account for 6.6 percent in New Zealand and by 2016 they are expected to become 9.1 percent of the total population of New Zealand. [1]

Among the immigrant population in New Zealand Indians constitute second largest group next only to Chinese. According to the 2001 census, among the Asian communities 44 percent are identified with the Chinese ethnic group, 26 percent with the Indian ethnic group, 8 percent Korean, 5 percent Filipino, 4 percent Japanese, 3 percent Sri Lankan, 2 percent Thai and 8 percent are other ethnic minorities. [2] The increase in Asian migration to New Zealand can be attributed to the encouragement of foreign investment in New Zealand.

The Indians, being second largest Asian ethnic minority, have established themselves as a culturally vibrant group. It has grown into integral part of New Zealand Society. Many traditions that were brought to New Zealand by Indian Diaspora have been maintained since the first settlement in the nineteenth century, especially within the community organizations.

Early Migration

Indians have migrated to New Zealand since late 18th Century. Before 1880 Indians were not identified in the census records, though their presence was noted. A man named Edward Peter (from Goa and also known as Black Peter) arrived around 1853 from India. Although the Australian Gabriel Reid is credited with discovery of gold at Tuapeka in Otago, it is believed that it was Edward Peter who told Reid where it could be found. [3]

The 1881 census recorded six Indian men, three of whom lived in Canterbury and were probably servants of wealthy English Settlers who had lived in India. Steadier Indian migration to New Zealand began in the 1890's. By 1896 the number of Indians had grown to 46. The numbers fluctuated over the next 20 years as people arrived and departed. But by 1916 there were 141 Indians including 14 women. They came mostly from the Navsari and Surat regions of Gujarat province. There are also Indians who migrated from Jalandhar and Hoshiarpur in Punjab. [4]

The first immigrants were wanderers rather than settlers, they intended to return to India once they had improved their financial position. They were almost all men. Many, especially Sikhs were employed as flax workers, drain diggers and scrub cutters. In fact, in 1916 most of the Indians lived in rural areas. They also built roads and made bricks. In urban areas they worked as bottle collectors and hawkers of fruits and vegetables. Apart from a small community in Christchurch, most of the Indians chose to live in the North Island, especially Auckland. [5]

Indian settlers encountered prejudice from the whites during the early years. During 1890's there were attempts to legislate against the activities of Indians and to limit their immigration. The immigration Restriction Act was passed in 1899. Before this act, Indians were allowed to enter New Zealand freely as British subjects, unlike other Asian migrants such as Chinese, who as 'aliens' faced restrictions from the

1880's. The new act made it necessary for anyone not 'of British birth and parentage' to fill out their immigration application in a European Language. But it proved only a minor barrier to Indians who were determined to go to New Zealand. Many simply memorized application information at special 'cramming schools' in Fiji, en route to New Zealand. [6]

The number of Indian Immigrants came down during the First World War as travel restrictions were imposed by the British on Indians. But the Indians found ways to sneak out of the country and reach New Zealand and other countries. By 1921, there were about 621 Indians in New Zealand. The increase in the Indian population created problems for the anti-Asian European New Zealanders. After the war a 'Reciprocity Principle' was established between British India and self-governing dominions of the British Empire such as New Zealand. This Principle stated that Indians, who were British subjects, could enter any other British country as visitors or temporary residents. It also allowed Indians living permanently in other British countries to bring their spouses and children. But New Zealand Immigration Act of 1920 made it possible to block Indian Immigration while maintaining the 'Reciprocity Principle'. The Act required anyone, not of British birth and parentage, to apply for a resident permit before entering New Zealand. The definition of British birth excluded Indians and other 'aboriginal natives' of British colonies or dominions. [7]

As a result of the 1920 Act, Indians were usually denied entry permits, but they continued to come by other means. As families of existing Indian residents were allowed entry under the Reciprocity Principle, many men chose to send for their sons. It also became very easy for resident Indian to bring in male friends or other relatives as his 'sons'.

Post-Second World War Migration

According to 1951 Census there were 2,425 Indians in New Zealand. By 1981 this number has swollen to 11,244 and by 2001 the number of Indian immigrants has galloped to 62,646. Until 1981 steady growth was attributed to many factors. The post Second World War saw the arrival of the wives and families of the first Indian immigrants. The political instability in the other Asia-Pacific nations also brought many Indians to New Zealand. The Indian women also arrived in great numbers to help their husbands. With the birth of children in New Zealand, the Indian community became more balanced and settled.

Between 1960 and 1970's it remained difficult for Indians not related to earlier immigrants to enter New Zealand. However, a small number of Fijian Indians arrived in the mid 1960's. In 1980's, with the relaxation of immigration laws towards Asian migration, many Indian business people arrived in New Zealand. Following the 1987 and 2000 military coups in Fiji, a good number of Fijians of Indian origin were provided immigration by New Zealand on humanitarian grounds. The boom in information technology in 1990's helped many Indians, especially professionals and skilled workers, to secure work permits to work in New Zealand. At present the Indian population in New Zealand is around 65,000 many of whom are permanent residents. [8]

Survival

The early years for the Indians were not easy, the winters were unbearable, early Indian migrants experienced the financial hardships, and the discrimination against the Indians was evident. Having little or no financial savings on arrival, even accommodation was not assured, some of the Indians slept under the open skies. They travelled on horse, trams and bicycles to various towns in search of employment. Even work was not easy to obtain as knowledge of English language was limited, at best a labour job was all that could be expected. Despite all these difficulties, life went on and these men tried as best as they could to assimilate amidst the people of New Zealand.

As understanding of Western culture became inevitable, these men ventured into business on their own, with fruit barrows and eventually set up their own retail stores. The early immigrants worked extremely hard for 12 to 18 hours a day for one to two pounds a week. [9]

In the early days, the pace of immigration was very slow with three to four people arriving into the country at a time. Those who had already settled would help the new comers with meals, accommodation and employment. From 1905 to 1927, Indians were meeting periodically at each others homes to share their views, concerns and values which were important to them all. As their material requirements were minimal, the need to preserve their culture and heritage was an important issue amongst the majority. [10] By 1927 there was increasing prejudice and fear about Asian migrants. The 'White New Zealand League' emerged in 1926 with the slogan 'keep New Zealand a white man's country'. It found strong support in the press and the local bodies. Indians were criticized for living in shacks and 'introducing alien views of life and standards of conduct'. The White New Zealand League warned that the intermingling of Indians with both Pakeha and Maori would result in the 'half-caste citizen of the future'. In some places where Indians were perceived as 'taking over', prejudices ran deep and lasted a long time. Indians were not allowed to join the local growers association, some land owners refused to lease them land, and they were not allowed into the balcony seats of the picture theatre. Until 1958, only one barber shop in Pukekohe was allowed to cut the hair of Indians. [11]

The discrimination Indian migrants encountered, and their increased determination to settling in New Zealand permanently, led to the formation of the New Zealand Indian Central Association in 1926 with Inder Singh Randhawa as its first General Secretary. Indian Associations sprang up in other places as well throughout New Zealand. Auckland Indian Association in 1918, Pukekohe Indian Association, Taranaki

Indian Association, Waikato Indian Association, Wellington Indian Association, Christchurch Indian Association etc. These associations also provided crucial social and cultural support. Their branches raised funds to establish community halls and buildings for religious and cultural activities. [12]

Religion and Culture

While the majority of Indians in New Zealand are Hindu, there are also Sikhs, Parsis, Muslims, Jains and Christians, to name the main religious groups. Most Indians of Gujarati origin are Hindu, although some are Muslim. Those from Punjab are mainly Sikh. Indians who have come recently to New Zealand from Fiji are both Hindu and Muslim. [13]

Early Hindu immigrants missed the colourful mass celebration of festivals such as Navratri (nine nights of folk dance and prayer), Diwali (festival of lights), Janmāsthami (Lord Krishna's birthday) and Ganesh Chaturthi (Lord Ganesh's birthday).

Nevertheless, before 1925 Hindu Indians in Wellington and Auckland met regularly to pray and listen to readings from the Bhagavad Gita, their central religious text. In the 1920s permission was received from some local authorities to conduct cremations according to Hindu and Sikh rites. Later, the regional associations organised Gita classes, and the community halls they built were used for festivals. In 1964 the Sanskara Kendra, a centre for religious instruction, was established in Auckland. Globalisation has also boosted religious enthusiasm for older Hindu sects and new syncretic movements.

Since 1980's an increasing number of religious swamis, devotees and yogis have visited New Zealand. The established Indian Associations built large multi-purpose complexes in the early 1990's, which included a mandir, such as the Radha Krishna temple at the Mahatma Gandhi Centre in Auckland. Other early temples were the Bharatiya Mandir in Auckland, opened in 1993, the Kurinji Kumaran Temple, started in 1992, and a Murugan temple erected by the New Zealand Hindu Association in 1995, both in Wellington. Hindu centres of worship and study are maintained by the Hindu Council of New Zealand, the New Zealand Hindu Temple Society, the Vedic Trust of New Zealand (Arya Samaj), the Bochasanwasi Shri Akshar Purushottam Swaminarayan Sanstha, regional Ramayana Sanstha communities. Many New Zealand Indians have long supported Satya Sai Baba, the Brahmakumaris, Gayatri Parivar and in lesser numbers, the International Society for Krishna Consciousness.

Sikhs celebrate festivals including Vaisakhi (a commemoration on 13 April of the establishment of a sacred community by Guru Gobind Singh), and guruparba, the birthdays of other gurus. In 1964 the New Zealand Sikh Society was formed to provide opportunities for religious and social interaction, and in 1977 the Sikh Gurdwara (temple) was opened at Te Rapa, just outside Hamilton. Now there are Gurdwaras in Auckland, Wellington and Hawke's Bay.

There were initially so few Indian Muslims that organised worship was almost impossible. The New Zealand Muslim Association was founded in 1950 and reconstituted in 1976, bringing together Muslims of all cultures and ethnic backgrounds. According to the 2001 census, Indians made up about 37 percent of New Zealand's Muslim population, but an estimate put the proportion as high as 50-60 percent. [14]

Among the religious festivals Diwali occupies important place among the New Zealand Indians as well as the local population. In New Zealand, Diwali has now moved from the relatively private sphere of ritual and performance within the Indian community to a public display and outward celebration. The festival has been held in distinct public places since 2002, with tens of thousands of people attending the event in Auckland and Wellington each year. Diwali maintains support not only from various Indian community groups, but is now a major public festival receiving generous assistance from a partly government-funded organization, two city councils, and from corporate, community and private sponsors. Diwali in New Zealand has been transformed from a local religious and cultural festival celebrated by one broad community, to an event that has become a mainstream public expression of Indian or South Asian identity. [15]

Language

Hindi is the most spoken language among the Indians in New Zealand followed by Gujarati, Punjabi, Tamil, Bengali, Telugu, Marathi, Malayalam and Kannada. In an attempt to promote Indian cultural identity, the 1950s saw the establishment of several centres for social and cultural activities. In the 1950's and 60's some of the Indian Associations started classes in Hindi and Gujarati languages and culture for younger people. For example, in Auckland, a community centre that served as the main meeting place for all the Auckland Indian Association activities was built in 1955. Named after Mahatma Gandhi (1869-1948), the Gandhi Hall was the site for language classes, especially Gujarati language. Many of these classes continue today. Other languages, such as Punjabi, Marathi, Bengali and Hindi, were maintained within families. Formal teaching of Hindi began in Wellington in 1985, and Fijian Hindi classes started in the 1990s. After the Second World War, Indian associations began to hire and screen films in Hindi to impart an idea of Indian culture to the younger generation. [16]

Arts

The first Indian immigrants to New Zealand did not come from parts of India that emphasized the classical traditions in art, music, literature and dance. Now that the Indian population is more diverse and established, there is considerable interest in dancing, music and other forms of arts. Several groups offer regional Indian dance classes, while institutions such as the New Zealand Academy of Bharata-Natyam and the New Zealand Carnatic Music Society (NZCMS) offer classical training in Carnatic Music.

The NZCMS which was registered in September 1999, is the first of its kind in New Zealand. The main aim of the Society is to propagate and encourage Carnatic Music in New Zealand. The NZCMS organizes at least two concerts every year by professional musicians from India. The NZCMS also promotes local artistes who have contributed to the growth of the Carnatic Music.

NZCMS has recently established its education wing, the 'Centre of Learning'. The Centre's objective is to motivate students and to encourage them to learn Carnatic Music. The theory and practical exams are for vocal and instrumental (string, wind and percussion) music and are held in Auckland. The Centre administers the Carnatic Music examination set by the London Academy of Fine Arts from grades 1 to 7 upon completion of which, students are awarded diploma in Carnatic Music. [17]

Sports

Sports especially hockey and cricket has always been important to the Indian community. In the late 1920's in Wellington and Auckland men would get together to play cricket, sometimes using the lids of banana boxes as bats. Cricket was the most important sport among the Indians and equally important was hockey. Early tours of Indian National teams to New Zealand began in 1926, next to come was the Dhyan Chand's All India side in 1935. These early tours were catalyst for the formation of Indian Sports Clubs in New Zealand. The Auckland Indians Sports Club was founded in 1936 with its founding members Khusalbhai Madhu, Parsotbhai Keshaw, Parbhubhai Dheda, Dajibhai Dheda and Bhanabhai Fakir. Christchurch Indian Sports Club was founded in 1937 and Wellington Indian Sports Club was founded in 1938.

Some of the people of Indian origin who represented New Zealand are Ramesh and Mohan Patel who were part of New

Zealand hockey team of the 1976 Olympic Hockey Team. Dipak Patel played cricket for New Zealand team for long time and presently Jeeshan Patel of Indian origin is part of New Zealand cricket team. [18]

Famous Indians in New Zealand

Along with Deepak and Jeeshan Patel there are also other personalities of Indian origin who represented New Zealand and who are placed in important positions in New Zealand. To name them Anand Satyanand, Governor–General of New Zealand, appointed on August 23, 2006. Dr. Ajit Swaran Singh was sworn in as a Judge in Manukau on 4 November 2006. Judge Avinash Deo Bhakta of the Auckland District Court is of Indian origin from Uganda. Sukhinder Turner, was the Mayor of Dunedin, New Zealand, from 1995 to 2004. Rebecca Singh is a news presenter on the New Zealand television station, TV3. Madeleine Sami is a New Zealand actor of Irish and Fiji Indian Heritage. Apart from those recognised, there are many Indians in New Zealand who are placed in important positions in New Zealand government and private sectors. [19]

Justice Anand Satyanand is the first person of Asian descent to be appointed as Governor General. He was born and raised in New Zealand by Fiji Indian parents. Until the early 1970's, the post of Governor General was reserved for the members of British Nobility, with the first indigenous Maori New Zealander, Sir Paul Reeves, appointed in 1980.

Indian Students in New Zealand

The number of Indian students heading for New Zealand has been increasing steadily. The New Zealand government is making efforts to improve the enrolments by marketing itself as an alternative to neighbouring Australia where many Indian students have faced racial attacks. Although Australia has 90,000 Indian students and New Zealand only about 6000, it is an improvement from a mere 500 in 1990.

According to New Zealand High Commissioner to India,

Rupert Holborow, "India has become an important source for students in recent years. The New Zealand government very much welcomes this growing Indian student body". New Zealand invests about NZ$3 billion annually in the tertiary (universities and polytechnics) education system where most of the Indian students are enrolled. Following a spate of attacks on Indians in Australia, the New Zealand government has asked its trade and enterprise office in India to market the country as a nation with a culture different from its neighbour. [20]

Indian students enter New Zealand through a one year student visa, which gets converted to a graduate open work visa for one year and allows them to opt for any part-time job. After one year they can apply for two-year work visa. After getting two-year work visa they can apply for permanent residency based on the points which they get in the skilled migrant category. [21]

Conclusion

Indians contributed their mite for the growth and development of New Zealand and won appreciation for their hard work and commitment. Growing number of Indian students are also going to New Zealand for higher studies as the atmosphere in Australia is not conducive. Though moved from their motherland, Indians followed faithfully Indian customs and religious practices. The fact that Anand Satyanand holds highest office in New Zealand speaks of the esteem in which Indians are held in New Zealand.

End Notes

1. www.wairua.co.nz/ruth/culture/asians.html.
2. *Ibid.*
3. www.theIndian.co.nz.
4. *Ibid.*
5. www.teara.govt.nz/NewZealanders/NewZealandPeoples/indians.
6. *Ibid.*
7. *Ibid.*

8. www.tepapa.govt.nz/learning/aaina/indians.
9. *Ibid.*
10. *Ibid.*
11. *Ibid.*
12. Brij V. Lal ed. *The Encyclopaedia of the Indian Diaspora,* (oxford University Press, New Delhi, 2007), p. 391.
13. www.theindian.co.nz.
14. www.hinduismtoday.com/archives/1990/06/1990-06-05.shtml.
15. Wardlow Friensen and Robin A. Kearns, "Indian Diaspora in New Zealand: History, Identity and Cultural landscapes" in Parvati Raghuram, et. al (eds.) *Tracing an Indian Diaspora,* (New Delhi, 2008), pp. 210-236.
16. www.teara.govt.nz/NewZealanders/NewZealandPeoples/indians.
17. www.nzcms.org/about percent20Society.htm.
18. www.wisc.org.nz/history.htm.
19. www.nriol.com/snippets.
20. www.indiaedunews.net/In-focus/july_2009.
21. New Zealand has unique points system for the issue of permanent residence. Under the Immigration act of 1987 (Immigration Act was amended several times) under which immigrants were selected. Any person who met specified educational, business, professional, and age or asset requirements was provided permanent residency regardless of race or nationality. For more details see www.teara.govt.nz/NewZealanders/NewZealandPeoples/indians.

Index

Index